Gender and Development

Gender and Development
The Role of Religion and Culture

Alice Peace Tuyizere

MAKERERE UNIVERSITY
Kampala

FOUNTAIN PUBLISHERS
Kampala

Makerere University
P.O. Box 7062
Kampala

Fountain Publishers Ltd
P. O. Box 488 Kampala
E-mail:fountain@starcom.co.ug
Website:www.fountainpublishers.co.ug

Distributed in Europe, North America and Australia by African Books
Collective Ltd. (ABC), Unit 13, Kings Meadow Oxford OX2 0DP,
United Kingdom. Tel: 44-(0) 1865-726686, Fax: 44-(0)1865-793298
E-mail: orders@africanbookscollective.com
Website: www.africanbookscollective.com

ISBN 978-9970-02-618-0

Contents

1
Introduction

According to Revelations 21:5-6 the one who sits on the throne said, "And now I make all things new!" He also said, "Write this because these words are true and can be trusted, and, It is done.' I am the first and the last, the beginning and the end, to anyone who is thirsty I will give the right to drink from the spring of water of life without paying for it." In John 10:10, He says, "I have come in order that you might have life in all its fullness." In Mark 9:38-40 John said to Him, "'Teacher, we saw a man who was driving out demons in your name and we told him to stop because he does not belong to our group.' 'Do not stop him,' Jesus told them. 'Whoever is not against us is for us.' (The United Bible Societies Good News Bible, 1999)

The objective of this book is to examine the religious, cultural, political, economic and social revolution in African society in the context of gender and development. The book addresses a number of misconceptions about feminist schools of thought and their relevance in the African context. In the recent past the African woman has seen many changes relating to development, gender, equality and power. Questions regarding the status of African women are raised, such as: Are women turning into men? Why do women no longer respect African culture and religious teachings? Why are women doing men's work?

Chapter One explains the relationship between religion, culture, gender and development in a patriarchal society. It defines gender in terms of religious and cultural concepts. It discusses religion and culture at length and explains how these two components force women into positions of subordination and inequality. Gender equality does not mean antagonism between men and women as individuals or domination of one over another, because gender inequality is a social phenomenon, not a personal one. This book explains that men and

1

women should be equal, not only in the egalitarian sense, but also in the socio-economic, political, cultural and political sense. In order for such equality to become a reality, a radical change should take place in the entire socio-economic order, including class, culture, religion and gender. The chapter stresses that in order to liberate women, particular beliefs, practices, customs and teachings at the level of culture and religion that emphasise or demand seclusion of women, should be subjected to a process of change. The book contends that development in the context of gender equality can only be achieved by total transformation of society and quality of life. Women should not be left behind in the development of the nation, but should enjoy the same rights and opportunities as men, thereby creating an egalitarian society.

Chapter Two addresses the assumptions, theories and philosophies regarding gender and how these impact on women in the development process.

Chapter Three discusses gender and society, roles, societal expectations, violence of various types and HIV/Aids and how these issues illuminate the domination of patriarchal ideology as an integral part of society. Attempts are made to answer questions such as: Why do men dominate women? Where do men obtain power from and how do they use it? What ideologies repress and place women in inferior positions?

Chapter Four discusses gender and sustainable development concerns such as politics, health, the economy, poverty and education.

Chapter Five explains religions like Hinduism, the Near East, Greek and Roman religions, Buddhism, Confucianism, Judaism, Christianity, the Baha'i and Islam faiths, which share a common factor namely male domination. The ideologies of these faiths strive to maintain women's inferiority at all levels, although they have the capacity to bring about women's liberation. However, it should be mentioned that some of these religions, especially Christianity, offer a faint light at the end of the tunnel as far as gender equity is concerned.

Chapter Six deliberates on women's liberation movements, their objectives, background causes and international laws addressing gender issues of equality, women's achievements and emancipation. It shows that women's movements in Africa arose from certain historical, religious and cultural perspectives. Women are struggling to liberate themselves from the religious, cultural and patriarchal systems that oppress them. Women are trying to liberate themselves from shackles such as poverty, illiteracy, forced marriages and labour, sexual abuse, exploitation, oppression and denial of opportunities.

Chapter Seven addresses the issues of gender empowerment and development. It discusses women as a disempowered force in a patriarchal society. In its struggle against patriarchy, women's empowerment is driven by women's organisations, participation in money-generating projects and employment. The chapter considers the significance of involving women in development projects and programmes and obstacles to their participation. The chapter outlines guidelines for integrating women into projects or programmes and how to implement, monitor and evaluate these projects. The book also addresses issues that continue to hinder gender equity and development such as electricity, poor agricultural methods and environmental degradation resulting from poverty.

Lastly, Chapter Eight shows that gender mainstreaming in all the programmes and projects of NGOs and the government could be the means to address gender concerns and imbalances. Decentralisation provides an entry point, since districts are in position to identify, analyse, examine and incorporate gender concerns in their programmes. Different gender-analytical tools and frameworks are discussed to assist planners in incorporating gender issues in their programmes and projects.

There is no doubt that this book is timely. It was written at a time when gender equity was stressed as one of the millennium goals, with its emphasis on quality of life for all. At the time of publication, gender mainstreaming (see chapter 8), is the theme song for the government and non-governmental organisations. A National Gender Policy has been enacted and the Ministry of Education and higher institutions of learning like Makerere University are in the process of gender mainstreaming to address the gender imbalances within the organisations.

The Relationship between Religion, Culture, Gender and Development

Right from the beginning of human history, religion has been the engine for gender violence and inequality. All over the world, cultures follow religious beliefs and these beliefs affect a society's development negatively or positively. Gender myths are socially and culturally constructed beliefs or ideas about men and women, which explain the origin, personalities and mental capabilities of men and women, and which control sexuality, access to food, roles and responsibilities. As most world religions developed from myths, people hold these myths to be true. Misinterpretation and misunderstanding of religious myths and sacred texts relegate women to a position of subordination, submissiveness and oppression, thus resulting in gender inequality and violence. Culture is the custodian of religious beliefs and its role is to implement these beliefs.

The sacred book of Genesis, Chapter 2, has been interpreted as reflecting man's superiority over woman because man was the first human creation of God. The Yahwist writer shows God making Adam out of the dust of the earth. Genesis 2:21 shows God making Eve out of Adam's rib. These verses have been a source of confusion and result from a misinterpretation of the original writer's idea of equality (Yahwist) of man and woman, leading to the unwarranted conclusion that the woman was formed from the man, she was not created, but made from the rib of a man. However, Genesis 2:23–24 says: "At least this is one of my own kind, bone taken from my bone and flesh from my flesh, woman is her name, because she was taken out of man. That is why a man leaves his father and mother and is united with his wife and they become one." The Yahwist, by showing that God created a woman from a man's rib, did not imply that man is dominant and that woman is inferior, but it indicated equality of humanity. The unity of male and female is today confirmed by HIV/Aids infection. The partner who is unfaithful infects the other and because the two have become one, both suffer the same consequences.

Genesis 3:6 declares that woman is the source of sin and suffering, a price which women continue to pay through gender violence, subordination and inequality. Genesis 3:16 declares woman's subordination, desire for and protection by man, "I will increase your trouble in pregnancy and your pain in giving birth. In spite of this you will still have the desire for your husband, yet you will be subject to him." According to Genesis 1:28, men and women were created as equal companions and given the same responsibilities to harness their environment and to preserve it. However, the creation of man followed by woman and the deception of Eve by the serpent, as recorded in Genesis 3, has, throughout human history, been taken as proof that man must exercise authority and domination over the woman (Corinthians 11:12). A mythological belief among the Bafumbira and Bakiga of South Western Uganda, that the woman is the origin of death, buttresses every reason for their suppression, oppression and discrimination. Genesis 3: 19 declares that man is the breadwinner, an institution which he must guard jealously by hard work. In most societies women who venture and excel in men's religious, political, economic and educational domains are called by different names such as igishigabo (Rufumbira), ninkomushaija (Rukiga), both words meaning a manly woman, or aine za Nyabingi (demon possessed), both languages from South Western Uganda. These different labels given to women who work on equal footing with men the society negatively praise them and are always a source of violence in cases where men try to protect their domain or when the empowered women undervalue the men, this may deter gender equity and development.

Religious teachings are the root cause of women's inequality in society, world over. The Bible is rooted in a patriarchal society. Both the Old and New Testament teachings are often taken to be the cause of the generally inferior position women hold in Christianised societies. Certain Bible passages, however uplift women and speak of their roles as equal to that of men. Women were subordinates in Hebrew society and this is true of most Christianised societies. In ancient Hebrew society, women were controlled by their fathers until they were passed on to their husbands by marriage. When they were widowed, they depended on their sons. It was a curse not to have a son. It was through men that women gained access to the economic resources of the community. In 2 Kings 4:8-37 the story of the rich woman of Shunem and prophet Elisha is recounted. The rich woman stood to lose everything if she lost her son. Widows without male support found themselves in dire straits, as Naomi did, in the Book of Ruth.

In the Ten Commandments (Exodus 20:17), women are listed among their husbands' property. Daughters were at their fathers' disposal (Exodus 21:7). Startling acts of sexual disposal of women by their fathers are reported in the story of Lot and his two daughters (Genesis 19:4-8) and in the story of the Levite and his concubine (Judges 19:22-29). Since a woman was a man's possession, the man could dispose of her at any time by divorcing her (Sirach 25:23-28).

Mananzan (1998) shows that all religions and cultures punished sexual transgressions by women. Adultery by a woman was ranked with murder as a major crime and called for the death penalty. The adulterous woman was either burned or stoned to death; she faced heavy punishment, not because she had committed a sin, but because her husband's property rights had been violated. However, men were not condemned for committing adultery, unless it was with someone else's wife or a betrothed woman. Men judged women who were promiscuous. Genesis 38:1ff, tells the story of the unequal nature of the punishments given to men and women who were promiscuous. Judah's son, who was married to Tamar, died before they had produced a child. Judah commanded his other son, Onan, to produce children on behalf of his dead brother with Tamar, but because Onan knew that the children would not be his, he spilled his semen on the ground during intercourse with Tamar. This action displeased God and He killed Onan. Because Tamar was desperate for a child from her husband's line, she disguised herself as a prostitute and sat down at the entrance to Enaim, where Judah found her. Tamar had sexual intercourse with her father-in-law on condition that he left his stick and the seal with her, a condition that Judah accepted. When it was reported to Judah that his daughter-in-law had become a prostitute and was pregnant, he ordered that she be killed. He did not know that he was responsible for the pregnancy. In Genesis 38:25 Tamar says, "I am pregnant by the man who owns these things, look at them and see whose they are, this seal with its cord and stick". When Judah recognises his property he is ashamed, but his society could not pass judgment on him as it had done on Tamar.

In accordance with Hebrew culture, women could not inherit property unless their fathers had no sons (Numbers 27:1-11). Women were dependent on male support. Discrimination against women was not only economic and social, but also religious. According to Genesis 17:10, circumcision was the only way to be initiated into the Israelite religious community, and since women were not circumcised, they were excluded from the religious community. In the temple women were confined to the court of women, which was 19 steps higher than the court of Gentiles but 15 steps lower than the court of the male Israelites. Only Israelite men were admitted to the court of Israel. Women who were within seven days of the end of their menstruation were denied entry to the temple, as were mothers within 40 days of the birth of a boy or eight days of the birth of a girl (Mananzan and Arche, 1998). The religious culture of Judaism is reflected in some modern religions, which forbid women to mix with men during church worship. In ancient Israel, menstrual women were forbidden to enter certain churches or to participate in the Holy Communion because they were considered unclean during this time, and this is why, even today, few religions ordain women as priests. Cultural and religious beliefs are detrimental to women's development and equality.

However, in Israel, women such as Jael and Deborah played roles reserved for men. Judges 4–5 describes Deborah as a prophet, judge, military leader, singer and poet, talents which she used to deliver Israel from its enemies, the Canaanites. As an exception, her presence as a military leader and hero among the biblical cast of male leaders and heroes calls attention to the more usual position of women in patriarchal societies. Her story serves as a critique of patriarchal structures that blocked the leadership by and independence and development of women. Other similar women who appeared in stereotyped roles, acted behind the scenes and ensured the welfare and fortune of their people. The courage of women like Deborah, Jael, Esther and Susan shows the underlying structure of the narrative and brings into prominence the unexpected power of women over men. God gave power to Israelite women rather than men in order to liberate Israel from her enemies. In this light, if women's potential can be harnessed to the full today, they would have the ability to shake up empires in the political, religious, educational, medical, social, economic and cultural realms. Women as a force that can effect change and development are under-utilized. Women's liberation and equality is based on the essential premise that we are all created in the image and likeness of God and we all have the potential, as men and women, to develop the world around us.

Mananzan (1998) reports that the oppression of women by religion was recognised in an ecumenical consultation of church women from seven Asian countries, held in Manila in November 1985. They wrote in their composite statement, "As church people we have come to realise that the highly patriarchal churches have definitely contributed to the subjugation and marganalisation of women. Thus we see an urgent need to re-examine the church structures, traditions and practices to remedy injustice and correct misinterpretations and distortions that have crippled us. We saw how theology itself has added to these distortions. We unearthed theological premises, traditions and beliefs that have prevented us from becoming fully human and blurred the image of God, throughout the church history".

Up to now biblical teachings have been used to justify the subordination of women and discrimination against them. On the basis of sacred teachings, men argue that it is divinely ordained that women should be inferior and dependent on men. Only a few women have been recorded as participating in the development of the history of their religions and the nation, but the majority of women, who are mostly the unlearned, live in precarious conditions of cultural and religious subordination. Research shows that in the Anglican Church of Uganda, most male clergy are educated, but their wives can hardly read or write or are primary or secondary school dropouts. This gap makes religious men, who are mostly preachers, think that everyone is dependent, uneducated and cannot contribute to social development. Religious leaders should help women to rise above their subordinate positions, so that they can contribute to the challenging and changing times.

One of the issues of religion that affect women is the prevailing notion of God as a male. In the monotheistic patriarchalism of the Hebrews, God was considered as a God of the patriarchs, not the matriarchs. He was referred to as the God of Abraham, Isaac, Jacob, Joseph and Moses. Nowhere in scripture is God mentioned as a God of women. Dorr (2002) says that the Israelites identified this God with masculine qualities like protector, father, lord, conqueror, defender, warrior, avenger, almighty, all-powerful and the punisher of evil, although there are scanty mentions of feminine qualities such as mother, life-giver, nourisher, comforter, merciful, gentle and forgiving. Because of these beliefs, there was a pronounced male domination over women in Hebrew society. This led to the establishment of a double standard of morality, favourable to men. Women's contribution to society involved bearing children, which explains why barrenness was considered a curse. Women could not participate in any societal activities. They were illiterates, while men were learned and leaders. According to Chapman (1989) patriarchy is a system of social structures and practices, in which men dominate, oppress and exploit women. Men are deemed to be superior and women require controlling. It is the foundation upon which gender relations are based. It governs how social and state institutions operate and the values and attitudes forming these operations. Patriarchy manifests itself in the culture and religion therefore men control the family property.

Mananzan (1998) and Dorr (2002) note that God inspired male writers to record His message. Although they were inspired by God as writers, they had human weaknesses, prejudices, ignorance and limitations. The authors of sacred scriptures were men of their cultures and their writings about women reflect cultural norms prevalent at the time of writing. Jewish culture was patriarchal and considered women to be inferior, thus women could not access opportunities that would promote their development. World religions have had a tremendous effect on women as far as accessing equal development opportunities is concerned. In this respect Mananzan (1998) quotes Denise Lardner Carmody as saying, "Beyond doubt, the major religions of the world have a dubious record with regard to women". She goes on to say that Buddhist women could not participate in the religious ceremonies of the community. Hinduism usually held women ineligible for salvation. Islam made a woman's witness only half the value of that of a man. Christian writing called a woman the weak vessel and the more blurred image of God. Jewish men thanked God for not having made them women. According to Jackson and Pearson (1998), some have suggested that it was the spread of Christianity and the destruction of pagan religions that produced the idea of a separate, dominant section of humanity. By destroying paganism, Christianity made it possible for men to exploit women. Pagan religions have female gods that inspire respect for women. But Christianity stressed the masculine God, who was represented by His son Jesus, and male leaders were to serve Him while women were subordinate and inferior to all men.

In 1 Corinthian 11:3-13, Paul confirms the subordination of women in society when he says: "But I want you to understand that Christ is supreme over every man, the husband is supreme over his wife and God is supreme over Christ". Verses 7-8 says that a man reflects the image and glory of God, but woman reflects the glory of men, for man was not created from woman, but woman from man. Nor was man created for woman's sake, but woman was created for man's sake. These teachings are still perpetuated by church leaders, even when some women have broken the yoke of oppression.

Radford (1996) indicates that religion, especially the Christian tradition, with its roots in the Hebrew and Greco-Roman worlds, has been named as a prime source of cultural symbols which inculcate the idea that women are inferior. The patriarchal God of the Hebrew Bible as the controller of creation, fused with the Greek philosophical dualism of the spirit and matter, is seen as the prime identity myth of the male ruling class. Male domination of females is delivered by the story of the Garden of Eden, which religiously underpins woman as the cause of man's suffering.

Most Christian religions insist that headship by men in the Christian family is natural, cultural or God-given, even when the man contributes nothing to the well-being of the family. Christian faith and identity remain intertwined with the socio-cultural regime of subordination. Theological and religious discourses reinforce the status of women as inferior objects, rather than interrupting the victimization of women and children. Religions do not question but reproduce prevalent socio-cultural prescriptions of femininity. Christian theology condemns oppressive forms of exploitation and victimization such as rape, incest, and sexual abuse but does not condemn the subordination of women. Radford (1996) says that the Christian proclamation of the politics of submission and its attendant virtues of self - sacrifice, docility, subservience, obedience, suffering, unconditional forgiveness, male authority and unquestioning surrender to God's will, covertly advocates in the name of God patriarchal practices of victimization of women as Christians. In so doing, religious regimes theologically reinscribe to the socio-cultural construction of femininity and subordination in order to maintain the heterosexist structures of subordination.

The church and many Christian families jeopardize the survival of the women who struggle at the bottom of the socio-cultural and economic-political pyramid of domination, by reminding them that their place in the society is reproduction, looking after children and domestic work. As long as such structural change does not take place, Christian theologies will continue to collude in the practice of physical, political, social, economic and religious violence against women. Feminist theological work on violence against women has four traditional theological discourses that serve as major hurdles in the way of abused women who seek to change their violent situations:

(i)   The subordination of women has its roots in the sacred teachings of Greek philosophy, Roman law, Judaism, Christianity, Islam, Confucianism, Hinduism, Buddhism and other world religions.

(ii) In 2 Corinthians 11:2-3 Paul relates the image of marriage between Christ and the church with Eve's deception, thereby linking the theology of submission with teaching on woman's sinfulness. Some religious leaders prescribe the silence of women and forbid them to exercise authority over men by claiming that not Adam, but the woman, was deceived and she became a transgressor (2 Tim 2:11-15). This is the origin of the cultural patterns which subject women to rape, incest, domestic violence and victimization. Women's submission has its roots in scriptural teaching that sin came into the world through Eve and that women obtain salvation primarily by bearing children, through whom they continue in faith, love and holiness. However, Genesis 3:16 gives woman cause to hope that she will one day be liberated and become victorious: "I will make you and the woman hate each other, her offspring and yours will always be enemies. Her offspring will crush your head and you will bite her offspring's heel."

(iii) Christian ministry and theology do not interrupt, but continue to foster the cycles of discrimination, subordination and violence engendered by social, economic, ecclesiastical, cultural and political disciplining practices.

(v)   When Christians continue to preach central Christian values such as love and reconciliation to men and subordinated women, they sustain relations of domination and accept domestic and sexual violence in the name of prayer and forgiveness. Thereby scriptural texts and Christian ethics perpetuate the cycle of violence. Christian teachings should address the root cause of women's subordination to effect equality in the development process. Prayer, forgiveness and tolerance, which priests use to counsel women in violent relationships, are tools for women submission.

(vi) There is a story of a couple in one of the sub counties of Kisoro district, Southwestern Uganda who married in church in the early 1980s. The religious leader who performed the service stressed

Paul's teaching in Ephesians 6:22-24, that of the submission of women. The preacher stressed to the congregation that women must submit to men, a tenet that is upheld by preachers even today. The newly married woman understood this message to imply that women should submit to whatever any man asked for. Two weeks after the wedding, the newly married man left his wife in the care of his father and brothers and went to work in town. In Western Uganda incest is rampant, and no sooner had the husband left for town than his father approached his daughter-in-law for sex. The woman remembered that she had been commanded to submit to men. Thus she submitted to her father-in-law's request and had sexual relations with him, conceived and produced a child. Her brother-in-law also asked her for sex. She complied because she was taught by the preacher to be submissive to men. She became pregnant by this man and produced another child. By the time her husband returned from town, she had two children. She was taken to a local court, chaired by the priest who married them. In her defense, the woman said that the man who was judging her was the same person who had ordered her to be submissive to male authority. She won the case, because scriptures do not explain the boundaries of submissiveness of women to men. The church should explain to women what it means to be submissive to men and to what extent they should be submissive in a changing society, that is faced with HIV/Aids, and promiscuity.

Many women are victims of sexual exploitation and abuse because culture and religion demand that they be submissive. Many women, whether married or not, when seeking for favors from men do not say "no" to sexual advances, especially if a man is of higher status, a family member, or a friend. As a result, women continue to be used by men who have more authority than they do; most of the victims are young girls, seeking employment, or marks from their teachers or lecturers. A culture that emphasizes submission tends to encourage naivety among women, so that they are unable to think on their own and make responsible decisions. Consequently, excessive cultural and religious submissiveness among women may harm the family. If a woman has an irresponsible husband who cannot make sensible decisions, the family may crumble. As religion and culture continue to promote their gospel of submissiveness, in modern society, there are situations where women need to take responsible and radical decisions. The following questions are raised about the submissive role played by the wife:

- How can a wife allow her husband to sell off family property, or prevent her from finding work outside the home when the family income is inadequate?
- How can women continue to engage in unprotected and dangerous sexual relations when they can protect themselves by using condoms?
- Why should a woman whose child is very ill wait for a husband who has gone to work to come and take the child to hospital, because she fears using his money without obtaining his permission first?

In such times of need, women have to act responsibility for the benefit of society and their families. The Bible shows women failing to make decisions about their sexual relationships with men. For example, in Genesis 35:22, Reuben, son of Jacob, made sexual advances to Billah, his father's wife, who could not turn him down. Although Jacob was furious about his wife having sexual intercourse with his son, Billah had to submit to Reuben's demands, since he was a man. 2 Samuel 11:1ff narrates how David used his authority as king to have sexual relations with Bathsheba, wife of Uriah. In this episode, we also see the God of the weak and oppressed passing judgment on the promiscuity of men. God punished David for using his authority to take Bathsheba from Uriah.

The Book of Esther 1:1ff tells the story of Queen Vashti, who defied the wish of her husband, King Xerxes, to display her as a sexual object. Esther 1:11 says "He ordered them to bring in Queen Vashti, wearing her royal crown. The queen was a very beautiful woman and the King wanted to show off her beauty to the officials and all his guests, but when the servants told Queen Vashti of the King's command, she refused to come." Queen Vashti's stand should be emulated by feminists. They should liberate women who are used as sexual objects, in display and dancing, in fashion shows, beauty pageants, in bars and hotels. Women should be empowered with skills and the confidence to stand on their own and to compete with men in the world of development.

African Ecclesiastical Review (1971) describes how the women of Iran rebelled against Islamic clerics in 1963 because Islam and Iranian culture treated them like third-class citizens. Changes are taking place in all religions and cultures, like Protestantism, the Catholic Church and other world religions.

However, civilizations tend to assign more or less rigid, specific and different roles and tasks to men and women. Thus, women's roles usually lie outside the fields of religion, politics and economic activities of the society. For instance, in most countries of the world women are excluded from the higher echelons of religious and political leadership. Nonetheless, it should be possible to enhance women's dignity at the social level and allowing the emergence of a more balanced image of the capacity of men and women in the management of both private and public affairs, without destabilising religious structures or importing foreign cultural values.

In the context of religion and culture men wish to control female sexuality and reproduction because male control enhances kinship systems preoccupied with purity of descent. Thus women are segregated or secluded, virginity tests are done and women suspected of adultery are socially sanctioned by punishments that could include death. In Judaism, Islam and other religious traditions, a woman caught in adultery or a girl who conceived before marriage was punished by death, and this still stands today. Paradoxically, many societies place a double burden on women - they are the carriers of tradition and the centre of the family, yet during periods of rapid social change, their actions and appearance change less quickly than that of men, or do not seem to change at all. Demands for family stability and unchanged roles for women may be strong when the processes of change are perceived as coming from outside the group, thus change is seen as alien and threatening to established patterns of life. These demands presuppose a high degree of female compliance and acceptance of male control and, in turn, provides men with a sense of mastery over events that seem to be out of control.

Moghadam (1988) reveals that women in Islamic states such as Iran, Pakistan and Afghanistan suffer untold oppression and subordination from males. He defines patriarchy as a kinship-ordered social structure with strictly defined sex roles in which women are subordinated to men. In the 1970s and throughout the 1980s, the female question assumed a paramount position in political discourse and religious and cultural battles.

Moghadam (1988) shows that in Pakistan, Iran and Afghanistan, males enacted laws to institutionalize female subordination and rule by men, in the same way as the creation of patriarchy by law in ancient Mesopotamia institutionalized female subordination and rule by men. The code of Hammurabi, the middle Assyrian laws, and the laws of the Hitites and Hebrews encoded male and female differences, especially sexual control of women. Moghadam (1988) defines a patriarchal society as one in which power is held by male heads of households, where there is separation between the public and private spheres of life and where power is shared between male patriarchs. No female holds any formal public position of economic, ideological, military or political power in Islamic states. Young brides, who marry into large families gain respect mainly via their sons and, later in life, acquire power as mothers-in-law. The patriarchal extended family gives the senior man authority over everyone else, including young men, and entails forms of control and subordination of women which cut across cultural and religious boundaries. In Russia, despite women's heavy agricultural burdens and functional importance in the household, women are considered second-class citizens and were placed under the authority of men.

In Muslim societies, low levels of proletarianization, industrialization and educational attainment inhibit women's active participation in the public sphere in the patriarchal community. In Islamic societies, patriarchal forms of control over women include the institutionalisation of extremely restrictive codes of behaviour for women, a practice of rigid gender segregation, specific forms of family and kinship and a powerful ideology linking family honour to female virtue. Men are entrusted with safeguarding family honour through their control over female members. In Muslim patriarchal societies the control of women is considered necessary because women are regarded as potential sources of Fitna, that is, capable of causing disorder or anarchy. Moghadam (1990) stresses that construction of gender identity and discourses about women are sometimes convenient weapons between contending political groups. Political elites may raise the question of women, or issues of morality and cultural identity, to divert attention from economic or political problems. Discriminatory personal status and laws which render women legal minors and dependants of men reflect and perpetuate patriarchy. In Islamic states, laws and government policies established by patriarchal states serve to limit women's autonomy, mobility and employment. Islamic fundamentalists struggle to maintain women in a state of subordination and fulfilling traditional sex roles.

Moghadam (1988) explains that the Iranian revolution of 1977 and 1979 against the shah was joined by women who wanted liberation from economic deprivation, political repression and identification with Islamism. Many women protested against the hejab (veiling). However, with the defeat of the liberal Muslims in 1981, Islamists made veiling compulsory. The Islamists in Iran felt that the genuine religious and cultural identity of Iranians had been distorted by westernisation or what they called Gharbezadgi. The unveiled, publicly visible woman was both a reflection of western subversion of indigenous culture and religion and the medium by which western influence was achieved. The growing number of educated and employed women terrified men, who came to regard the modern woman as the manifestation of westernisation and imperialist culture and a threat to their own manhood. Thus, in 1979, the constitution of the Islamic Republic of Iran set out the place of women in an ideal Islamic society under the Iranian government. In the Iranian constitution, motherhood and domesticity were described as socially valuable roles for women. The Islamic Iranian Republic emphasized the distinctiveness of male and female roles and thus stressed a preference for the privatisation of female roles, the desirability of segregation in public places, modesty of dress, demeanor and in media images. Moghadam (1998), describes the laws relating to women that were enacted in the Iranian Islamic constitution. The Family Protection Act of 1967 which gave women additional rights and limited those of men was abrogated in favour of laws which closely linked Islamic norms and canon law. The marriageable age for girls was lowered from 18 to 13 years. Polygamy and temporary marriage were reinstated. Abortion was declared illegal and contraceptive devices were banned. Divorce and child custody became the unilateral rights of men.

Hejab (veiling) was made compulsory. When in public, women were to wear the all-enveloping chador, or a large head scarf covering all hair and pushed down to the eyebrows, along with loose clothing and dark stockings. Make-up, especially lipstick, was forbidden. Male guardianship was reintroduced, rendering women legal minors and dependants. Written permission by a man was required before a woman could travel or obtain employment.

While women were not banned from the labour market, written permission by a male guardian was required. Women were barred from certain occupations and professions such as judge, agricultural extension worker and mining engineer. Childcare centers were closed. A law was introduced limiting young mothers to part-time work only. Women were not to be seen nor heard on radio and television. The result of these laws was a drop in female labour participation.

The Shariat (Islamic canon law) was strengthened. The ancient law of retribution was introduced which, inter alia, imposed stoning for adultery and restored the practice of payment of blood money. In the case of the latter, the woman's value was set at half that of a man. Unmarried political prisoners awaiting execution were raped before their execution on the Islamic grounds that virgins ascend to heaven. Coeducational schools were converted into single-sex schools and textbooks were revised to show pictures of women playing only domestic roles. A woman's opportunity to obtain a university education was limited.

However, events in modern Islamic Iran indicate that the dressing code has relaxed and women can now initiate divorce, although they may not wear cosmetics in public. Educated and working women and their presence in the Islamic Republic has undermined the patriarchal ideology of domesticity. The gender code has also been modified and women are allowed to work in public places. Female members of parliament and female Islamist intellectuals continue to defend the cultural and religious use of the veil and insist that women's liberation can only come about within the Islamic context. Women in parliament and magazines continue to criticize discrimination against women and complain of obstacles to the realisation of their rights under Islamic faith (Moghadam, 1988).

Moghadam (1988) describes how, during the reigns of Ayub Khan and Zulfiqar Ali Bhutto, women obtained university degrees, joined professions and became active in politics. However by the 1980s, Pakistan still had the highest female illiteracy rate and a high fertility rate among poor and illiterate women. The lives of the majority of Pakistani women has been described thus:

> Rural women are subjected to exploitation as unpaid drudges and child bearers by their own men and as sexual quarry by the rural aristocracy, a floating reservoir of unorganised cheap domestic and industrial female labour. Some of their children labour is available owing to urban migration... In the absence of social services and social security, poor widows and deserted women are reduced to near-destitution... The majority of Pakistan's women live on the edge of poverty in a male-dominated environment where the average number of surviving children is seven per family (Moghadam, 1988)

Pakistan has one of the highest population growth rates in the world. The traditional view that a woman's modesty can best be protected if she remains within the confines of her home is still reported as the main impediment to female participation in education, industrial employment and government. Although Prime Minister Benazir Bhutto expressed her commitment to women's rights during her brief tenure, no concrete steps were taken to alleviate women's subjugation.

In social structural terms, most Pakistani women, regardless of their socio-economic status or class, remain dependent on the domestic group for survival. Economically and socially, most women remain dependent on men throughout their lives and most derive identity from the family circle as mothers, wives, daughters and sisters.

According to Moghadam (1988) the Islamic society of Afghanistan, has experienced drastic changes in favour of women, although Islamic fundamentalism tends to resist these changes. In 1978 the government of president Noor Mohammad Taraki enacted legislation to raise women's status through changes in family law, and practices and customs related to marriage, female education and employment were encouraged. The Afghan state was motivated by a modernizing outlook and socialist ideology, which linked Afghan backwardness to widespread female illiteracy and the cultural and religious practice of exchanging girls for bride price. The leadership resolved that provision of women's rights to education, employment, mobility and choice of spouse would be major objectives of the national democratic revolution. Decree Number Seven of the constitution was intended to enhance equal rights between men and women; it also forbade the exchange of a woman in marriage for cash (pride price). Alongside this decree the government embarked on an aggressive literacy campaign, led by the Democratic Women's Organisation of Afghanistan, whose function was to educate women, bring them out of seclusion and initiate social programmes. Throughout Afghanistan, classes for men and women were established. This audacious programme for social change was aimed at the rapid transformation of the patriarchal society, but it faced resistance by Muslim fundamentalists, who used threats to discourage women from appearing in public places and gatherings for lessons. Some women literacy workers were killed as an act of resistance against the new revolution that encouraged women to appear in public and exercise equal rights to men. There was universal resistance to the abolition of the bride price. Most Muslims insisted that it should be paid to the bride's father as compensation for the loss of his daughter's labour in the household unit. It was also argued that compulsory education for girls and marriage regulations could lead to women refusing to obey and submit to family and male authority. Changes led to the rise of a tribal Islamist opposition in 1979 that took up arms against the government, and led to the death of President Taraki. The previous government's efforts to raise women's status regarding marriage, education, participation in public affairs and religion by law, was stymied by patriarchal structures highly resistant to change. Both in Pakistan and Afghanistan, conservative Islamists stress compulsory veiling, gender-segregated education and a separate curriculum for girls. Neither Pakistani Islamists nor Afghan Mujahideen allows women to assume positions in their administrative structures, which are patriarchal. In some Islamic states women's liberation and emancipation is still a dream.

Developing states like Uganda have much to learn from Islamic states. It is significant to note that illiteracy among women hinders development. Results of the population census of 2002, indicated that Uganda's population stood at 26 million. Despite the prevailing war in northern Uganda, and HIV/Aids, poor and illiterate women in rural areas produce many children, yet they do not possess land, are unemployed and lack resources. There is a need for nation-wide female and male education to check the existing imbalances that prevent women from using contraception and having a say in the number of children they produce.

Women's liberation is a continuous process, but the government and men should lend a hand to women feminists to liberate all humanity that is enslaved. Religious and cultural dictates that subject women to reproduction should be addressed so that women's quality of life can be improved.

Gender and Church History

The religious teachings of Jesus caused changes in religious thought of the time. When he began his ministry, he called 12 male disciples, although he frequented the company of women like Martha, Mary Magdalene and Salome. By choosing the disciples as future leaders of the church, the disciples of Christ followed his example, and understood that only men could lead the church. Most church leaders to the present have been men. For example, all Uganda Catholic and Protestant bishops today are men, nor is there a woman mufti in Islam. Only the Protestant church and charismatic religions have female pastors.

According to Mananzan (1998), the New Testament shows a shift in its attitude towards women largely as a result of Jesus' own pro-woman stance. Matthew 10:37-39 and Luke 14:26 records how he tried to dismantle the rigid patriarchal system of his time. The Hellenistic culture, within which Christianity took root and spread, also provided for a relatively liberal and high status for women. Women had extensive economic rights, they could buy, own and sell property and goods. In Hellenistic culture there were wealthy women, who attended social gatherings, participated in the Olympic Games and pursued careers in medicine, science, literature and philosophy.

Jewish culture, from which the Christian religion originated, was conservative regarding women's rights. Paul's teaching in 1 Corinthians 11:26, where he advised women to cover their heads and be silent in church, and in Ephesians 5:21-23, where he orders women to be submissive reflects a preoccupation with maintaining the social order and distinctions. Throughout the spread of Christianity, patriarchal culture subverted the gospel and turned it around as a complex, idealizing subordination of women. Christianity played a large role in dislodging women from positions of leadership and placing them in silent and subordinate positions, by basing their teachings on 1 Corinthians 14:33-35, Ephesians 5:21-23, Colossians 3:18-25, Titus 2:3-9 and 1 Peter 3:1-7. The culture of the Bible, in its reading, preaching and interpretation, stresses the subordinate position of women and most of the (male) preachers continue to sow seeds of inequality through 'their' gospel.

Throughout the history of the church, the Bible, from which the "gospel of good news" for liberating humanity from slavery is preached, has been used to justify the subordination and discrimination of women. The fact that ecclesiastical affairs were led by men meant that women were excluded from offices, leadership and participation in public roles. Throughout church history, women have lagged behind in the development process. Women had to conform to their stereotypical role in patriarchal culture. It was no longer woman's call to discipleship that brought her salvation but her prescribed role as wife and mother.

The move towards an ecclesiastical patriarchal society continued relentlessly throughout church history. The fathers of the church, in reaction to Gnosticism, which accepted the possibility of the existence of a female godhead, became increasingly misogynistic in their writings. According to Mananzan (1998), one of the Church fathers, Tertullian, lashed out at Gnostic women, labeling them heretical, bold and immodest because they presumed to prophesy, teach, exorcise and baptize. Thus he, as priest, addressed women with harsh words:

> Women, you ought to dress in mourning in rags, representing yourselves as patients bathed in fears and redeeming, for the fault of having ruined the human race. You are the door of hell, you finally are the cause why Jesus Christ had to die.

Mananzan (1998) also says that the Church fathers such as Origen castrated themselves because they believed that marital relations lessened the efficiency of prayer. St John Chrysostom blamed women for the sins of David and Solomon and described them as a storehouse of spittle and phlegm. Father Augustine also vowed "l know nothing much that brings the many men's mind down from the height, more than a woman's carelessness and that joining of bodies without which one cannot have a wife." In this context many males joined the celibacy life so as to avoid the evil that comes from a woman through sexual intercourse. The doctors of the early Church were no better than the Church fathers. One of the Church doctors, Thomas Aquinas, considered women as misbegotten males, thus he propounded that: "Different kinds of temptations make war on man in his various ages, when he is younger and when he is very old, but women threaten him perpetually. Neither the youth nor the adult, nor the wise nor the brave, nor even the saint is ever safe from the woman', (Mananzan, 1998).

The writer of Proverbs warned young men to avoid adultery with evil women. Proverbs 5:3 says, "The lips of another man's wife may be as sweet as honey and her kisses as smooth as olive oil, but when it is all over, she leaves you nothing but bitterness and pain." Proverbs 7:6ff also says:

> 'A foolish young man walked along the street near the corner where a certain woman lived. As he passed near her house in the dark, dressed like a prostitute, making her plans, she was a bold and shameless woman, who threw her arms around the young man, kissed him, looked him straight into the eyes and said, I have made my offering today and have meat from the sacrifices. So I came out looking for you, I wanted to find you and here you are. I have covered my bed with sheets of coloured linen from Egypt. I have perfumed it with myrrh, aloes and cinnamon. Come on, let us make love all night long, we will be happy in each other's arms. My husband is not at home; he has gone on a long journey.'

Religious teachings do not warn women about adulterous men, yet women are often victims of rape and other sexual offences. In this context, many early Church fathers championed the oppression of women because women were regarded as a source of evil. Many patriarchal societies believed that women have an evil power which they could use to seduce men and uproot them from positions of power. For example, in Judges 16, Delilah made Samson, the man of God, fall from grace. Jezebel used Ahab, the king, to lead Israel into apostasy. The wives of Solomon made a significant contribution to the decline of Israel as a nation of God. Nations use women as spies in order to undermine structures or kingdoms.

Mananzan (1998) reports that in the middle ages, a systematic persecution of charismatic women who were regarded as witches emerged. In 1484 a tract entitled Malleus Maleficarum, was published. The title means the hammer against witches, and this anthology was the product of fevered imaginations regarding the alleged habits, characteristics and evil techniques of females given over to Satan. Between the 13th and 18th centuries, about one million women, including Joan of Arc, were burned as witches by church fathers. Nevertheless, during this era some women rose above repressive circumstances to achieve greatness, such as Juliana of Norwich, a famous mystic, St

Gertrude, St Mechtide and St Theresa of Avila, who were famous for their scholarship. St Catherine of Siena had a tremendous influence on popes and bishops regarding important ecclesiastical matters affecting women.

The Protestant revolution did much to promote the role of women in society. Martin Luther was reported to be ambivalent about women. He failed to see the sexism in biblical patriarchalism. Like the church fathers, he preached that the role of women was procreation and nurturing. However, the emerging Lutheran and Calvinist churches recognised the social and theological role of women in the development process. They accepted women preachers in the 17th century. The Quakers recognised sexual equality and produced great women preachers like Elisabeth Houston, Mary Dyer and Elizabeth Fry. In the 19th century, Mary Baker Eddy founded Christian Science and renewed the father–mother image of God. Likewise the Catholic women of the counter-reformation, such as Angela Meric and Louise de Marillae, broke through the restrictions of the patriarchal society to engage in social services. In the 20th century, at the advent of the feminist movement, the participation of women in the church began in earnest.

Mananzan (1998) states that, before Christianity was introduced in the Philippine Islands, Filipina women enjoyed equal rights with men. They received equal inheritances; their training was the same as that of males. The wife enjoyed the same rights as her husband in marriage, including the right to divorce. Women participated in managing the domestic economy as well as agricultural production. They had opportunities for political leadership. But she laments that, in the 16th century, when the Spaniards introduced Christianity and western civilization, with its patriarchal attitudes to the Philippines, they introduced the misogynistic trend of female subordination and male supremacy. Christian missionaries instructed the priests in the colony that:

The woman is the most horrible animal in the whole nature, bad tempered and worse spoken. To have this animal in the house is asking for trouble in the way of faulting, tale bearing, malicious gossip and full of controversies, for wherever a woman is, it would seem to be impossible to have peace and quiet. Not only should the parish priest abstain from employing any woman in his house but he should not allow them to enter it, even if they are only paying a call.

Such an utterance from a missionary leaves a lot to be desired as far as preaching of the gospel is concerned. Some religious beliefs consider woman to be a source of bad omens and misfortune. However, a propaganda movement under the leadership of the Philippine people tried to awaken the national consciousness of the people and denounced Christian teachings that exploited and domesticated women. Some women began a revolution and preached against the parish priests, encouraging the Philippinos to reject the western religion of the Spaniards, namely Christianity, because it undermined the status which they had enjoyed previously. However, today few women in the Philippines continue to defy domestication and the oppression preached by Christianity. In spite of the growth of the women's movement, the majority of the women in the church have internalized the stereotyped roles which the church and society have assigned them.

The gospel of Christ as preached is supposed to liberate the oppressed, chained, discriminated against, downtrodden and despised. Instead, in modern society, it stresses their bondage. Christianity has continued to champion women's oppression, discrimination and subordination by emphasizing women's submissiveness and subordination. Christian women have continued to accept such discriminatory preaching from men and have not challenged it on the basis of the teachings of Jesus. Christianity has led to a patriarchal society. Males tend to preach the gospel that will favour them – it is to their benefit to be served and cared for by women. This helps men retain their positions of authority as they continue to enslave women as servants in the name of Christianity.

Mananzan (1998) comments that the Catholic Church still holds a conservative view of women. It does not allow them to use artificial family planning methods, only permitting natural methods of family planning, neither has it lifted its ban on divorce. Catholic moral theology still focuses on sins of the flesh, with a certain bias against woman as "Eve the Temptress". Women are expected to behave as Mary, a virgin mother, did, which is obviously impossible for Catholic women to emulate. The Catholic hierarchy may not ordain women as priests or bishops yet women are the most active in church services, functions and activities. Women are deprived of participation in the major decision-making processes. Catholic priests do not allow women to preach, give sacraments as baptism, preside over weddings, say Mass, or officiate at funeral ceremonies.

Catholic priests continue to enforce rules and prescriptions governing marriage and family life, without considering how they impact on women. Women are given minor roles in the liturgy, but they shoulder the greater burdens of the church. Religious women, especially nuns, continue to play a vital role in the church. They participate actively in educational, medical, social and religious programmes that liberate the poor. Some nuns are becoming aware of themselves as women concerned with the feminist question and are contributing to the liberation and emancipation of women towards a full development of their humanity (Mananzan, 1998). The Protestant Church is less hierarchal than the Catholic Church. Some women who compete with men are ordained as priests and they play the same roles as men. Other women are deacons and church wardens; however, they are still the minority in church ministry and no woman has yet been appointed bishop.

Protestant congregations have a greater number of women members than men, but in most jobs and decision-making bodies the minority leads the majority. However, new developments in the Protestant Church and relating to women's emancipation and gender sensitisation encourage women to participate actively in church activities. The Church stresses that every committee should contain at least one woman. The Protestant Church is becoming gender-sensitive, although its teachings are still conservative (Mananzan, 1998).

The Feminist Theology of Liberation

Feminism is a complex movement comprising many layers and advocating the liberation of women from religious and cultural oppression. It can be defined as a movement with liberal democratic societies for full inclusion of women in political, religious and political rights and access to equal opportunities. It is defined more radically by socialist and liberationist feminism as the transformation of the patriarchal socio-economic system, in which male domination of women is the foundation of all social, religious and political hierarchies. Feminism can also be studied in terms of religion, culture and consciousness, charting the symbolic, psychological and cultural consciousness and cultural connection between the definition of women as inferior, mentally, morally and physically weak, and male monopolization of knowledge and power (Radford, 1996).

It has been pointed out that the roots of women's oppression are grounded in religion. To remedy this situation, Christian women should participate in women's movements. Women theologians should preach the gospel that liberates their fellow women from domination and subordination. The Christian gospel should bring about total transformation of the Church. Women should examine the biblical passages that men use to relegate them to subordinate positions critically and use these very passages to preach a liberating gospel, hence the feminist theology of liberation. Mananzan (1998) quotes Rosemary Ruether, a feminist theologian who delineates the critical principles of liberation theology:

> The critical principle of feminist theology is the promotion of the full humanity of women. Whatever denies, or diminishes, or distorts the full humanity of women is therefore appraised as not redemptive. Theologically speaking, whatever diminishes or denies the full humanity of woman must be presumed neither to reflect the divine nor an authentic relation to the divine nor to reflect the authentic nature of things, nor to be the message and work of an authentic redeemer of the community of redemption.

Feminist liberation theology requires Christian leaders to reinterpret Scriptures in relation to the history of the church doctrine and from women's point of view. The Church's discriminatory and sexist preaching must be scrutinized, and attention should be paid to the tradition of addressing the congregation of men and women as "fellow men" or "brothers". Certain Bible texts reflect the way sexism affects the lives of women and relations between men and women. These passages reflect ancient Jewish culture and are still used today to justify the oppression of women in society, within the Church and the family. When the gospel is taught, it should not present the relationships between men and women from the perspective of ancient Jewish culture. Jesus' message of liberation for the whole person and community cuts across cultures and makes people more human. (Mbuya-Beya, 1998).

Female theologians should not be satisfied with profound exclusive utilitarian services in church, because church activities and services are profoundly affected by gender discrimination. Feminist theologians should challenge religious beliefs that discriminate women (Mat.15; 10-11, Mark. 7; 14-23)

Jesus challenges men that "true defilement comes from the heart of a man". Many female theologians lament that religions oppress women, but Jesus openly allowed them to approach and discuss with him the message of liberation.

Mbuya-Beya (1998) mentions that feminine theology is also concerned with the life of all women, whatever their levels of education and their social positions. As Africa is struggling and fighting to free herself from fear, hunger, racism and political, economic and religious oppression, Christian women should also risk their lives to defend the rights of the weak and oppressed, so that the gospel seed may be broadcast and take root in African soil. The Christian gospel should liberate women from poverty, illiteracy, ignorance, poor health and dependence on men.

Religious institutions should preach the gospel that liberates men and women from the need to dominate one another. Considering the fact that illiteracy is high in Africa, it is essential for women in Africa to have access to the press and media, of all types. Religious institutions should promote educational programmes that address gender imbalances. Religious leaders should defend the weak and the most vulnerable in the face of dictatorial and political power and should protect people against oppression. Religious institutions should encourage women to enroll for further studies, especially courses like sciences and sacred subjects, in order to counteract the silence many women keep (Wayne, 1998).

When Jesus cured the woman whose back had been bent a long time, he was saying to all women: "Straighten your back, my daughter, walk, erect now, be proud of being a woman, a daughter of God." When he talks of adultery and promiscuity Jesus says "Any man who looks at a woman lustfully has already committed adultery in his heart" (Matthew 5:28). In this context Jesus was condemning the prostitution of men that is in the mind and the heart and that drives men to abuse women sexually. In the cases of the woman who sinned (Luke 7:36-50) and the adulterous woman (John 8:1-11), Jesus did not condemn them, because the patriarchal society only condemned women as prostitutes, not their male accomplices. Because Jesus was filled with pity for the way men treated women in the Jewish culture, he invited women to a true conversion of the heart and to have a personal relationship with him. In Jesus' judgment, both men and women were guilty of promiscuity, something that men resist even today.

Mark 2:27 reports how Jesus opposed traditional and cultural taboos that were an obstacle to life and liberation. He declared that the Sabbath was made for man, not man for the Sabbath. He awakened the consciousness of his own people to the unique and supreme value of the human person, the value that must be considered superior to any religious practice. He criticized the purely external religion of the Pharisees, together with religious practices that ignored the necessities of life (Mbuya–Beya, 1998).

Today, Jesus still criticizes cultural taboos and the external religious practices of religious institutions that ignore the needs of women. In the same way that Jesus warned the Jewish people, he also warns people today that the liberation of all women and all men comes through the cross, through breaking away from anything in societal traditions which is not the source of abundant life. In Matthew 76:24, Jesus challenges his disciples to take up his cross if they wished to follow him. It is the way of the cross that will make people break away from cultures and religious teachings that relegate women to positions of inferiority. Through the cross of Christ, the African woman will liberate herself and in this way she will contribute to the liberation of all humanity in Jesus Christ.

The feminist theology of liberation provides a unique opportunity to ignore the differences between men and women and to dare to leave the beaten paths and reveal Christ so that he may empower both African men and women to live their lives in full, as men and women and children of God. The principal message of Christianity is the good news of salvation that liberates the whole being not only from sin, death and hell but from all dehumanizing influences, including oppression, domination, exploitation, injustice, discrimination and poverty.

For the feminist theology of liberation to be realised, a process of evangelization and preaching in the context of the total environment – economic, social, political and religious – should take into consideration historical factors that affect human destiny. Salvation should liberate men and women from all that hinders their development. The prophetic teachings of human liberation shared this basic insight regarding salvation being concrete. Prophet Isaiah announced liberation for Jews exiled in Babylon. Jeremiah spoke of the homecoming of the scattered sons of Israel. Ezekiel announced that Yahweh would give people a new life and a new spirit. Luke 4:18-21 reports Jesus announcing a liberation gospel, "The spirit of the Lord has been given to me, for He has anointed me, He has sent me to bring the good news to the poor, to proclaim liberty to captives and to give the blind new sight, to set the downtrodden free and to proclaim the Lord's year of favour." Female theologians should proclaim this message that will open the eyes of those who are gender-blind, so that both men and women receive total liberation and salvation.

> Patriarchy is the basic principle underlying not only the subordination of women to men, but of one rule to another, of colonies to master, of children to adults, of monarchs and subjects, of being believers to clergy. In other words patriarchy is racism, classism, colonialism and clericalism as well as sexism. Fundamental patriarchy is a masculine power structure in which all relationships are understood in terms of superiority and inferiority and social cohesion is assured by the exercise of dominative powers.

Women keep these patriarchal structures intact, therefore female theologians have the task of unmasking the patriarchal connections in culture and ideology.

The hierarchy in Ugandan church structures and kingdoms such as Buganda, Bunyoro and Busoga reflect dominance by some men over other men, as well as over women. For example, men should prostrate themselves before their kings, the clergy should obey bishops, bishops should obey the Pope, cardinals and archbishops, thus dominance by men impinges on all areas of life, not only on women. Feminine theology cannot be realised until the patriarchal structures that bring about sexual inequality are addressed by both men and women.

In January 1983, a conference of the Ecumenical Association of Third World Theologians (EATWOT) was held in Geneva. One-third of the participants were women. It was agreed that a women's desk be established in church institutions for the purpose of developing a theology of liberation for Third World women. Some of the tasks for the women's desk in the church were to conduct a structural analysis of the rights of women in terms of their economic, political, socio-cultural and religious situations. The desk was also mandated to discuss the patriarchal element in theology and to reformulate theology from the perspective of a full humanity. The EATWOT of 1983 gave birth to a commission of women theologians. During development of a feminine liberation theology for Third World countries, the following issues were to be addressed.

(i)   Ways in which women are oppressed and their response to it in society and the church.

(ii)   Social analysis of women's economic, cultural, political and socio-cultural situations.

Mananzan (1998) reports that a continental Christian conference for women was held on in November 1985, at which 27 women representing churches from Hong Kong, India, Japan, Korea, Malaysia, Sri-Lanka and the Philippines met in Manila to share their insights into feminine liberation theology. These women denounced various types of oppression and dehumanization originating from foreign economic domination, state repression and racial strife. The delegates condemned vehemently the following injustices visited upon women by men:

(i)   In India, the dowry system, bride burning, forced sterilization and sexual discrimination.

(ii)   In the Philippines, job discrimination, exposure to health hazards in factories, institutional prostitution due to sex tourism, torture and rape during military interrogations.

(iii) In Malaysia, religious fundamentalism, and diminishing political freedom.

(iv)   In Japan, the continuing male-oriented imperial system and the development of highly dangerous technology with its concomitant deadly hazards to health, pollution of the environment resulting from industrialization

(v)   In Korea, the painful separation caused by the division of the homeland, growing militarism and the continuing grip of Confucian family law, which makes the male the absolute master.

The delegates concluded that patriarchal churches in their countries of origin contributed to the subjugation and marganalisation of women. The courage of these women delegates should serve as an example for theologians and Christian women in Uganda and other countries, to inspire women to liberate their sisters who are dominated, suppressed and oppressed by a patriarchal society. Among the many challenging issues that dehumanize women in our society and that need to be addressed by theologians, are the following:

(a)   What contribution have Christian women made in the church to liberate women from the slavery of poverty, domination, poor health and illiteracy?

(b) · Have Christian women participated in liberating women from the dehumanizing activities of the Lord's Resistance Army in Northern Uganda? In this part of the country, women live in camps without sufficient food or scholastic materials, they are raped or abducted; children are defiled, suffer amputations, burns and death. What have female theologians done to combat this situation?

(c) Many young girls have been forced to engage in prostitution. Others, in institutions of higher learning and secondary schools, prostitute themselves to make ends meet. What have the Christian women done to curb these dehumanizing situations? Remember that these women are the mothers of the future.

(d) Sexual harassment in offices, homes, streets, marketplaces, classrooms and lecture rooms, availability of pornographic literature, nude dancing and dressing of mini skirts. Will Christian women keep on turning a blind eye to these evils as the God given dignity of women is being eroded and attacked? Cultural dictates such as female genital mutilation, dowries, early marriages, and children being denied education continue to undermine women's liberation and equality. How can female theologians address these issues?

(e) What role have Christian women played in keeping families?

(f) How can female theologians break into male-dominated structures? Will there come a time when women are appointed bishops and priests?

(g) How can female theologians break the culture of male domination in politics, public office, education and the marketplace?

(h) What role have female theologians played in building fruitful relationships between men and women in all situations?

In December 1994, an international conference took place in Costa Rica to discuss issues such as dowry, female circumcision, suttee, sexual harassment, prostitution, and women as victims of war, rape, and incest, wife-beating or domestic violence. The issues were discussed in cultural, ethnic, social and religious contexts.

In a society like Uganda, where women are oppressed, the church and society should encourage women to take courses in theology so that they are on equal footing with men in the church ministry. Theology should be attuned to the realities of life to make it effective. Considered from a feminist orientation, theology becomes sensitive to the situations of women and encourages them to be committed to work for the transformation of all created beings. Religion, which is the root cause of male domination and female oppression, also has the capacity to liberate the underprivileged, the downtrodden, despised and the poor in society, especially women. For equity to be realised in society, the root cause of gender imbalance, which is manifested in religious teachings and cultural dictates, must be addressed and uprooted for once and for all.

Feminist Theology in Islam

Riffat (1998) describes women such as Khadijah and Aishah (wives of the prophet Mohammed and Rabiaal-Basri) as outstanding in early Islam. However, Islamic tradition has remained strongly patriarchal. The Qur'an, which is the source of Islamic tradition and God's word, was transmitted through the Angel Gabriel to Muhammed Sunnah (practice of prophet Mohammed), Hadith (the oral traditions which are attributed to prophet Muhammad) and Fiqh (jurisprudence) have been interpreted only by men who have arrogated to themselves the task of defining the theological, sociological and eschatological status of Muslim women. Riffat (1998) outlines three basic theological assumptions of Islam that are similar to Jewish teachings and upon which the super structure of men's alleged superiority has been erected:

(i)   That God's primary creation is man, not woman, since woman is believed to have been created from man's rib, hence the woman is derivative and secondary.

(ii) That woman, not man, was the primary agent of man's fall or expulsion from the Garden of Eden; hence all daughters of Eve are to be regarded with hatred, suspicion and contempt.

(iii) That woman was created not only from man but also for man, which makes her existence merely instrumental and not fundamental.

Islamic, Jewish and Christian belief in the myth that Adam was God's primary creation and that Eve was made from Adam's rib is rooted in the Yahwist account of creation given in Genesis 2:18-24. However, an analysis of the Qur'anic descriptions of human creation shows the Quar'an using both feminine and masculine terms and imagery to describe the creation of humanity from a single source. In Genesis 1:25ff, the priestly writer shows that God created man and woman as equal partners and in His image. Implicit in a number of Quranic passages is that God's original creation was undifferentiated humanity, neither man nor woman. Riffat (1998) raises a fundamental question: If the Qur'an makes no distinction between the creation of man and woman, why do Muslims believe that Hawwa was created from Adam's rib?

Riffat (1998) shows that it is more likely that the mention of the rib story entered the Islamic tradition during the early centuries of Islam, after being incorporated in the Hadith literature. In this context there are six Hadiths important to Islamic faith, which are recited in Sahih-al-Bukhari and Sahih Muslim, which Sunni Muslims regard as the most two authoritative collections and whose authority is exceeded only by the Qur'an:

(i)   Treat women well for woman was created from a rib. The most curved portion of the rib is its upper portion which, if straightened, will break, but if it is left as it is, it will remain crooked.

(ii)   The woman is like a rib. If you try to straighten her, she will break. So if you wish to derive benefit from her, do so while she is still slightly bent.

(iii) Whoever believes in Allah and the Last Day should not hurt his neighbour.

(iv)   Woman is like a rib. If you attempt to straighten it, you can break it, but if you leave it alone you could benefit and the crookedness will remain in her.

(v)   Woman has been created from a rib and will in no way be straightened for you. If you wish to benefit by her, benefit by her while crookedness remains in her. And if you attempt to straighten her, you will break her and breaking her is divorcing her.

(vi)   He who believes in Allah and the hereafter, if he witnesses any matter, he should talk in good terms about it or keep quiet. Act kindly towards women, for a woman is created from a rib and the most crooked part of the rib is its top. If you attempt to straighten it, you will break it and if you leave it, its crookedness may remain; therefore act kindly towards women.

The above Islamic teaching leaves many unanswered questions for life in modern times.

(i)   If the woman was made from a man's crooked rib, did the man remain with straight ribs that do not need straightening?

(ii) Physically and biologically, does a man have straight ribs and the woman crooked ones?

(iii) If both have crooked ribs, don't they need straightening?

(iv) If they cannot be straightened, don't they both need to be treated with care, love and kindness?

Theologically, the history of women's inferior status in Islamic (and Jewish and Christian) tradition began with the story of Hawwa's (Eve's) creation from a crooked rib, although in Jewish and Christian creation history Genesis 3 mentions how woman took the lead in the fall of man. The negative impact of these stories on the life of the Jewish, Christian and Muslim women is impossible to overstate. From the beginning of human history these stories have affected the status of women in terms of politics, religion, economy, culture and social activities, and have definitely hindered women's development. Riffat (1998) insists that the rib has no place in the Qur'an, which upholds the view that man and woman were created equal by God. The existing inequality between men and women was not mandated by God but must be seen as a subversion of God's original plan for humanity. The Qur'an does not discriminate against women. The cumulative Jewish, Christian, Roman and Hellenistic biases that existed in the early years of religious expansion infiltrated the Islamic tradition through Hadith literature which undermined the intent of the Qur'an to liberate women from the status of chattels or inferior creatures. The Qur'an emphasizes righteousness for both men and women and affirms equality of both and their fundamental rights to realise the human potential that women share equally with men. Qur'an teachings go beyond egalitarianism.

It exhibits particular solicitude towards women and other classes of disadvantaged persons. It provides particular safeguards for sexual and biological functions such as carrying, delivering, suckling and receiving offspring.

The God who speaks through the Qur'an is a God of justice, thus cannot promote unfairness, oppression, subordination, discrimination or wrongdoing. The Qur'an as the Word of God cannot be made a source of human injustice, to which Muslim women have been subjected. The goal of Qur'anic Islam is to establish peace, which can only exist in a just environment. It is important for Muslim feminist theologians to read, interpret and understand what God is talking to them in the Qur'anic teachings and in the context of the Islamic tradition to liberate not only Muslim women, but also Muslim men, from unjust social structures and systems of thought.

The United Nations Conference on Population and Development which was held in Cairo in September 1994 was an important landmark for raising global consciousness about a number of issues. Delegates deliberated about the agonizing issue that women were traditionally identified with their bodies, rather than their minds and spirits, yet they are not the owners of their bodies because they were controlled by men, the church, the state and the community. Muslim women delegates challenged the tradition of being identified with the body and also the control of their bodies by men. They stressed that issues of population control could not be discussed independently of development issues which focus on the whole person.

At this conference, Muslim women lamented that they were being monitored by men and that they were poor and illiterate and live in precarious environments. They stressed that the 1948 United Nations Declaration of Human Rights should be realised by every Muslim women.

Black Feminist Theology

Experiencing black women bearing numerous responsibilities, holding the family and the church together, with little money and under white oppression in America, Williams (1993) laments the enigma of being a black woman in a racist society. She recognises forces in the African-American community working to conquer black women's power to resist and rise above obstacles.

Black women suffered dual violence, from white people and black men. Some black men in America wanted to conquer black women, by destroying their ability to resist and rise above trouble. They were beaten by their black husbands, forced to hand over their salaries, and the result was frequently divorce. The physical violence to which black women were subjected was only matched by emotional and psychological pressure (Williams, 1993).

In the era of segregation, some black men who were in charge of selecting black women to fill posts would distribute the jobs to women on the basis of the women's willingness to submit to illicit affairs with them. Racism and male supremacy in the courts and in social service offices left black women without legal recourse.

Many African-American denominational churches prohibit black women from asking critical questions about women's oppression and about the way the Bible and by the Christian church, in all its male-dominated forms, supports and reinforces that oppression. Relatedly Lipsitz Bem (1993) shows that the first women liberation movement that began in America stressed for liberation of the African -American slaves and the white women from patriarchal oppression.

Against this background, black feminist theology attempts to help black women to see, affirm and have confidence in the importance of their experiences and faith for determining the character of the Christian religion in the African-American community. It challenges all oppressive forces impeding black women's struggle for survival and for the development of a positive and productive quality of life conducive to freedom and well-being of women and the family. It opposes all oppression based on race, sex, class, sexual preference, physical disability and caste. It assumes the necessity of responsible freedom for all human beings. It concerns itself with faith, survival and the freedom struggle of African women the world over. It identifies and criticizes black male oppression of black females, as well as white racism that oppresses Africans, both female and male. It affirms the full humanity of women. (Williams and Lipsitz Bem 1993)

Women's liberation among black-Americans arose from a slave heritage. The book of Genesis, Chapters 16 and 21, tells of Hagar and Sarah. Sarah gave Hagar to Abraham to continue his lineage as Sarah was barren. But when Hagar became pregnant she despised her mistress, and this led Sarah to chase her away. When a child of promise was born to Sarah, Hagar and Ishmael were chased away on the orders of Sarah, but God also blessed Hagar and her son in their state of need, when they were stranded in the wilderness. As a slave, Hagar was brutalized by Sarah, her owner.

Similarly, black-American women slaves were treated cruelly by husbands and wives of their owners and white female employers. As a slave, Hagar had no authority over her body; it belonged to her owner, whose husband ravished Hagar. Ishmael was fathered by Abraham, but because Ishmael's mother was a slave, Ishmael was chased away with his mother. Black-American women were treated as brutally. Their bodies were owned by their masters because they were slaves. Black feminist theology sees the God of Hagar in the wilderness as a liberating God who does not abandon slaves to suffering. From Hagar's story, female slaves learnt that God responds to pain and bondage. He also understood the suffering of black women under slavery and servitude and liberated them.

According to Genesis 16:1-16 and 21:9-21 Hagar's predicament involved slavery, poverty, ethnicity, sexual and economic exploitation, surrogacy, rape, domestic violence, homelessness, single parenting, alienation and a radical encounter with God. God approached Hagar with a recourse that gave new hope and vision for survival. God would be instrumental in the development of Ishmael and Hagar's quality of life. Genesis 21:20 explains that, as Ishmael grew up he was with God; he became an archer; God responded to Hagar and Ishmael's situations and heritage. Today, Hagar's situation is similar to that of many African–American women's predicament of poverty, sexual and economic exploitation, surrogacy, domestic violence, homelessness, motherhood, single parenting and ethnicity, but in all these most encounter the God of Hagar, who meets their needs in the wilderness that is slavery in America.

Surrogacy has been a major theme in African-American women's history. Like Hagar, African-American slaves had little control over their bodies or labour. They were exploited in any way their masters desired. Their reproductive capacity belonged to the slave owners. They experienced sexual exploitation. Black female slaves were forced to substitute for slave owners' wives in nurturing white children. Black women worked for longer hours than men in plantations.

The highest position a slave could attain was that of driver or overseer. Women made pregnant by owners were often abandoned. They would haul logs, drive out hogs and set posts into the ground for fences. They drove ox-wagons, tended mills and ploughed like men. They milked cows, penned sheep, grazed cattle, staked them, fed and rubbed down their masters' horses. They prepared beds and undressed children and tucked them into sleep. Williams (1993) tells the story of a slave woman who met her death at her master's hands:

> Hetty's death was hastened by the dreadful chastisement she received from her master during pregnancy. It was as follows: One of the cows had dragged the rope away from the stake to which Hetty had fastened it and got loose. Her master flew into a rage and ordered Hetty to be stripped quite naked, notwithstanding her pregnancy, and to be tied to a tree yard. He then flogged her as hard as he could lick, both with a whip and cowskin, till she was all over streaming with blood. He rested and then beat her again and again. Poor Hetty was delivered after severe beating and labour of a dead child. She appeared to recover after her confinement but her body and limbs swelled to a great size and she lay on the mat in the kitchen till water burst out of her body and she died.

Such brutal treatment of black women by whites is condemned by women the world over. Women, irrespective of colour and class, require proper treatment, respect and protection.

Williams, (1993) says, because their slave masters used them for sexual liaisons they are labeled i.e. "loose, over-sexed, erotic, easily responsive to sexual advances of men, especially the whites and the immoral." Slave women were mated with studs, dogs and horses on the orders of whites.

Genesis 16 and 21 provides evidence of women surrendering their bodies to their masters against their will. Isaac and Jacob were also given slave girls for sexual pleasure. King David, in his old age, was given a young girl to keep him warm.

Williams (1993) says that Africa, the source of black-American heritage, is depicted in many American sources as a wilderness, a continent inhabited by sub-human savages and not civilized according to white standards. Blackness is looked upon with disdain. In North America, popular culture, religion, science and politics have worked together to assign a permanent negative value to the black colour. This has led to the formation of an American consciousness that considers black people as frightening, dangerous and repulsive. In a subtle way, the repulsion the colour black is communicated in every aspect of American culture. For example, whites put on black when mourning the dead, thus black is equated with death, misery and sorrow. Americans assign black to evil, for example hero is believed to be black. Such words as 'blackmail' and 'black book' show that black is something related to evil. On the other hand, white symbolizes purity, angels, heaven and perfection. This is confirmed by the Protestants' song which says; Are you washed in the blood of Jesus? Are you washed as white as snow? And wash me whiter than snow, Lord or white wash me than snow." These two songs associate white with purity and perfection, a basis which white men use to oppress black women.

Biblical interpretation of black people is based on Genesis 9:20-27, where Noah cursed Ham or Canaan for looking upon his father's nakedness, decreeing that he shall be a slave of slaves to his brothers. Colonialists interpreted this story to equate blackness with slavery. The perpetual enslavement of blacks was thus ordained by God and was a curse, thus the enslavement and backwardness of black people was intended by God, as recorded in the scriptures. Amos 9:7 records that God was angry with the Israelites and said to them: "You are no more to me than these Cushites." The Cushites were darker-skinned Ethiopians.

Jesus assures the enslaved that his divine righteousness will alleviate their suffering. In Luke 4:18-19, Jesus said:

> The Spirit of the Lord is upon me, because He has anointed me to preach the Good News to the poor. He has sent me to proclaim release to the captives and recovery of sight to the blind, to set to liberty those who are oppressed, to proclaim the acceptable year of our Lord.

Black women need to encounter God, the creator of all races, who transforms the consciousness of people. The power of the liberating God is not limited to any space or time.

Female theologians the world over should use religion and other measures to liberate women who are experiencing harsh conditions, so that suffering women can participate in the development processes of their societies. The Gospel of Christ should be preached to suit present concerns and issues. Reconciliation, forgiveness, confidence, self-acceptance, determination, love and commitment should be the overriding virtues as black women struggle towards liberation worldwide. Women should desist from harassing other women wherever they are, because this hinders struggle for liberation.

The God who liberated the Israelites from Egyptian, Assyrian and Babylonian slavery is the same God who is ready to liberate black women today, in whatever circumstances. Women the world over are being oppressed, but God is the redeemer, liberator and the source of peace, and identifies with women in situations that overwhelm them.

Gender and Culture

Many people today are worried that modern developments, technology and science, feminist movements and emancipation and promotion of gender equality are interfering with culture. Therefore some traditionalists feel that, for ethical and religious reasons, gender equality should not be promoted. Elsewhere, the cultural values of any society are described as a major constraint to attempts to promote gender equality.

Nida (1983) defines culture as all learned behaviour which is socially acquired, that is the material and non-material traits which are passed from one generation to another. Culture is both transmissible and cumulative and the traits are cultural in the sense that they are transmitted by the society, not by genes. This makes the transmission of culture different from the biological heritage of human beings or animals. Culture is a way of behaving, thinking and reacting to situations. Unlike biological traits, culture changes with time. Culture refers to the norms and practices of a society as defined by a prevailing ideology. Such practices include turning women into commodities through bride price, inheritance of widows, and use of girls to appease vengeful spirits in the form of sacrifice, polygamy and the replacement of dead married daughters with their younger sisters. The man is the head of the family whether he is handicapped or not.

Sigmund Freud claimed that human culture began when young males, who had been kept from the women possessed by their father, plotted against him, killed and ate him. Because of this, the young men became remorseful and expressed their feelings by sacrificing a totemic animal, which had become for them a father substitute. Having come into possession of their father's wives, they developed a Oedipus complex and created the laws of incest. Freud's theory, based on the Oedipus complex (antagonism to one's father and sexual attraction to one's mother), is appealing to people who take for granted that the patrilineal family, following the father's line, with strong paternal domination, is a characteristic of all peoples. In matrilineal societies, status and property are inherited through the mother's line. The Oedipus complex explains some psychiatric phenomena in culture. This text is based on certain fundamental questions that arise from the definition of culture given above:

(i)   How are men and women expected to behave in a given culture?

(ii) What is the relationship between sons and fathers and sons and mothers, and daughters and brothers?

(iii) What is the relationship between men and women?

(iv) What is the nature of the societal assumptions about gender relations?

(v) What is the relationship between children and the community?

(vi) What cultural practices bind women in the societal setting?

(vii) What is the relationship between gender and culture?

(viii) Are development initiatives culturally neutral?

(xi) Does culture empower or disempower women?

Expectations about attributes and behaviour appropriate to women or men and relations between men and women are shaped by culture. Gender identities and gender relations are critical aspects of culture because it shapes daily life in the family, the wider community and the workplace. Gender, like race or ethnicity, functions as an organizing principle for society because of the cultural meanings assigned to being male or female. This is evident in the division of labour based on gender. In most societies, there are clear distinctions between women's work and men's work, both in the household and in the wider community and cultural explanations of why this should be so. The patterns and explanations vary from society to society and change over time.

While the specific nature of gender relations varies among societies, the general trend is for women to have less personal autonomy, fewer resources at their disposal and limited influence over the decision-making processes that shape their societies and their own lives. This pattern of disparity based on gender is both a human rights and a development issue.

Societies and cultures are not static. They are living entities that are continually being renewed and shaped. As with culture, gender definitions change over time. Change is shaped by many factors. Cultural change occurs as communities and households respond to social and economic shifts associated with globalisation, new technology, environmental pressures, armed conflict, development projects, etc. Today the employment sector attracts more women into the labour force. The involvement of women in the labour sector has had an influence on women roles at home and brings about criticism from the wider community, since they tend to leave domestic work and child care to house maids.

The greater presence of women in formal employment sector influences public perceptions of the roles women play in the family and the workplace. Efforts to reshape values relating to women and gender relations have focused on concerns such as the number of girls participating in universal primary education (UPE), secondary education, tertiary and other institutions of higher learning, women's access to paid work, entrepreneurship, the employment sector and the public's attitude towards violence against women. Many people have embraced the changes in cultural attitudes towards these issues, while others resist.

Cultural values are being re-interpreted continually in response to new needs and conditions in a society. The Canadian International Development Agency (2001) shows a member of the Cambodian government who used to avoid using the image of women when describing the need to question cultural norms that reinforce gender inequality. She says the aim is not to overturn the cultural identity of a nation, but to focus on the elements within it that oppress women;

> There is a Cambodian saying that men are a piece of gold and women are a piece of cloth. The piece of gold, when it is dropped in mud is still a piece of gold, but a piece of cloth, once stained is stained forever. If you are a prostitute, if you have been raped, if you are a widow, you are no longer that virginal piece of cloth. But men, whether they are prostitutes or criminals, they are still pieces of gold. When there is such a saying and perception, then there is something wrong with that culture that is when you want to change it.

The Canadian International Development Agency (2001) states that changes in gender relations are highly contested, partly because such changes have immediate implications for everyone, as both men and women are affected equally. Gender roles, especially women's roles as wives and mothers, can be potent symbols of cultural change or continuity. People are advocating change to cultural values that relegate women to subordinate positions. Most women are agitating for their freedom and dignity. Women's organisations and movements are struggling to gain recognition from male-dominated society through their participation in the labour market, politics and education and by agitating for human rights.

Culturally speaking, in a patrilineal society, status and property are inherited through the father's line. According to Chapman (1989), sons in patrilineal societies are potential rivals for their fathers' status and the property they will inherit. As a result, fathers in patrilineal societies tend to be domineering, inspiring reverential fear in their sons and being jealous of them. The wives in patrilineal societies are never fully integrated into their husbands' lineages. This explains why women do not inherit their husbands' properties at their death. Children born into a patrilineal line belong to the fathers' line. For this reason wives in patrilineal marriages have no children of their own but produce to extend the lineage of the man's clan and when divorced, they go back to their birth families.

A woman is not shared by men but can be inherited at the death of her husband. In some cultures, such as among the Banyarwanda of Rwanda (Nida, 1983) a man could loan his wife to his male visitors for a night. In other cultures men are expected to share their wives with particular men, and can expect the favour to be returned. If women are surrendered for sexual union with other men by their husbands they have no right to object.

According to Chapman (1989), culture determines that men and women do not compete for the same occupations. Their roles are differentiated according to their physical constitutions. Traditionally, male and female occupations were linked to their family roles, which were differentiated by sex, and involved rigid and clear-cut gender-related division of labour. Childbearing, breastfeeding, child rearing, caring for the extended family, cooking and production of crops were women's work, and meant that women were not available for social or political activities outside the family circle. Most cultures have a history of gender inequality. The research carried out by the writer of this text in Apac, Kisoro, Kabale, Mbarara and Kapchorwa districts and central part of Uganda, the following cultural practices illustrate the perceived inferiority of women:

- Women are expected to kneel before men while serving food, welcoming or talking to men or asking for something. Women are not permitted to look directly into the eyes of men when talking to them. Women are expected by the culture to carry water for their husbands' baths.
- Less compensation is paid for the murder of a woman than for that of a man. Female relatives receive a smaller share of the bride wealth of a daughter than male relatives do.
- A man is compensated for his wife's adultery while he is permitted to be promiscuous and polygamous. A man may beat his wife if she is caught in adultery; he may even divorce her, but women are expected to tolerate and endure polygamy or promiscuous behaviour.
- Culture demands that a wife confesses to her husband even when she is not in the wrong, but a man would not confess to his wife.
- Women may not initiate divorce.
- Women have no public or political roles, but are responsible for agriculture and are only housewives.
- The husband is the head of the family. This headship denies women equality with men in most aspects of life. The woman is treated like a child.
- Polygamy is an acceptable and common form of marriage. Childlessness in marriage is blamed on women.
- The birth of a baby boy is received with more joy than that of a girl (Chapman, 1989; Kwesiga, 2000).
- In Kapchorwa, female circumcision is obligatory; the rationale is to check promiscuity.

However, in patriarchal societies women are afforded the highest status from the point of view of motherhood. The mother is regarded as the effective symbol of life. Children honour the mother more than they do the father (Chapman, 1989).

As a result of man's activity, the environment is in constant change, hence culture is dynamic. Research carried out by the writer of this text in Hoima, Bushenyi, Kabale, Mbarara, Kapchorwa and Arua found that, although the Ugandan constitution gives women the same rights as men before the law, societal ideas, attitudes and customs have ensured and perpetuated a negative image of women. The fact that most ethnic groups in Uganda are patriarchal in nature has ensured male authority over women in the home and dominance in all important social institutions, such as marriage, policy-making at all levels and administration. This state of affairs is supported not only by men, but also by women.

Cultural practices in most parts of Uganda hold women not as equal partners to their counterparts, but as subordinates. Women are seen as workers who were married so that they could labour in homes and the fields, or as a necessary source of wealth, as they bring bride price on marriage, or they are perceived as mere reproduction agents. Traditionally, they are expected to fulfill the roles of mother, housewife, family worker and agricultural labourers. Kasekende (1991) says that 80 per cent of Uganda's agricultural labour is provided by women, who are not paid for their labour. They prepare the land, sow, plant, weed, harvest and store crops. The harvest is used to feed husbands, children and extended-family dependants. Women do all household chores related to feeding, such as fetching water and firewood and washing up utensils. In Karamoja, women are responsible for building houses for their husbands and children. Cultural attitudes towards women have doubtlessly contributed to and perpetuated the image of women as inferior in most African countries.

Cultural expectations are that women should be good wives, thus a good wife in an African cultural setting should be able to endure drudgery and hardship without complaining. She must have the ability and stamina to endure physical and emotional pain. She must ensure that her husband and the entire clan are well cared for. When her husband disciplines her, she must be grateful because "a good beating is a symbol of love, it shows that a man cares", a saying in most African societies. A good wife takes care of her husband as she does her children, she teaches her children to stay out of sight when their father is tired, indisposed or busy. If the husband suddenly and inexplicably disappears for a few nights or even a year, this is her opportunity to demonstrate her faithfulness and commitment to the marriage. She must not consort with other men (Gallin, 1986; Bagyendera, 1991).

Culture prescribes that a good wife remains on duty late at night, waiting for her husband who has gone drinking and returns late. She should not sleep before the man returns, so that she opens the door for him, baths and feeds him and, if he imbibed excessively, to undress him and put him to bed. If the husband wakes with a hangover, the wife must prepare something good for him to eat. A good wife must look beautiful and be cheerful and tolerant no matter when the husband returns, as men do not like sulky wives. She must never inquire about the husband's comings and goings, this is construed as nagging. If a man obtains another wife, the wife may not complain because this is a right afforded men by the culture (Bagyendera, 1991).

The culture prescribes that a good wife should not keep the company of emancipated or rebellious, divorced or progressive women. If she does so she will be spoilt by the ideas of these women, and this may eventually ruin her marriage. Bagyendera (1991) explains that a good wife is a skilled and imaginative cook and knows what the husband requires, thereby keeping him away from other women. Under no circumstances must she ask a domestic worker to cook, because men enjoy eating food cooked by their wives, this is one of the reasons they married.

If the husband talks to other men, a good wife will keep a low profile and keep away from them because men's issues are beyond women's understanding. She must never contradict her husband as men do not like intelligent women. Beauty and good performance in the bedroom are all that are required from a woman. As a wife, her manner of dress must be modest – she must not be mistaken for a prostitute. A good wife will not use make-up, as it may mean she wishes to seduce other men. She should wear clothes that match the standard set by her husband (Bagyendera, 1991).

Culture prescribes that a good wife's work is not affected by pregnancy. She must work hard up to the birth. She must follow the example set by her mother-in-law, who was never weakened by pregnancy. She should not relax at home, dodging work, with the excuse that she is pregnant. She must never show signs of fatigue. A good wife must work, even under stress, if she shows signs of fatigue she will be replaced by a young bride or the husband will go to his other wives. Men cannot abide sickly wives. Wives should never be arrogant or conceited. If food is scarce, the wife feeds her husband first, then the children; good wives are able to withstand hunger and material deprivation graciously. A good wife is expected to ensure that her children are clever and disciplined, because such children are a credit to her husband. She must decorate the house and keep it clean so that her husband can take pride in bringing his friends home. When her husband's boss visits, she must be full of life but appear docile at the same time. This balance is necessary, otherwise she might ruin her husbands career by exposing her ignorance. If the husband allows her to take up paid employment, the job must not prejudice her performance at home. Money earned must never be spent without his permission. She must not be overambitious, because this may influence her work at home (Gallin ,1986, Bagyendera; 1991).

Culturally, good wives are always obedient to their husbands' mothers and fathers in law, relatives and the entire clan. She must be submissive and maintain a good relationship with her mother-in-law, at all costs she does not talk much when the husband is talking, because he is the head of the house. It is summed up by the saying, "A home must have only one boss, just as two cocks cannot crow in the same compound and a woman should speak once but the husband twice."

According to the culture, a married woman may not sue her husband, either in court or at a clan meeting, unless the complaint is serious. Even in such circumstances judgment at the local setting will always favour the man. It is a bad omen for the woman to win a case against her husband. In the past women have been unable to sue their husbands, even when they have been battered (Gallin, 1986). Cultural attitudes present obstacles to the dissemination of legal information, its reception, demystification and the issue of equal protection before the law. Attitudes also play a role in the continued lack of legal awareness among women.

Concerning marriage, it is customary for a man to make the first move to commence proceedings. If a woman did so, she would be out of order and could be labeled a prostitute. Women are on the whole on the receiving end of initiatives and must remain there. When a man makes the first move towards marriage, the woman is expected to decline the first time. She should pretend to ignore her suitor by evasive tactics. She is expected to take her time before announcing her decision because this shows the man she will be slow to speak to her husband once married. If a woman says "yes" after the man's first move, he may take flight. If a man asks for a woman's hand in marriage or makes sexual advances, the woman should not reject the man outright but should find ways of avoiding him, such as ignoring his letters, phone calls, etc. In a society rampant with HIV/Aids, promiscuity, defilement, rape and other forms of sexual abuse, parents should be aware of cultural practices that expose girls to danger. Parents should teach their daughters to say "no" to men. However, they should also teach their daughters to say "yes" for example, to an offer of marriage. Both young boys and girls need guidance by their parents on fair treatment of members of the opposite sex.

Ugandan culture does not encourage parents to discuss sex with their children. However, parents should talk to their children, especially to adolescents, winning their confidence, being aware of their needs, discussing the emotional and physical changes they are going through, talking about the sexual feelings and development they are experiencing and advising them on coping with it. Parents should not take their children for granted as they used to do in traditional societies. Today many things undermine the family, such as sexual harassment, violence and rape, which parents should talk about freely, to prevent their children from becoming victims.

Kawamara (1991) discussed punishments meted out by the Bakiga of Rukungiri to women who conceived out of wedlock. Girls who fell pregnant before marriage were punished by being thrown off the River Kisizi falls. Girls would be wrapped in banana leaves and led to their death by their own brothers. This disciplinary measure was aimed at preventing young girls from indulging in premarital sex. The punishment was barbaric and discriminated against women, as the boys or men who were responsible were spared. On such occasions, hundreds of spectators would gather to condemn the young girls and their irresponsible mother for failing to raise them properly. The congregation would cheer the brothers for their bravery. Women had no power to oppose such evil practices because, culturally, they had no say in beliefs and practices affecting their lives, they implemented cultures that undermined them.

It was considered a blot on the family name if a girl fell pregnant before marriage. Mothers would be scorned by their neighbours and surrounding villages while the men who were responsible laughed at the victims. Girls who perished over the centuries by being tied to trees, abandoned in forests, rivers and lakes, flung over cliffs became a ransom for many girls who meet their death for producing outside since today many girls who give birth before marriage continue living with their parents. Christianity played a role in preventing such barbaric practices by heathen cultures.

Sometimes mothers would help their daughters to abort in order to spare them embarrassment. According to EDIRISA (2000), in southwest Uganda, Bakiga women who fell pregnant out of wedlock were tied to trees on isolated islands to warn others. A man who had no cows to pay a bride price could go to the island and fetch such a girl, if nobody fetched her, she would die. The men who made these girls pregnant were not punished.

According to Chapman (1989) customs of eating and drinking has much to say about societies' social structures in African setting. Women and girls used to have separate fireplaces for cooking their food, and their food came from different gardens from that of men. Women had a poorer nutritional status than men. For example, women were barred from eating eggs, goat's meat, fish, milk, grasshoppers and butter.

Kurz and Prather (1995) observed that, in Pakistan, boys were breastfed longer than girls and, in India, women curtailed breastfeeding of daughters so that the woman could fall pregnant again in order to bear a son. Kathleen also reports that boys received more expensive, high-calorie foods such as milk, butter and eggs than girls. She says that, in Bangladesh, severe malnutrition was reported in 14% of girls but only 5% of boys. In most African families men are served the best pieces of meat and larger portions than the women and children. If the food is not enough for the family, the wife is more likely to remain without so that the husband and children can eat.

Ssemanda (2003) reports that, in most African societies, men are served before the rest of the family. Men receive the best pieces of meat, while women and children are served soup. If food is scarce, it is reserved for men. Women are not supposed to eat before men. Women have to wait for their husbands to return from drinking before they eat, regardless of the time the man returns.

Ssemanda (2003) reports on the cultural practice of the Baganda called *okufumba/okuzza omuziga*, which involves a newly married woman preparing food for her in-laws, and the men eating the best parts of the meat while women sit and watch. This makes men very greedy. This unequal access to food constitutes violence against women. Since men are served great quantities of good quality food, women lose the strength required to carry out heavy tasks. Because of differential feeding practices, girls have less energy than boys, so cannot participate equally in societal activities or defend themselves.

Susie (1992) explains that, in Zimbabwe, bride price payments were crucial underpinnings of women's social position. Bride price was the basis of marriage and its dissolution. Research carried out by the author of this text in Uganda revealed that in Arua, Mbarara, Kapchorwa and Hoima, the payment of dowry was important because it provided the man and woman with status and cemented relationships. A woman acquired social status through hard work and the bearing of children, particularly sons. Barren women were divorced or their husband married other women who would produce sons. In all African cultures a wife lacked permanent authority over her children; if divorced she would be forbidden access to her children. Men had exclusive sexual rights over their wives, but women had no such rights over their husband. A woman was advised never to refuse her husband's sexual demands. Among the Batooro of western Uganda the saying 'Omusajya tayangwa' literally means that a man cannot be denied sex.

According to Preston (1984) a woman is sexually available only to the man she marries and then on demand, while promiscuity in a man, whatever his matrimonial and family commitments, is widely accepted as confirming his masculinity. Catholicism, along with other Christian religions, idealizes the purity of womanhood and the sanctity of motherhood, placing the mother on a pedestal from which she can only fall, while the man is free from the risk of such condemnation. It is widely accepted that a Catholic marriage subordinates the woman to her husband's will and care.

Preston (1984) explains that Latin American culture requires women to care for their husbands and children, yet they are considered to have an inferior body and to be physically weaker than men. They are also perceived to have a lower intellectual capacity and less admirable personalities. Women are expected to be submissive to male authority and seek male permission to carry out any activity on their own account. Preston goes on to report that, among the Ecuadorians, social convention does not allow a rural woman, if married, to leave her home for work, or visit relations away from the immediate neighbourhood, without first obtaining permission from her husband. Social convention allows men to be mobile, with no limitations on their freedom. It is mainly men who migrate in search of employment, while women do domestic work and assume responsibility for smallholdings while men are absent.

Susie (1992) explains that it is rare for the Zimbabwean state to consider women's concerns existing outside the spheres of biological reproduction and production of labour. Households are culturally divided by gender and the Shona-Ndebele societies are strongly male-dominated. However, women do have limited rights and a degree of autonomy. Although the society is patrilineal, polygyny was accepted and male elders controlled access to the means of production and the labour of junior men and women in their lineages. Through marriage women moved into villages in which they were strangers and in which men belonged to one "blood". This made women more vulnerable to control by the husband's family and more prone to witchcraft accusations, in most African societies it is mostly women who are associated with witchcraft.

Among the Shona and Ndebele, although men participated in agricultural tasks like ploughing and harvesting, women did the bulk of the agricultural work. As household heads, men used their position to distribute small pieces of land to their wives or inherited widows. Zimbabwean women, unlike those of other societies, could dispose of any produce from their plots and control granaries of staple foods, but a woman had the obligation to feed her husband and children since she had to till and work on the husband's field. Shona women did have several rights. For instance, they could dispose of income from their crops, beer brewing, handicraft and midwifery. They had rights to a satisfactory sexual relationship, to have children and to refuse remarriage upon widowhood, but these rights were eroded by colonialism and the spread of Christianity that stressed that men were the heads of families, providers, security, and controlled the activities of the family women inclusive.

Culturally, Zimbabwean women's economically-based power and social esteem were limited. Men had authority over land use and could use it to acquire more wives. Women were likely to lose access to their plots if widowed or divorced. A woman acquired social status through hard work and through the bearing of children, especially sons. Women had no permanent authority over children and if divorced, they would lose access to them. Men had exclusive sexual rights over wives, but women had no such rights over husbands and a woman was enjoined never to refuse her husband's sexual demands under any circumstances, (Susie, 1992).

Susie (1992) explains that, during the colonial era, Zimbabwean women were not incorporated into the proletariat, thus women were left in barren reserves along with children and elderly men. Colonialism deprived women of access to land, since only men and whites were allocated land. Women participated in the struggle for independence by the Zimbabwean people as messengers and feeding and clothing guerillas; even participating in military activities, but their efforts were not recognised. Black women were more affected by colonialism than men, since they were left on barren reserve land while men migrated to work for money. Women were legally subordinated and lacked employment opportunities in urban areas. In urban areas even domestic work was monopolized by men, because they could earn salaries. Like African women elsewhere, Zimbabwean women lacked substantial property, income and decision-making powers. They were denied white-collar jobs because of their illiteracy. Feminists had to address the structures that oppressed them, including dowry.

Most laws reflect the culture of a society supporting patriarchal ideologies, for example many laws legitimize subordination of women notwithstanding the equality guaranteed under the constitution. Violations of women's rights in a patriarchal society have one thing in common: the violations all originate from the viewpoint that women are owned by men. The cause of violence against women is the unequal relationship between men and women in society.

When women are raped, they are blamed, not the men who committed the rape. A letter written to the editor of the New Vision (Munyambazi, 2004) echoes the viewpoint of other African men who blames women for instigating men to rape them by raising the following issues:

(a) Was she in a disco, alone and after 02:00 a.m ?
(b) Was she in the company of people she does not know and did she accept their offer of a drink and a lift?
(c) How was she dressed? Were her knickers showing? Was her navel and breasts exposed? Was she wearing a see-through dress, exposing her body to the public?
(d) Did she go to a teachers' residence for coaching at night?
(e) Did she go to a video club or to view a blue movie in the company of boys?

Munyambazi (2004) concludes that women have lost their dignity, leading to "rotten values and behaviour", especially among the youth. Women should restore their lost dignity. He challenges women, as the backbone of the family, to go back to the cultural roots that subordinate them.

The views held by Munyambabazi (2004) are a reflection of a culture that is gender-biased and expects women to be at home by 06:00, to retain their virginity and to avoid leisure activities. On the other hand, in certain cultures for example, Karamoja, men and women go about naked, but there are no reports of women being raped because men are attracted by women's nakedness. In other societies, like Buganda and Kasese, women move around half-naked in their gomesi with breasts hanging out during the hot season, but they are not raped.

Men and women today are lost in a world between modern and traditional culture. There are increasing reports of fathers raping their daughters and young girls being defiled by those in whose care they are entrusted. Men defile children as young as three months and women as old as 70 years. God created humanity to rule over creation, to reason, apply intelligence and make choices. Even animals that cannot reason and make choices are sexually abused by human beings. The state should enforce laws that protect the weak and the defenseless, in order to curb rape and defilement.

Religious and cultural leaders should uphold values that ensure equality and human dignity. Men and women all need to come together to address the issues that undermine their dignity, such as homosexuality, rape and pornography.

Cultural and religious prescriptions that set women up as the only role models should be addressed. Both men and women should set examples to children in every aspect of life. Couples should talk to their children, raise boys and girls equally so as to counteract the factors that have a negative effect on the morals of both youth and adults. Female liberation will be realised only if men and women begin to treat each other as equal human beings who have dignity that is worth preserving. Isaiah talks of a peaceful kingdom from the royal line of David. Isaiah 11:3b-9 says:

> He will not judge by appearance, he will judge the poor fairly and defend the rights of the helpless. He will heal his people with justice and integrity. Wolves and sheep will live together in peace and leopards will lie down with young goats. Calves and lion cubs will feed together and little children will take care of them. Cows and bears will eat together and their cubs and calves will lie down in peace. Lions will eat straw as cattle do. Even a baby will not be

harmed if it plays near a poisonous snake. The land will be full of the knowledge of the Lord.

Religious leaders and feminists should preach the gospel that liberates humanity from evil, selfishness and self-centeredness. The liberation of humanity should lead to harmonious relationships based on equity in all aspects of life, at all times and places. Humanity should work to overcome the animal instinct that makes us abuse the dignity of others and ourselves. The prophetic voice of Isaiah 11:3-9 should be realised in human relationships.

Research conducted in Uganda, specifically Kigezi, Ankole and Buganda, found that girls are sacrificed to appease spirits and gods. At birth, Bakiga girls are "booked" for spirit appeasement and when they reach the age of 12-15 years, they are married to old men as sacrifices to native gods. Byamukama (1999) stunned the international community when he reported the Baganda cultural marriage of the 13-year-old Sarah Nakku to the Kabaka (King). He reported that Sarah Nakku of the Buganda *Fumbe* clan had been identified and given up by her father to fulfil the cultural dictates of becoming the 44-year-old Kabaka's ritual wife. The Kabaka was expected to abstain from sexual intercourse with her during and after the ceremonial installation, she was expected to remain a virgin throughout her life, she would be isolated from her family members and stay in Ganda, and she would leave school. She would remain a virgin, unmarried and without children because of the "prestigious status bestowed upon her as the Kabaka's first wife". This incident shows gender discrimination based on sex. Many cultures consider women to be "property" which men pass on to their fellow men in bars, to return a favour or as an expression of thanks. Nakku was given away as a ceremonial offering because she is a female with no rights, whose existence and wellbeing only depends on culture and male domination. This cultural mock marriage is a manifestation of the discrimination against women worldwide. Culture enslaves women, whose well-being is dictated by men. A cultural ceremony such as this is a violation of the fundamental human rights of freedom, protection, expression, movement, assembly and association provided for under article 29 of the Uganda constitution. It undermines the status of women, their liberation and equity. It is against the African Charter on the Rights and Welfare of the Child. Article 21(1) of the Charter states that governments should eliminate harmful social and cultural practices affecting the welfare, dignity, normal growth and development of children, particularly customs and practices which are prejudicial to children on the basis of sex. Cultural and religious practices that are based on sex affect women and hinder equity and participation in the development process.

Culture and Female Genital Mutilation

Female genital mitilation (FGM) refers to the removal of part or all of the female genitalia. The most common type of procedure is clitoridectomy or excision that is cutting off the clitoris and most of the external genitalia. The most extreme form of this procedure is known as infibulation or pharaonic circumcision, involving the removal of the clitoris, the inner labia and the internal part of the outer labia. The remnants are then sown together, leaving a small hole through which urine or menstrual blood can pass (Nandutu, 2004).

Research carried out by Nandutu (2004) revealed that circumcision for both men and women is obligatory in rural Kapchorwa. Uncircumcised men and women are not permitted to participate in important clan meetings. It is a rite that introduces youth to adulthood and transforms them into respected members of society. Girls interviewed by the researcher lamented that they would not be accepted as family members unless they were circumcised – they might even fail to find husbands. Uncircumcised women are not allowed to fetch water, collect food from the granary or clean the kraal. This is because uncircumcised women are not considered to be "full" women. While human rights groups are trying to help communities that practice FGM to find other ways to celebrate girls' womanhood without causing harm, young girls in Kapchorwa are still being subjected to this extreme procedure that can cause infection, severe breeding and even death. FGM affects menstruation, makes sex difficult and painful and may cause problems during child-bearing. The continued practice of FGM has caused major public health and human rights concerns. Many human rights activists have condemned it as a violation of women's rights (Nandutu, 2004).

Elderly respondents who were interviewed about the reasons for female circumcision indicated that it was introduced to instill faithfulness in women. Some elders reported:

> A long time ago, our ancestors used to go to war and would take so long, then men of that age thought of ways of keeping their wives sexually inactive until they would come back. They came up with circumcision.

NGOs and Reproductive Educative and Community Health (REACH) programmes funded by the United Nations Population Fund (UNFPA) have been organizing women in Kapchorwa to oppose FGM. The traditional adherents of circumcision argue that REACH and UNFPA represent whites who wish to destroy indigenous culture, and that it is essential that women are circumcised for them to marry and remain faithful to their husbands. Some traditionalists argue that girls who have listened to REACH and UNFPA campaigns against their culture have encountered problems in their marriages. They argue that these uncircumcised women come for circumcision when they encounter problems in their marriages.

The process of circumcision begins with gifts given to candidates and parties being held in honour of those intending to be circumcised. The gifts take the form of goats, chickens and money from relatives. Relatives are united to participate in the ceremony. These incentives motivate and encourage girls to be circumcised.

Candidates for circumcision move in groups of 2-6 girls and sometimes boys accompany them. They wear beads around the waist, neck and wrists and go dancing for about four days. On the eve of circumcision the parents, relatives and mentors sit around a pot of beer drinking all through the night. The girls are smeared with millet flour and dance all night. Just before dawn, the mentors take them to a river where they are immersed in cold water at 05:00 to cool their bodies to reduce pain during circumcision. Nandutu (2004) reports that women of 40-70 years perform the circumcision and the healing process takes about two weeks to one month. Herbs are used for treatment but girls are encouraged to let urine go into the wounds to aid rapid healing.

Research shows that a man who is to marry a circumcised woman takes her to his home before she has healed to avoid any other person from having sex with her. Most men want to take girls who are freshly circumcised to their homes and keep them there till they are healed. As the girls heal, mentors keep them indoors to teach them about marriage issues (Kakaire, 2004).

Some mentors of circumcised girls who were interviewed revealed that many women are crippled as a result of female genital mutilation because when they cut off too much flesh, the outlet is very small after healing. When a woman has to give birth the outlet tears, causing severe bleeding, which can lead to death or permanent paralysis?

Some elders report that circumcised women have no desire for sex. Women who have been convinced of the negative effects of FGM condemn the practice and argue that it leaves scars on the private parts of women, causing unbearable pain during childbirth because the skin is no longer elastic. Furthermore, sexual intercourse is painful due to scarring. Because a circumcised woman's libido is low, she cannot enjoy sex, and her unsatisfied husband seeks sexual satisfaction outside the marriage. Research carried out among couples with circumcised women found that decreased libido among circumcised women causes domestic violence because women infrequently welcome their husbands' sexual demands (Kakaire, 2004).

Culture, Media and Gender

Cultural beliefs are instilled to the youth through agents of socialisation. Socialisation refers to pressures of reward, punishment, ignoring and anticipating values that push the child towards an acceptable response. The major agents of socialisation include the family, the church/ mosque, school and the peer group. Currently the media is also an influential agent of socialisation, thereby affecting African culture. Through the culture of socialisation children acquire characteristics that make them successful in a given culture. Men are discouraged from developing certain traits such as tenderness and sensitivity, just as women are discouraged from being assertive and independent. Because people internalize cultural values, media personnel invest in women stereotypical feminine image. The media stereotype men and women both deliberately and unconsciously, but it affects women more than men which is harmful to their development (Mugenyi, 1991).

Mugenyi (1991) describes two myths that exist in most African cultures; the myth of female weakness and the myth of female strength. Culture alleges that women are weaker and inferior. However, the same culture that assumes women to be weaker is threatened by and suspicious of women's potential. Mugenyi (1991) quotes a psychologist, Jean Baker Miller, who wrote a book on a new psychology of women, and explains the myth of female weakness. Jean suggests that societies have two categories of people, the dominant and the subordinate, who behave in different ways. Dominants are powerful and they assign to themselves jobs that are high in status and material reward. On the other hand, the less valued jobs are assigned to subordinates who are encouraged to develop certain characteristics or traits such as submissiveness, dependence and passivity. Subordinates quickly learn how to use this behaviour for protection. The subordinate group, unable to make demands or reach openly for power, become experts at manipulation. They know much more about the dominants than themselves because their survival depends on them. They become highly attuned to dominant players and they are able to predict the dominants' reactions of pleasure or displeasure. This is, according to Miller, the origins of feminine intuition and wiles. From early childhood, females learn that they have a duty to raise children and look after husbands. It is not female genes that make females subordinate or caring, but cultural socialisation.

The second myth that Mugenyi (1991) describes is that of female strength. Deep-rooted in African culture is the notion that, if women obtain political power, the world will fall into chaos and women themselves would suffer. Culture always reminds women that they are delicate and do possess the courage and determination of men. Culture also reminds women that, if they set their goals too high, they will develop health problems, heart attacks and ulcers and die young. These warnings are normally aimed at women heading for prestigious positions, yet they are not warned that domestic work is tedious, and strenuous. Mugenyi (1991) continues to say that many educated men marry village girls or less educated women who are submissive and do not question male authority as constituted by culture. Men consider women who excel in society as possessing the wrong genes or hormones, or faults in the structure of the brain.

Both the electronic and print media have a role to play in changing cultural attitudes and expectations of modern women who have been exposed to opportunities. The mass media should help to shape new attitudes towards women by portraying the societal roles they play. It should encourage women to break away from traditional roles and assume new ones in community and national development. Women should be educated through radio, television, the Internet and newspapers that they can be mothers and homemakers as well as working outside the home for family, community and national development. The mass media should shape new societal attitudes towards women, instead of portraying women as merely good for sex, as Red Pepper and East Africa Television do. Mass media should facilitate the integration of women in development. It should address issues like contraception, health and nutrition information, modern farming techniques, credit schemes, participation in politics and education (Mugenyi, 1991).

Media programmes should emphasize women's contribution to society in order to rectify the distorted image of women presented by culture and media. The mass media have a role to play in changing the roles of men and women as well as encouraging both husbands and wives to share domestic responsibilities because today many women work outside home in the employment sector. The media should desist from promoting traditional roles for women. In this respect parents should train both boys and girls in all the social roles without basing roles on sex. It is at the domestic level that gender inequality is rooted and also where socialisation of girls and boys begin, an issue that media should address.

In some cultures women serve as scapegoats for men and society to explain certain happenings e.g. women are responsible for infecting their husbands with HIV/Aids or they are accused of witchcraft. Culturally women are perceived as homemakers who cannot discuss anything in public but who are guilty of spreading gossip, while men's work is viewed as the economic foundation of society. Men's contribution to society is recorded in history, sung in songs and included in riddles, but women have no history. Cultures grant men fundamental benefits, like the right to own and inherit property, marriage rights, family headship and religious rights. The media can be influential in improving the dignity and power of women in society.

The media should address the cultural myth that men should dominate women. If a man does not dominate his wife in the family but assists her with chores, he is viewed as henpecked, bewitched and a public embarrassment. Men are encouraged not to socialise with women; those who do so are also called names (Mugenyi, 1991).

The government, NGOs and religious leaders should censor newspapers such as Red Pepper, that carry articles and pictures that portray women as foolish people whose interests are centered around men, falling in love and worrying about children. It is unfortunate that many companies use women in their advertisements and for nude dancing. While men are fully clothed, women working in hotels and bars dress scantily to attract male customers and to entertain men. These cultural stereotypes about females should be addressed through the media. Liberated women should be committed to the liberation of other women from all types of bondage as a prerequisite for democracy and self-actualization. The status of women in society is a barometer, the lens of democracy of any state and an indication of the respect given to human rights. Women liberation is an ongoing struggle. Freedom is never given, it is always sought. Women will have no freedom as long as they are handicapped by legal lack of education and social imbalances. Women, who form 80% of the labour force in agriculture in rural Uganda, should be given access to means of production such as ownership of land and credit facilities through loans. It is necessary to improve the conditions under which women shoulder their heavy workload of food production, child-bearing and sustaining the family.

NGOs, stakeholders and feminists should make use of the media and the press to influence the public and opinion leaders to change their attitudes. It will be a slow process but can play a liberating role. The media can play a positive role in enhancing freedom of expression and promoting a positive image for women. Through the media, Ugandans can be challenged to redress inequalities based on sex.

Radio, television and computers (the Internet) can be effective instruments for promoting social change, education and economic development. Mugenyi (1991) describes the important role women can play in the development of Uganda. Through its portrayal of women, the mass media can either undermine or foster women's dignity and roles in the development process. If the media portrays women only performing their traditional roles, society's attitudes and women's expectations will be confined to these roles. The media that portrays women as mere sexual objects and a source of entertainment for men undermines women's dignity and poisons the youth psychologically and emotionally. If the image of women presented by the media reflects the range of contributions women are capable of making to society, social attitudes towards women will be broadened correspondingly.

The media can undoubtedly make a crucial contribution towards the promotion of gender awareness. The media can instill in the public the fact that women's participation in political life is an essential part of democracy. The media can play an important role in removing cultural and religious discrimination against women. It can be used to promote the culture of participation in social affairs by women. It can widely publicize the contributions that women have made to the development of human civilization and history, present positive images of women, encourage women to build their confidence, raise women's participation and awareness and deplore discrimination of any kind and conduct that is detrimental to women's interests (Inter-parliamentary Union, 1994).

Since the first international women's conference was held in 1975, heated debates, discussions and actions have taken place on gender inequality in the development process. Consequently, the Women's Second Decade has been a period of deepening social awareness, which has sharpened the international community's perception and the role of gender in social change and development. The women's conference that was held in Nairobi in 1985 made many resolutions centered on empowering women socially, culturally, politically and economically (Sanga, 1995).

In her study on women and gender relations in Tanzania, Sanga (1995) observes that, although the government is committed to the women's cause as far as equality between males and females is concerned, progress is slow owing to religious, cultural and historical prejudices and double standards with regard to women, which is difficult to change because the Tanzanian government is male-dominated. Sanga (1995) accuses Radio Tanzania of sexism by distorting the image of women and portraying them as dependents and objects of male pleasure and violence. Even today, most radio stations in Uganda, especially during the day, present women's programmes with topics relating to motherhood, housewifery, sengas, sex scandals, etc. Most radio stations still portray women as inferior beings who are intellectually and physically dependent on men. The radio songs cherished by both males and females reinforce this dependency syndrome. On television, women are portrayed negatively by showing them half-naked, dancing and advertising products. This encourages women to dress up to attract men and male customers. Most local bands play and praise women as beautiful objects to be admired, touched and cherished by men. Some songs portray women as flowers, who have the capacity to blossom, as delicate, no one is like them; their figures, eyes, hips, cheeks are all subjects of praise. Other songs portray women as treacherous, having double standards, lacking in trustworthiness, satanic and evil. However women also sing songs portraying men according to stereotypes Mbughuni (1979) argues:

> The most popular image of a woman in Kiswahili literature seems to be Eve. A woman appears as a destructive element in society.

She threatens the stable and civilized male order, often leading them, the heroes, into a life of crime and moral turpitude.

These deep-rooted cultural and religious beliefs and attitudes can only be addressed through education of community members by the media. This education must be centered on the need to cultivate mutual respect and harmony based on equality between the sexes. Cultural dictates make women less assertive than their male counterparts, which hinders the women's cause. The press, radio and television should be transformed to accommodate positive gender relations. Management should be sensitized about gender issues in order to enhance gender transformation. Sanga (1995) shows that history has proved that women are a powerful force, both in terms of production and reproduction. Kingdoms have risen and fallen because women persevered. Utilized carefully, media have great potential to change cultural and religious attitudes and practices that deny women participation in the developmental process.

Considering the power of the media in communicating messages, the practice of portraying women negatively may have far-reaching effects on society if it is not checked in time. The media should sensitize the public about equal participation of both sexes in science, engineering, environment, politics, economy, education, medicine and economics. However, if women themselves do not oppose the negative portrayal, oppression and subordination of and discrimination against women, which is deeply rooted in culture and religion, the battle, will be lost. Those working with the media are challenged to create an enabling environment for men and women so that the sexes can live in equality, peace and unity and develop equally.

The relentless negative portrayal of women in commercial advertisements, pornographic literature, tabloids such as Red Pepper and East Africa Television is probably encouraged by the presence of few women in top decision-making positions in the media or, if there are women in these positions, they are not sufficiently assertive owing to cultural upbringing. We need female reporters and producers, editors and subeditors who can influence decisions regarding what is reported by the media. Unfortunately the majority of the media staff are males. Women working in the media should be sensitized about "women's values" in the advertising industry.

Although women are involved in the communications sector, few have attained positions at the decision–making level or serve on the governing bodies that influence media policy. The lack of gender sensitivity exhibited by the media is shown by the failure to eliminate gender stereotyping in the content of public and private local, national and international media products, including the continued projection of negative and degrading images of women in the media, and internet. Violent and degrading or pornographic media products have a negative effect on women's development and participation in society. The worldwide focus on consumerism has created a climate in which advertisements and commercial messages often portray women primarily as consumers, targeting girls and women of all ages with inappropriate images.

Women should be empowered by enhancing their skills, knowledge and access to information technology. This will strengthen their ability to combat negative portrayals of women internationally and to challenge instances of abuse of power by an increasingly important industry. Self-regulatory mechanisms for the media need to be created and strengthened and approaches developed to eliminate gender-biased programming. Most women in developing countries such as Uganda are unable to access the expanding electronic information highways and therefore do not have alternative sources of information. Women therefore need to be involved in decision-making about the development of the new technologies in order to participate fully in women's growth and impact.

In order to address the issue of mobilisation of the media, the government and NGOs should promote an active and visible policy of mainstreaming a gender perspective on policies and programmes. The government and NGOs should also:

1. Support women's education, training and employment, to promote and ensure that women have equal access to all areas and levels of the media.

2. Counteract all the cultural, religious, economic, political and social obstacles that expose women to abuse in the media.

3. Support research into all aspects of women and the media so as to define the areas requiring attention and action and reviewing existing media policies with a view to integrating a gender perspective.

4. Promote women's full and equal participation in the media including management, programming, education, training and research, aim at gender balance in appointments to all advisory, management, regulatory and monitoring bodies, including those connected to the private and state or public media.

5. Encourage media to address women's needs and concerns in a positive way, recognise women's media networks and new technologies of communication as a means of disseminating information, exchanging views at all levels and supporting women's groups active in all media and systems of communication.

6. Encourage women to express their concerns in the media, freely and with equal participation in decision-making by both sexes, to monitor whether concerns are portrayed properly by the media.

7. Train women to make use of information technology for communication and media at all levels.

8. Encourage the media and educational institutions to develop arts and media in appropriate languages, storytelling, drama, poetry and songs reflecting all cultures, and utilizing these forms of communication to disseminate information on gender development and social issues.

9. Counteract the negative portrayals of women on the Internet and the use of vulgar language that undermine women's equity and development.

10. Promote the equal sharing of family and office responsibilities through media campaigns that emphasise gender equality and non-stereotyped gender roles of women and men within the family and workplace. Disseminate information aimed at eliminating spousal or women abuse in all forms.

11. Sensitise the public, local people, institutions of learning and workplaces of all categories about women's rights.
12. Support the development of women's groups and dissemination of information about their concerns down to the grass-roots level. Develop approaches and train experts to apply gender analysis with regard to media programmes.
13. Censor those media outlets that portray acts that undermine women.
14. Encourage and support women to participate in literature and writing.

Culture and Development

Culture has been defined as that complex that one acquires as a consequence of being a member of a particular society. It may be material, as is reflected in ways of dressing, works of art, greeting and feeding habits. It may also be immaterial, involving ways of behaviour and values, among others.

Development, on the other hand, refers to both qualitative and quantitative improvement in the standard of living of a given people. It implies quality of life in terms of income, employment, reduction in death rates, unemployment, better health services and education for all and increased participation by the masses in the governance and decision-making of their society. Women play a significant role in their society through the triple roles of production, reproduction and community maintenance.

Empowerment of women is the process by which women take control and action in order to overcome obstacles. Empowerment refers to collective action by the oppressed and deprived to overcome the obstacles of structural inequality which have previously placed them in a disadvantaged position (UNICEF ESARO, 2000).

Despite the pivotal roles that women play in their societies, they are disempowered by cultural dictates. Culture constrains their efforts towards development. It has been stated that societies are world over patriarchal in nature. A belief in the superiority of men over women undermines women's development. Because women are considered inferior, authority lies in the hands of the so-called superiors and men have placed themselves in influential positions; these men sabotage women's efforts to rise above their circumstances, so as to maintain the status quo.

Most men tend to be assertive in their homes because they are income-earners and disregard their wives' contribution, even if the wife is also in gainful employment. Because culture has socialised women to be submissive and less assertive, they are susceptible to men's wishes, demands and decisions, which increases their dependency. Culture enslaves women to still believe that they cannot stand on their own in the development process. The state and NGOs should address the issue of culture because it contributes to constraining and disempowering women in development. It is necessary to change society's attitude about women and develop appreciation of the role women play in development. Women should be seen as equal partners with men in development. The historical and gender imbalances that disadvantage women in the name of culture should be addressed (Kakwenzire ,1991, Kamya, 1999).

In Uganda the government has expended considerable effort to redress gender imbalances through affirmative action, constitutional provisions and the actions of women activists. However, much needs to be done to manage cultural heritage. Modern trends of development indicate that culture has had a serious impact on women's empowerment. According to Ocheng (2000) cultural impediments to women's emancipation and empowerment include:

- Inhibiting the education of the girl-child in most rural areas of Uganda.
- Less education of women, which has decreased their participation at strategic decision-making levels; consequently women have not enjoyed the critical majorities to influence policies.
- Culturally ordained, unlimited male power over women has led to the oppression of women by males in all aspects of life.
- Less economic power resulting from low educational attainment, thus most women find themselves in helpless situations.

- Culturally induced blindness regarding their rights, allowing men continue exploiting and oppressing women.

Ocheng (2000) shows that the legacy of cultural beliefs is still very strong in Ugandan society and needs demystifying. The way forward to demystifying negative aspects of culture with regard to women is to recognise the problem and address it without altering the positive values of cultures. Education as a means to women's empowerment and demystification of negative beliefs would be the solution if geared towards addressing the following:

(a) Negating historical factors like customs and traditional beliefs which have, for a long time, restrained women.

(b) Prioritising the education of the girl-child and retaining her in school, so that she can compete on equal terms with her male counterparts.

(c) Enforcing constitutional provisions for women's rights and upholding affirmative action in areas of need.

(d) Providing assistance in the form of micro-finance to make capital accessible to the most disadvantaged rural and urban women, to make empowerment a reality.

Education should serve as a springboard for sensitizing men and women about the necessity for new era of Cultural Revolution which regards women and men as equal partners in development (The pope speaks to women, 1996). UNESCO (2000), in its world report on the right to education, emphasizes education for all, irrespective of sex, status or race.

The Canadian International Development Agency (2001) comments that development is dynamic. Development initiatives by governments, NGOs or development agencies consist of investments in promoting social and economic change. Some development initiatives aim to change values and practices that shape social relations, e.g. family planning affects cultural beliefs about the number of children a family should have. Development models also incorporate cultural values, for example concern about the transition to market economies and support for private property. Development has an impact on culture, e.g. improving road networks linking rural and urban areas. New roads allow greater mobility of people and goods. Many villages benefit from better access to markets for their agricultural products, health services and schools for their children. Improved rural roads lead to rural-urban migration, exposure and the existence of more households with absent men, forcing women to take charge of farms and families. Decisions made in the planning process have an effect on gender equality, so women should be involved in planning processes so that their issues are addressed. The Canadian International Development Agency (2001) policy on gender equality requires explicit consideration of gender equality issues in the planning process and a decision-making process that supports progress towards gender equality. Countries like Uganda have undertaken commitments and action in support of gender equality. The commitments are stated in the national constitution and international instruments such as the United Nations Convention on the Elimination of Discrimination Against Women (CEDAW) and the Platform for Action (PFA). These commitments to gender equality were reaffirmed in June 2000 at the special session of the general assembly that reviewed progress in the implementation of the PFA. These instruments reflect a broad international consensus on the elements of gender equality and the steps required to achieve it.

Actions by the government to promote change in cultural values and practices include changes in laws relating to marriage, property inheritance, etc., public education and campaigns about domestic violence; women's right to education and health care, and programme redesign, e.g. incorporation of gender equality themes into HIV/Aids prevention initiatives. Women's organisations in partner countries are at the forefront of efforts to define gender issues and gender equality strategies.

Many women's organisations are seeking to understand and respond to the complex interconnections between gender and nationality and religion. It remains a struggle for women's organisations to make their voices heard by the mainstream media and influential institutions. The United Nations Convention on the Elimination of All Forms of Discrimination Against Women (CEDAW) has been ratified by three-quarters of United Nations members. The convention:

(i) Includes articles on the elimination of discrimination in public life, civil status, education, employment, health care and other aspects of social and economic life.

(ii) Goes further than other human rights standards by requiring states to take measures to eliminate discrimination.

(iii) Requires states to take action to modify social and cultural attitudes that disadvantage women.

(iv) Applies to discriminatory actions, by private organisations and enterprises as well as by the state.

The Platform for Action (PFA) was adopted by the governments of all countries at the United Nations Fourth World Conference on Women in 1995. The Platform for Action:-

(i) Outlines strategic objectives and actions in relation to the critical concerns, namely; poverty, education, health, violence, armed conflict, the economy, power and decision-making, government structures to support equality, human rights, media, the enrolment of boys and the girl-child.

(ii) Emphasizes the responsibility of governments to promote equality between women and men.

(iii) Emphasizes the relevance of gender equality commitments to government policy and programmes in all sectors.

(iv) Outlines responsibilities of NGOs and development agencies as well as governments. The government and NGOs should enhance strategies that support women's empowerment, which can contribute to women's ability to formulate and advocate their own visions for their societies, including interpretations and changes in cultural and gender norms.

2

Philosophical Teachings and Theories on Gender

Ancient Greek Philosophy and Gender

According to Greek mythology, Pandora was the first woman on earth, created on the orders of Zeus in order to punish Prometheus for stealing fire from heaven and giving it to man. Because Zeus' intention was to create an evil being that all men would find desirable, Pandora was created in the image of goddesses, each of whom gave her some special gift, like beauty, to enhance her attractiveness, thus Pandora means "all gift". Pandora was given a box which she was warned never to open. After her marriage to Prometheus' brother, she became curious and opened it, left it open unintentionally and all the vices of sin, disease, troubles and death, which were imprisoned in the box, escaped. She closed the box again and all that remained in the box was hope. According to ancient Greek philosophy and ancient Judaic tradition, the first woman on earth was held responsible for the banishment of humanity from paradise. The Greek writers of the 4th and 5th BC, such as Sophocles, Socrates, Plato and Aristotle, defined woman in the same way the andocentric (patriarchal) writers of the Jewish-Christian tradition have defined her, namely that she is an inferior departure from the male standard and a subordinate within the male-dominated society, whose specialized functions were to provide legitimate heirs, produce children and look after them and perform various domestic chores (Lipsitz Bem, 1993). The Greek mythological belief, that woman is a source of evil, is shared by other societies in Africa.

Plato and Gender

Plato's conception of woman as inferior to man is communicated clearly by his own creation myth (Hutchins, 1952a: 640-799). He describes two kinds of human nature: men are the superior race and women the inferior race. According to his myth, woman was created from the man, as it is described in Genesis. Furthermore, she was created from those men who were cowards or led unrighteous lives during their first existence on earth. Plato believed in communal activities, thus emphasised that child rearing also be done communally. He eliminated the private life and the private child, thus women had no role in bringing up children; the only role they played was in becoming pregnant, bearing children and producing milk. In this social context, Plato envisioned an extraordinary new role for women, that women should play the same role as men. Women would participate fully in the military, while men participated fully in communal child-rearing.

Plato argued at length that, once women are removed from the traditional role of private wife and given the same education and training as men, women would be capable of performing the full range of activities and functions that men performed. However he maintained that woman was inferior to man because the male sex possessed all the gifts and qualities to a higher degree than the female.

In the context of his description of life, Plato saw his andocentric concept of woman as a subordinate within a male-dominated society come to fruition. Women were denied the most basic civil and legal rights, e.g. the right to own property, to inherit or to give evidence in a court of law, they were segregated and secluded within the household, where they carried out only three primary functions:

(i)   Attending to domestic chores
(ii) Bearing children
(iii) Looking after infants.

Within the context of child care, women's functions did not extend to anything intellectual, such as giving children their lessons, thus educational and public roles were reserved for men. Plato saw women as the private property of individuals. He said that women, like all kinds of property, including servants and children, could be given away legally by their male relatives, i.e. they had no choice about whom to marry. Plato was the first male writer in history who seriously wondered whether females and males could be similar enough in their natures to fulfill similar roles in society.

Aristotle and Gender

According to Aristotle the world is a unified structure whose constituent parts are organised hierarchically, hence there is a natural and orderly relation among the parts, with some being higher or superior and others being lower or inferior (Hutchins, 1952b: 225-331). Aristotle stressed that, in the world of both nature and art, the inferior always exists for the sake of the better or superior and the superior is that which has a rational principle. In other words, those beings that are capable of reason or deliberative thought are at the top of the hierarchy and general function of everything and their inferiors help them in the fulfillment of their specific destiny. In this hierarchy women are positioned relative to men. According to Aristotle: "The male is such in virtue of a certain capacity and the female is such in virtue of an incapacity, i.e. the female character is naturally deficient, it is an impotent, or mutilated male whose deliberate faculty is without authority."Woman exists as a natural necessity among all those beings that reproduce sexually, but she is born of the same circumstances at conception that also produce deformed children and other ministries. She is thus one of those cases in which nature has, in a way, departed from type. Aristotle stressed that what follows from a woman's natural inferiority is that she exists for the sake of her superiors. Like a slave, her general purpose in life is to enable the male to live a better rational, deliberative and orderly life. Aristotle sees the woman, unlike the slave, as able to care for children and maintain the stability of the household. The household itself is a hierarchy, with the father having authority over the son, the master over the slave and the husband over the wife.

From Plato's and Aristotle's understanding of gender arose a conflicting legacy which later cultures had trouble reconciling i.e. hierarchy, status and natural differences. Society had a hierarchical structure and a person was seen as having a natural level of virtue that determines his or her status within the hierarchy; lower persons were seen as naturally serving the interests of higher persons. The ancient

Greeks took their notion of natural hierarchy for granted, so they applied their notion of democracy and equality to only the elite group at the top of the hierarchy. Many years later, other philosophers, such as Thomas Hobbes and John Locke, stressed that all individuals are equal in nature, thereby demolishing the ancient rationale for giving some individuals more political rights than others. The ancient Greek assumption that natural differences justify political inequalities has penetrated the writings and the constitutions of all modern democracies in the world. For example, in the United States constitution the most basic of all political rights, the right to vote was denied to all women, blacks, slaves and whites who owned no property until 1848, when the Seneca falls conference was held where women opposed injustices towards them in a male dominated society.

Jean Jacques Rousseau

Jean Jacques Rousseau is regarded as the enlightened theorist who transcended the ancient Greek assumption about natural difference to justify political inequality. Because women are sexually attractive, Rousseau considered them a threat to men. He saw in them great power and the potential to destroy men's structures of power. Rousseau was an advocate of women's subordination; he argued that, because women use their sexual attractiveness to men to establish their empires, men must subjugate women in all spheres of life if they are to preserve a balance of power. He was against political equality for women, and resurrected the ancient Jewish definition of a woman as an evil sexual temptress. Rousseau's philosophy led to women being excluded from the public sphere in the United States, because they were considered inferior (Hutchens, 1952 b).

Freudian Psychoanalytic Theory and Gender

Lipsitz Bem (1993), quotes the theories developed by Freud (1965, 1977) and lists two explanations for men's and women's different and unequal natures. Freud's first explanation of inequality was that, by nature, God created them differently. Freud's argument corresponds with Genesis

2, which says that God created the male and female differently and that he created the woman out of the man's rib. Freud's second reason is that the two sexes develop their different and unequal natures gradually in the course of their psychological development as children.

Freud argues that, during the oral stage, the child's sexuality is primarily focused on the act of sucking. During the anal stage, it is primary focused on holding and expelling faeces, and during the phallic stage, the child is primarily focused on fondling the genitals. According to Freud, it is during the phallic stage, which lasts from 3-6 years, that the child usually develops a feeling of sexual attraction towards the parent of the opposite sex and awareness that the two sexes have different types of genitalia. Discovering this difference has drastically different consequences for the psychosexual development of the two sexes. For the boy, whose own penis is a prized possession, the sight of a girl's genitals fills him with the kind of, either, horror inspired by a mutilated creature, or triumphant contempt for her. The boy also convinces himself of a very real risk to his own penis, as he fears castration seeing a vagina or has masturbated, or because of his sexual interest in his mother, or both. Because of this fear, he represses his sexual feelings towards his mother and identifies with his father, and through the process of identification resolves his Oedipus complex and develops normal masculinity and a strong superego (Freud, 1965, 1977).

On the other hand, the girl, who has so far been "a little man", engaged in masturbation with her "penis equivalent", experiences not the threat of a dreadful castration upon the discovery of genital difference, but the desire for the superior organ, i.e. the penis. Freud describes that the girl, after noticing her brother or playmate's penis, striking, visible and large, realises that she does not have a penis. Thus the girl instantly becomes a victim to "penis envy". The penis envy in the girl paves the way for normal femininity, just as castration anxiety in a boy paves the way for the development of normal masculinity. Freud outlines six psychological consequences of the girl's penis envy, which aid her in developing femininity:

(i)   Firstly, as soon as she becomes aware of the injury to her narcissism, she develops a scar and a sense of inferiority.

(ii) She experiences her lack of a penis as a punishment, but soon, realising that all girls lack penises, realises that sexual character is universal.

(iii) Even after penis envy has been abandoned, its true object continues to exist in the character trait of jealousy.

(iv) The girl gives her affection to her mother, whom she considers responsible for her lack of penis.

(v)   Because of the sense of humiliation she feels over the inferiority of the clitoris, she gives up clitoral masturbation, thereby making room for the development of her vagina and femininity.

(iv) Lastly, she gives up on the possibility of having a penis and begins desiring a child, thereby turning to the boy "who brings the long penis with him".

Freud also argued that the girl's discovery that she has been castrated develops self-love as compared to the boy who has his superior equipment. She therefore represses a great deal of her sexual needs, which leads to "sexual inhibition or neurosis". The girl also develops a powerful masculinity complex, refusing to accept that she is castrated, and hardens herself in the conviction that she does not have a penis. Thus she behaves as though she is a man.

Freud's psychoanalytic theory portrays a woman as an object for the male sexual appetite. He posits a passive and masochistic woman whose sexual gratification finally established itself after a tortuous process of psychosexual development, not in her "masculine clitoris", but in her feminine vagina. He defines woman in terms of her reproductive and domestic functions in male-dominated society. He also says that a woman's nature makes her unsuitable for carrying out activities outside the home. He saw women as, by nature, possessing less capacity than men for sublimating their instincts and this ability to transform the instincts is precisely what is required for cultural achievements outside the home.

Freud defines woman as an inferior departure from the male standard, which he developed through the concepts of male castration, anxiety and female penis envy. He presupposes that female genitalia are a castrated or mutilated version of male genitalia. Freud's theory naturalized female inferiority, because he claimed that very young children of either sex recognised it instantly. His theory clearly explains why there is more joy in African society at the birth of a baby boy than the girl. It also explains why, as they grow up, girls are denied many opportunities while boys are indulged. His theory also supports oppression of women worldwide. Some males use their "penises" to harass women and to show them that they are inferior. For example, men demand sex from women in exchange for favors such as promotion, money, marks and jobs. Women are raped if they challenge men and they may be denied sex by their spouses in the case of a quarrel. In her research, Nassali (2000) quotes various women who found that men use sex to show women that they are inferior and cannot be equal to them. The East African Standard (2004) shocked the world with the headline, "Gunmen raped my wife, says Ngugi". Ngugi's story illustrates the savagery and impact of his ordeal at the hands of four gunmen, who raped his wife in his presence. His wife, Njeeri, emphasised that she wanted the world to know that she was raped, a fact that is seldom made public. This case offers an example of a female victim punished and humiliated by men's penises, which could also be used to break up families, defile young girls and inflict political humiliation.

On the same event, Lirri (2004) reports that the Uganda Women Writers Association (Femrite) condemned Njeeri's rape as an assault on womanhood. The patron of Femrite, Ms Mary Karooro, said "The use of the penis as an instrument of torture and humiliation to silence and destroy the spirit of the woman, her family and the entire community is repugnant, sickening and demonic." Research has found that young boys intimidate female playmates with their penises. In times of war, men rape women and children, thereby using their penises as weapons to humiliate their opponents. Women are thus not only threatened by firepower, but also by the penis and the havoc it wreaks - HIV/Aids, psychological torture and trauma.

During childhood development, parents are duty-bound to educate their children about sex differences and its significance, so that a society is created where men and women are equal and the penis is used to bring about life, happiness and stability instead of threatening women, as theorized by Freud (1965,1977).

Feminist Reactions to Freud's Theory

Several feminists reacted to Freud's andocentric analysis of psychosexual development. Feminists like Ernest Jones, Karen Horney and Melanie Klein found his analysis of women to be unduly phallocentric. These theorists declare that the male psyche is organised around what the penis symbolises and what man can make, whether he destroys or builds. The female psyche is organised around the uterus, which symbolizes a biological, psychological and ethical commitment to take care of human infants. A girl's femininity develops progressively, not from a phallocentric process of psychosexual development, but from the promptings of an instinctual female constitution (Lipsitz Bem, 1993). All psychological sex differences result from a combination of cultural conditioning and life in a male-dominated society not, as Freud claimed, because women lack penises. In keeping with this reasoning, Millett (1969) criticizes Freud for having confused biology with culture and anatomy with status and for having squandered an excellent opportunity to study the effect of male-supremacist culture on the ego development of the young female, preferring to sanctify his oppression in terms of the inevitable law of biology.

Lipsitz Bem (1993) quotes Millett (1969):

> Girls are fully cognizant of male supremacy long before they see their penis. It is part of their culture that this is entirely present in the favoritism of school and family, in the image of each sex presented to them by all media, religion and in every model of the adult world they perceive. That to associate it with a boy's distinguishing genitals, girls would since have learnt other distinguishing sexual marks by now, therefore it would be irrelevant. Confronted with so much evidence of the male's superior status, sensing on all sides the depreciation in which they are held, girls envy not the penis, but only what the penis gives one social pretentions to.

Freud's theory on how female sexuality and unconsciousness are shaped is also criticized. He is accused of failing to create a theory explaining how female sexuality and unconsciousness are mis-shaped by a patriarchal culture. Feminist psychoanalysts emphasize Freud's fundamental premise that masculinity and femininity are made, not born. They support the French psychoanalyst, Jacques Lakan, who views the penis as psychologically important to children because of the precise role given to the phallus as symbol within the patriarchal society. They argue that women do not envy the penis, but are envious of what it gives men in terms of power, status, education and economic opportunity.

Feminists oppose Freud's theory, arguing that differences are socially, not biologically determined. In her study, Sayers (1982) observes that mothers treat their girls differently from boys. The feminist theorists criticize Freud for believing that women are sex objects for men. It is clear that today, women's liberation movements are not fighting to become men or have penises, but to be treated equally in terms of education, health, politics, social and economic opportunities and cultural exposure and human rights.

Fatima (1991:141), a feminist active in the 1960s and 1970s, considered gender not as a grammatical term but as an analytical tool to help distinguish between a biological dimension (sex) and a cultural one (gender). According to this distinction, a person is born female or male but through the influence of society becomes feminine or masculine. Some feminists extrapolated from this viewpoint that, in order for women to be equal to men, they should be equally masculine. Thus some feminists adopted the definition which replaces sex with gender on the assumption that gender is a cultural concept. However, this definition does not provide a sufficient answer to those who propose that the oppression of women is the result of their biological makeup, the implications of which are obvious. Why should women fight their oppression and seek their liberation when their oppression stems from their genetic makeup? What good would it do to change society if women cannot change their biology? It is obvious that females are biologically different from males, in that only the female sex possesses the organs and functions necessary for maternity. But it is not true that nature is responsible for the oppression of women. Women's degradation is exclusively the result of a man-made patriarchal society. It is no less false to say that biology is woman's destiny, than to say that biology is man's destiny. Such assumptions reduce humans to the level of animals, for if women are nothing but breeders, men must be nothing but studs.

Gender equality means that all members of society should be equal, not in an egalitarian sense but in a socio-economic and political sense. In order for such equality to be achieved, a radical change in the entire socio-economic order, including social strata on gender, should take place. On the cultural level, certain practices, customs and beliefs that discriminate women should be changed so that women can be liberated from violence and oppression by men.

Biological Essentialism Philosophies and Gender

The second half of the nineteenth century was a time of great social upheaval in the United States (Lipsitz Bem, 1993). Not only did the women liberation movement, lead to the freeing of slaves and granting of the vote to black men but it also altered the relations between races dramatically. These events spurred feminists like Elizabeth Cady, Santon, Lucretia Mott and Susan B. Anthony to challenge the legal and social inequalities between the sexes as well. In 1848, Stanton and Mott convened a women's rights conference in Seneca Falls, the first of its kind in the world, where Stanton demanded women's suffrage, along with a range of marriage reforms. By 1869 Stanton and Anthony had founded the National Women's Suffrage Association. This was the beginning of a full-fledged women's rights movement in the United States that was demanding the right to vote, to be educated, to speak in public, to own property, practice law, wear trousers and to participate in all public affairs of the society.

The feminist challenge so threatened the social order that biological theorizing and philosophizing about men and women intensified in the 1870s. Biological theories tried to reveal how science was intertwined with cultural ideology. Six scientists developed theories which were intended to keep women in their traditional cultural roles. These theories were developed by Edward Clarke, Herbert Spencer, Charles Darwin, Patrick Geddes and J. Arthur Thomson, Lionel Tiger and, Edward Wilson.

Edward Clarke's Theory

In 1852 a German physicist and physiologist, Hermann von Helmholtz, measured the speed of a single nerve impulse. He assumed that this vital force was some form of electrical energy and, concomitantly, that the nervous system was itself governed by the same conservation of energy principle that was already known to govern heat, light and electromagnetism. The conservation of energy principle, also known as the first law of thermodynamics, states that the total amount of energy in a system always remains constant because energy can be neither created nor destroyed. The conservation of energy principle was used to naturalize a great number of beliefs in the 19th century. Beginning with Edward Clarke's publication on sex education, the conservation of energy principle was used to naturalize the anti-feminist belief that higher education was not a suitable activity for women.

Clarke's theory is based on the belief that the nervous system has a fixed amount of energy. Any energy spent on the development of one organ reduces the amount of energy available to other organs. Because education diverts a women's energy from the development of other organs to the development of her brain, it is harmful to a woman's health to be educated. He urged that education is especially harmful to a woman during her menstruation period, because a woman's reproductive organs require energy at that time. Clarke's theory later formed the basis for denying women participation in education. In Uganda, however, cultural factors prevented girls from being educated. The idea that education was dangerous to a woman's reproductive system was also voiced by other writers of the 19th and 20th centuries, such as the British psychiatrist Henry Maudsley and the British philosopher Herbert Spencer.

Herbert Spencer's Theory

The argument that education was dangerous to a woman's reproductive system was presented also by Herbert Spencer. Like Clarke, Spencer used the conservation of energy principle to naturalize beliefs towards and the roles of men and women. The second law of thermodynamics states that, even though the total amount of energy in the universe is always constant, that energy becomes less and less over time. In contrast, Spencer argued that, for biological and social systems alike, the persistence of force, or the conservation of energy, always and inevitably produces progress. The persistence of force inevitably produces a shift from uniformity to specialisation, as can be seen in both the evolution of humans from single-celled organisms and the evolution of a class- and sex-based division of labour from an undifferentiated social organisation. Spencer emphasised that evolution is inherently progressive, thereby reinterpreting Malthus's population theory, arguing that the harshness of the struggle for existence amidst scarce resources, inevitably produces, not the misery and vice that Malthus predicted, but "the survival of the fittest".

Applying the progressing theory of evolution to class and sex, Spencer concluded that the existence of a class- and sex-based division of labour in society was biologically ordained. He also concluded that biology moulds classes and the sexes to fit their respective social roles, making men more competitive and women more nurturing. He stresses that, because biology has made women more nurturing and charitable, they must be denied the right to vote, for they might interfere with the natural course of progress by giving state help to those who would otherwise be unable to survive the struggle of existence. Spencer's theory represented a serious setback to women who were struggling to obtain human rights, including the right to vote. Later, Spencer's theory was used by politicians to exclude women from public life and from participating in politics, especially through voting.

Charles Darwin's Theory

Darwin was not a political activist, but his theory of evolution and the evidence he provided gave scientific legitimacy to the conservative politics of the period and his theory has stood the test of time.

Unlike Herbert Spencer, Charles Darwin (1859 and 1871/1952) was more interested in the evolution of animal and plant species than in the evolution of human social organisation. He, too, constructed a theory of evolution that naturalized the sexual inequalities in society. Darwin's evolutionary theory had three primary ingredients, i.e. endless variation among individuals, both natural and sexual selection of certain variants and the continued survival of the selected variants only. In natural selection, it is assumed that some variants are more successful than others in relation to the physical conditions of life, hence those variants are more likely to survive and to produce offspring. In sexual selection it is assumed that some variants are more successful than others in mating, hence those variants are also more likely to produce offspring. Darwin's theory developed the view that the males of each species are subject to more selection than females are, as a result the males of each species are more highly evolved than females. Darwin posited that males are subject to more sexual selection than females because, among other things, they have to both drive away or kill their rivals and excite or charm their sexual partners. This state of affairs results from the fact that, among other things, males have to defend their females as well as their young from enemies of all kinds and to hunt for food. This requires the aid of higher mental faculties, namely observation, reason, invention, or imagination. These faculties will be put to the test continually and selected during manhood.

The result of all this unequal selection among humans is that a man can attain a higher eminence in whatever he takes up than a woman can, whether requiring deep thought, reason, and imagination, use of the senses or the hands. He stresses that, ultimately, man is superior to woman. Darwin's theory supports the African cultural belief that women are physically weak, inferior, have feeble mental faculties and cannot reason. In a society where there is movement towards gender equality, Darwin's theory must be challenged for the purposes of good governance, ensuring access to equal opportunities for both genders and harmony among people. If his theory is supported, it will cause problems of confrontation, mistrust and selfish tendencies among men and women. Feminists criticize Darwin for upholding that men are superior to women, beliefs which are passed on to children.

Patrick Geddes and J. Arthur Thomson's Theory

These two biological essentialists argue that, if the germ plasma remains constant from generation to generation, then the differences between males and females must be as old as life itself and must also stem from differences in the sperms and the eggs themselves. They argue that there is a difference between the sperm and the egg. The sperm and its metabolism are "katabolic", that is, it is active, energetic, eager, passionate and variable. On the other hand, the egg and its metabolism are "anabolic", that is, it is passive, conservative, sluggish and stable. Geddes and Thomason's theory naturalized sexual inequality by distorting biological essentialism. From the eighth to the 20th century many philosophers applied man-made knowledge to abuse biology, basing their theories on biological differences which they theorized to promote gender inequality (Lipsitz Bem, 1993).

Lionel Tiger's Theory

Lipsitz Bem (1993) reports that one of the first biological challenges to the women's liberation movement occurred in 1970, when Lionel Tiger wrote an article supporting the exclusion of women from the military decision-making process which, he claimed, did not result from male chauvinism or from a coercive process of socialisation, but from a genetically programmed "behavioural propensity" for males to create bonds with one another. He argued that male bonds are intrinsically related to political, economic, military and police activities, thus men expressed themselves in power/dominance-centered subsystems and unequal female colleagues. Contrary to this theory, today women participate in the military world-wide.

Edward Wilson's Theory and Gender

Edward Wilson was a social-biologist who declared that both human social behaviour and organisation were encoded in the genes. Socio-biology contributed to the ongoing cultural debate about men's and women's roles with a new evolutionary perspective on the origins of sexual differences and inequality. Wilson's theory explained sexual differences and inequality on the basis of the fact that the number of offspring a male can produce is biologically limited only by the number of fertile females he can inseminate, whereas the number of offspring a female could produce in her lifetime was limited. In 1978 Wilson said:

> One male can fertilize many females but a female can be fertilized by only one male. Therefore if males are able to court one female after another, some will be winners and others absolute losers, while virtually all healthy females will succeed in being fertilized. It pays males to be aggressive, hasty, fickle and undiscriminating. In theory it is more profitable for females to keep their virginity until they can find or identify males with the best genes. It is also important that females select males who are more likely to stay with them after insemination.

This argument was used by socio-biologists to explain promiscuity in males, rape, abandonment of children borne out of wedlock, inter-male aggression and intolerance for female infidelity, the sequestering of females, the killing of stepchildren and universal male dominance. This was also why females retained their virginity for as long as possible, were faithful, selected the best partners, invested their time in producing children and looking after them, stayed with a single man, cared for him and deceived males with respect to paternity.

Wilson's theory of sexual difference and inequality is supported by Ugandan society. Males are sexually promiscuous, they rape, abandon children borne outside marriage, inseminate many women, are aggressive towards each other, especially when fighting over women. According to Wilson's theory they are competing for scarce reproductive resources. Most men in Ugandan society are intolerant of female infidelity, are polygamous and universally dominant over females because male reproductive strategies highly select them for that particular trait. Ugandan society today also supports Wilson's theory where females are encouraged to keep their virginity until marriage, fidelity is strongly emphasised, women are raped, they produce and look after children, promiscuity is highly condemned and women are blamed for being barren and for not producing quality children or boys. In the African cultural setting, the bad behaviour of a child is blamed on the mother, not the father

The Sexual Universals of the Human Social Organisation Theory and Gender

According to Lipsitz Bem (1993), this states that, at one time, there were indisputable and universal differences between men's and women's bodies, with only women being able to fall pregnant and breastfeed, while men became bigger and stronger. Through breastfeeding and continuous production of children in the absence of family planning, women became weaker and weaker, thus were unable to participate in public affairs. Lipsitz Bem (1993) explains that, in this socio-historical context, physical differences between the sexes made it likely that most women would be either pregnant or breastfeeding during most of the years from menarche to menopause. It was also likely that society developed a division of labour based on sex, with women being responsible primarily for caring for children, while men were responsible primarily for physical defense and hunting, because men were stronger and their mobility was not limited by the presence of children. In addition to developing a sex-based division of labour, the majority of human societies also developed an institutionalized system of male political power.

Gender differences and inequality became institutionalized. The sex-based division of labour and the system of male political domination gave rise to a system of cultural beliefs and social practices. This theory of sexual universals of human social organisation explains why many employers in some societies are unwilling to employ women. The argument raised is that they are always pregnant, on maternity leave and looking after children.

The Sexual Differences of Individual Psychology

The constants in human history and culture that seem to provide the best explanation for sexual differences relating to individual behaviour and psychology are the sexual division of labour and the institutionalized system of male political dominance, which was created by the interaction of biology and history, which programmed such different life experiences for males and females that men and women developed masculine and feminine traits. Lipsitz Bem (1993) quotes Maccoby and Jacklin (1974), who state that it has been proved scientifically that:

(i)   Evidence exists to prove that males are more aggressive than females in all human societies.

(ii) The sex differences are found early in life and differential socialisation pressures have been brought to bear by adults to shape aggression differently in the two sexes.

(iii) Aggression is related to levels of sex hormones.

Maccoby and Jacklin (1974, quoted by Lipzitz Bem, 1993) state that, while they are being reared, sons are handled more roughly than girls. In all societies, in the past ,males assumed the roles of warriors, leading to sex differences. Men are physically aggressive towards each other, directly involved in fighting, killing and heavy work, while the female roles of looking after children and pregnancy reduce aggression. The sexual differences of the individual psychology theory explains why, in most societies world-wide, women are assigned responsibilities relating to child care, while male roles are outside the home.

Religious Theory and Gender

Philips (1984), in his richly documented study of the Eve myth, observed that biblical interpreters throughout the ages have been unanimous in supposing that the serpent, being shrewd, recognised that the woman was the weaker of the two humans, thus the serpent seduced Eve because of her weakness and she was able to seduce her husband because she was filled with the power of the devil. According to this theory, the origin of gender differences and inequality is sin, as explained in Genesis 3:16, where the writer says: "God said to the woman, I will increase your trouble in pregnancy and your pain in giving birth; in spite of this you will still have to desire for your husband, yet you will be subject to him."

Religious theory shows clearly that, from the beginning of creation, woman was a subject of man. She is an inferior creation whose existence and production of children depends on desire for the man (sexual fulfillment). While the man was cursed to toil for a living, he is the breadwinner for the family.In Genesis 3:17-18, God said to the man, "You will have to work hard all your life to make the land produce enough food for you. You will have to work harder and sweat to make the soil produce anything for you, until you go back to the soil from which you were formed." This passage has been used to deny women equality with men. Women have been harassed for causing men's suffering. Genesis shows clearly that Eve took the lead in causing the fall of man. Most religions in the world believe that the female is the weaker sex and must be submissive to man.

Lipsitz Bem, (1993), says that the story of Adam and Eve's fall brings into focus the theme of inequality and introduces the definition of woman as a sexual temptress. The fall from the grace of God began when Eve was persuaded by the serpent to eat from the forbidden tree of knowledge. Some historians claim that the serpent recognised Eve as the weaker of the two humans and this was because "she was a less than perfect approximation of her creator, inferior to God and to Adam as well, a dilution in power, rational faculties, self-control, piety and moral strength. Theologians preach that Adam's transgression was due to Eve's seductiveness. As a special instrument of Satan's will, she possessed a heightened sexuality that inevitably lured Adam to destroy the state of paradise.

This assumption that Eve was the source of evil has caused problems for women. For instance research carried out in western, central, eastern and northern Uganda found that, when calamities or misfortunes befall men, women are blamed. A woman may be beaten if a man's business fails, if he fails to be promoted, fails examinations or is unsuccessful in politics. Genesis 2:18 shows that woman was created from man's rib to be his helper. Man also named her. Having been created to be man's helper, she was subordinated and defined in terms of her childbearing function. This explains why some husbands deny their wives the right to work and limit their activities to house work and child bearing, claiming it to be prescribed by God . When women work to provide food and shelter for their families, they face resistance from their husbands, who feel that women are intruding in the man's God-given realm. The biblical account of creation shows that not only was Adam explicitly mandated to name and desire every creation including woman, but he was also unambiguously said to be created in God's image. The woman was formed, not created (Genesis 2:21). Woman came into existence to be a helper or man's companion, and to bear children. She did not participate in naming God's creation (Genesis 2:8-23) and was made from the rib of man.

The religious creation theory stresses that the creator of man and woman is a masculine God. He is addressed as "he" throughout the scriptures. The inferior female who tempted the male away from the path of righteousness was punished by God by being made inferior to man (Genesis 3:16). According to religious theory, only men could be religious leaders and would be circumcised as a sign of identity. Only men received revelations from God, for instance Moses, Nathan and the prophets, while some women were only used by God as judges. Women were not counted during censuses. As reported in the New Testament, the saviour of the world was a male. Jesus called 12 disciples, who were all men.

However, modern society challenges the religious theory. Many women are breadwinners of families, fill positions of responsibility and are leaders of men and women. Some families are headed by women, because factors such as poverty, retrenchment and disease such as HIV/Aids prevent men from supporting their families. Women are not the source of evil as it is assumed in religious teachings since today men lure young girls into sex, rape, defile, buy sex from prostitutes and cause wars. All these issues need to be addressed in the context of their cultural and religious implications to promote development. This text tries to address these issues.

Feminist Theories

Feminism started as a social movement in the 18th century in England that aimed to achieve equality between the sexes by broadening the horizons for women. Its original causes were in the fields of voting, education, politics, public life and the professions. It is a movement that works to challenge the oppression of women wherever they are. Its overall goal is the liberation of women from oppression. In this context a feminist is an individual who is aware of the oppression, exploitation or subordination of women within society and who consciously acts to change or transform this situation (Ssali, 2004).

According to Giovana (1985), a feminist analysis of society is one of a variety of critical social analyses that take a historical and political-economic view of human social relations and of the structures and problems that arise from them. Feminist theory encompasses components of other theories such as Marxist socio-economic theory, psychoanalytical theory and radical humanist theory, including class, race, sex, age, etc., by illuminating the gendered construction of all such social categories.

Feminism rejects the division of labour based on gender. It rejects biological determinism, which argues that anatomy is the destiny of humanity. It maintains that gender differences are socially constructed and are therefore susceptible to transformation and that the sexes do not necessarily have to conform to gender stereotypes. Feminism argues that these socially constructed differences in gender roles between men and women work systematically to the advantage of men, so that the two sexes have unequal power relations, opportunities and social status.

Feminism presents an analysis of the gendered roles of men and women and an account of how these social constructions have shaped society, its institutions and practices throughout history. It is the study of men as well as women. Feminism believes that men must recognise and understand the gendered construction of their positions in society, that is, they must understand that they are located in the gendered category and do not represent the genetic category of humanity.

Feminism stresses that the two categories of masculine and feminine are not merely opposites but equivalent concepts, which men and women must understand that the power and privileges bestowed upon the historically designated masculine gender and the inferior status likewise accorded the feminine gender, are socially and culturally created irregularities and are not determined by natural law.

Feminism aims to understand the patriarchal underpinnings of society and how it created the invisibility of women; it questions the adequacy of cultural, religious and theoretical assumptions, methods and frameworks for both understanding and living in the world. Feminism aims to explore ways in which current practices in society might be changed in order to dismantle those gendered structures and ideologies that subordinate, oppress and exploit women and other major social categories of race and class. Feminist theories aim to challenge assumptions and theories and present alternative interpretations and discourses of reality and what it means to be a social human being.

Feminist theory seeks to explain women's oppression and subordination and advances proposals on how it can be mitigated. Different strands of feminist thought on gender issues have been developed, most emphasizing different issues although, in principal, all are concerned with:

(i)   Women's liberation from oppression and subordination.
(ii) Women's access to the same education afforded to men.
(iii) Equal participation in politics, decision making and administering laws.
(iv) Abolition of gender stereotypes and division of labour based on sex.
(v)   Deconstructing the faces of femininity and masculinity.

Feminist theorists work to achieve equal rights with men in the public sphere and recognition of women's differences from men, with the objective of enhancing women's positions in the private sphere or the family.

Liberal Feminism

Liberal feminism's tenets are based on liberal political thought. It believes the oppression of women arose from women's exclusion from opportunities available to men, such as education. It is criticized for accepting male values as human values. It emphasizes nature (biology) over nurture (socialisation). It overlooks the cost of equality and the effect of socialisation.

Socialist Feminist Theory

Socialist feminist theory became prominent in the 1970s, and combines Marxist, radical and psychoanalyst notions. It locates women's oppression in their dual oppression by class and patriarchy. It sees capitalism and patriarchy as Siamese twins that oppress women. This school of thought is criticized for:

(i)   Failing to challenge the Marxist view of material social relations.

(ii) Stressing that women experience alienation differently.

(iii) Failing to specify women's oppression outside the family for example, offices, markets, classrooms, etc.

Socialist feminism works to link gender relations to the wider social sphere and asserts that other factors, such as socio-economic class and race, interact with gender to produce complex patterns of dominance and subordination in society. This theory focuses mainly on the analysis of historical and socio-economic class factors that relate to the position of women in a capitalist society. Socialist feminists aim to understand the relationships among different types of class struggles over the control of the means of production in a given capitalist society and the gendered nature of the social relations of production in that society. Socialist feminists seek to understand how the gendered construction of society under patriarchy interacts with other social forces of domination and subordination under capitalism.

Socialist feminism urgues that the division of labour based on sex perpetuates patriarchal capitalist values because different types of labour are neither equally valued nor equally compensated. Socialist feminism maintains that women in their domestic role have an important place in the maintenance of capitalism, although they are unpaid. Capitalists benefit not only from exploiting the labour of waged workers but also indirectly from the cheap labour provided by women in reproducing the labour force. It is assumed that such labour is paid for out of men's wages. Men, although exploited, benefit from the fact that women are primarily responsible for domestic work and the family. Not only are isolation and many stresses and strains involved in domestic work, which is largely avoided by men, but women find themselves in a position where they, together with their children, are legally and economically dependent upon men. Many women play a vital part in the reproduction of the labour force, while they are also involved in waged labour, often in the home. In theory, the woman does not need to work for wages because she is supported by her husband's wage. However, hidden structures of socio-economic systems are becoming increasingly visible world-wide as the numbers of families headed and supported by women expand yearly. Socialist feminism focuses on the history and economics of the gendered work force in capitalist societies and attempts to shed light on current issues, like global environmental problems and the role of gender.

African Feminist Theory
African feminist theory arose from discontent with earlier feminist movements, most of which were perceived as Eurocentric. African feminism arose to highlight issues related to the oppression of African women, including poverty, colonialism, post-colonialism, culture, race, war and underdevelopment. It raises gender issues that led to women's oppression and subordination, such as culture (dowry, female genital mutilation), heterosexuality (p olygamy) and marganalisation by socio-cultural, economic and power structures. It arose out of a history within corporate and agrarian societies that possess strong cultural heritages that experienced traumatic colonization by the West. It criticizes African leaders for managing economic crises by exploiting women, through proving cheap labour in the informal and formal sector.

Black Feminist Theory

Black feminism as a movement started in the USA and focuses on black women's oppression by class, sex and race. Slavery in the USA dehumanized black women, who have been, raped, overworked, segregated, despised, forced by whites to have sex with animals, battered, etc. Black feminists oppose all oppression that is based on sex, race, class, sexual preference, physical disability and caste. It agitates for the freedom of all human beings. It criticizes both white and black male domination over women.

The Marxist-Feminist Approach

Marxist-feminist theorists attribute gender inequalities to the rise of capitalist and class societies. They see the family as a unit linked to the labour market by the husbands and his relationship to production. Women produce the labour force biologically by child-bearing and socially by child-rearing, in addition to caring for men. Women are consumers of the products of capitalism and are a source of psychological and material comfort for alienated male workers. The argument is that the class structure itself is responsible for women's inequality. The capitalist system exploits women, but Marxist feminists believe that, one day, gender inequality will be eradicated. Marxist feminists argue that education reinforces the division of labour in the economy and the family. Certain courses of study are offered on the assumption that the different sexes have different needs and interests, thus technical and vocational school are reserved for males. In criticism of this approach is the view that it cannot address gender inequality in a non-capitalist state because, even before capitalism, women were subordinates of men (Kwesiga, 2002). The theory is situated in Marxist political thought which finds the cause of women's subordination in class relations, leading to the sexual division of labour, locating women in the domestic sphere, and not in the labour force.

Marxist feminist theory has been criticized for being gender-blind because:

(i)   It assumes an original sexual division of labour.
(ii) It rejects the biological basis for gender differences.

(iii) It reduces gender relations to relations of production.

(iv) It downplays women's oppression due to class differences.

(v) It focuses on women's reproductive functions.

(vi) It overlooks specific contexts in which gender operates.

However, the Marxist feminist theory advocates the abolition of class if gender oppression is to be overcome and women are to be included in the labour force. It argues that class best explains women's status and functions, thus it views patriarchy as a product of class and the relation between the propertied husband and the propertyless wife. It highlights the differences and experiences between the rich and the poor (Ssali, 2004).

The Radical Feminist Approach

Radical feminism was strengthened by the women's liberation movement in the West and calls for direct political action, such as increasing women's wages and promoting their businesses. Its core is the exploitative nature of patriarchy. This approach embraces the Marxist view, since it accepts that capitalism exists alongside patriarchy. It believes that the state plays a role in the reinforcement of patriarchy. Radical feminists point to schools and colleges as shaping female identity and encouraging subordinate roles for women. School experiences encourage women to accept this "inferiority". They argue that men control and define knowledge through curricula and that teaching methods exclude women. Harassment in classrooms, such as sexist jokes, abuse and degrading remarks, exacerbate the situation. Patriarchy assumes the superiority of men in all aspects of cultural and institutional life (Kwesiga, 2002).

Radical feminism examines the interrelationship between the two genders and the ways in which these interrelationships operate to benefit men and subordinate women. Radical feminists call this the most fundamental cause of social divisions and conflict in a patriarchal society and it explains why sex (a biological fact) becomes gender, a social phenomenon. Giovana (1985) quotes Kate Millet (1977) as saying:

> Our society, like all other historical civilizations, is a patriarchy.
> The fact is evident at once if one recalls that military industry,
> technology, universities, science, politics, economy and finance and
> every avenue of power within the society, including the coercive
> force of the police, is entirely in male hands.

Radical feminism focuses on the historical development of culture and
how certain views of reality and natural order of things based on sexual
divisions have become embedded in our socio-cultural discourses and
practices. Radford (1971) says that sexual symbolism is foundational
to the perception of order and relationships that has been established
in cultures. The psychical organisation of consciousness, the dualistic
view of the self and the world, the hierarchical concept of society, the
relations of humanity and nature and of God and creation, have all
been modeled on sexual dualism.

Radford (1975) suggests that the melding of the world view of sexual
dualisms and a hierarchal ordering of inferior and superior creates
a symbolic cultural model of domination and subordination which
legitimates the subjugation of the lower race class, sex and tribe. These
symbolic, psychical and religious roots of patriarchy form the foundation
of the radical feminist concept of the nature/culture dichotomy. Man
has been identified with culture, the mind, the intellect, autonomous,
spiritual and the transcendent God the father, while woman has been
identified with nature, the body, passivity, sensuality, dependent
fecundity and Mother Earth. Through its genesis, the Judeo-Christian
doctrine decrees the father God and the rights of males to dominate
females, children, peoples of other colour and other religions and at
the bottom of the hierarchy, nature.

The language of domination and man against nature and woman is
evident in socio-cultural metaphors such as conquer and subdue, the
earth and nature, wilderness, manage, exploit, use, mastery over nature,
etc. The language master of nature is imaged as a patriarchal despot
whose subjugation of nature is expressed in the language of domination
over women and slaves. The language is that of both despotism and
sexual aggression. Radical feminists picture nature as a fecund female
slave whose children are used by rulers while the slave is reduced to

a condition of total submission. The radical feminist critique of the patriarchal dualism of nature (woman) versus culture (man) finds expression in the philosophy of eco-feminism.

Eco-feminists argue that there is a dialectical relationship between the polar masculine and feminine principles. At some point in history, sexual differentiation occurred in human societies and each culture imposed its own values and definitions on the masculine and feminine. Simultaneously, these concepts were identified with biological maleness or femaleness.

Radical feminists are convinced that women are increasingly discovering their own oppression and the oppression of others worldwide. Many women the world over, are rising up to fight the anti-nuclear, so as to bring about peace and equality. Women worldwide are fighting problems of inequality, opposing nuclear war, overpopulation, hunger, illiteracy and the desolation of the planet. Women have sought to raise the status of all women by becoming part of the masculine world, e.g. Margaret Thatcher and Indira Gandhi. Coming to terms with and relating to the masculine world as women is part of a crucial development process that women should aspire to, both collectively and individually. Women must lose all their fears about speaking up, in demanding what is theirs and should try to forge new ways of wholeness, balance decentralization, preservation, mutual interdependence, co-operation, gentleness, non-possessiveness and soft energies so as to change the environment around them for equality and development. Women should not be enslaved by religion, culture, nature or men, but must be set totally free from all oppressive structures. Radical feminists say that division of labour based on biological sex marks out the woman as the other, while men are accorded high status.

Radical feminism advocates:

(i)   a gender-based division of labour analysis.
(ii) Valuing of women's domestic work and equal pay for both genders.

(iii) A struggle against sexual abuse and harassment, exploitative pornographic literature, art and movies, prostitution and trafficking of women.

(iv) A struggle against the idea that motherhood is a natural need among women, that heterosexuality is a natural order.

(v) Creation of women's sphere and space, on the premise that patriarchal institutions such as churches and schools are gender-blind, hence need sensitisation.

However, radical feminist theory is criticized for:

(i) Not empowering women.

(ii) Ignoring cultural diversity in patriarchy.

(iii) Celebrating lesbianism over heterosexuality.

(iv) Universalising and generalizing gender experiences.

Ugandan women, like others worldwide, continue to experience various forms of subordination and exploitation. The theories of feminism and experiences of women in other countries may contribute to understanding and providing solutions for existing gender inequality while taking different cultural settings into account.

Feminism originated around 1700 as a result of women's subordinate status and oppression. It assumes total subjection of women and stresses conscientisation and sensitisation to liberate women's psyches. It focuses on women's universal oppression, subjugation and subjection. It welcomes ideas from men who are gender-sensitive and calls for political struggles to end women's suffering. On the other hand, the theory focuses on relations between women and men. It emphasizes participation by men and women in public activities and the development process. It addresses issues related to gender inequality.

Equity Theory

The aim of this book is to accelerate religious, social, economic and political equity for all women at all levels and at all stages of their lives and development. The underlying assumption of gender equality is that the international instruments of equality of life that have been developed for human rights should be applicable to women, like it is to all sectors of society. Equal partnership between men and women is the ultimate goal for the writer of this book.

Although education has brought some women onto the educational, political, medical, and economical scene at the grassroots, women need education regarding their rights. Women need to participate actively in everyday issues that affect them, like decision making, elimination of all forms of discrimination, violence and denial of human rights. They need to achieve and accelerate the educational, medical, economic, social, religious and political empowerment of women at all levels, enabling them to stand on an equal footing with men, becoming active contributors to and beneficiaries of national development (African Platform for Action, 1994). Women and children are the major victims of ethnic and civil strife, including religious extremism. In the ongoing process of conflict prevention, management and resolution, women should be closely and actively involved and consulted at village, sub-regional, regional and national levels. Priority action should be taken to protect the human rights of girls and to ensure that they receive adequate nursing care and educational opportunities for achieving their full potential alongside their brothers. Denying girls access to education will hinder the realisation of equity with their brothers (African Platform for Action, 1994). The gender perspective and its incorporation in all policy decisions is of paramount importance to engender equality, development and peace.

Social Theories of Inequality
Schmuck (1986) classifies the theories of inequality into individual socialisation processes, organisational constraints to women's mobility and gender-based career socialisation. Drawing from this classification, the theories are examined and analysed under the headings:
(i)   Overt and covert discrimination.
(ii) Organisational constraints, with the implication that it is the culture that should change, not women.
(iii) Theories of socialisation of women which carry the implication that women should be re-socialised.
(iv) Male cultural domination.

Overt and Covert Discrimination

Despite the fact that Uganda's Sex Discrimination Act (1975) forbids direct or indirect discrimination, women find discrimination and prejudice as the greatest obstacle to career progression. In their interviews with nearly 700 female managers and 185 male managers, Davidson and Cooper (1992) found that sex was a disadvantage regarding job promotion/career prospects. They reported:

> The usual employer attitude towards women is that women are poor training and promotional investments who leave work on marrying, which is particularly detrimental to those who work continuously after marriage. Many employers prefer to use single women who are also sexually harassed.

Organisational Constraints

At every level of an educational or other organisation there are barriers to the advancement of women. These include barriers at the point of application for a promotion, in planning a career path, differential levels of opportunities within the post, differential expectations of others and, partially resulting from these expectations, the stereotypical roles that men and women tend to adopt in management. Such organisational barriers may operate, not only against women, but may favour men. Schmuck (1986) says that, at each stage of administrative preparation for job-seeking and selection, there are organisational processes which clearly indicate a preference for males.

Schmuck (1986) and Gray (1989) say that sex bias exists in the training offered by higher educational institutions. Males are sent to mentor other males, there is a lack of female role models in senior management, more opportunities are provided for males to exhibit leadership and males dominate selection committees, leading to discrimination against females. Men also hold more positions of responsibility than women and tend to set standards regarding what is expected from a manager. It is claimed that men are "gatekeepers to the profession". Kanter (1977) says that if barriers to women's advancement are inherent in the institution, there is evidence to show that the lack of opportunities may result in women adjusting their aspirations accordingly. Thus people who have very little opportunity to move up the hierarchy disengage in the form of depressed aspirations.

Davidson and Cooper (1992) show that women are unfairly penalized by employers for taking a career break such as maternity leave, thus many employers in some sectors may resist employing women. It is also claimed that men are given extra responsibilities compared to women. Some men in society still find it hard to cope with working with women as equals, having been burdened with their conditional stereotypes of women being mothers, wives, or secretaries.

Theories of Socialisation

Women are less likely to be promoted because of the way they have been socialised. Shakeshaft (1989) says that, essentially, the victim blames her lack of achievement in leadership on the social structure. The remedy is to re-socialise women, so that they fit into the male world.The presumption that a woman can succeed in management only by a re-socialisation process and the adoption of male styles of management has been countered by the recognition that more feminine traits involving participatory management and respect for relationships should be valued.

Male Cultural Domination Theory

Shakeshaft (1987) states that men and women divide labour on the basis of sex and male tasks are more valued than female ones. The theory of male domination of society and culture is applied to all areas of life, including the world of education. Such theories of patriarchy and androcentrism hold that a male-centered culture invests worth in male values and regards female values and experience as less significant. This approach, which is based on male domination, needs to be opposed and more women must be involved management.

Male Domination of Management Theory

In developing theories of administration, researchers did not look at the context in general and, therefore, did not document how women experienced the world in a different way (Shakeshaft, 1987). When women's experiences differ from those of men, it is ignored or its importance is diminished. Some of the most widely accepted theories and concepts used in educational management are criticized as being androcentric. Shakeshaft criticizes Fielder's theory of leadership effectiveness which is based on the male-dominated corporate world of big business. He argues that, while the theory is concerned with the interplay of situational variables and the relationship between the leader and followers, no account is taken of the situational variable of gender. Shakeshaft (1987) also criticizes Maslow's theory of motivation which, by placing social needs well below self-realisation in the hierarchy of needs, appears to indicate that self-actualization through home and family is inferior to the full humanness of the male. He concludes that Maslow appears to devalue the female experience since the theory implies that women may evolve beyond feminine fulfillment to the public world of the male.

Gender inequalities are consistent in social, political, economic and cultural disparities between men and women across societies. Many people have tried to trace the origin of inequality between men and women. They have found that these range from religious and cultural beliefs to philosophies like those of Plato, Freud, Aristotle and others.

3

Gender and Society

The Concept of Gender

According to Gallin and Ferguson (1989), gender is a social construct. The term is used to denote socially and culturally determined differences between men and women as opposed to biological differences determined by factors which are chromosomal, anatomical, hormonal and psychological. In this sense women and men are made rather than born. Women's and men's identities are developed through a complex process in which separate gender scripts appropriate to a culture are learned. Gender systems are binary systems that oppose male to female, masculine to feminine, and usually not on an equal basis but in a hierarchal order. Gender systems reflect an asymmetrical cultural valuation of human beings, in which the ranking of traits and activities associated with men are normally given higher value than those associated with women. Gender is a powerful ideological device which produces, reproduces and legitimates the choices and limits that are predicated on sex category, and the outcome of these male processes is male privilege. In most literature the term "gender" is interpreted or approached in three different ways i.e. as a social role, relations and as a practice.

Gender as a Social Role

Gender as a social role is used to describe what women and men do, thereby implicitly defining gender as a socially learned behaviour and activities associated with women versus men. Anderson and Chen (1988) call for a shift in the development paradigm by using a gender lens when they say,

> It has become clear that women's roles are essential and important in production. It has also become clear that a gender division of

labour exists in all societies and that it is necessary to factor the gender variable into our analysis (collect gender-disaggregated data) in order to plan and execute development projects with a higher power of predictability and effectiveness.

The term gender is used to highlight the roles and responsibilities that differentiate women from men. Gender encompasses more than a notion of roles for example, in development projects women need to access and control projects. They also need equal rights with men and an equal share of the benefits of the development. Approaching gender as a social role draws attention to differences between women and men.

Writers such as Ferree and Hess (1987) identified the problems inherent in gender as a social role and which underpin this interpretation. Firstly, the role theory emphasizes stability and continuity throughout the life course. Those who subscribe to the notion of gender as a social role do not ignore change. They tend to view change as something that impinges on roles and change comes from outside, as when economic change demands shifts in the roles people occupy. According to Connell (1985), role theory underpins the politics of liberal feminism thus: Women's disadvantages are attributed mainly to stereotyped customary expectations, held by both women and men, which keep them [women] from advancement and create prejudice and discrimination against them." In principle sexual inequality can be eliminated by measures to break down stereotypes and redefine roles. Processes and relations are gendered and that the term gendered indicates that gender-based beliefs and images along with gender-based asymmetries in power rewards immediate relations (Connell, 1985).

Secondly, the role theory rests on the assumption that people choose to maintain existing customs, thereby ignoring structural constraints and presuming that people conform to role expectations voluntarily.

Thirdly, according to Stacey and Thorne (1985), role theory tends to differentiate the issues of power and inequality. The use of the term "role" tends to focus attention more on individuals than on social strata, and more on socialisation than on social structures, thereby deflecting attention from historical, economic and political questions.

Gender as Social Relations

Gender is a constitutive element of social relationships, based on perceived differences between the sexes, and is a primary way of signifying relationships of power (Scott, 1986). The experience of womanhood and manhood are inseparable from relations of power and domination.

Some analysists, like Pearson, Whitehead and Young (1984), use the term gender relations to convey the general character of male-female relations within the household. Others use it to suggest that gender relations are embedded in economic and political structures as well as in the relations of everyday life, that relations of power enter into and are constituent elements of every aspect of human experience. Analyses deconstructing the household reveal the way hierarchies within the household structure gender relations. By examining the relationships between men and women, the way strategies of control embedded in marriage are implicated in household patterns becomes clear. Within most households only one person makes decisions and the less-empowered household members follow and implement these decisions. Household strategies embody relationships of power-domination and subordination. Colonialism and capitalism restructured traditional economies in a way which had a profound impact on women's economic activities, on the nature of the division of labour and on all the social and political notions which remained open to women.

Gender as a Practice

Gender as a practice is the notion that women are social actors who use systems to achieve ends. This approach focuses on what people do by way of shaping the social relations they live with (Connell, 1985). The theorists acknowledge that the system has a determining effect on social action and even lead women to connive in their oppression. This system of inequality, constraint and domination enables women to resist and shape the form of domination (Collier and Yanagisako, 1988). The literature contains many examples of women's resistance, solidarity and collective action against male domination. There are descriptions of women mobilizing for change and challenging power relations as members of collectives that range from informal to formal organisations.

It must be noted that there are ties that bind women and lines that divide them (Caplan, 1982). Women are not a homogenous group, nor do they share the same interests. Some women oppress their fellow women and men. In many societies older women wield power over young women, while rich women oppress the poorer. Social relations coalesce and the hegemony of some women is built on distinctions based on race and class, some women are not oppressed, while others are more oppressed than others. Age, class and race may override women's solidarity, distinguishing an ally from an enemy. Approaching gender as a practice portrays that women are not passive bearers of gender but powerful actors who are involved in oppression. Strategies focus on the need for these actors in oppression to transform the system. The goal of gender as a practice is the collective mobilisation of women to challenge their subordination by men. It homogenizes women and obscures not only the differences between them but also the strategies of control that are implicated in their relationships. It makes efforts to extend women's rights, so that they share equally in the benefits of development, based on the assumption of sameness. However this may perpetuate women's subordination by treating the effects of inequality rather than its causes (Anderson and Chen, 1988; Tinker, 1990).

Difference between Gender and Sex

Gender refers to social and cultural rolesA role is an expected behaviour, for example could be women are expected to feed the family, fetch water, collect firewood, care for children and cultivate fields, while men could be expected to inspect the fields and socialise. Gender expectations often lead to attitudes which equate women and their activities with low social status and men with high social status.

Gender describes the socially constructed roles, activities and responsibilities assigned to women and men in a given culture, location or time. It differs from sex, which describes biological and genetic differences between men and women. Gender is learned and changes over time. Gender functions at the household, community and national levels and this is embedded in social, cultural, economic and political systems. These systems are based within a given legal framework, which includes not only laws and regulations but institutions which enforce or act to enforce them. Gender identities influence how men and women perceive themselves, think and behave. Gender differences interact with other inequalities such as race, age, social class and ethnicity. Rwendeire (2001) defines gender as differences between men and women which have arisen as a result of socialisation, and which are not biologically constructed. She says gender allocates to men and women different complementary, but often overlapping roles, responsibilities and activities. Gender relations are unequal. In many societies women are subordinate to men and depend on them traditionally. In these societies women are susceptible to overwork, exploitation, oppression and violence. She stresses that gender relations are not static, that they are created by society, and can thus be changed. This gives an explanation why correcting gender imbalances that exist in societies is emphasised today.

According to UNICEF (2002) gender refers to the asymmetrical power relations between the two genders. It refers to the amount of social power one has, based on her or his gender. Being boys or men and girls or women involves entering into power relations. In many societies boys/men occupy high status and highly paid positions and they regulate and control sexual relations; while girls/women are expected to engage in unrecognised and unrewarded activities. Women's task is to provide the domestic labour for their families and male partners. They are the servants of men to enhance the good living of men.

Gender also refers to those characteristics that are culturally and socially assigned to and associated by specific cultures with notions of masculinity and femininity, in contrast to biologically determined sex. At birth a baby is identified as male or female on the basis of its genitalia, i.e. whether it has a vagina or a penis. On the basis of this classification, the child is taught directly or indirectly what the society expects of her or him. As the child grows up she/he internalizes the kind of behaviour, values, attitudes and roles associated with being male or female in that particular society. For example, female children in many cultures learn to be submissive, dependent and prepare for child-rearing, while male children in a similar environment learn assertiveness, independence and how to work with machines. This means that male children learn to assume socially powerful values, attitudes and behaviours, while female children learn socially less powerful ones. However, assigned roles may be resisted or contested.

Lungaho (2001) defines gender as attribution of male and female labels to social roles and attributes as they arise from sexual differences. These attributes are acquired through the process of socialisation, while gender roles are classified by sex based on social, not , biological, differences. For instance, child rearing is classified as a female role and not a male sex role, but child-rearing as a role can also be fulfilled by men. Lungaho (2001) defines gender division of labour as a means to give differential treatment to individuals on the basis of their gender.

UNICEF (2002) defines patriarchy as the male domination of ownership and control at all levels of society, which maintains and operates the system of gender discrimination. This system of control is justified in terms of patriarchal ideology, a system of ideas based on a belief in male superiority. This ideology includes the belief that gender division of labour is based on biology and scripture.

Gallin and Ferguson (1992) define gender as a social constituent. The term is used to denote socially and culturally determined differences between men and women as opposed to biological differences and determined factors, which are chromosomal, anatomical, hormonal and psychological. In this sense women and men are made rather than born. Rita and Ferguson define gender as a social relation that constitutes an element of social relationships based on perceived differences between the sexes.

Gender-patterned, socially constructed distinctions between male and female and feminine and masculine are key concepts for understanding how religion, culture and society treat individuals and how some feminists counteract the religious and cultural dictates that relegate to women positions of inferiority, subordination, oppression and the periphery .

Gender refers to the economic, social, political and cultural attributes and opportunities associated with being male or female. In most societies men and women differ in the activities they undertake, as a result of differential access to and control of resources and participation in decision-making. The differences between men and women that are changeable over time differ more widely among different cultures. Gender is a socio-economic and political variable that is used to analyse roles, responsibilities, constraints and opportunities. Gender as a concept refers to the roles played by men and women. Gender is therefore socially constructed, it is affected by many factors and varies regarding place, time and context.

The identities of women and men developed through a complex process in which separate gender scripts appropriate to their culture and religion were developed. Sex is God given. It cannot be changed. Humans are created either male or female. Sex is the concept relating to the biological differences between male and female, (Mombasa Proceedings, 1995). An understanding of the distinction between gender and sex will help to understand the concept of gender, culture, religion and development. The emphasis on gender is based on the recognition of gender as a development concept, in identifying and understanding the social roles and relations of men and women of all ages and how these impact on equity and development and, if misunderstood and misinterpreted, could lead to violence against one of the sexes. Sustainable development necessitates maximum and equal participation in society by both genders.

Table 3.1: Identifying Sex and Gender Differences

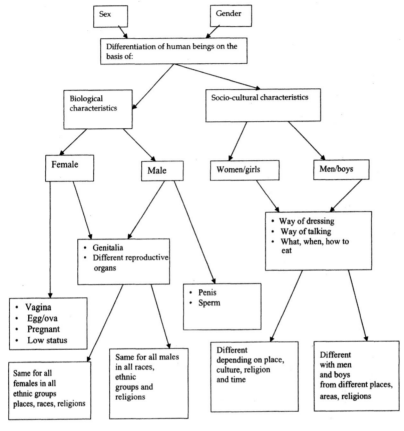

Source: Wamahiu and Miriti (2001)

Figure 1 shows the defining dimension of gender. From this definition it is seen that:

(i)   Sex is the central determinant for differentiation of gender expectations and behaviours.

(ii) Gender is socially constructed thus bound to change.

(iii) Gender is not limited to space, time, race or culture.

According to Gray (2000), difficulties in relationships between men and women are caused by lack of understanding and acceptance of the difference between the two sexes. Gray shows that men are from Mars and women from Venus; he portrays both men and women in neither a good nor a bad light. Gray (2000) mentions the following differences between men (Martians) and women (Venusians):

- Men like to help women by fixing problems while women like to help men by improving their problems.
- Men do not like women's attempts to improve them; they feel humiliated and offended.
- When men feel depressed, they want women's loving acceptance, not their criticism and unsolicited advice. Men want to be trusted and admired. When women are depressed, they like to talk about their problems. They want men to be sympathetic listeners, not necessarily to offer solutions to their problems.
- Men are goal-oriented problem-solvers, women talk about their feelings. Women need to be heard and understood instead of being busy figuring out how to solve their problems. Men should show their acknowledgement vocally or through nodding and brief eye contact.
- Men talk to exchange information, women talk to express feelings.
- Men need to be alone sometimes especially when under stress. They need to retreat to their "cave" and do not want to be disturbed. Insisting on helping them before they are ready to emerge from the "cave" can make them feel harassed. Women under stress and in other difficult times like to seek out contact and make human connections.
- Men are often disconcerted by women's emotions. Women tend to use dramatic expressions such as "You always forget", or "You never listen to me!"
- Men and women, even when they speak the same words, may speak different languages.
- When men are corrected, challenged and criticized by women, they feel offended, while women who are criticized by men will struggle to improve (Gray, 2000).

Sexuality and Gender

Mueller (1993) defines sexuality as the social contraction of a biological drive. Sexuality is distinct from gender yet intimately linked to it. An individual's sexuality is defined as being female or male. Sexuality is more than sexual behaviour and is multi-dimensional and dynamic. Explicit and implicit rules regarding sexuality imposed by society and relating to gender, age, economic status, ethnicity and other factors influence an individual's sexuality. The components of sexuality are practices, partners, pleasure, pressure, pain, procreation and power.

According to Weiss and Raogupta (1998) power is the most important component of sexuality. The power underlying any sexual interaction determines how all the other powers (components) are expressed and experienced. Power determines whose pleasure is given priority and when, how and with whom sex takes place. Each component of sexuality is closely related to the other. The balance of power in sexual interactions determines its outcome. Weiss and Raogupta also show that power is fundamental to both sexuality and gender. The unequal power balance in gender relations that favors men translates into an unequal power balance in heterosexual interactions, therefore male pleasure supersedes female pleasure and men have greater control over women in terms of when, where and how sex takes place. An understanding of individual sexual behaviour among men and women necessitates an understanding of gender and sexuality as constructed by a complex of social and cultural forces that determine the distribution of power.

The imbalance of power between women and men in gender relations curtails women's sexual autonomy and expands male sexual freedom, thereby increasing women's and men's vulnerability to HIV/Aids.

Reproductive health is a human right. According to the World Health Organisation (1968) and the United Nations Declaration on Human Rights, reproductive health is defined as a state of complete physical, mental and social well-being in all matters relating to the reproductive system and processes. Reproductive health therefore implies that people are able to have satisfying and safe sex lives and that the ability to reproduce and the freedom to decide if, when, where and how often to do it, it is the right of men and women to be informed of and have access to safe, effective, affordable and acceptable methods of fertility regulations of their choice and the right to access medical care.

Weiss and Raogupta (1998) stress that reproductive health in the context of primary health care should include family planning, counseling, information, education, communication, services for antenatal care, safe delivery and post-natal care, prevention and appropriate treatment of infertility, abortion and its prevention, treatment of reproductive tract infections, sexually transmitted diseases and other reproductive health conditions, counseling on human sexuality and responsible parenthood. Sexual health means that people should be able to have a safe and satisfying sex life, including a healthy psycho-sexual development. Reproductive rights mean that couples and individuals decide if and when they want to have children, without any discrimination, coercion or violence. Reproductive rights apply to all sexually mature women and men irrespective of civil status and include the right to knowledge about sexuality, reproduction and to reproductive services, including fertility regulation.

Sexual rights include all people's rights to decide about their sexual lives, with full respect for the integrity of the partner and the right of girls/women to refuse sex. These include religious and cultural norms that hinder women and men from taking responsibility for their sexual behaviour. In this respect, societies must take action to eliminate coercive laws and practices that undermine one's rights. Equality for men and women should enable individuals to make free and informed choices and decisions in all spheres of life, free from coercion and discrimination based on gender. Men and women need sexual and reproductive security, which includes freedom from sexual violence and coercion, and the right to privacy. Women should have the right to reproductive decision-making as far as their sexuality is concerned. This includes voluntary marriage, family formation and determination of the number, timing and spacing of children and the right to access to the information and means needed to exercise voluntary choice. (Hill, and Upchurch, 1995)

Gender and the Socialisation Process

Socialisation is the process of passing to people or children the roles, customs and traditions of society. As children grow up, they are taught what society expects of them, they are rewarded for approved behaviour and punished for incorrect performance. In this way each child learns to value certain things and refuse or dislike others. Socialisation takes place throughout an individual's life and society influences the process, although the most crucial socialisation takes places in the family. It is the process by which attitudes and behaviours are encouraged or discouraged (Ebila and Musiimenta, 2004).

Socialisation is the process of learning to become a member of society. When new members are born into a society, they are expected to do what the society expects of them and to shun what it disapproves of. The new members are taught openly and subtly or unconsciously what society expects of them. In the process of this teaching the growing child learns to depend on approval from his or her fellows and of the things the society values. Children learn their gender roles from birth, they dream about how they should live in order to be perceived by others and themselves as masculine or feminine throughout their lives. Parents, peers, religious leaders, culture and society reinforce this.

Gender is learnt through a process of socialisation and through the culture of a particular society. In the Western world the baby boy receives gifts that are blue in colour. By giving the boy such gifts the child is being taught to regard blue as a sign of masculinity. Boys are also given toys like bicycles, cars, aeroplanes, guns, donkeys and horses. On the other hand, baby girls receive pink gifts, this makes them conscious of their role as women. Girls are given toys like dolls and, cooking utensils to prepare them for feminine roles (Lipsitz Bem, 1993). The kinds of discipline given to boys and girls emphasise femininity and masculinity. Girls are punished lightly and talked to, while boys are harshly punished and taught to be assertive.

In the socialisation process, women in most African societies are socialised to remain silent, to avoid responding to men when the men speak and not to retaliate if they are beaten. They should not look men straight in the eye and when a man looks a woman straight in the eye, she should look down, or sideways. Women are trained by society to speak softly, slowly, to be obedient, kneel down before men, including their brother. Cultural traditions and customs stress that women must humble themselves before men to the extent of feeding them, carrying their water to bathrooms and in some cases bathing them, carrying their towels and soap to bathing places and picking them up after the men have finished bathing. In some polygamous societies men even demand to be carried on the backs of women, to be paid tax and be collected from bars each time they are drunk (Oduyoye, 1997).

Men and women are brought up and socialised differently. In most cases the socialisation process promotes social inequalities between men and women. This leads to women's subordination, not only within the family but also in society and the church and mosque (Lipsitz Bem, 1993). In many cultures boys are encouraged to participate in activities regarded as displaying manly traits, e.g. to be fearless, refrain from crying or displaying excessive emotion and should venture into risky situations, while girls are encouraged to undertake activities considered to be feminine.

Gender equality refers to enjoyment of opportunities, socially valued goods, resources and human rights at the same level by both men and women. Gender equality does not mean that women become men or vice versa, but that they have equal access to opportunities irrespective of sex. Most societies are still carrying a heavy burden of outmoded notions about women and men in the socialisation process. These beliefs include the following:

(i)   Every woman must depend on a male provider.
(ii)   Few women are economically active.
(iii) If women work, they are taking jobs that belong to men.
(iv)   It is a waste of money to educate women because they will waste their education by marrying, becoming pregnant and ceasing work outside the home.

(v) Religion and tradition teach women to stick to their husbands, to suffer in silence and to endure everything so as to save their families, particularly the children.

(vi) Women have inadequate legal protection because issues involving husband and wife are usually considered private (Mbuya-Beya, 1998).

The gender rules of the socialisation process are inculcated by parents, teachers, peer groups and the whole society.

Agents of Socialisation

Family
The family controls emotions and what girls and boys may and may not do. Each sex is socialised to behave according to the expectations of society. Girls do most of the domestic work while boys go out to play, have fun with friends or read their books, listen to the radio, and watch television.

School
As an agent of socialisation the school plays a considerable part in the formation of the character of boys and girls. Teachers encourage girls to take subjects like home economics, typing, needlework, religious education, history and geography, while boys are encouraged to take mathematics, physics, chemistry and biology. In boarding schools boys' dormitories are never closed, thus allowing them to come and go as they please. In some mixed schools and single-sex schools of Uganda, girls peel matooke and sweet potatoes while boys are left to read. Most schools have only a few female teachers, and these few teach the lower classes. In primary schools there are few female teachers teaching mathematics and science to help the young girls grow liking the science subjects. Most books used in schools have pictures of boys driving, riding, playing with machines and commanding girls, while girls are shown cooking, sweeping or carrying babies. Girls are expected to kneel for teachers while boys are not. In classrooms boys fight for front seats, while girls hide at the back. In religious schools, Muslims

and Catholics are stricter with girls than boys. Most student leaders are boys, while the girls are deputies.

Peers

At school, boys do not sit with girls, whether in class or the compound. They distract girls so that they do not beat them academically by, for instance, nicknaming and teasing them. The stereotype for girls is that they eat less than boys, sweep classrooms and perform poorly in class. In most mixed schools girls avoid eating foods like posho and beans, lest boys nickname them so as to scare them from eating much food or going to dining halls for meals. On the other hand, the stereotype for boys is that they are shabbily dressed, eat a lot, beat girls academically and supervise girls as the girls sweep classrooms. Boys tease girls and in most cases refuse to talk to them. In homes and even schools boys are served by girls, thus they are brought up knowing that they possess power.

Church

The Christian church is gender-insensitive. Biblical accounts, like the creation of woman from Adam's rib and the story of the fall, place women in subordinate positions. In Islam, men may marry up to four wives, but women may not marry more than one man. Religious teachings continue to uphold the inferior status of women in sermons, teachings and the leadership hierarchy. Through religious socialisation women are led to believe that they are the weaker sex and should be cared for by men, who are the heads of families and providers.

Gender Roles

The Role of Women in the Family and Socialisation

According to United Nations (1994), African societies are products of a common historical evolution enriched by diverse cultures and languages and composed of different ethnic or religious communities. Individuals within these societies have collective identities as members of families, communities, ethnic or religious groups, nations and an increasingly globalised society. The delicate balance between the rights of the individual society and the groups within a society should be respected by every one irrespective of sex. There should be active encouragement of the social integration of the disadvantaged, especially women and the marginalised, in society, in order to reconnect and integrate them into the community through the enhancement of their potential and by making all the institutions of society more accessible to them. It is important to promote an equitable society that ensures respect for the marginalised.

Women play a considerable role in the socialisation of children. They pass values on to girls that consign them to a position of subordination. Women play a critical role in holding the family fabric together. Women who also work outside the home have had their working hours increased, as they usually also have to attend to domestic responsibilities, while men spend their evenings and weekends at leisure. Men should share family responsibilities with their wives to redress this imbalance, for the well-being of the family. At the same time, a number of cultures perpetuate traditional practices that are harmful to the health of women like circumcision, and dowry payments that put women in the position of over working. Measures should be taken to eliminate such cultural practices.

The family is the basic unit of society, applies an established system of ethics, cultural values, and behavioural attitudes and patterns to influence the conduct of individuals. In Uganda, the fabric of the family has become greatly challenged by prevailing problems associated with poverty and economic deterioration – which continue to impoverish many households–unemployment, retrenchment, internal displacement, terrorism and the need for money to maintain the family. This has disrupted family relations and social systems. As a consequence, family members have lost the social, economic and emotional support of those closest to them, and young children often fall victim to delinquent behaviour and drug abuse.

In addition, recurrent natural disasters such as floods, earthquakes and drought, civil strife, war and conflicts such as those in northern Uganda, have created serious problems for families and the cultures that bind African families. The displacement of families during these crises deprives them of family support and this has serious social and cultural implications. Science and technology has also undermined the family fabric, as the young are exposed to pornography through the media and the Internet. Parents are no longer as effective in passing cultural traditions to their children because of the influence of formal education. As a result the young are torn between western and African culture, they seem to be lost. Since women are the custodians of culture, the government should support social protection schemes and programmes that target women. Single parents should be assisted so that they can support their families financially and socially.

As seen earlier, socialisation is the process by which a child is taught the roles she or he ought to play in society. This process determines how adult men and women behave as chief agents of socialisation in families, schools and communities. In Africa, the roles assigned to men and women are predetermined and different. The family, as an agent of socialisation, assigns different status, values and roles to girls and boys. In many societies, discrimination against women and girls starts before birth, with parental and societal attitudes that promote a preference for sons rather than daughters. Young women and girls should be given equal opportunities to grow and develop to their full potential in their reproductive and productive roles. This should be enhanced by women who socialise the young in their roles. Women and men should promote a cultural environment within which girls and boys grow and work together as equal partners for sustainable development and peace.

In many African countries, women's culturally disadvantaged positions, low self-esteem, lack of confidence, coupled with lack of time and low motivation, limit their capacity to take advantage of opportunities available to them to eradicate poverty and conquer oppression. Social and cultural traditions, customs and practices should be reformed so as to uphold the dignity of women as equal partners with men in the family. This should include the removal of gender bias in matters of marriage, divorce, child custody, property rights and inheritance. As socializing agents, women should expose their male and female children to all family responsibilities and housework equally, without demarcating different work for boys and girls. Mothers should train their boys in cooking, washing, cleaning the house and other related jobs, while girls should be exposed to slashing the compound, fetching water, etc. This will promote gender equality at family level and can then be extended to the wider community.

Gender roles refer to job behaviour in a given social context. Gender roles are socially defined and prescribed and they shape and condition tasks and responsibilities into masculine or feminine. Gender roles are affected by factors such as age, class, religion, ethnicity, race, regional origins and history. It can also be affected by changes brought about through development interventions or efforts.

Throughout the African continent, roles are divided according to sex. African society is patriarchal in nature, where men are seen at the centre. It is a culture that oppresses women. Gender has been defined as a set of roles which, like costumes or masks in the theatre, communicate to other people traits which are masculine or feminine. These include appearance, dress, attitudes, personalities, work (both in and outside the household) , sexuality and family commitments.

Most religious teachings have encouraged maintenance of traditional male and female roles. Most of the religious theologies, ideologies, cultures do not focus on cultural transformation of the gospel and religious ideologies hinder change. For example, in the Catholic Church, women cannot be ordained as priests, there are hardly any women bishops in the Anglican Church or any women muftis in Islam.

Female roles in most African societies include cooking, doing housework, looking after children, fetching water, collecting firewood, digging, making pots and mats and grinding grain. Male roles include hunting, fishing, going to market, making weapons, building boats and mining (Mbuya-Beya, 1998).

In Uganda most of the agricultural work is done by women. In the research conducted by the writer of this text in Kigezi, it was found that most men spend their time drinking in bars although, in some cases, they clear the bush. Men are responsible for marketing what their wives harvest. Women are also responsible for weeding, harvesting and processing the agricultural produce. At the family level, males play a dominant role in decision making while women have little or no say in family matters, whether in terms of agriculture, politics, etc. Women are responsible for most of the domestic and household work.

According to Diehl-Huwe (1991), gender roles change over time and have wide variations both between and within cultures and environments. Gender roles are also interchangeable between women and men. For example, an African man may involve himself in "feminine" activities while in a foreign country, but when he returns to his country he will stop performing the "feminine" activities in the presence of his wife and children. In hotels, for instance, men cook because they are paid to do so, but when they return home they do not cook because they are not paid to do so. According to African culture family headship is a role performed by men, but in modern times it is increasingly being performed by women.

Gender Roles in Traditional African Society

Traditionally, in African societies, women were beasts of burden; they engaged in agriculture, cooking, child-bearing and all the domestic work. Among the Maasai, women's work also included building houses for the family. This division of labour was inherited by modern women, especially in rural areas, where they have little time to participate in public affairs. They are unable to compete with men who are exposed to current events. Women were responsible for teaching and guiding the girl-child. They would counsel them about social affairs, like how to greet, take care of children, cook, when and how to speak and how to conduct themselves in the presence of men.

In traditional African society men and women played different roles, which were clearly defined by society. Men's roles were taught by fathers, uncles and grandfathers, while women's roles were taught by mothers, aunts, grandmothers and other females within the society.

It was the duty of men to protect the family. They provided security for their families by, for example, making bows, arrows and spears to be used in defense of the family in the case of attack. Men were the heads of the family. They made the decisions that affected the family. They would choose partners for their daughters and sons. They provided shelter for the family, most societies required them to build houses for their families; they also participated in hunting, which was strictly a male activity.

Politically, women had no political, public or leadership roles. They would not participate in wars or gatherings, as these were roles reserved for men. Political issues were discussed by men around pot of beer in areas like Kigezi, Teso and other parts of eastern and northern Uganda, and women were not permitted to sit near men when they were drinking beer. The role of women was to prepare the beer but they would not drink it.

Women had the role of feeding the family by growing crops. They had to ensure that there was enough food for the family throughout the year, thus a lazy woman was greatly despised.

In traditional African society women could not own property, women were considered to be part of the household property. If the husband died, his relatives would take over all the property and even inherited the woman. In some cases, women performed religious rituals like being medicine women, rain-makers, etc.

Education in traditional African society was task-oriented. The daughter was educated in society according to the tasks she was expected to carry out, such as child care e.g. caring for a baby and food production, while boys were introduced to the roles of hunting and security. Boys and girls were trained to respect the spirits of ancestors and were given religious roles to play. Morality was emphasised and every individual was expected to be responsible for upholding it. The youth were taught the moral values of the society by both parents.

Rites of passage introduced the youth into adulthood, e.g. circumcision. Other rituals were conducted for pregnant mothers, the new-born children, etc. The rites of passage would start at birth and continue through marriage, until death (Mbiti, 1988).

Sex Roles

Sex roles refer to the function that a female or male performs by virtue of his/her biological makeup. For example, only males have they chromosome that is needed to produce a male child. Only women can become pregnant, go through the gestation period and produce children. Sex roles are unchangeable. They are universal and fixed by nature. They do not vary in any society. They are limited to human reproduction and are not affected by the environment. Sex roles raise the question of sex identity. The physical makeup of someone determines his/her sex. At birth the child is identified by either a penis or vagina. In this way a new-born baby is classified as male or female. Sex identity at birth brings about problems of sex preference and this has consequences for women's social security and health. Some societies tend to prefer boys to girls, an indication that girls are not valued. From birth, sex identity determines allocation of family resources and all forms of power in favour of males. A woman who does not produce sons may be beaten, abused or divorced, or her husband may marry other wives who can produce sons (Bem, 1972).

Sex roles encourage stereotypes, which are rigid and oversimplified beliefs that men and women, by virtue of their biological makeup, possess distinct psychological traits and characteristics, e.g. men are portrayed as independent, emotionally strong leaders while women are portrayed as dependent, emotionally weak followers. Stereotypes originate from division of labour between men and women and the socialisation process, and are perpetuated and transmitted from generation to generation by social institutions, including the family, church, the school system and political parties. Stereotypes are reinforced by parents, teachers, curricula, peer groups, religious leaders, the mass media and language (Fredrick 1968, Freedman 1990).

Stereotypes influence society's attitudes towards men and women, applied as standards to evaluate people. They tend to lead to prejudice and discrimination against a particular sex. Most stereotypes applied to males are positive and give them greater opportunities for advancement than those applied to women. Stereotypes influence decision making about the distribution of resources, e.g. political power and productive resources like land, credit, education, training, employment, etc.

Gender Relations

The concept of gender relations refers to the relations of power and dominance within a structure and the life choices of women and men. The general character of gender relations is one of male dominance and female subordination. In patriarchal society two main structural processes disempower women:

(i)   The structural process of male superiority, based on the male's physical and intellectual ability.

(ii) The control exercised by men over the prime factors of production and economic factors.

Gender is about social relations between males and females and how they relate to each other. Men and women are born in a gendered world. Upon ascertaining biological sex, gendered relations begin in the household.

Gendered relations are subtle, although some are explicit, as are entitlements. But both influence emotional, psychological, social and cognitive development. Gendered relations and entitlements transcend their household origins and intrude into the wider socio-economic units, like churches, medical institutions, workplaces, even markets, as long as there is social interaction. Gendered relations and entitlements influence opportunities, justice and equality. In society, interactions occur at multitudes of power levels, with people experiencing equality and inequality at different levels of power. The nature of gender relations in the wider society needs to be changed to enhance opportunities, justice and equality for all through gender mainstreaming, sensitisation and gender awareness. The ideology of male dominance and oppression of the female in all spheres of leadership and power, needs critical analysis and redress for equality to be realised.

Gender issues are revealed when relationships between men and women, their roles, privileges, status and positions, are identified and analysed. Thus a gender issue arises from the different treatment of individuals or groups of people on the basis of social expectations about men and women, which may lead to gender discrimination, oppression and subordination. Gender issues are raised as a result of gender awareness. Gender issues cut across all sectors and social settings and affect men and women in their relations with each other; most affected are usually women. Women are oppressed in many societal structures and are most disadvantaged (Ebila and Musiimenta, 2004).

Women become less important as society views men as more important. Women are treated as secondary citizens by a male-dominated society, a cultural belief that will always lead to discrimination against women in all spheres of life.

Gallin and Ferguson (1992) agree with Pearson et al. (1984) and Scott (1986) that gender relations are embedded in economic, social and political structures as well as relations of everyday life. Relations of power enter into and are a constituent element of every aspect of human experience. Gender as power is a socially constructed relationship of inequality. It labels men and women as representing different power structures. It establishes gender power hierarchies and institutionalizes and naturalizes gender discrimination. Gender as discrimination shows masculine as rational, dependable, resolute, aggressive, competitive, assertive, clever, dominant, shrewd, physically strong, restrained and composed. On the other hand, it shows feminine as emotional, flexible, fickle, passive, co-operative, naïve, compliant, relations oriented, instinctive, loving, caring, verbal, expensive, extravagant and weak.

Culture and social institutions are gendered by norms, values, social discourses and practice. To foster gender equality, it is necessary to address these cultural values, practices, norms and structures. Perceptions of gender are influenced by factors such as power relations and patriarchy, and often make up the prevailing social structure in society. The socialisation process is an overarching theme of UNESCO's (2001) effort to promote gender equality). Socialisation concerns all members of society including men, women, boys and girls. The process of socialisation takes place at the individual level, thus affecting the public community in all of its levels. There is a need to examine and evaluate the role of culture and societal institutions as major contributors to women's inequality and lack of status.

Article 5 of the Convention to the Elimination of All Forms of Discrimination Against Women, concerns the modification of the social and cultural patterns of conduct of both men and women. The aim is to promote equality among men and women through research that examines the role of culture and societal institutions as contributors to inequality. There is a need to address the interrelationships between culture, tradition, stereotypes and images that impede access to and the enjoyment of human rights by women. Stakeholders should address the role of culture, social institutions and violence against women. Stakeholders should also raise awareness among the general public on the causes and social structures that foster gender inequality and violence against women.

Women have an enormous impact on the well-being of their families and societies, yet their potential is not realised because of discriminatory social norms, incentives and legal institutions. Although women's status has improved in recent decades, gender inequalities remain pervasive. Gender inequality starts early and keeps women at a disadvantage throughout their lives. In some countries, infant girls are less likely to survive than infant boys because of parental discrimination and neglect. Girls are more likely to drop out of school and to receive less education than boys because of discrimination, educational expenses, household duties and early marriages. Literacy is a fundamental skill necessary to empower women to take control of their own lives and to engage directly with authority to give them access to the wider world of opportunities. Educating women and giving them equal rights improves their relations in society and increases their productivity, thus raising output and reducing poverty. It promotes gender equality within households and removes constraints on women's decision making, thus reducing fertility and improving maternal health. Educated women can do a better job of caring for children than uneducated women, thereby increasing children's chances of survival and living healthier and better lives. Educated women also have better relations with those with whom they come into contact with than illiterate women.

Gender relations have important implications for globalisation. The global pursuit of profit has opened up employment opportunities for women around the world, thereby facilitating their economic and social independence and challenging long-established patterns of division of labour based on sex.

New approach to gender and development tries to explore the gender dimensions of current processes of development and globalisation. It looks at the way gender relations are being shaped and reshaped in global development. It also looks at the way these changes shape and challenge some of the traditional presumptions of western feminism. It considers the critiques of a global feminism that presumed that women throughout the world showed the same preoccupations and experiences and the critiques of a cultural relativism that implies an excessive distinction between the rest and the West (www/msc gender development and globalisation. html+gender+and+develop ment &hl =en&be= UTF page 1 of 1. MSC Gender, Development and Globalisation).

Matriarchal Society

This is a society where women are leaders and in which power passes from mother to child. Property belongs to women rather than men, men have no right to chastise their wives, women are protected by their male relatives. A woman's position is more honourable than in a patriarchal society. In matriarchal families, women are permitted to rebel against their husbands, they have supreme power in families and could even beat, spit on, abuse and oppress men. Children born in these societies belong to the line of the woman (Chapman, 1989). However, in practice, there are few matriarchal families in Africa. The only examples cited are in Zambia and Ghana.

Androcentric (Male-centred) Society

Androcentrism is male-centeredness, it is patriarchal in nature. Patriarchy is a social system based on male privilege and power, in which women are regarded as secondary and as created for the service of men. It depends on hierarchy on relationships of domination, subordination, on ranks, titles and correct dress (Sandra, 1993). In some families, small boys are discouraged from playing with dolls but are forced into rough and tumble games, taught to fight their friends and are prepared for protecting their future families. The masculine is defined according to the stereotype intelligent, strong, courageous, in control, non-emotional and leader (Lipsitz Bem, 1993).

Females and males' experiences are treated as sex-specific deviations from that allegedly universal standard. In a patriarchal society, the military, industry, technology, universities, science, police, etc are entirely in male hands. The concept of the andocentric culture is that men are placed in a superior position, while women are companions and subordinate assistants. Women have always been considered to be below men, before them, behind them or beside them. Although women in patriarchal societies may have certain powers, like becoming heirs, being elected heads of societies, becoming millionaires or academics, regarding their status or situations, they still live under the power of men. Women have little control over their lives no matter what professional position they hold in society.

The andocentric culture stresses a masculine culture in excess and this leads to a theory of inequality. In most societies males represent a positive designation of human beings (Lipsitz Bem, 1993). Absolute masculinity exists, this humanity is male and man defines woman as relative to him. She is not regarded as an autonomous being; she is incidental, she is a subject and man is the absolute. The central image underlying the concept of androcentrism is that males are at the centre of the universe looking out at reality from behind their own eyes, describing what they see from an egocentric or andocentric point of view. Men define the woman in terms of her domestic and reproductive functions within a male-dominated society or in terms of power to stimulate and satisfy the male's sexual appetite. An andocentric society is a patriarchal society.

A patriarchal society will have laws supporting a patriarchal ideology that is laws legitimizing the subordination of women. Women are considered to be men's property. The cause of violence against women is the unequal relationship between men and women. Women are not involved in making decisions in the democratic process and other discussions that affect society.

Feminists believe that self-deception among men is greater than that among women and that patriarchy destroys humanity. Today many young parents are trying to raise their children in non-sexist ways, so that they can value members of the other sex and enhance their awareness of sexual differences in society. Many feminists believe that children are brought up within different cultures according to their sex. Girls are trained to be dependent and nurturing, while boys are trained to be self-reliant and competitive and are socialised into acting like men. They are forbidden to use the healing process of tears but are, instead, supposed to hide their feelings. Boys are expected to suppress their emotions of anger, fear and a sense of inadequacy and aggression is admired and seen as a male birthright (Lipsitz Bem, 1993).

The result of aggressive training is violence. Many aggressively trained men find outlets for their aggression in sports, politics and the money market. Patriarchal values lead to competition and sets man against man. Violent men are usually the by-products of a patriarchal culture, while the gentle, non-aggressive men are the misfits, who may fail to fit in society. Society labels them as gays, wimps, or women. A capacity for violence has been instutionalized and men are expected to kill on demand. Soldiers are meant to be heroes who do not break down under stress, hence the way many people have been killed in male-dominated countries like Uganda, Rwanda, Zaire, Ireland, Bosnia, South Africa, Somalia, Iraq, Palestine and Israel.

Violence becomes more personalized in the act of rape, which is not a response to sexual urge, but is fired by the urge to dominate, control and demean another. Bedridden women of 90 years and toddlers of eight months are raped. In a patriarchal society men associate masculinity with sexual activity and will turn to pornography or prostitution for a sexual outlet. They use women like drugs to anaesthetize themselves against their inner sense of frustration (Fiorensa, 1987; Fredrick, 1968).

Dignity of Women and Their Vocation

Women have dignity and were created in the image and likeness of God. This is affirmed in Genesis 1:26-27:

> And now we will make human beings, they will be like us and resemble us and they will have power over the fish, the birds and all animals domestic and wild, large and small, so God created human beings making them to be like him, male and female.

Women have a God-given right to live in dignity and equality with others. Both men and women are endowed with the responsibility to change the world around them through co-creating with God (Genesis 1:28).

However, the questions that are raised by modern women include: Are women aware of their God-given gifts – talents, abilities, contributions to the society and to religious institutions like the church or mosque? Do women have confidence in themselves to participate in the world of development? Are girls and women taught their human value, dignity and equality in the home and religious places; in classrooms and the community? Why are women treated like children by society? Why do men regard them as sex objects? Are women the weaker sex? What about those women who have the qualities of Jael, Esther, Deborah and others, who did what men failed to do? Do we have women with the cunning of Delilah and Jezebel, whose plans were so destructive? What about those women who have leadership qualities, are they still regarded as the weaker sex? Where is the authority of men? Can women venture into this realm of authority and protect themselves against violence?

CEDAW (1992) defines gender-based violence as a form of discrimination that seriously inhibits women's ability to enjoy their rights and freedoms and equality with men. The Ministry of Gender, Labour and Social Development (1999) defines violence as the use of force and other ways of causing suffering and pain to a person or people. According to Diehl-Huwe (1991), and Shisanya (2001), gender violence is any activity that is intended to keep women in a subordinate and submissive state so as to perpetuate their dependence on men. It is a universal reality that is the consequence of the historical inequality of power relations between men and women. It arises from the patriarchal system which, since time immemorial, has extended control over women's lives. The most seriously affected, are, however, those who live in precarious conditions or are discriminated against on the basis of race, language, culture, opinion, social condition, religion or membership of a minority group. Gender violence violates and impairs or nullifies the enjoyment by women of their human rights and fundamental freedoms such as the right to education, owning property, health and freedoms of association.

UNICEF (2002) defines gender violence as acts of violence inflicted on one sex because of their gender and sexuality. It includes physical, psychological, social, political, educational and religious violence. These acts of violence are manifested in the form of coercion or arbitrary deprivation of liberty and knowledge, whether occurring in either public or private life, of denial of medical services, political participation, possession of land, property and land inheritance: Violence against women poses as an obstacle to achieving the objectives of equality, development and peace. Persistent failure to protect and promote the fundamental rights and freedoms of women leads to violence against women, and this is a matter of concern for all states. Violence against women encompasses physical and sexual aggression, psychological battering, sexual abuse, dowry, marital rape, female genital mutilation, sexual harassment in the workplace and public places, trafficking in women, forced marriage and prostitution, violation of human rights in armed conflict, murder, rape, sexual slavery, forced pregnancy, denial of opportunities such as education and health and preventing women from participating in economic activities and politics, forced sterilization and abortion, coercive and forced use of contraceptives, female infanticide and antenatal sex selection (United Nations, 1994). Some women belonging to minority groups, indigenous women, refugees, migrant workers, poor women in rural or remote areas, housemaids, female children and women with disabilities, the elderly, the displaced, the repatriated, the imprisoned or in detention, women in conflict areas or areas suffering foreign occupation, wars of aggression, terrorism or hostage-taking are all vulnerable to violence, which undermines their dignity.

Acts or threats of violence, whether occurring within the home or in the community and whether perpetrated or condoned by the state or not, instill fear and a sense of insecurity in women and constitute obstacles to the achievement of equality, development and peace. Fear of violence and harassment acts as a permanent constraint on the mobility of women and limits their access to resources and basic activities. Violence is one of the crucial social mechanisms by which women are forced into subordinate positions. In many cases violence against women and girls occurs in the family or within the home, where violence is often tolerated. The neglect, physical and sexual abuse, rape of girls and women by family members and other members of the household as well as incidents of spousal and non-spousal abuse often go unreported or are difficult to detect. Even when such violence is reported, the community often fails to protect the victim or punish the perpetrators.

Violence against women is a manifestation of the historical imbalance in power relations between men and women, which has led to domination over and discrimination against women by men and the prevention of women's full advancement. Violence against women derives essentially from cultural and religious patterns, in particular the harmful effects of certain customary practices and all acts of extremism linked to race, sex, language or religion, that perpetuates the lower status accorded to women within the family, the workplace, the community and society as a whole. Violence against women is exacerbated by social pressures, that they can not denounce certain acts that have been perpetrated against them, women's lack of access to legal information and protection, ignorance about their rights, lack of laws that prohibit violence against women, failure to reform existing laws, inadequate efforts by public authorities to promote awareness of and enforce existing laws, and the absence of educational and other means to address the causes and consequences of violence. Media images of violence against women, e.g. depictions of rape, sexual slavery, nude dancing, using women and girls as sex machines and objects, including pornography, are factors contributing to the continued prevalence of such violence, and adversely affects the community at large, especially children and the youth (United Nations, 1994)

CEDAW (1999) decries the increasing violence against women and girls, which has reached alarming proportions over the world. Reports of domestic violence from all over the globe confirm that it has become an international epidemic, affecting women, girls and children regardless of their religion, culture, class or race. It affects both rural and urban women and children, whatever their class. It kills, tortures, maims victims physically, psychologically, sexually and economically. Abuse by male partners or husbands is one of the commonest forms of gender-based violence, yet it is often dismissed as a family affair rather than a criminal offence or a human rights issue. Poor women are particularly vulnerable to abuse, owing to the fact that they lack resources or jobs that would enable them to leave abusive situations and relationships. Even economically independent women could be victims of domestic violence, because their economic independence is considered a threat by their male partners.

CEDAW (1999) laments that systematic violence against women violates many fundamental rights supposedly guaranteed by international human rights instruments, like the Universal Declaration of Human Rights, the International Covenant on Civil and Political Rights and the African Charter on Human Rights. Violence against women is a form of discrimination which hinders the ability of women to enjoy rights and freedoms on an equal basis with men. In November 1979, the General Assembly of the United Nations adopted the Convention on the Elimination of All Forms of Discrimination Against Women (CEDAW). The Convention catapults women's rights into the sphere of human rights guaranteed to all human beings and the Universal Declaration of Human Rights (UDHR). The UDHR affirms everyone's entitlement to all rights and freedoms without discrimination based on sex. The main thrust of CEDAW is to eliminate all forms of discrimination encountered by women in all areas affecting their lives. It urges state parties to embody the principle of equality in their national constitutions or other instruments and to adopt appropriate legislative measures, if necessary, to ensure women's full development and advancement. In the CEDAW recommendations, Article 1 defines gender-based violence as a form of discrimination which seriously hampers women's ability to enjoy rights and freedoms on a basis of equality with men. Article 2 of CEDAW states that, while state parties condemn discrimination against women, they have to adopt appropriate legislative and other measures, including sanctions, which prohibit all discrimination against women.

In 1993, six months after the Vienna World Conference on Human Rights, the United Nations General Assembly adopted the Declaration of the Elimination of All Forms of Violence Against Women (DEVAW). This was the first UN document which addressed the issue of violence against women exclusively and it was a major step in the striving to protect women from all forms of violence. This Convention defines violence against women as an act of gender–based violence that results or is likely to result in sexual, physical or psychological harm to or suffering by women, including threats, acts such as coercion or arbitrary deprivation of liberty, whether occurring in public or private. DEVAW also identifies the family, among others, as one of the places where women and children are subjected to violence, and recognises that violence against women within the family by spouses and partners and other members of the family constitutes a violation of human rights. It calls upon state parties to condemn violence and to avoid invoking custom, tradition or religion to avoid their international obligation.

According to one of the articles of DEVAW, some forms of violence to which women are subjected include:

(a) Physical, sexual and psychological violence occurring in the family, including battering, sexual abuse of female children in the household, dowry, marital rape, female genital mutilation and other traditional practices harmful to women, non-spousal violence and violence related to exploitation.

(b) Physical, sexual and psychological violence occurring within the community, including rape, sexual abuse, sexual harassment and intimidation at work, in educational institutions and elsewhere, trafficking in women and prostitution.

(c) Physical, sexual and psychological violence perpetrated or condoned by the state wherever it occurs.

CEDAW (1999) states that women in violent relationships are unable to negotiate safe sex with their partners. This exposes them to high risk of infection by sexually transmitted diseases. Cultural and religious attitudes and practices relegate women to subordinate positions and contribute to women's increased risk of contracting HIV/Aids. Violence against women can be equated to torture.

Culture and religion have served as obstacles to programmes aimed at developing women worldwide. Women's dignity has been often unacknowledged and their prerogatives misrepresented. Women have been often relegated to the margins of society and even reduced to servitude. This has prevented them from truly realising themselves and has resulted in the spiritual imprisonment of humanity (Pope John Paul II, 1995).

The gospel of Jesus is about freeing women from every kind of oppression, exploitation and domination, thus transcending the established norms of his own culture and the religion of his own people. Jesus treated women with openness, respect, acceptance and tenderness. In this way he honoured the dignity of women. Although women have contributed to history as much as men, very little of women's achievements have been recorded by history. Pope Paul John 11, (1995) laments that women have been and continue to be valued more for their physical appearance than their skills and professionalism, their intellectual ability and their deep sensitivity. There are obstacles in many parts of the world that prevent women from being integrated fully into social, political and economic life.

The gift of motherhood is often penalized rather than rewarded. Mothers are discriminated against and dominated in patriarchal societies. As far as the dignity and rights of women are concerned, there is an urgent need to achieve real equality in every area, equal pay for equal work, protection for working mothers, fairness in career advancement, equality of spouses and family rights and the recognition of every aspect that forms part of the rights and duties of citizens in a democratic state. Women have always played and continue to play a role in solving serious problems in society, including problems related to social services, drugs, health care, ecology, HIV/Aids, poverty, democracy and the environment.

Pope Paul John II (1999), comments that the underground history of violence against women is in the area of sexuality. To promote the dignity of women, stakeholders and the community must condemn sexual violence and the widespread hedonistic and commercial sexual culture which encourages the systematic exploitation of sexuality that corrupts young girls into allowing their bodies to be used for profit and tourism. Acts that undermine the dignity of women, such as rape, abortions and aggressive male behaviour, should be condemned.

States, non-governmental organisations and international institutions should make every effort to ensure that women regain their dignity. Feminists should continue defending the dignity of women by fighting for their basic social, economic, political and religious rights. Obstacles in many parts of the world prevent women from being acknowledged, respected and appreciated in their own right. Pope Paul John II (1999) shows that, within Christianity, more than in any other religion, women have been invested with a special dignity of which the New Testament shows us many facets.

Genesis 1:28 shows man and woman as possessing the same dignity. God gave the first couple the power to procreate as a means of perpetuating the human species. He also gave them the earth, charging them with equitable and responsible use of its resources. In Genesis 1: 27, God's purpose of man and woman's dignity is stressed in creating them in his own image. Man and woman form the apex of the order of creation in the visible world. The human race, which has its origin in the creation of man and woman, crowns the entire enterprise of creation. Both man and woman have equal dignity as human beings and both were created in God's image. God entrusted dominion over the earth to the human race, to all persons, to all men and women, who derive their dignity and vocation from the common beginning which is God's creation and command (Genesis 1:27-28). However, Genesis 2:18-25 is misinterpreted to mean that the woman was created from the man's rib, therefore she is his property and should be dominated by man. Genesis 2:18-25 says: "I will make him a helper fit for him", which is interpreted to mean that the woman must serve the man. In this verse both man and woman are called to interpersonal communion, marriage is a fundamental call in which men and women develop their dignity and human relationships. It also shows the beginning of the call to both women and men to share intimately in the life of God himself. The creation of man and woman is the start of the history of salvation.

Genesis 3:15 shows how woman lost her dignity and how she became subordinate to man. Sin brought about the disruption of the original unity which the first parents enjoyed in the state of original justice. The sin of Genesis also brought about differences in the roles of men and women. In Paul's letter to Timothy he makes this distinction between men and women, when he says (Timothy 2:13-14) that Adam was formed first, then Eve and "Adam was not deceived but Eve, the woman, was deceived and became a transgressor."

Sin undermined the dignity of women, as reported in Genesis 3:16, when God said to the woman, "Your desire shall be for your husband and he shall rule over you." This pronouncement by God to the woman has posed a serious threat to women's dignity. Domination by men of women started with sin and indicated the disturbance and loss of the stability of that fundamental equality which man and woman possessed at the beginning of creation. It was a disadvantage to the woman because the pronouncement diminished the true dignity of all women. These words of Genesis 3 led to a situation in which the woman remained disadvantaged or discriminated against owing to the state of being a woman.

Today women movements object to the statement of Genesis 3:16, "He shall rule over you." Pope John Paul II (1995) says that women's movement must not, under any circumstances, lead to masculinisation of women in the name of liberation from male domination. Pope Paul John II (1995) expressed the fear that if women engage in masculisation, they will not attain fulfillment but instead will deform and lose what constitutes their essential richness. He stresses that man and woman are different. Therefore the woman must understand her fulfillment as a person, her dignity and vocation on the basis of God's commandment in Genesis 3 and according the richness of her feminity, which she received at creation, which she inherited and which is expressed in her particular image, which mirrors that of God. It is significant to note that the agenda of women liberation movements does not include turn women into men, or reengineering women to behave like men, but to create conditions that will enable women to share in the privileges and opportunities men access because they are men. Women are trying to overcome the evil they experienced in Genesis 3:16 and which undermines their dignity.

In the New Testament Jesus restored the dignity of women. Mary, the mother of Jesus, became the first to witness the new beginning of women's liberation and the new creation. She became the first woman priest in salvation history by receiving the good news that she would produce the saviour of the world. As sin came into the world through Eve, the first woman, the liberation of humanity also came through Mary, through the birth to Jesus. According to Paul's letter to the Galatians (3:28), there is neither male nor female. In the Old Testament God addressed himself to women, as in the case of the mothers of Samuel and Samson; and he did the same to Mary, the mother of Jesus.

In the New Testament Jesus restored the dignity of women and he became a promoter of women's dignity and vocation, which often scandalized people and caused them to wonder. For example, in John 4:27 it is reported that people marveled because Jesus talked to a woman and his behaviour towards women differed from that of his contemporaries. Jesus restored the dignity of women who were regarded as outcasts and prostitutes. In Mathew 21:31 Jesus stresses that tax collectors and harlots would go into the kingdom of God before those who called themselves righteous. Jesus was aware of the consequences of the sin committed in Genesis 3, thus he promoted dignity for women by stressing permanent marriage and condemning adultery and divorce. The gospels show Jesus interacting, healing, conversing and working with women, contrary to the cultural and religious expectations of the time. To those who were prostitutes and adulterous, he restored dignity. The sinful woman who was caught in adultery became a disciple of Christ and proclaimed him to the inhabitants of Samaria at the well of Sychar. Jesus talked to this adulterous woman about the mysteries of God and God's infinite love which was like a spring of water welling up to eternal life. He revealed himself to this woman as the Messiah. Women like Mary listened to the teachings of Christ, as Martha was preoccupied with domestic matters as the culture of their day demanded (African Ecclesiastical Review, 1971).

The gospels portray women as steadfast at the foot of Jesus' cross. The disciples of Christ, all men, ran away at his hour of need but the women remained faithful. At the time of the crucifixation of Jesus, the test of faith and fidelity proved the women to be stronger than the apostles. At the moment of danger, those who loved Jesus deeply succeeded in overcoming their fear. Thus, in his hour of need the women wailed and lamented for him.

According to the report about the resurrection, women were the first to arrive at the tomb and to find it empty. They were the first to hear the good news that Jesus was not there, that He had risen (Matthew 26: 61). Matthew 28:9 reports that they were the first to embrace Jesus' feet. They were also the first to announce the resurrection to the disciples. These events indicate that, by restoring the dignity of women, Jesus was commencing a new era, in which the downtrodden would participate as apostles, disciples, priests and evangelists in announcing his resurrection. It fulfilled Joel's prophecy of 3:1 that, "I will pour out my spirit on all flesh, your sons and daughters shall prophesy." It was now time for faithful women to prophesy as priests, prophets and disciples about the goodness and liberation of Jesus Christ, who restores the dignity of the downtrodden. Jesus promoted equality between men and women. He also showed that both men and women are equally capable of receiving the outpouring of divine truth and love in the Holy Spirit and equally receive his salvation and sanctifying visits. The fact of being a man or woman involving no limitation, just as the Slavic and sanctifying action of the spirit in people, is not limited by being a Jew or a Greek, a slave or free, woman or man, "For you are all one in Christ Jesus" (Galatians 3:38).

God calls men and women to serve Him equally in all respects. Unfortunately, the Catholic Church does not ordain women as priests in the service of God. In this new millennium, God's outpouring of the Holy Spirit should break the barriers that divide men and women, including service to Him. The Catholic Church promotes motherhood and virginity of woman, as seen in Pope John Paul's apostolic letter on the virginity of women (1995). Women should rise above the virtues that enslave them and serve the wider public using their intellects and the Spirit of God, thereby liberating women who have lost their dignity.

The Catholic Church does not ordain women as priests on the premise that Jesus called only twelve apostles, all men, and who participated in the Eucharist. By calling only men as his disciples, Catholics argue, Jesus was stressing the vocation of women and their dignity which is outside the priesthood (Pope John Paul II, 1995). However, the assumption that he called only men to be his apostles in order to conform with the widespread notion of his times does not correspond to Christ's way of acting and relating with the people of his time. Matthew 22:16 says: "Teacher, we know that you are true and teach the way of God truthfully and care for no man, for you do not regard the position of men" (The United Bible Societies, Good News Bible with Deutoronomic Books, 1999).

Pope John Paul II (1995) argues that only 12 disciples, who were all men, were with Christ at the Last Supper and they alone received the sacramental charge "Do this in remembrance of me" (Luke 22:19 and Corinthians 11:241). According to John 20:23, on Easter Sunday night, they received the Holy Spirit for the forgiveness of sins: "If you forgive peoples sins, they are forgiven, if you do not forgive them, they are not forgiven". According to some people's interpretation of this scripture, only men have the power to forgive people their sins, one reason why there are no women priests and why Catholic nuns cannot officiate at the Eucharist and forgive people their sins. Jesus commanded only men to officiate at the Eucharist and to forgive people their sins. Pope John Paul II (1995) says that, since Christ linked the Eucharist with the service of the apostles, it is legitimate to conclude that he wished to express the differences between man and woman, between what is feminine and what is masculine. It is a relationship willed by God, both in the mystery of creation and in the mystery of redemption. It is the Eucharist, above all, that expresses the redemptive act of Christ, the bridegroom, towards the church, the bride. It is a clear and unambiguous belief and practice when the sacramental ministry of the Eucharist, in which the priest acts in persona Christ, is performed by a man. This explanation confirms the teaching of the declaration "Inter insignioues" published at the behest of Paul IV in response to a question concerning the admission of women to the ministerial priesthood. It is worth noting that the first 11 apostles that Jesus called to his service were all circumcised Jews, except Judas, who was a gentile and who eventually betrayed his master. Because the gospel of Christ is a gospel of liberation, it is also extended to the gentiles, who were despised by the Jews, yet Jesus allowed gentiles to serve him as priests without discrimination. The reason for Jesus dying on the cross was to break the barriers that divided men and women, so that we may serve him as priests and disciples irrespective of our sex. Women, as well as all non-Jewish men, were removed from the goodness of God, but because of God's grace and redemption through his son Jesus Christ, all men and women meet at Calvary to serve him as priests. Christ also calls each one of us to forgive those who sin against us, irrespective of our sex. Women are challenged to keep up the struggle to liberate women completely and to understand what the gospel of Christ is saying to them. The patriarchal selfishness that was extended to the Church to promote male dominion over women should come to an end. The mainstream Protestant and charismatic churches that ordain women as priests should be emulated by those churches that still regard women as important only for serving the needs of men, motherhood and virginity.

Violence against Women in Patriarchal Society

Types of Gender Violence

Domestic Violence

Domestic violence covers all forms of abuse, whether educational, physical, social, political, economic or religious. Domestic violence remains the most invisible crime of our times. Radford and Elisabeth (1996) and Mukasa (1999) agree that domestic violence is the major source of harassment that women experience.

Domestic violence has become a public issue. Women who feel threatened by their intimate partners are always tense and suffer from stress. Reports from the Ministry of Gender Labour and Social Development (1999) support Dossier (2002), which says that abuses by male partners or husbands are one of the commonest forms of gender-based violence. In similar vein, Ultimate Media (2003) reports that many women the world over are tortured by their husbands, who force them into sex. This kind of emotional and physical torture erodes woman's dignity. Marital rape could be equated with murder, especially if the partner is HIV positive or if the woman has recently produced a baby. According to Ultimate Media (2003) a woman who reports domestic violence to courts of law is often harassed by society and her case dismissed. It quotes the Kiganda saying "Ebyomunju, tebittottolwa" which literally means "bed affairs remain in bed".

In most African communities, domestic violence has its origins in the norms of African customary traditions and practices which regard wife-beating as a husband's right. He paid, and still pays, bride wealth. Consequently, most African societies view the wife as her husband's chattel and that entitles him to treat her as he pleases. He may chastise her and whatever form the chastiment takes, it would be deemed to be acceptable. To justify violence against a spouse, some men argue that a woman needs beating periodically to keep her on the straight and narrow path. The notion that a woman is her husband's chattel devalues her dignity and may lead her believing that she is inferior to her husband, making her accept violent conduct against her. In many cases, women in violent relationships opt to suffer in silence, avoiding involvement by law or the police, for fear of inciting more violence, as they may have no safe place to go to upon leaving the matrimonial home. As the family is considered a private place, a battered wife will suffer in silence to shield the family's private life from public scrutiny. Where the woman lacks economic security, she may suffer in silence because, if she reported the matter to the police and the husband, who is the aggressor, is arrested and imprisoned, the family will suffer owing to his inability to work in order to provide for family needs.

This publication describes domestic violence against women as a form of gender discrimination which inhibits the ability of women to enjoy rights and freedoms on an equal basis with men. The authors are in agreement with Dossier (1991), Kurz and Prather (1995), who quote emerging evidence on violence against women which suggests that domestic relationships are considered private, not in the domain of law enforcement. Wife-beating is often an accepted cultural norm. Women are considered to be the property of men, as evidenced by a Chinese proverb: "A wife married is like a pony bought, I will kill and whip her as I like." Women are at greatest risk of violence from men they know. A Brazilian study of 2,000 cases of battery found that 70% of violence against women took place in the home.

The *Star* and *Sapa* (2003) analysed violence against women perpetrated by the Lord's Resistance Army rebels in Uganda. Many women who have been abducted as fighters, raped and kept as concubines will bear the scars for years to come, even after escaping from their captors. Some are traumatized and can only speak in monosyllables, while others have to come to terms with bearing children fathered by rebel commanders. In northern Ugandan society, any woman who bears a child out of wedlock is frowned upon and these women suffer from extra stigma of being women of rebels. Even when women escape from the rebels, they are constantly reminded of the past. Men tease them, saying, "Maybe she will kill you". This kind of teasing results in violent marriage relationships. Some young mothers are emotionally detached from their children and are thus unable to display affection.

The Mifumi (2003) project in Tororo district declares domestic violence a crime and prohibit it in accordance with the prohibited Uganda constitution and the Penal Code Act. They quote evidence that domestic violence as an area where women's situation is worsening globally. It remains one of the most common crimes, yet the most invisible. Domestic violence inhibits women's fundamental enjoyment of their human rights. It restricts the realisation of their potential and full participation in society. Domestic violence destroys women's health and confidence. It also affects children's survival and confidence. Domestic violence has a negative impact on society and hinders development. In Ugandan society domestic violence is exacerbated by factors such as cultural practices that underscore the subordinate position of women, economic conditions and inadequate laws. Police records in Tororo show that 20 incidents of domestic violence resulted in homicides since 2000. Of the victims, 10 were women, 6 were children and 4 were men.

Ocwich (2003) reports that the United Nations condemns violence against women, describing it as an age-old scourge which has, in the 21st century, become as serious a pandemic as HIV/Aids and even more complex. In a message to mark the International Day for the Elimination of Violence against Women in 2004, the United Nations Secretary General, Kofi Annan, called for a bold transformation in men's attitudes and behaviour, so that women can become equal partners. According to the Executive Director of the United Nations Women's Fund, at least one-third of the world's female population is exposed to violence, which is attributable to lack of empowerment of women.

Causes of Domestic Violence

The causes of domestic violence are rooted in cultural and religious beliefs about gender and the position of a woman in society, and include:

(i) **Arrogance:** When a man or woman has more money than the partner, or have a better job, that spouse may behave arrogantly towards the other, thus leading to domestic violence. Some partners want to control each other's incomes, or monitor movements, which may erupt into conflict.

(ii) **Irresponsibility of one of the couple:** Some people resort to gender violence to solve family problems such as alcohol abuse, jealousy, lack of money, denial of sex, insults or failure of the wife or husband to carry out his/her duties.

(iii) **The unequal position between men and women:** The husband considers himself the head of the family because he paid a dowry, married the woman and built her a house, so the wife must be submissive, dependent on the man for his land, money and other property. She should not have her own money or other property besides what he has given her. The woman is not allowed to make physical contributions towards the well-being of the family. The children do not belong to her. If a woman behaves contrary to these societal expectations, she may be beaten up or divorced, or live in a miserable marriage.

(iv) **Stress:** Men and women transfer tension caused by work, lack of money, retrenchment, demotion, poverty and others reasons to their spouses.

(v) **Lack of communication between husband and wife:** In the past there was much less need for direct communication and sharing of ideas and feelings between a husband and wife because of strict segregation of men and women. Because of polygamous marriages, husbands and wives often lived apart. Owing to cultural traditions, men seldom associated with women. Many customs endorsed the maintenance of distance and respect between a husband and a wife. Marriage was a work partnership rather than a love partnership. However, in modern times, husbands and wives want to have close emotional relationships with each other, but they don't necessarily have the communication skills they need to talk honestly with each other about their feelings and about dealing with the problems they face in modern life.

(vi) **Culture and aggression:** In some African cultures wife-beating and abuse are accepted as a way of settling problems. Some people believe that, if a man beats his wife, it is an indication that he loves her. Wife-beating is also considered acceptable because men have paid the bride price, are breadwinners and heads of families.

(vii) **Nagging wives or husbands:** Sometimes wife-beating is followed by a gift like a *gomesi*, money, or an outing, to silence and appease the woman. Because women are spoilt like children after the appeasement, they forget about the beating. Some women are proud of being beaten because this provides them with an opportunity to have a good meal or to acquire money or a new dress. Women do not report their husbands to the police because they fear being divorced, rebuked by society or, if the man is jailed, managing without his support.

(viii) **Social attitudes and norms towards non-enforcement of the law:** Women who are victims of domestic violence do not seek legal redress because abuse is taken as a normal, culturally and socially acceptable way of disciplining women. A wife who reports her husband to local authorities for beating her may face social stigmatization for exposing matters relating to her family to the public. In an effort to curtail domestic violence, the government has established a family protection programme up to the national level and a gender desk at each district police headquarters. The Ministry of Gender, Labour and Community Development (1999) has carried out gender sensitisation of law enforcement agencies, like the judiciary, the police and local councils. Police officers have been trained to monitor domestic violence cases at every level of the community.

Characteristics and Techniques of Domestic Violence

Schuler (1992), Miranda (1994) and Alda (1995) identify the following techniques used by men to control women:

(i) **Male privilege:** In most societies men use their authority to treat women as servants, defining women's and their own roles, making all decisions and reminding women that they must be subservient.

(ii) **Coercion or threats:** Men use threats to hurt women. They threaten to abandon them or to commit suicide if they are abandoned. If a women lays a charge against her husband, she may be threatened with violence. A man may threaten to embarrass his wife at her workplace, to harm coworkers and even to prevent her from associating with others. The husband may threaten to harm family members or his wife herself. He may dismiss domestic workers who assist his wife with the housework.

(iii) **Intimidation:** While in a public place, a man may threaten his wife using gestures or words, proverbs and riddles. A man may threaten to destroy things that are important to the woman, such as her clothes, photographs, certificates, passports, identity cards or office files. A husband may threaten her with a weapon, like a gun, panga or spear. Husbands sometimes threaten to divulge family secrets or other information about their wives that will embarrass or shame them. Husbands may threaten to expose their wives' secrets, so that friends terminate their association with her.

(iv) **Economic depression:** Some husbands prevent their wives from working, finding jobs, keeping their own accounts or having their own money to buy cars or even clothes. They wish to keep women dependent and under control. Some husbands demand that their wives turn over any money earned. The wife must give him money for drink when he demands it, otherwise he could prevent her from going back to work. Other men prohibit women to go to school or to study further, or may stop them from finishing school or finding gainful employment.

(v) **Emotional abuse:** Some men make their wives feel bad about themselves by calling them names, making them think that they are crazy, destroying their image in the eyes of their friends by telling lies, making the women feel guilty and inferior, calling them prostitutes, dirty, shapeless, smelly, unappetizing or ugly. Men accuse their wives of going out with other women's husbands or their own friends, discourage them from wearing certain clothes or using makeup, because they allegedly intend to attract other men. They prevent women from visiting relatives and friends, even those who are ill. They may prevent their wives from attending burials of relatives and friends or workshops and seminars. Wives may be accused of using witchcraft, or feeding their husbands potions. Other men associate closely with domestic servants to torture their wives psychologically, to the extent of having sexual relations with the worker in the presence of the wife. Domestic workers may take over the responsibility of daily shopping, drawing up domestic budget and taking water to the bathroom.

(vi) **Using children:** A husband may abuse the wife in the presence of their children, spit on her, slap her, knock her around and ignore her, only talking to the children. He may threaten to take children away from the wife and placing them in boarding schools. She may not be permitted to visit them at school, or even talk to them. The husband may discuss his wife with the children, causing her to feel guilty and tormented. He might deny having fathered some children, calling them bastards or attributing their paternity to other men.

(vii) **Isolation:** Husbands may harass their wives by controlling them by monitoring what they do, who they see and where they go, thus limiting their activities outside the home. They will use jealousy to justify actions, isolate wives from friends and family, read their mail, forbid them to possess phones, monitor who rings them, check the names recorded in mobile phones, prevent them from going to work, church service and trips, cut them off from supportive persons and have them spied on when they go out. Husbands may refuse to sit with their wives at public gatherings like prayers or weddings.

(viii) **Belittling, disregarding and blaming wives for everything that happens to the family:** Husbands ignore their wives' concerns by shifting responsibility for abusive behaviour, blaming them for family breakups and the children's misbehaviour.

Physical Violence

African women are frequently beaten by their husbands. The motive behind wife-beating is to maintain women in a dependent and submissive state. Wife-beating is culturally acceptable in most parts of Africa, it is considered to be a normal way of life. Some men are said to enjoy wife-beating and may consider it as a "sign of love".

Physical violence against women may take various forms:

(i) **Physical beating:** which may lead to bodily injuries and deformity. Some women die as a result of beatings from their husbands.

(ii) **Treating women as beasts of burden:** They do a lot of work both at home and beyond without assistance from their husbands and if they are beaten, they are weakened further.

(iii) **Men having affairs with other women** and infecting their wives with sexually transmitted diseases. Women are not supposed to refuse sex, even if their husbands come home from visiting a prostitute. A wife refusing sex may lead to a beating or even divorce.

(iv) **Women are slapped, spat on, knocked around, threatened with pangas, guns, spears, knives, sticks and metal rods** (Eastern and Central African Women in Development Network, 1997).

(v) **Girls are physically forced into sex by males,** who are stronger than they are. This could result in unwanted pregnancy or infection with HIV/Aids or any other sexually transmitted diseases.

(vi) **Many men engage in adultery:** They leave home and return late at night or not at all, sleeping with other women or prostitutes, leaving children and wives without support.

Psychological Violence

Psychological abuse includes:

(i) **Verbal abuse:** Many women are psychologically tortured with words e.g. "You are always dirty, you are not meant for me, you are not like other women, you are dense, stupid, foolish, you can't reason, you are a woman, no wonder you did not go to school, I did not know that you were that ugly, you are so thin, you look sick, you are as fat as a pig, you do not satisfy me sexually."

(ii) **When women produce only girl children, they are blamed:** The fact that men prefer sons is used to torture wives psychologically, since women feel that the children they have borne mean nothing.

(iii) **Daughters and women are often considered as good-for-nothing and not worth educating:** Women may be prevented from working because their financial contribution is considered negligent. Some husbands restrict their wives' movement and prevent them working. Men hire people to spy on their wives. The women have to request permission before going anywhere and they are told what time to return. Coming late may lead to a beating or divorce. Women live in fear of being beaten, chased away and harassed.

(iv) **Fear of husbands:** When wives have problems, they avoid sharing them with their husbands for fear of the consequences.

Cultural Violence

Cultural violence varies from society to society but it is mainly manifested in the following forms:

(i) Girls are prepared for womanhood by being conditioned to please men sexually. Women must make sure that they satisfy men sexually, otherwise they are divorced, or men visit prostitutes.

(ii) In most societies, women are divorced if they do not conceive, or the man may take a second wife. It is only the woman who is harassed for failing to produce children, not the man. It is assumed that men are all fertile.

(iii) Young girls are forced into marriage at an early age by the parents for the purpose of receiving a bride price.

(iv) The payment of bride price lead men to regard wives as their property.

(v) Polygamy is approved of and a woman in a polygamous family who does not work hard is tortured. Furthermore, some married men and even their wives consider it normal for husbands to have extramarital affairs. They feel it is normal for a man to have "girlfriends", hence the African saying: "No man eats one dish every day".

(vi) A wife can be inherited after the death of her husband. If she refuses, she can be labeled a witch and harassed by her in-laws. She is accused of being responsible for the death of her husband and her late husband's family may lay claim to her property and chase her away.

(vii) Women are not educated because parents view educating a girl as a waste of resources, owing to the belief that the girl will get married and take her education elsewhere.

(viii) Women face dietary restrictions for example, women in Uganda may not eat eggs, pork, chicken or goat meat - these products are preserved for men. Women may not eat before men and men should be served the best of the dishes cooked.

(ix) Women are regarded as rumour mongers. They are warned by their husbands not to disclose what happens at home.

(x) Men have all the decision-making powers, including the right to determine the number of children the family will have. Poor health will not be regarded by husbands as a valid reason for fewer children, the women may be divorced if they cannot comply.

(xi) Women continue to undergo female genital mutilation.

(xii) Some cultures like that of Baganda of Uganda demand that women kneel before men.

Social Violence

Women do not play a role in decision making in the home, leading to institutionalisation of their inferior status. Parents send their sons to school at the expense of their daughters. Some schools encourage girls to take courses that are traditionally seen as suitable for girls, such as home economics, needlework, religious education and health science, while boys are encouraged to study mathematics, physics, chemistry and biology.

Men may attempt to undermine women who have managed to reach positions of authority. Men and women in authority do not enforce laws that support women's rights. The police or local councils tend to ignore women's complaints, often relegating it to the sphere of domestic affairs.

In the religious sphere, Christian and Muslims councils urge women to keep quiet about domestic affairs, and advise them to pray about problems instead of taking action. Even when women are pregnant or ill, men expect them to look after the husband. The husband will rarely care for an ill woman, abandon them to the care of their mothers, sisters or domestic workers instead.

Sexual Violence

Sexual violence against women in a patriarchal society includes rape, even in the context of marriage. Women cannot demand sex in marriage, but have to submit to their husbands' demands. If women demand sex, they are regarded as little better than prostitutes. The sexual act only considers a man's satisfaction. A woman may not complain that her husband fails to satisfy her sexually.

Women may be promised jobs or promotion in return for sex, if they refuse, they are denied jobs or promotion or are harassed. Sexual violence continues to militate against women's equality. Ultimate Media (2003) refers to sexual violence faced by women. If women refuse to have sex with their husbands it may be for valid reasons, like recent childbirth, poor health, recent surgery, or because they fear to be infected by HIV/Aids. However, women can be forced by their husbands to have sex. This can be seen as emotional and physical torture and undermines the dignity of the victim.

A study about the effects of violence on women in Uganda, released by Human Rights Watch in 2003, cited marital rape as an influential factor in the spread of HIV/Aids among women, owing to their inability to refuse sex or to enforce condom use. The Ugandan constitution does not give women the right to deny their spouses sex, and marital rape is not recognised by the law.

Ssali (2002), in his observations on street children, documents that girls are subjected to sexual violence. He observes that teenage girls are raped by the boys they stay with on the streets, commenting that "the guys are like cocks chasing hens". The street boys say proudly that girls are their blankets at night. Many street girls have turned to prostitution to survive.

In Peru, one out of every four children is a victim of sexual abuse before she reaches her 16th birthday. Thirty-three percent of all adult women in Peru report having been forced to have sex against their will. In Toronto, Canada, 40% of 420 women studied reported at least one episode of forced sexual intercourse since the age of 16 years. A survey in Santiago revealed that 80% of women are victims of violence and rape in their own homes. A representative sample of 612 men and women from Kiisi district of Kenya revealed that 42% of women reported being raped and beaten by a partner, with 58% being beaten often (Arise, 1999). These violent acts against women promote gender inequity and hinder development.

According to Ninsiima (2001) African women are sold in European countries as sex slaves or prostitutes. Women are trafficked from Nigeria, Ghana, Senegal, Cameroon and the Ivory Coast. In transit many women are gang-raped. Similarly Nansubuga (2002) reports that hundreds of Ugandan girls are trafficked as sex workers, a practice also common in Sudan, Democratic Republic of Congo, Nigeria and Cameroon. These girls are promised jobs as domestic workers, waitresses or beauticians, but they end up as sex workers. This wave of violence against women is degrading and humiliating, especially if women are forced into it. Women are not protected from this dehumanizing and violent act.

Over 20,000 Muslim girls and women were raped in Bosnia and Herzegovina during the Balkan wars. More than 15,000 girls and women were raped in one year during the Rwanda genocide of 1994. Girls are often abducted by soldiers to serve as domestic servants, spies and sex slaves. During post-conflict reconstruction efforts, many girls and women are rejected by their communities, brutalized, stigmatized and viewed as outcast mothers with sexually transmitted infections. In Uganda, as many as 15,000 children were abducted by the Lord's Resistance Army over a period of 20 years, many were raped and forced into marriage, while in Sierra Leone, over 5,000 children have been kidnapped by rebels (Barton and Mutiti, 2000).

According to the World Bank (2002), 32% of schoolgirls and 15% of schoolboys in one district in Uganda reported that they had been sexually abused, mainly by teachers. In South Africa, 40-47% of sexual assaults are perpetrated against girls of 15 years or younger. Fifty-five per cent of adolescent girls in rural Malawi are reported to have been forced to have sex by their teachers.

According to Dossier (1991), in South Africa one adult woman out of every six is assaulted regularly by her partner. In at least 46% of these cases, the men involved also abuse their children sexually. A woman is raped in South Africa every ninety seconds totaling approximately 320,000 women being raped every year.

In Kenya, 71 girls were raped and 19 others died at St. Kizito Boarding School. Girls were attacked by boys when the girls refused to take part in a štrike against the headmaster. The deputy principal commented: "The boys never meant any harm to the girls. They just wanted to rape."

According to Kurz and Prather (1995), young brides in India are burnt if they bring inadequate dowry. The Mexican Federation of Women Trade Unions reports that 95% of female workers are victims of sexual harassment. In India, a woman is beaten every 15 seconds, a rape takes place every six minutes and a woman is killed by her partner every four minutes, while violence occurs in at least 67% of all marriages. In the USA domestic battering is the single most significant cause of injury to women, more than vehicle accidents, rapes and muggings combined.

Christianity teaches that God gave sex to humanity as a gift intended to serve Him in the procreation process (Genesis 1:27-28). According to Dortzbach (1996), God designed the sexual union uniquely for exclusive enjoyment in marriage. This explains why Leviticus 18:6-8, 19:21 and 1 Corinthians 5 and 6 condemn adultery, incest, homosexuality, prostitution, rape and fornication. People have to be educated about the importance of equity and dialogue regarding sexual matters, as emphasised by St. Paul in 1 Corinthians 7:1-5.

> A man does well not to marry, but because there is too much immorality every man should have his own wife and every woman her own husband. A man should fulfil his duty as a husband, a woman should fulfill her duty as a wife and each other's needs. A

wife is not the master of her body but her husband is, in the same way a husband is not the master of his own body but his wife is. Do not deny yourselves to each other, unless you first agree to do so for a while in order to be kept from giving in to Satan's temptation because of your lack of self-control.

Paul's teaching on the equality between spouses in sexual matters is significant. It enhances equity, equal participation and mutual understanding in marriage. It is a tool against unfaithfulness and the spread of HIV/Aids infection among couples.

Women's Vision (2003) reports a new wave of violence against women. Many men who loose their spouses to HIV/Aids are marrying uninfected women. They tell these women that their wives died of witchcraft, malaria or tuberculosis, or even that they have not been married before. Owing to lack of knowledge about the causes, symptoms, stages and preventive measures against HIV/Aids, women often marry and have sexual relationships with infected men. Most women lack bargaining power with their sexual partners, and have sex with infected men because they lack the power to convince them to use condoms. Feminists urge that women have been taught that they must be subordinate and remain in the marriage, even though it may mean exposure to HIV/Aids infection.

The Programme of Action of the International Conference on Population and Development of 1998, the Vienna Declaration, the Programme of Action adopted by the World Conference on Human Rights and the Fourth World Conference on Women all affirmed that reproductive rights rest on the recognition of the basic rights of all couples and individuals to decide freely and responsibly about the number, spacing and timing of their children, having the information and means to do so and the right to attain the highest standard of sexual and reproductive health. It also includes the partners' rights to make decisions concerning reproduction, free of discrimination, coercion and violence.

In an address on World Peace Day, 1996, Pope John Paul II drew attention to the exploitation of women and girls that exists in every part of the world. He decried the sexual exploitation of women and children, the trivialisation of sexuality, especially by the media, and the acceptance, in some societies, of sexuality without moral restraint and without accountability to women, which increases the challenges women face in sustaining their personal dignity and service to life. The Pope condemned abortion as a so-called solution to the unwanted results of sexual promiscuity and irresponsibility. He challenged the violence embodied by women being abandoned by men who made them pregnant, or women pressured into terminating the life which has already started. Women are abandoned while pregnant and bear the burden of sexual promiscuity alone. A radical solidarity with women requires that the underlying causes of the phenomenon of unwanted children be addressed. There will never be justice, equality and peace for men and women unless there is an unfailing determination to respect, protect, love and serve life.

All types of sexual violence that imprison women as sexual objects must be condemned and effective laws must be enacted to protect women from such violence. Girls learn that sexual violence and abuse are an inescapable part of going to school, so some avoid going to school. Sensitisation and education of girls are powerful tools for slowing down and reversing the spread of HIV/Aids and reducing the vulnerability of women. Gender sensitisation and education of girls are factors that contribute to reducing poverty and gender equality and raising awareness of human rights and sexuality.

UNICEF (2002) indicates that the HIV/Aids epidemic is presenting special challenges to gender issues and the education sector. Violence and sexual harassment are widespread in sub-Saharan African schools and many parents wish to protect their children, especially daughters, from these risks. If enrolment rates among girls are to be increased, and HIV/Aids fought, sexual violence in secondary schools is an issue that will have to be addressed. Teachers should be reminded of professional ethics and should be forbidden to engage in any type of sexual relationships with students, or to perpetrate sexual harassment. Instead, teachers should take part in solving the problems introduced by HIV/Aids and sexual harassment, and promote positive social values that enhance gender equity.

Teenage girls are physically and psychologically tortured when men introduce them to sexual relations at an early age. Consequently they can no longer concentrate on their studies. Unmarried teenage girls who become pregnant are forced to drop out of school. It is true that, while girls are forced to deal with sexual harassment or unwanted pregnancy, the males who are responsible go unpunished. This has negative repercussions for gender equity. Boys are able complete their education and compete in the world of employment, while girls who drop out of school become mothers at an early age, and because they have no qualifications, they become domestic workers or prostitutes, or are left destitute.

Christian Teaching on Sex

The sanctity of sex finds its fulfillment in the act of marriage where there is a sacred and intimate relationship shared uniquely by a husband and wife in the privacy of their love. Genesis 1:28 explains that God designed sexual relationships for married couples. It is a sacred experience that appears in God's first commandment to humanity: "Be fruitful and multiply and replenish the earth". Sexual intercourse and procreation were divinely instituted and ordained by God at the time of creation. It is through lovemaking that man and woman populate God's world. God designed sexual intercourse for procreation and enjoyment. It is a relationship where man and woman experience a unique and strong experience of unity, soul-to-soul and body-to-body, without shame, guilt or condemnation.

After blessing the institution of marriage and sex, God looked at everything that He had created and was very pleased because it was good (Genesis 1:31). In Matthew 19:5 Jesus confirms the sacred union of marriage of Genesis 1:28 when he says,

> And God said for this reason a man will leave his father and mother and unite with his wife and the two shall become one, so they are no longer two but one. No human being must separate then, what God has joined together.

Hebrews 13:4 declares the holiness of sex in marriage: "Marriage is to be honoured by all and husbands and wives must be faithful to each other. God will judge those who are immoral and those who commit adultery". This text implies that coitus in marriage is honourable and undefiled. Married partners who engage in sex are aware of the possibility of the God-given privilege of creating new life – another human being – as a result of the expression of their love.

The Book of Proverbs warns against taking up with the strange woman (prostitute) but, in contrast, the writer challenges a husband to rejoice with the wife of his youth, by letting her breasts satisfy him at all times and be ravished always with her love (Proverbs 5: 18, 19). The lovemaking experience should make humanity rejoice, conferring upon them ecstatic pleasure, as it is an experience intended for mutual enjoyment. In this context rape and denial of sex by one partner is condemned, thus sexual intercourse is not only designed for propagation of the human race but also for enjoyment by the partners (Lahaye and Lahaye, 1997).

The writer of Proverbs 1:9 records the inspired words of Solomon, the world's wisest man, to his son, teaching him to handle his sex drive and to avoid being tempted into using it improperly. Solomon wanted his son to enjoy a lifetime of legitimate use of that drive by confining it to the act of marriage. Solomon states that an enjoyable, satisfying married love is the wellspring of wisdom. Extramarital love is presented by Solomon as the way of folly, offering short-time pleasure but bringing destruction, heartache, guilt, sorrow, regret and, in the end, death.

Genesis 4:1-2 reports that Adam had intercourse with his wife and she became pregnant and bore a son and said, "By the Lord's help I have acquired a son". Genesis 26:6-11 says: "When Isaac had been there for some time, King Abimelech looked down from his window and saw Isaac and Rebecca making love." In Deuteronomy 24:5, God commanded Moses to inform Israel young men were exempted from military service and business responsibilities for one year after marrying, so that the couple could get to know each other at a time when their sex drives were strongest and under circumstances that would provide ample opportunity for oneness. In 1 Corinthians 7:9, Paul warns Christians that it is better to marry than to burn, because there is one legitimate way, a God-ordained method, for releasing the natural pressure He created in human beings and that is the act of marriage. God intended that husband and wife be totally dependent on each other for sexual satisfaction. In 1 Corinthian's 7:2-5, Paul says:

> But because of immoralities, let each man have his own wife and let each woman have her own husband. Let the husband fulfill his duty to his wife and likewise also the wife to her husband. The wife does not have authority over her own body, but the husband does and likewise also the husband does not have authority over his body but the wife does. Stop depriving one another except by agreement for a time that you may devote yourselves to prayer and come together again, lest Satan tempt you because of your lack of self-control.

Lahaye and Lahaye (1997) delineated four central principles concerning sexual union taught in 1 Corinthians 7:2-5:

(a) Both husband and wife have sexual needs and drives that should be fulfilled in marriage.

(b) When one marries one forfeits control of one's body to one's partner.

(c) Both partners are forbidden from refusing to meet the mate's sexual needs.

(d) The act of marriage and sexual union are approved by God.

God condemns the sexual exploitation that exists in our society. God never intended that sex be displayed publicly in movies, magazines and on television in a cheap and perverted way. This is the result of man's depraved nature, destroying the good things that God has given. God intended the act of marriage to be the most sublime experience between a husband and wife, where equality is realised. The purpose of sexual union in marriage is to:

(a) Satisfy men and women's sex drives. Both men and women find fulfillment in the act of marriage through sexual union.

(b) Realise womanhood and manhood. Men and women feel intricately confident after a fulfilling sexual union. They enjoy a strong self-image. A sexually satisfied husband or wife will rapidly develop self-confidence in other areas of his or her life. A partner that is not sexually satisfied always brings his or her sexual frustration to her place of work, workmates, social gathering, etc. Lahaye and Lahaye (1997) comment that a man can endure academic, occupational and social failure as long as he and his wife relate well together in the bedroom, but success in other fields becomes a hollow mockery if he fails in bed. To the man, being unsuccessful in his bedroom signals failure in life. Failure by the man or woman to fulfill his or her sexual duties leaves a psychological gap that torments the affected partner in every aspect of life.

(c) Enhance love for one another. When sexual intercourse is satisfying, it drives away fears, depression and anger. When sex provides merely gratification and is followed by guilt, it makes a mockery of what God intended to be a very satisfying experience. In Romans 1:1ff Paul says: Because they do this God has given them to shameful passions. Even the women pervert the natural use of their sex by unnatural acts. In the same way the men give up natural sexual relations with women and burn with passion for each other. Christianity condemns rape, homosexuality, defilement, adultery and bestiality.

(d) Reduce friction in the home. A satisfying relationship between couples reduces minor irritations in the home. A sexually satisfied man is usually a contented man. Lahaye and Lahaye (1997) comment that most of the men's unexplained irritations in public places could often be traced to an unsaturated sex drive, but when there is sexual harmony a man's difficulties shrink to life-size.

(e) Provide life's most exciting experience. The titanic emotional and physical explosion that crowns the act of sex for the husband and wife is the most exciting experience, the most beautiful aspect of all that God has created for the man and woman to share. It creates a warm and affectionate relationship that enriches the entire married life. Lahaye and Lahaye (1997) quote Napoleon Hill, in his book for businessmen, Think and Grow Rich, saying: "A sexually satisfied husband is a motivated man" and "a sexually frustrated man has a hard time concentrating, is prone to be edgy and harder to work with and finds it difficult to retain lasting goals. Likewise, a woman who is not sexually satisfied, or if she does not succeed in the bedroom, will fail in other areas of life. Sexually frustrated women have the lowest self-esteem and image".

(f) Reassures the couple of their compassionate, companionate, romantic, affectionate and passionate love.

(g) Relaxes the nervous system. Impotence and frigidity invariably produce nervousness. It is therefore important that the couple learn healthy modes of sexual expression towards each other. God has made it possible for couples to enjoy a hygienically relaxing experience in marriage. Good sex promotes fidelity and fulfillment and also acts as a much-needed relaxant for the nervous system.

Gender, HIV/Aids and Violence

In many African societies HIV/Aids poses a threat to transformation. It is also linked to poverty, and the most vulnerable groups are women and girls. Research shows that the economic vulnerability of girls makes it more likely that they exchange sex for money or even small favours, and are less likely to negotiate for protection measures. For example, statistics reveal that, by 1997, about 1.7 million Ugandan children had been orphaned by HIV/Aids (UNICEF, 2001).

Mannathoko (2001) says that, in Africa's most affected countries, HIV/Aids is having a devastating impact on education systems, schools and learning. It is also having a devastating impact on the demand for education, its supply and quality and educational planning and management capacity. In addition, HIV/Aids is impacting negatively on all sectors, thereby hampering development and capacity-building.

Emasu (2004) reports findings from Mifumi, where domestic violence among women living with HIV/Aids is on the rise. Women living with HIV/Aids suffer more domestic violence than their counterparts because most infected men live in denial. Today, most women opt for voluntary HIV testing after losing a baby, when a co-wife dies or when they become sickly. These days many women seek family planning advice or information on positive living. Women are abused when they ask their husbands how they acquired the virus, while others are jilted for suggesting or insisting on protected sex. Women are blamed for anything that affects the sexuality of the couple. In addition to increased physiological susceptibility to HIV/Aids infection, violations of rights of women living with HIV/Aids heighten their vulnerability. Domestic violence exposes women to HIV/Aids infection and prevents them from accessing information freely, negotiating condom use, practicing family planning and resisting unprotected sex with HIV-positive partners. Women seldom subject their husbands to domestic violence, however, women have abandoned their spouses after mistreatment or forced, unprotected sex. A 2003 study by Human Rights Watch confirms that infected women suffer more domestic violence than men because they constitute the biggest proportion of people living with HIV/Aids. The 2003/2004 UNAIDS global estimates of HIV/Aids states that of the 37.8 million people living with HIV/Aids, 17 million are women.

Women's subordinate position in marriage, discrimination, unequal access to economic opportunities, information, education and legal rights are among the factors that sustain the escalation of the pandemic. The Mifumi report (2003) blames increasing abuse of infected women on the economic dependence of women, which compounds their vulnerability and leaves them unable to escape from harmful marriages. Thousands of Ugandan women are becoming infected with HIV and will eventually die of Aids because the government fails to protect them from domestic violence. Women whose husbands rape, physically attack or intimidate them are unable to protect themselves from HIV infection. The reluctance of state officials to intervene in domestic matters and to reduce male authority in the home implies that battered women are left unaided and condemned to endless abuse.

In order to protect women from violence in the home and to decrease their vulnerability to infection and discrimination, the enactment of comprehensive domestic violence laws which punish offenders and compensate victims is critical.

The gender gap in Africa entrenches gender discrimination and violence within the education system and societies, which impact on the quality of life of girls in schools and communities. Conflict and emergency conditions require a gender lens and a rights-based perspective to analyze the different impact it has on boys and girls. Gender violence worsens the impact of HIV/Aids for both male and female adults, children, politicians, medical workers, teachers, managers, parents and communities.

Unequal power relations, highlighted by culture and religion, in boys and men's domination of physical space and control of sexual relations, constantly remind women of their submissive position. The opportunistic use of traditions by men and women indoctrinated in a patriarchal religious culture deny girls and women control of their sexuality. Most men present themselves as upholders of religious doctrines, culture and tradition and they consequently control female behaviour and assert male authority while succumbing to tensions caused by differences in traditional and modern values, which is used to explain the practice of adult men having sexual liaisons with teenage girls. The situation is worsened by sexual abuse and sexual harassment of girls and young women. Many schoolgirls become pregnant after sexual abuse and, in most cases, contract HIV/Aids and give birth to babies who are also infected with the virus, thus creating a triple burden (Mannathoko, 2001).

The focus on HIV/Aids and other gender and sexuality issues should be expanded to include men. Mannathoko (2001) argues that it is men that drive the HIV/Aids pandemic, even though women are the most vulnerable to HIV/Aids. Thus, to control HIV/Aids, the most vulnerable, that is women and girls, must be protected. It is necessary to understand how the power relations between males and females manifest themselves in villages, families, offices, public places, streets and between young lovers.

Battered and depleted women and girls are faced with an urgent need for new innovations in education, medical, social, and economic spheres so as to reach out to the young people with knowledge and life skills to protect themselves from men with a high libido. The curriculum development process in schools, institutions of higher learning and in other sectors, should be gender-responsive, rights-based and participatory. Management systems at the state, district and village levels must be reshaped in order to reduce the vulnerability of girls and women to sexually transmitted diseases (STDs) and HIV/Aids. In the process of programming and monitoring gender and HIV/Aids in society, it is important to focus on and address societal problems. Mannathoko (2001) raises fundamental questions about gender and HIV/Aids:

(i)   What is the role of the government, education, managers, community-based organisations and cultural and religious leaders in breaking the silence and eradicating the stigmatization of vulnerable people?

(ii) How can we ensure that HIV/Aids strategies strengthen the broad-based participation of the youth and children, women, the disabled, orphans, children in refugee camps and conflict areas, children in exploitative labour and highly vulnerable street children?

(iii) How can concrete and workable links be established between higher, secondary and primary education and basic education on HIV/Aids issues such as orphans, young girls, the disabled and gender violence?

(iv) What are the strategies required of African governments to strengthen legal frameworks that can protect girls from sexual abuse by adult men in their families, schools, as domestic workers, in offices and communities? On this note, Ssejoba (2004) reports the shocking news of a Catholic priest from Luvule Parish in Masaka, who was found in a lodge defiling a 15-year-old girl, while another young girl of 16 years was in the next room awaiting her turn.

(v)   How can we incorporate HIV/Aids concepts in the school curriculum?

HIV/Aids is robbing our society of its cream and in the process imposing untold suffering on children, men and women. Many households are now headed by children. This has affected girls' education through increasing absenteeism. Women in HIV/Aids-afflicted families care for sick relatives and even take over responsibility for farming and domestic work. It has led to many girls leaving school to assist with caring duties. When parents die, children are withdrawn from school to go and stay with relatives and grandparents, and the most affected are girls.

HIV/Aids tends to worsen existing gender inequalities, increasing women's vulnerability and exploitation. For example, when a husband or child is infected with HIV/Aids, a wife usually absents herself from work or stops working altogether in order to care for sick family members. However when the wife falls ill, the husband continues his work and abandons her at home or in hospital to the care of female relatives. School-going girls are withdrawn from school to look after family members who are ill, while brothers continue with their education (Anarfi, 1994; Freeman, 1996; UNICEF, 2002).

Freeman (1996) and UNICEF (2002) declare that women's vulnerability to societal exploitation and quality of life are bound to lead to gender violence and inequality. Widespread evidence from the majority of African countries indicate that the health and quality of life of girls become more precarious at adolescence as they are faced with the risks of exploitation and unwanted pregnancy, abortions, prostitution and violence in various forms, leading to rejection by the family and community. Faced with rejection by an unsympathetic society, young girls enter prostitution in order to survive and are at risk of acquiring STDs.

Cultural and religious practices that include assumptions that women are weak and inferior aggravate women's physiological vulnerability to HIV/Aids infection. Women's needs are more often than not neglected and open discussions about safe sexual behaviour between men and women are not encouraged. The first official report of HIV/Aids was published on 5 June 1981. HIV/Aids has since spread all over the world. According to UNICEF (2002), relationships, together with psychological differences, determine, to a great extent, women's and men's vulnerability to infection, their ability to protect themselves effectively and their respective share of the burden of the epidemic. HIV/Aids is therefore a gender issue.

In his address at the Beijing +5 conference, Kofi Annan, the United Nations Secretary General, stated that there were many challenges that hinder women's equality with men. He cited HIV/Aids as affecting more women than men. He noted that 40 percent of pregnant women were HIV positive and more than 10 million children had lost their mothers to HIV/Aids (United Nations, 2000). There is therefore a need for special emphasis on educating girls and women about risk patterns and safe practices, alongside efforts to encourage men to be better informed and to adopt patterns of behaviour that reduce the spread of HIV/Aids. By promoting a culture of rights and gender equity, responsibility and choice in relation to HIV/Aids, empowerment, communication and education can play a significant role in ending women's overwhelming biological, social and economic susceptibility to HIV/Aids (UNICEF 2002).

Gender stereotypes permit women to be blamed for spreading HIV/Aids. In some families where a couple is found to be HIV positive the wife is blamed by relatives for bringing it to her husband. If the man dies before the wife, she is harassed for killing the man. Usually women are tested for HIV before their husbands, because of pregnancy or because they gave birth to a sick baby. When found positive, they are the first to be blamed for acquiring or causing the infection. Health violence continues to be a contributory factor to women's inequality. Women are beaten, abused and even killed by people who blame them for causing the death of their husbands. Many women have a poor understanding of their own bodies, mechanisms of HIV transmission and the level of risk involved in unprotected sex.

Economic factors make women more vulnerable to HIV/Aids than men. Because of poverty, many families are unable to provide necessities for their children. This leads some women and children to engage in risky activities like prostitution in order to survive. According to Anarfi (1994), Freeman (1996) and Shisanya (2001), women find it difficult to obtain medical treatment once they have been infected with HIV, while their husbands treat themselves and their children. Men prolong their lives at the expense of their wives. Many women who are HIV positive are marganalised at their places of work. When their husbands die, they are left with orphans, with no money to look after them.

Besides, women become infected at a younger age than men since girls become sexually active earlier than boys. In Kenya, in most cases, the girls' first sexual intercourse is forced because of the belief among some Kenyans that sexual intercourse with virgins cures HIV/Aids. Subsequently many vulnerable young girls, such as orphans, are raped by HIV positive men. In addition, many young girls are raped in their own homes by domestic workers or relatives, leading them to contract HIV/Aids and/or become pregnant.

The reality of sexual activity among girls is confirmed by the prevalence of premarital pregnancies, abortions and sexually transmitted diseases. Unmarried girls who conceive are exposed to violence, as they are expected to bring up these children single-handedly, as their male partners usually refuse to provide support. Teenage pregnancies cause frustration, shame and anxiety, making girls seek out abortions (Anarfi 1994; Shisanya, 2001).

Shisanya (2001) says that teenage girls in Kenya are prepared for maternal roles through clitoridectomy, a form of female genital mutilation. This practice constitutes violence against the initiates, because they are often infected with HIV/Aids during the procedure, as the same blades are re-used.

Violence against women is also illustrated by practices encouraging women to serve as sexual objects to please men. This violence is effected in some communities by prescribing women to apply vaginal agents to give men maximum sexual satisfaction (Anarfi, 1994). The male sexual prowess and need to glorify virility exerts pressure on men to demonstrate these virtues through sexual conquests and a multiplicity of sexual partners. If polygamy is furthermore condoned, women have no assurance that faithfulness in marriage will guarantee that they avoid contracting HIV/Aids. Men infect their wives because the latter have no control over their sexuality. Payment of bride wealth and the dependence syndrome causes women to be defenseless. Women have to fulfill their conjugal duty irrespective of the sexual practices of their husbands. According to Freeman (1996), the pervasive threat of physical violence or divorce makes women surrender to unsafe sex with their husbands. Violence against women is also evident in the failure of men to disclose the nature of their ailments to their spouses, to enable them to employ safety measures to avoid infection. Some Infected men cannot use condoms to save their wives, who have limited autonomy to decide on sexual matters that relate to them.

Patriarchy and religion provides men with too much power over women. The church has the capacity to protect its followers from reckless living. The church can negate gender imbalances by emphasizing the biblical teaching of Genesis 1:27, that male and female are created in God's image and are equal. The church should raise men and women's consciences by stressing the scriptures, promoting equity between genders, rather than practices that promote the superiority of males over females (Shisanya, 2001). This understanding would enable women to compete for opportunities on equal footing with males in all spheres of life, for instance educational, economic, social and political. Women's resulting improved socio-economic status will empower them, which will enable them to avoid situations that render them vulnerable to HIV infection. The church is responsible for re-educating its flock about the moral values preached by religion.

According to the United Nations Commission for Africa (1994), women's health and reproductive rights are central to the realisation of their potential and the improvement of their health and their ability to exercise control over their fertility, which is a major step in enabling women to make the right choices in other areas. African women's inability to control their own fertility is associated with unacceptably high levels of infant, child and maternal mortality. This results from the interplay of a variety of inappropriate, unaffordable and inaccessible services and the persistence of traditional mentalities which hinder contraceptive practices.

Adolescent sexuality and fertility pose considerable health risks. This contributes significantly to girls' inability to attain high levels of education and to the commission of unsafe abortions, which lead to maternal mortality and morbidity United Nations Commission for Africa, (1995); Mbuya Mbeya, (1998); UNICEF, (2002).

According to the United Nations commission for Africa (1994), mortality problems relating to malaria, malnutrition, anaemia, tuberculosis, maternal ailments and sexually transmitted diseases, still continue to preoccupy women. It prevents Ugandan women from attaining equality with men. A large proportion of women who are of child-bearing age are infected with HIV, and many young women are seriously debilitated by HIV/Aids. The political, economic and social consequences of HIV/Aids are mostly felt by women, with serious repercussions for elderly women, who are left to care for the orphans when they are least capable. Because women play such key socio-economic roles, it is necessary to address women's vulnerability to HIV/Aids. Education and information campaigns should target the sexual and reproductive health of women.

Mwagale (2004) links faithfulness, like abstinence, with culture. Women are culturally mandated to be faithful to their husbands, yet it is culturally acceptable for men to practice polygamy. Being in a polygamous marriage predisposes women to HIV infection more than men, even though these women do not have multiple partners. The 2004 World Aids Day identified women as the most vulnerable to HIV infection and the most seriously affected by the scourge.

Mwagale (2004) reports that the rate of infection among young people aged 15-24 years is growing rapidly at a rate of 67% per year, and the escalating risk is evident among this group, who make up 64% of the young people living with HIV/Aids in developing countries. Heterosexual sex accounts for the vast majority of causes of HIV transmission in sub-Saharan Africa, and today African women are being infected at an earlier age than men and the gap in HIV/Aids prevalence between the two sexes continues to grow.

In Uganda, statistics from the Aids Control Programme in the Ministry of Health indicate that females accounted for 55.2% of the 56,451 cumulative adult Aids cases recorded in 2003. In 2002, HIV/Aids killed 28,760 females compared to 23,560 men (Mwagale, 2004). Women's educational levels have been found to play a vital role in the spread of HIV/Aids. Most girls who are educated to secondary level have acquired certain skills, so that they are more assertive, are able to make informed decisions and understand the importance of behavioural change to avoid the spread of HIV/Aids. Educated girls also face less risk of marrying early and depending on their husbands for support.

This reduces their risk of being subjected to violence in relationships, which is one of the major factors predisposing women to HIV/Aids.

Mwagale (2004) says that the Ugandan Ministry of Health is working to prevent the transmission of HIV from mother to child. They have instituted health programmes to improve health care for HIV infected mothers and their families. Records from the Ministry of Health indicate that over 400 women and their families are receiving anti-retroviral drugs free of charge. In addition to receiving this therapy, women and their families receive counseling and psychosocial support. The government should, however, increase its support to women by ensuring that everyone infected with HIV has access to ARVs.

Some reports have indicated that, if the Aids epidemic is to reduce, women have to take control of their sexuality. Women continue depending on male cooperation to protect them from HIV/Aids. A good number of men are unwilling to use condoms because they say it interferes with the natural enjoyment of sex. Thus most men would rather be infected than be denied unprotected sexual contact. The current male condom is not user-friendly for women, since it is the man who decides whether to use it or not.

Through gender mainstreaming, specific gender approaches and actions should be used to solve family issues. The government, NGOs and cultural and religious leaders should work together to free women and girls from political and socio-economic issues that predispose them to being infected with HIV/Aids. More education is required and girls and women must be sensitized about the urgent need for behavioural change. More women and girls must be involved in HIV/Aids prevention and control programmes. The Guardian (2004) reports that UNAIDS has urged government to reform inheritance laws and make rules against domestic violence. In sub-Saharan Africa, where the pandemic is most advanced, 57% of those with HIV/Aids are women. In Zambia, Zimbabwe and South Africa 77% of all HIV/Aids sufferers are women. East Asia has experienced a 56% rise in the number of HIV positive women over the past couple of years while, in Russia, the proportion of infected women has risen from 24% to 38% in only 12 months. In every region of the world Aids is a significant killer.

Reuters (2004) reports that worldwide violence against women, is fuelling the spread of HIV/Aids. Amnesty International says that, if governments are serious in their fight against HIV/Aids, they have to deal with another worldwide pandemic, which is violence against women.

Reuters (2004) and The Guardian (2004) quote the annual report released by UNAIDS and the World Health Organisation, which shows that the number of adults and children living with HIV/Aids reached higher levels in 2004, to an estimated 39.4 million, compared to 36.6 million in 2002. Women comprise nearly half of the 37.2 million adults living with HIV/Aids. Traditional practices such as female genital mutilation, early marriages and widow inheritance by male relatives also increase women's exposure to the epidemic. Many women feel inhibited about seeking medical advice after rape because they are afraid of being stigmatized within their communities.

To check the increasing spread of HIV/Aids governments and other institutions should:

(i)   ensure the involvement of women, especially those infected with HIV/Aids or other sexually transmitted diseases or those affected by the HIV/Aids pandemic, in decision-making relating to the development, implementation, monitoring and evaluation of policies and programmes on HIV/Aids and other sexually transmitted diseases.

(ii)   combat practices that contribute to women's susceptibility to diseases such as HIV and other transmitted infections, including enacting legislation against those socio-cultural and religious practices that contribute to it. They should also implement legislation, policies and practices to protect women and girls from discrimination related to HIV/Aids.

(iii) develop gender-sensitive multisectoral programmes and strategies to end the social subordination of women, promote economic empowerment and equality and facilitate promotion of programmes to educate and enable men to assume responsibility in preventing HIV/Aids and other sexually transmitted diseases.

This should include the provision of resources and facilities to women who find themselves the principal caregivers or economic supporters of those infected with HIV/Aids or those affected by the pandemic.

(iv) promote mutual, respectful and equitable gender relations to meet the educational and service needs of the youth, to help them deal with their sexuality in a positive and responsible way.

(v) ensure the provision, through the primary health care system and universal access of couples , to appropriate and affordable preventive treatment for sexually transmitted diseases including HIV/Aids; expand voluntary counseling and confidential diagnostic and treatment services for women and men; ensure accessibility to anti-retroviral drugs (ARVs) and high quality condoms; sensitise people to the possibility of contracting HIV/Aids by the intravenous use of substances or unprotected and irresponsible sexual behaviour and advise men and women to implement appropriate preventive measures.

(vi) support strategies that empower women so that they can protect themselves against HIV infection.

(vii) support research addressing women's needs and situations, including research on HIV/Aids and other sexually transmitted diseases.

(viii) increase financial support to preventive and appropriate biomedical, behavioural, epidemiological and health services, research on women's health issues and on the social, economic, political and cultural causes of women's health problems and their consequences. This would include the impact of gender and age inequalities, especially with respect to chronic and non-communicable diseases (particularly cardiovascular diseases and conditions), tuberculosis, malaria, reproductive health infections and injuries, HIV/Aids and other sexually transmitted diseases, domestic violence, occupational health, disabilities, environmentally-related problems and tropical diseases.

(ix) ensure targeted measures for HIV/Aids, with a view to promoting awareness, education and protection.

(x) ensure that, by 2020, every individual youth and adult is aware of how HIV/Aids is acquired and transmitted and how it can be prevented.

(xi) ensure the availability of various methods, programmes and policies for creating awareness, disseminating information, educating and protecting against HIV/Aids.

(xii) emphasise the significance of living with HIV/Aids, good nutrition and sharing with others about HIV/Aids.

(xiii)utilise all types of media to transmit information about HIV/Aids.

Human Trafficking and Gender

Maicibi (2005) comments that human trafficking can be defined as the recruitment, transportation, transfer and harboring of persons by means of threats or force or other forms of coercion, of abduction, fraud, deception, abuse of power, a position of vulnerability or of the giving or receiving of payment or benefits to achieve the consent of a person and having control over another person for the purpose of exploitation. It is mainly women who are trafficked for sexual exploitation, forced labour, or servitude, or trade in human organs.

Children are sometimes sold by unsuspecting guardians or parents who believe that their young will be cared for and enrolled in schools abroad. Trafficking in persons is caused and aggravated by poverty in the countries of origin. Maicibi (2005) notes that poor people are especially vulnerable, as their desperate situation makes them believe the false promises made by human traffickers.

Unemployment is another major cause of human trafficking. Many jobless primary, secondary school and tertiary graduates are unemployed in both rural and urban areas. Because these children lack accommodation, food and transport money, they become vulnerable to the machinations of human traffickers, who promise them a better life in the developed world.

Disruption of traditional livelihoods, resulting mainly from the movement of the youth and educated people from rural to urban centers, has caused a labour drain in rural agrarian communities. For example, the absence of young people in rural areas means that the elderly are responsible for farming and continuing to earn a living for the household. This results in low output, due to low labour input, mainly due to the age of the labour force. In the same way, women who are educated tend to leave their traditional agricultural roles in search of paid jobs, thereby disrupting traditional family livelihoods. As a result, when an opportunity avails itself, unsuspecting parents volunteer their children for slavery through human traffickers, who either sell the children into prostitution or use them as organ donors.

Another cause of human trafficking is the economic disparity between men and women. In most developing countries, men have higher literacy rates than women and more men are found in salaried positions. The disparity between men and women in terms of economic power has led to women being more vulnerable to human trafficking than men.

Human trafficking affects the most vulnerable in society, those who lack money and education, such as children, women and poor men. The United Nations Information Service (2002) reports that more than 700,000 women and children are trafficked every year for sexual exploitation, forced labour, forced marriage and forced adoption. Research shows that Asia, Eastern Europe, Latin America and Africa continue to experience human trafficking. UMCER (2000) estimates the figure of enslaved children alone at more than 200,000 worldwide.

Annual research carried out by the United States Department on Human Trafficking quotes a figure as high as 200,000 to 900,000 men, women and children who are trafficked into slavery internationally every year. Research also shows that:

(i)   The United States alone receives 18,000-200,000 trafficked people (United States Human Rights Watch, (2002).

(ii) Pakistan has over 100,000 trafficked children. Japan and Saudi Arabia are other destinations for trafficked people as reported in the Human Rights Watch document (1999) and on the Internet in June 2002.

(iii) Argentina, Brazil and Bolivia are involved in human trafficking (Human Rights Watch, 2002).

(iv) In 2000, Europe, Italy, Germany and the Netherlands were the most popular destinations for trafficked persons (This Day, 2000). Maicibi (2005) says that many drug traffickers have abandoned the drug trade in favour of human trafficking because it is more lucrative and relatively risk-free. This has turned it into the fastest-growing type of organised crime.

The United Nations African Institute for the Prevention of Crime and the Treatment of Offenders in 2003 stated that the African region most affected by human trafficking is West Africa. UNICEF (2002) estimates that up to 200,000 children are trafficked from West Africa alone every year. These trafficked people are forced into prostitution, pornography, forced and domestic labour and farm labour, especially for cocoa farms in the Ivory Coast. Maicibi (2005) says that On 17 April 2001, a commercial vessel heading to Gabon was impounded. It was found to be carrying 43 minors; 13 from Benin, 8 from Togo, 17 from Mali and five from other countries. In 1998, between 250 and 500 children were trafficked from Nigeria into Italy for sexual exploitation. According to This Day newspaper of 3 August 2000, among 454 trafficked Nigerians who were returned, the majority were women and children. They had been taken to five foreign nations between 1999 and July 2000. Of the 454 victims, 62 were men while 392 were females who had been deported from the USA, Italy, Germany, Saudi Arabia and the Netherlands. Within the same period, Italy alone had deported 368 comprising 4 males and 364 females. While the Netherlands had deported 39 people, 20 males and 19 females. Germany deported 26 males in April 2000, Saudi Arabia 17 females on 19 March, 2000 and the USA deported 12 males in January 1991.

Human trafficking must be condemned by all lovers of peace. It is a type of gender violence and a crime against humanity. Every country should therefore enact legal and other preventive measures to protect its citizens from this criminal act.

Human traffickers, mostly men, should be punished severely if found guilty. Countries that receive these human slaves must abide by the law and return trafficked people to their countries of origin. Parents, the community and school should equip learners, especially girls, with skills to detect, counteract and report those planning to sell them to other countries. Victims of human trafficking should be protected and their rights should be observed by the receiving countries.

According to the United Nations Centre for International Crime Prevention (2002), Kofi Annan, the Secretary General of the United Nations, describes trafficking of persons, particularly women and children, as the most blatant violation of human rights now confronting the United Nations. He urges member countries to ratify not only the protocol, to prevent, suppress and punish those involved in trafficking humans, but also to support the United Nations Convention against this transnational crime and to reinforce the fight against organised crime. In order to control trafficking of human beings, a plan of action should be established in each concerned country, including the implementation of the United Nations protocol and convention before the evil spreads to all other countries. Countries should also verify and implement the optional protocol on the rights and sale of children, including the International Labour Organisation Convention (Maicibi, 2005).

Governments and other institutions should eliminate trafficking in humanity and should assist victims of violence and abuse by:

(i) Ratifying and enforcing international conventions relating to trafficking in persons and slavery.

(ii) Taking appropriate measures to address the root causes and factors that encourage trafficking.

(iii) Allocating resources to provide comprehensive programmes designed to heal, rehabilitate and integrate into society victims of trafficking, including job training, legal assistance and confidential health care. Both governments and other institutions should provide social, medical, educational and psychological care for the victims of trafficking.

(iv) Developing educational and training programmes and policies and enacting legislation aimed at preventing sex tourism and human trafficking, thereby protecting those vulnerable to human trafficking.

The Family as an Arena of Masculine Violence

The family is one of the main arenas for masculine violence. For many men, their roles are those of producer, provider, protector and sustainer. While men often consider marriage secondary to work, for most women it is the most important institution in their lives. Men are usually the breadwinners. Patriarchy identifies a man by his position, and men are supposed to work to support their families. When a man is unemployed, made redundant, retired or retrenched, he loses his sense of importance to the community. In such a situation, a man may become ill or mentally sick, he may even commit suicide (Action Aid Uganda, 2003).

The family, which is regarded as the ideal basic unit of society for providing support, love, understanding and care, can also be the most oppressive institution, harbouring serious violence, hostility and conflicts. These negative emotions and behaviour may be prevalent in the long term, and could lead to separation or divorce. Ninety percent of violence perpetrated against women and girls occurs in the family.

Solutions to Family Violence

Education regarding the rights of women is essential at family, community and society levels. Families must be made aware of situations that promote violence and how to avoid them. All efforts should be geared towards promoting family values of love, sharing, tolerance, peace, honesty, fidelity, justice and compassion. Justice and peace, communication and harmony should coexist in the family.

Violence by Women against Women

Many liberated women who are leaders and are well-placed begrudge other women participation in societal activities. Many women employers mistreat their domestic employees, subjecting them to hard labour, abusing them or denying them food. Women promote traditional African rites that hinder full participation of women in society, e.g.

circumcision, forcing girls to marry at an early age, etc. Women do not recognise the abilities of their fellow women, such that when a woman competes with men in politics, women will not vote for the woman. They tend to prefer men because of the traditional belief that only men can deliver. They harass and abuse them, referring to them as prostitutes or failures in life. Women have to change their attitudes towards other women so that they can all compete equally with men. Women should realise that they are not always obliged to say "yes" as tradition demands. Women must learn to understand, forgive, support, trust and respect each other. They must learn to accept that they are different but able to complement each other. Women should not waste time monitoring other women whom they suspect of seducing their husbands, fighting and abusing them, but must learn to take care of their husbands, compete in the world of work and earn a living. Women also harass and kill each other in the course of fighting for lovers and husbands thereby undermining women's state of equality (Tibatemwa-Ekirikubinza, 1999).

Impact of Violence on Women
Physically, violence causes injuries which can lead to permanent disabilities or even fatalities. Many women die following beatings by their husbands and in most cases men are released by the court after the woman has been buried. Psychologically, a woman will experience intense fear that violence will happen again, she may suffer from low self-esteem, guilt, shame and depression, feel that she has been treated unjustly, helplessness and harbor feelings of hatred and revenge. Spiritually, women may experience spiritual hunger and a need for support, they may feel unappreciated in society and not recognised in the church. Psychological, economic, social and cultural violence may hinder women from carrying out their gender roles. Violence undermines the woman's confidence and security, socialisation and development (Fredrick, 1968; Fiorensa, 1987).

Preventative Measures against Gender Violence
Developing a holistic and multidisciplinary approach to the challenging task of promoting families, communities and states

that are free of violence against women is necessary and achievable. Equality, partnership between women and men and respect for human dignity must permeate all stages of the socialisation process. Educational systems should promote self-respect, mutual respect and cooperation between men and women. The absence of adequate gender-disaggregated data and statistics on the incidence of violence makes the elabouration of programmes and monitoring of changes difficult. Lack of documentation and research on domestic violence, sexual harassment, violence against women and girls in private and in public workplaces impede efforts to design specific intervention strategies. But experience shows that women and men can be mobilised to overcome violence in all forms and effective public measures can be taken to address both the causes and consequences of violence against women or marginalised groups. Both women's and men's groups need to be mobilised to challenge gender violence and to bring about social, political, cultural, religious, economic and educational change.

Women may be vulnerable to violence perpetrated by persons in positions of authority in both conflict and non-conflict situations. Training and sensitizing all officials in humanitarian and human rights law and punishment of perpetrators of violent acts against women should check violence that takes place at the hands of public officials whom women should be able to trust. These include teachers, lecturers, the police, prison officials and security forces.

The effective suppression of trafficking in women and girls for the sex trade is a matter of pressing international concern. The implementation of the 1949 Convention for the suppression of the traffic in persons and of the exploitation of prostitution and sex slavery, as well as other relevant instruments, needs to be reviewed and strengthened. All states should condemn forced prostitution, rape, sexual abuse and sexual tourism. Women who are victims of this trade are at an increased risk of further violence, as well as unwanted pregnancy and sexually transmitted infections including HIV.

In addressing violence against women, governments and other institutions should promote an active policy of mainstreaming a gender perspective in all policies and programmes so that an analysis may be made of their effects on women and men respectively before decisions are taken. Drastic and interrelated measures to prevent and eliminate violence against women by governments and other institutions or non-governmental organisations should include the following:

a) Condemning violence against women and refraining from invoking any custom, tradition or religious acts that cause violence, as set out in the Declaration on the Elimination of Violence against Women. Refraining from engaging in violence against women and exercising due diligence to prevent, investigate and, in accordance with national legislation, punishing acts of violence against women, whether those acts are perpetrated by the state or by private persons.

b) Enacting and reinforcing penal, civil, labour and administrative sanctions in domestic legislation to punish and redress the wrongs done to women and girls subjected to any form of violence, whether in the home, the workplace, the community or society.

c) Adopting, implementing and periodically reviewing and analyzing legislation to ensure its effectiveness in eliminating violence against women, emphasizing the prevention of violence and the prosecution of offenders. Taking measures to ensure the protection of women subject to violence, access to just and effective remedies, including compensation and healing of victims and rehabilitation of perpetrators.

d) Working actively to ratify and implement international human rights norms and instruments as they relate to violence against women, including those contained in the Universal Declaration of Human Rights, the International Covenant of Economic, Social and Cultural Rights and the Convention against Torture and Other Cruel, Inhuman or Degrading Treatment or Punishment. Implementing the Convention on the Elimination of all Forms of Discrimination against Women, taking into account general recommendations adopted by the Committee on the Elimination of Discrimination against Women at its eleventh session.

e) Promoting an active and visible policy of mainstreaming a gender perspective in all policies and programmes related to violence against women. Actively encouraging support and implementing measures and programmes aimed at increasing the knowledge and understanding of the causes, consequences and mechanisms of violence against women among those responsible for implementing these policies, such as law enforcement officers, policy-makers, personnel, medical and social workers, those who deal with minority, migration and refugee issues; and developing strategies to ensure that the revictimisation of victims of violence does not occur because of gender-insensitive laws or judicial or enforcement practices.

f)   Providing women who are subject to violence with access to the mechanisms of justice as provided by national legislation and to just and effective remedies for the harm they have suffered; and informing women of their rights in seeking redress through such mechanisms. Enacting laws and enforcing legislation against the perpetrators of practices and acts of violence against women. Formulating and implementing at all appropriate levels, plans of action to eliminate violence against women.

g)   Providing well-funded shelters and relief support for girls and women subject to violence as well as medical, psychological and other counseling services and free or low-cost legal aid where it is needed, as well as appropriate assistance to enable victims to find a means of subsistence.

h)   Establishing linguistically and culturally accessible services for migrant women and girls, including women migrant workers who are victims of gender-based violence. Recognizing the vulnerability to violence and other forms of abuse of women migrants, whose legal status in the host country depends on employers who may exploit their situations.

i)   Supporting initiatives of women's organisations and non-governmental organisations all over the world to raise awareness on the issue of violence against women and to contribute to its elimination. Organising, supporting and funding community-based education and training campaigns to raise awareness about violence against women as a violation of women's enjoyment of their human rights and mobilizing local communities to use appropriate gender-sensitive traditional and innovative methods of conflict resolution.

j)   Recognising, supporting and promoting the fundamental role of intermediate institutions, such as primary health-care centers, family-planning centers, existing school-health services, mother and baby protection services, centers for migrant families and in the field of information and education related to abuse.

k)   Organising and funding information campaigns and educational programmes to sensitise girls, boys, women and men to the personal and social detrimental effects of violence in the family, community and society. Teach them how to communicate without violence and promote training for victims and potential victims so that they can protect themselves against violence. Disseminating information on the assistance available to women and families who are victims of violence.

l)   Providing funds and encouraging counseling and rehabilitation programmes for the perpetrators of violence and promoting research to further efforts concerning such counseling and rehabilitation to prevent the recurrence of such violence.

m)   Raising awareness of the responsibility of the media in promoting non-stereotyped images of women and men as well as in eliminating patterns of media presentation that generate violence. Encouraging those responsible for media content to establish professional guidelines and codes of conduct. Raising awareness about the important role the media plays in informing and educating people about the causes and effects of violence against women.

n)   Promoting research, collecting data and compiling statistics, especially concerning domestic violence relating to the prevalent forms of violence against women, and encouraging research into the causes, nature, seriousness and consequences of violence against women, and the effectiveness of measures to prevent and redress violence against women. Supporting and initiating research on the impact of violence, such as rape, on women and girls and making the resulting information and statistics available to the public.

o) Encouraging the media to examine the impact of gender-role stereotypes which foster gender-based violence and inequalities and how they are transmitted during the life cycle, and taking measures to eliminate these negative images with a view to promoting a violence-free society.

p) Eliminating trafficking in women and assisting victims of violence due to prostitution and trafficking. Addressing the factors that encourage trafficking in women and allocating resources to institute comprehensive programmes designed to heal and rehabilitate into society victims of trafficking, including job training, legal assistance and confidential health care and taking measures to co-operate with non-governmental organisations to provide social, medical and psychological care for the victims of trafficking. Developing educational and training programmes and policies and enacting legislation aimed at preventing sex tourism and trafficking. (http: /wwwlin.org./womenwatch/daw/beying/platform/ violence/ htm, pages 1-7 of 9).

Domestic Relations Bill and Gender Issues

According to Nalugo (2004), the Domestic Relations Bill seeks to consolidate all laws relating to marriage, separation and divorce and provide for types of recognised marriages, marital rights and duties, grounds for the breakdown of marriages and the rights of parties on the dissolution of marriages. The Bill's main purpose is to harmonize all laws relating to marriage. It proposes ownership of property between spouses and specifies that men who wish to practice polygamy must obtain permission from their first wives to do so.

Traditionally, in African societies, women suggested that their husbands took second wives if the first wife was ill, overworked or elderly. These days, this is unacceptable because of the existence of sexually transmitted diseases and the social and economic costs involved. Why would the husband, who has overall authority over the woman, who is considered to be inferior to him, seek permission from his inferior for a second wife? How can a husband, who is a breadwinner, provides everything for the family expect an unbiased opinion from his first wife on whether he should marry a second wife or not? The man could tell his wife that, if she cannot tolerate a co-wife, she should simply leave the house but leave his children behind.

The Domestic Relations Bill argues that polygamy violates women's rights of equality with men in marriage, infringes on women's rights and the exercise of equal responsibilities as parents and impairs the rights of the most vulnerable family members. The advocates for the domestic relations bill also reason that polygamy accelerates domestic violence and increases the risk of contracting HIV/Aids and other STDs, hence violating the right to health. Some people in society feel that they cannot do away with polygamy. There are women who do not resent polygamous marriages. Some men argue that there are more women than men, and polygamy offers a solution.

According to FIDA, the bill does not address gender violence, especially domestic violence, but looks only at marital rape. It does not address other gender issues like the spacing of children, mobility, family names and the rights of spouses to employment outside the home, wife-battering and denial of opportunities. Whereas women believe that men are responsible for the domestic violence in the home, there are also women who batter their spouses, yet the Domestic Relations Bill does not address this issue.

The Bill fails to address many issues of concern to rural women, who have not been consulted for their inputs. Relationships in families are built on love, mutual respect, faithfulness and trust. Marriage relationships are institutions that are divinely instituted and natural but not artificial. The Domestic Relations Bill should promote laws that enhance quality of life for both husbands and wives, and equality between them. It should promote human rights based on love, mutual understanding, dialogue, openness and equal access to opportunities and responsibilities in families. It should also propose solutions that promote the equality of both sexes in all aspects of life because, in some cases, both men and women experience gender violence.

The Domestic Relations Bill recognises the non-monetary contribution of spouses to marital property. However, women and men should be educated on the need to have all their property registered in the names of both spouses to check appropriation of property by relatives upon the death of either spouse. Dialogue and communication should be encouraged in marriages so that spouses can declare their property without fear of each other, or even make wills.

The Bill decrees that the legal age for marriage be set at 18, that women have an equal right to determine what happens to property acquired jointly by the couple, that grounds for divorce be equal and that either partner can refuse to have sex on reasonable grounds, especially because of fear of disease. It calls for a radical overhaul of domestic law, which would enable women to sue their husbands for rape. The Domestic Relations Bill proposed a two-million shillings fine for men who have sex without the consent of their spouses (marital rape), but what about women who force their husbands into sex without their consent? What will be the barometer (evidence) for marital rape in marital relationships? Where and how does marital rape begin and end? It is true that many women suffer marital rape and die in silence, but how will the law establish evidence? Most men do agree that a woman refusing her husband sex is the most violent thing she can do. Some men say, "How can a woman, for whom I paid dowry, who stays in my house and who I look after, refuse to have sex with me? If she cannot meet the sexual responsibilities then she is failing in her marriage." Some men also argue that there are women who demand for too much sex from their husbands and are constantly abused by their husbands, thus the Bill is unfair to men, since their issues are not addressed. The Bill is opposed to widow inheritance, a practice that makes women vulnerable to HIV/Aids infection and degrades them to the status of material property that can be handed from one person to the other (Byamukama-Asiimwe,and Kiyimba,1999).

Dualism of Humanity

The dualistic character of human nature is based on the premise that we are created in God's image and we are a fallen humanity who are sinners. Dualism also shows that humanity consists of male and female. We are created in God's image, and God has two faces – one male, the other one female.

In the early years of Christianity, the female face of God was recognised, but as time passed, more emphasis was placed on the male face. Since most of the preachers were also males, only the weak traits of woman were emphasised. Some church writers, like St Augustine and Thomas Aquinas, taught that women were created from the weak or low part of nature, as seen in Genesis 2:21: woman was made from the rib of man, thus she is inferior. This religious teaching was upheld by men to oppress women.

These churchmen also emphasised that women are easily tempted into sin, as was the case with Eve as reported by Genesis 3; thus a woman cannot be the real image of God. Thomas Aquinas added that female bodies are used only for passion, lust, sex and wrong love and that a woman is a bodily representation of that which is weak and inferior, its only reflection of God's image is minor.

Thomas Aquinas said that, biologically, the seeds of life belong to the male and the female is a mere recipient of the seeds, thus she is inferior. According to him, a woman contributes positively to the matter of reproduction, but otherwise she is inferior in body, mind and morals and belongs to the weaker sex.

In the modern world, the human image of God is derived from Judeo-Christian thought. This represents God's image as being transcendent. The male God image is intended to show how God blessed males to conquer nature and in this respect the conquest symbolizes superiority in the principle of motherhood. To understand the roots of this thought we have to consider patriarchal monotheism, i.e. the world view that sees life from the perspective of men.

Male Monotheism

The notion of male monotheism represents God as belonging solely to one gender. Such an image indicates a sharp departure from the female principle. The idea of a male God originates from the cattle-keeping societies of the Middle East. These cultures did not have important female roles. Male monotheism reinforces the social hierarchy of the patriarchal societies and so God is modeled on a patriarchal culture, and thus God addresses men directly as his sons. Females are not referred to as God's daughters; therefore females no longer stand directly in a relationship with God.

According to male monotheism, women are contacted by God through men. This male monotheism was common among the Jews and in African society. Paul said:

> Christ is supreme over every man, the husband is supreme over his wife and God is supreme over Christ. A man has no need to cover his head because he reflects the image of the glory of God, but the woman reflects the glory of man, for man was not created from woman, but the woman from the man. Nor was man created for woman's sake but woman was created for man's sake. On account of angels, then, a woman should have a covering over her head to show that she is under the husband's authority (1 Corinthians 11:1-9)

Table 3.2: Male Monotheism

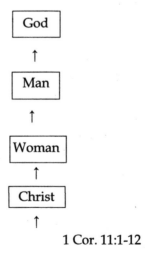

1 Cor. 11:1-12

Likewise, in Ephesians 5:21-33, Paul emphasizes male monotheism when he says that wives should submit to their husbands as to the Lord, as a husband has authority over his wife, just as Christ has authority over the Church. Wives must submit completely to their husbands just as the Church submits itself to Christ. 1 Peter 3:1-7 also stresses the male monotheism, namely that wives must submit to their husbands so as to win them to God. Sarah obeyed Abraham and called him master, and men are reminded to live with their wives with the proper understanding that women are the weaker sex. In the religious circles of male monotheism, there are surely men who are weaker than women. Are all men strong in the actual sense of what makes a man? How should women refer to those men who are weak and women who are stronger by comparison?

4

Gender and Sustainable Development

Gender, Education and Development

Education is an essential tool for achieving the goals of equality, development and peace. It is a useful tool for addressing the religious and cultural impediments that deny girls access to education. Non-discriminatory education benefits both boys and girls and ultimately contributes to the establishment of more equal relationships between men and women. Equal access to and attainment of educational qualifications is necessary if more women are to become agents of change. Literacy in women is important for improving health, nutrition and education in the family and empowering women to participate in decision-making in society. Investing in informal and non-formal education and training for girls and women, with its exceptionally high social and economic returns, has proved to be one of the best means of achieving sustainable development and economic growth.

In most societies, including Uganda, girls experience inequality at an early age and the discrimination persists well into adult years. The impact of this discrimination is acute in the area of education. Boys outnumber girls at every school level. Girls comprise 45% of the pupils at the primary school level, 30% in lower secondary school and only 20% in upper secondary school. Fewer than one-third of pupils enrolled in school complete primary education, while 75% of girls drop out, compared to 64% of boys. The average gross enrolment rate for girls is only 69% compared to 79% for boys. This trend is the consequence of a number of factors, among which are quality education, poverty, harmful cultural practices and beliefs, pregnancies, early marriage and the effects of the HIV/Aids epidemic (UNICEF, 2002).

Traditional practices which affect girls negatively are very noticeable in the education sector. In rural areas girls drop out to marry so that they can earn money for their families. Parents consider girls' education as less essential and they encourage girls dropping out to help with farming, or to care for children or ill family members.

Girls are more vulnerable to societal pressures than boys. In Uganda, for example, girls aged 15-19 years are exposed to sexual abuse by older men, their colleagues or teachers. Women are therefore more likely to acquire HIV/Aids than boys from the same age group. An estimated 1.2 million Ugandan children are orphaned, so girls drop out of school to head their families and take over responsibilities of their dead parents who, in most cases, died of HIV/Aids.These young children who are heads of families seldom receive love, guidance, counseling and nurturing from their relatives. Because they lack guidance from elders, they indulge in activities that make them vulnerable to HIV infection.

Many teachers at primary schools are untrained and in some schools the environment is not conducive for learning to girls. Facilities such as latrines are shared with boys, are inappropriate or nonexistent. The curricula tend to be gender-biased and insensitive and teachers are unskilled and poorly equipped to deal equitably with boys and girls. Cases of sexual defilement and abuse at schools are some times reported. Teachers are reported to abuse girls sexually, causing parents to prevent their girls from attending school as a protective measure. In addition, school obligations like tuition fees, contributions to building funds, uniforms, books, food for lunch, PTA and other levies limit the number of children parents can afford to send to school. If resources are limited, boys are given preference (UNICEF, 2002).

The challenges faced by people in Karamoja, North-eastern Uganda, relate to the traditional economic practices of a nomadic population. While boys move from place to place with herds of cattle in search of pasture and water, girls and women do the bulk of domestic work, including the construction of family huts. Because of the division of labour in this region, more than 75% of children between 6-12 years have never enrolled in school, even when the education is free (UNICEF, 2002).

According to the United Nations Economic Commission for Africa, African Centre for Women (1994), gross enrolment ratios are consistently on the decline, while attrition rates, for particularly girls, have been on the increase, while the quality of education has been declining. Girls are disadvantaged in terms of the quality, relevance and appropriateness of the education and training they receive. There is a pronounced discrepancy in educational attainment between rural and urban communities and between males and females. Africa's education system is pyramidal, with a broad base at the primary level, declining through the secondary level to a narrow apex at the tertiary level. Women's access to education is concentrated at the lowest level. Approximately 23% of primary school graduates enter secondary institutions, while less than 3% continue to the tertiary level. Africa's adult female literacy level is less than 50%, the lowest in the world. In 1990 the adult literacy rate in sub-Saharan Africa was 61% for men and 39% for women. The high level of illiteracy among women is a serious impediment to development and equality. In most countries, the number of women enrolled in the formal education system is low to affect the absolute number of illiterates significantly, while non-formal education programmes are not sufficiently widespread to compensate.

The educational process reinforces existing inequalities, which in turn shape the perceptions that influence curriculum designers, textbook writers, designers of audiovisual aids and teachers and pupils. Curricula and teaching materials remain, to a large degree, gender-biased and are rarely sensitive to the specific needs of girls and women. This reinforces traditional female and male roles that deny women access to opportunities for full and equal partnership in society. Lack of gender awareness among educators at all levels strengthens the existing inequalities between men and women by reinforcing discriminatory tendencies and undermining girls' self-esteem. Science curricula, in particular, are gender-biased. Science textbooks do not relate to women's and girls' daily experiences and fail to give recognition to women scientists. Girls are often deprived of basic education in mathematics, science and technical training, subjects which could provide the kind of knowledge girls can apply to improve their daily lives and enhance their employment opportunities (Kwesiga,1998).

Girls and women are expected to manage both educational and domestic responsibilities, often resulting in poor scholastic performance and early dropout from the educational system. Creation of an educational and social environment in which women and men, girls and boys, are treated equally and encouraged to achieve their full potential, a system that respects freedom of thought, conscience, religion and beliefs and within which educational resources promote non-stereotyped images of women and men, and eliminates the causes of discrimination against women and inequalities between women and men effectively.

Nevertheless, socio-cultural constraints impede women's access to vocational and technical training and education, thus making it difficult for them to acquire higher and relevant technical training. States have instituted initiatives to strengthen the capacities of African women. This includes training of women in vocational and technical subjects, and training in gender analysis and planning, importing of skills in entrepreneurship and management, provision of extension services, access to credit and introduction of new technologies and research and policy support. Some bilateral agencies, the United Nations and sub-regional and regional organisations have instituted efforts to strengthen the capacities of women farmers and entrepreneurs by training staff, extension workers and women in technical and income-generating skills and food-processing. Women's groups and non-literate women are trained with the aid of audio-visual materials. Vocational and technical education must be integrated as part of mainstream education.

Women should be viewed as users and agents of change in science and technology. Their technological and scientific knowledge and managerial skills should be improved to enhance their participation in industrial production and design, innovation, adoption and production. Measures that could increase women's participation are revision of school curricula, the promotion of equal opportunities in vocational training and the introduction of appropriate technology. The involvement of women in science and technology and their contribution to the process of industrialization are still minimal. Women's participation in science and technology subjects at higher levels, and their participation in scientific research and the formulation of science and technology policies, should be promoted. Advanced study in science and technology prepares women to take active roles in the technological and industrial development of their countries. Technology is changing the world rapidly. It is therefore essential that women not only benefit from technology but also participate in the process, from the design to the application, monitoring and evaluation stages.

The application of science and technology should benefit women in both the formal and informal sectors. In both rural and urban areas women shoulder heavy and labourious tasks in agricultural production, which could easily be eased by the adoption of appropriate, environmentally sound technologies. This implies women's involvement in the transformation, conservation and increased commercial exploitation of locally available materials (United Nations Commission for Africa, 1994).

Access to education and retention of girls and women at all levels of education should be addressed. Women who produce children in the course of their education must be encouraged to continue their courses.

The mass media are a powerful means of education and can act as a useful medium for educationists, governmental and non-governmental institutions. Computerized education and information systems are becoming an increasingly important element in learning and the dissemination of knowledge. Information technology could have a considerable impact on people in terms of shaping their attitudes and perceptions about women and girls.

Resources allocated to education, particularly for girls and women, are insufficient in many countries. Such insufficient resource allocations have a long-term adverse effect on the development of women.

In addressing unequal access to and inadequate educational opportunities, governments and other role players should promote an active and visible policy of mainstreaming a gender perspective into all policies and programmes so that, before decisions are taken, an analysis is made of the effects of gender imbalances.

Universal primary education has increased girl-child enrolment, but there are insufficient secondary schools and secondary school requirements exclude girls from continuing their education. Girls who are in schools are seduced by men of all types. Some of these men are HIV-infected and may promise these girls marriage. There are too few female teachers or guidance counselors, especially in rural areas, and some schools have no female teachers available to deal with girls' problems. Faced with physical and sexual threats from male teachers and other men, girls feel unprotected since there is no trusted adult person at school who can be approached for advice. When a girl is raped, she will hesitate to inform her parents for fear of being abused.

Girls, especially in rural schools, do not have access to sanitary towels, and they don't go to school when they menstruate. Furthermore, when menstruation begins, parents realise that the girl is ready for marriage and to "fetch" cows. Some parents will remove the child from school, saying that she must help her mother with agricultural work, while the parents wait for a suitor. In parts of Uganda, such as Kabale and Kisoro districts, girls frequently marry at merely 12-15 years. Few girls are still unmarried at 18 years.

Many rural areas lack positive female role models. Because girls fall pregnant while at school, the general perception is that sending girls to school turns them into prostitutes who will come back home with babies. Some rural areas have no educated female role models from whom others can learn and be inspired.

A clear girls' education policy, incorporating the goals of gender equality and human rights, would indicate that a government recognises the need for and is committed to planning appropriate strategies for achieving education for all. Such a specific education policy is a critical step for mainstreaming gender into the educational system. Certain countries, including Uganda, have started developing and implementing gender policies, leading to an increase in the number of girls at school. For example, in Uganda, of the four children from every family eligible for universal primary education, two must be girls. At Makerere University, girls are awarded an extra 1.5 marks to increase the intake of female students to the University.

Developing countries are experiencing financial constraints consequently public expenditure in the social and health sectors stagnate, even in countries where it should increase annually due to population growth. This has, in turn, affected the availability and quality of education, impacting negatively on girls' access to and benefits from education.

Social, cultural and religious practices militate against girls' education, among which are female genital mutilation, early marriages and payment of bride price. Once a girl has been circumcised she is regarded as mature enough to marry, regardless of her biological age, so a circumcised girl will drop out of school to marry.

The practice of paying bride price has implications for the retention of girls in school. In most rural areas where cash and cows serve as bride wealth for girls, a girl's level of education forms the basis of negotiation for the amount to be paid by the groom.

In western and eastern Uganda, gender socialisation has established the notion that girls are assets to their families, as they can be exchanged for cows or cash. The socialisation at home and in the community, teaches children about gender-stereotyped roles, attitudes, values and norms. According to these stereotypes, girls are, for instance, poor at science, mathematics and technology-oriented subjects, and should concentrate on subjects that will prepare them for motherhood, like cooking, needlework and agriculture. This stereotypical attitude causes underachievement and failure to prepare girls for careers.

Poverty is another impediment to gender equality in education. Many rural parents and urban slum dwellers are too poor to afford education for all their children. Extreme poverty, compounded by wars and displacement, inadequate food, lack of arable or fertile land, drought, famine and lack of scholastic materials and clothes are all factors that hinder girls' participation in the education system.

Child labour, which is closely related to poverty, ranks high as a cause of school dropout among both girls and boys. Girl-headed households are common today because of the death of parents due to HIV/Aids and warfare. Girls assume responsibility for their siblings' welfare and leave school to care for them. Owing to non-parent guardianship, education for the girl-child is a low priority under such circumstances. The guardian may not pay sufficient attention and motivate her to continue her schooling. Research shows that girls generally fail the Primary Leaving Examinations, while boys perform better. Thus girls in primary schools exhibit low literacy and low skills achievement levels (UNICEF, 2002)

Strategies for Improving Girls' Education

UNICEF (2002) suggests the following strategies for improving girls' education:

(i) Promotion of the health, sanitation and nutrition sectors in school in order to improve the learning environment and adapt it to the learners' needs.

(ii) Promotion of a unified education system that includes formal and non-formal strands in which learners can move from one strand into another.

(iii) Enhancing sustained capacity building through gender sensitisation and training of policy-makers, educational researchers, programme workers, curriculum developers and all other educational professionals.

(iv) Advocating affirmative action policies for girls and women in the education system and applying a gender mainstreaming perspective.

(v) Advocating the articulation and implementation of policies for girls who leave school due to pregnancy.

(vi) Supporting a review of the curriculum and adopting new teaching methods to enhance the relevance of learning, taking into account the HIV/Aids pandemic, health and nutrition. This would involve introducing new life skills in the curriculum for the empowerment of girls and boys and guidance and counseling programmes.

(vii) Promoting changes in attitudes and behaviour among both teachers and pupils.

(viii)Advocating a comprehensive view of quality education, including provision of support to child-friendly school initiatives in the education systems.

(ix) Advocating the elimination of child labour, and sensitising communities about the need to share costs between girls and boys.

(x)   Providing income, shelter, fees and food to orphaned girls, so that they can remain at school. Workshops should be presented for disadvantaged girls to equip them with leadership skills and knowledge about HIV/Aids, and to empower them with skills to handle threatening situations of a sexual nature.

(xi) Sensitising the community by means of radio, television, community workshops, etc. about the importance of educating girls.

(xii) Presenting gender training for teachers, managers, parents and administrators about gender issues in their society.

(xiii)Ensuring that girls complete basic education, acquire fundamental skills and achieve nationally determined goals in literacy, numeracy and life skills. This entails ensuring that girls gain access to and remain in school. The need is to:

    a) Develop and support reforms that improve the learning and achievement of girls, paying particular attention to the gender dimension and quality of life.

    b) Pay attention to the education of adolescent girls by addressing issues of gender disparity in the transition from primary school to the next level and from school to work.

c) Introduce gender-responsive monitoring of learning achievement in literacy, numeracy and life skills in the lower and middle levels of primary school.

(xiv)Improve teachers' teaching methods, especially in science and mathematics, so that all pupils can participate equally.

(xv) Sensitise girls and boys about sexual abuse and the threat posed by HIV/Aids, and the necessity to report sexual abuse to authority figures. http;11www.un.org,/Women watch /daw/beijing /platform/decision,htm.(2005) makes general suggestions that governments and other role-players in education could implement:

a) Advance the goal of equal access to education by taking measures to eliminate discrimination in education on the basis of gender, race, language, religion, national origin, age or disability, or any other type of discrimination at all levels. Making education physically accessible, providing child care facilities and parental education and encouraging those who are responsible for caring for children, to return to school after giving birth.

b) Improve the quality of education and promote equal opportunities for women and men in terms of access, in order to ensure that women of all ages can acquire the knowledge, capacities, and ethical values needed for full development and participation under equal conditions, in social, economic and political matters.

c) Eliminate the gender gap in basic and functional literacy, as recommended in the World Declaration on Education for All. Disparities between developed and developing countries, rural and urban areas and men and women must be addressed.

d) Eradicate illiteracy among women by encouraging adult education.

e) Promote, alongside with literacy, life skills and scientific and technological knowledge, and work towards an expansion of the definitions of literacy, taking into account current targets and benchmarks.

f) Improve women's access to vocational training, science and technology by:

- Developing and implementing education, training and retraining policies for women and men entering the labour market by teaching skills that meet the needs of changing socio-economic circumstances, in order to improve their employment opportunities.
- Sensitising women to the benefits of vocational training in science, and improve access for and retention of girls and women in vocational training in fields like mathematics, engineering, environmental sciences and technology and information technology.
- Developing a science curriculum and materials that are gender-responsive, to allow for the participation of both women and men, create an environment conducive to interest in science, develop training programmes and materials for teachers, educators and learners that raise awareness about the status, role and contribution of women and men to the family, society, national and international development. Promote equality, cooperation, mutual respect and sharing of responsibilities between girls and boys, women and men, in homes and at the workplace.
- Increasing training in technical, managerial, agricultural extension and marketing areas, so that women are equipped to work in agriculture, fisheries, industry and business and arts and crafts. Increase income-generating opportunities, women's participation in decision making at all levels and their contribution to production, marketing, business and science and technology.
- Provide equal opportunities to training for female and male leaders, administrators, lecturers and professors at all levels in the world of science and technology, including research and academe.
- Developing peace and human rights education programmes that incorporate the gender dimension at all levels of education. Remove legal, regulatory and social barriers to sexual and reproductive health within formal education programmes.

Sensitise women to the importance of developing self-esteem, avoiding unwanted pregnancy, HIV/Aids infection and sexual abuse and violence.

- Incorporating the needs of rural women, supporting a multicultural approach to education, and encouraging them to send their girls to school. This means that cultural and religious issues that hinder gender equality must be addressed at all levels. Non-formal education should be provided to rural women so that they can realise their potential with regard to health, micro-enterprise, agriculture and legal rights.
- Allocate sufficient resources for and monitor the implementation of educational reforms by:

(i) Providing budgetary resources to the educational sector and increased funds for basic education, and by creating mechanisms at appropriate levels to monitor the implementation of educational reforms and measures to relevant ministries.

(ii) Cooperating with multilateral development institutions such as the World Bank.

- Promote lifelong education and training for girls and women by offering a broad range of educational and training programmes that enable women and girls to continue to acquire knowledge and skills required for living in, contributing to and benefiting from their communities. The need is for flexible lifelong education, training and retraining programmes that facilitate transitions between women's activities at all stages of life. (http.//www/un.org./womenwatch/daw/beijing/ platform/education pages 1 of 10. With regard to the promotion of education for women and girls, UNICEF (2002) adds that:

(i) Education should be rights-based and grounded in human rights, as stipulated in the Convention on the Rights of Children and the Convention on All Forms of Discrimination against Women (CEDAW).

(ii) All education programmes should be gender-responsive. All education programmes must be designed, implemented, monitored and evaluated from a gender perspective to enhance gender equity, equality and balance.

(iii) Girls' education programmes should be concerned about quality in terms of content of education, thus teaching and learning methodology and the school environment must be gender-friendly.

(iv) Education should be broad-based and employ a holistic approach in which parents and the communities are involved to adopt a multi-sectoral approach in response to multi-sectoral barriers to the education of girls.

(v) Community-based feeder schools should be promoted to reduce distances between the home and school. The government of Uganda has achieved this objective by establishing primary and secondary schools in virtually most sub-counties.

- According to the Inter-parliamentary Union (1994) a rapidly changing and unstable world demands that education and training should be broad-based and launched as a lifelong learning process, striking a balance between practical and academic skills. Furthermore, education should be linked with sustainable development. This would require, among other things, fresh policies to close the gap between male and female involvement in all programmes. The Union admits that equal access to schooling by boys and girls is not yet a reality. Therefore it recommends measures to facilitate access to schooling for girls under legal and practical conditions identical for both girls and boys. It also recommends that:

(i) In countries where the rate of school attendance by girls is lower than that for boys, the government, community and grassroots organisations launch campaigns to overcome prejudice and to encourage families to send their girls to school in the same way as boys. In some cases, special provisions, such as the awarding of grants or special allowances for girls' schooling or the supply of free educational materials, could be adopted to overcome material obstacles.

(ii) An identical and mandatory period of schooling should be introduced for boys and girls.

(iii) Governments should draw up and implement adult literacy programmes to promote women's participation in political life.

(iv) All educational materials should be gender-sensitive; to eliminate every suggestion that man is superior to woman, and boys and girls should use the same educational materials. In teacher training colleges special attention should be paid to promoting the principle of equality between men and women and the concepts of parity and partnership. Furthermore, at appropriate levels of education, the rights of the person should be established as a discipline, which would contribute greatly to the further emancipation of women.

(v) Parents failing to send children to school should be punished. At least 50 per cent of children of school-going age should complete primary education. Governments should ensure that, by 2015, the gender gap in primary and secondary schools has disappeared. They should also provide universal secondary education by 2025.

(vi) In all institutions of learning gender disparities should be eliminated by ensuring that women have equal access to career development, training, scholarships and fellowships; furthermore, a gender-sensitive educational system must ensure equal educational and training opportunities and full and equal participation by women in education, administration, policy and decision making.

(vii) In collabouration with parents, non-governmental organisations (including youth organisations), communities and the private sector, young women should be provided with academic and technical training, career planning advice, leadership and social skills and work experience to prepare them to participate fully in society.

(viii) Enrolment and retention rates of girls must be increased by allocating adequate budgetary resources and by enlisting the support of parents and local communities through campaigns, flexible school schedules, incentives, scholarships and other means.

The cost of girls' education to their families must be minimized and parents must be encouraged to choose education for the child. Women and girls' rights to freedom of conscience and religion must be respected by educational institutions by elimination of all discriminatory laws or legislation based on religion, race or culture.

(ix) An educational setting that eliminates all barriers that impede the education of pregnant mothers should be promoted.

Gender, Health and Development

The message of Uganda's Minister of Health, Jim Muhwezi, on the occasion of World Health Day (3 May 2005), was that healthy mothers and children are the bedrock of a healthy and prosperous nation. He reported that millions of women die from pregnancy-related causes, while 10.6 million children die, 40% of them in the first month of life. Many more suffer from ill health and malnutrition. Ugandan women die in childbirth due to low utilisation of healthy facilities for example, 63 out of every 100 babies are delivered by an untrained attendant. This increases the mother and baby's risk of premature death. In rural areas, few pregnant mothers visit health centers during pregnancy. In addition, poverty and social exclusion, low levels of education and domestic violence are powerful underlying causes of maternal death and disability. Women who become pregnant when they are very young, who give birth to too many children, give birth too often, suffer from infectious diseases such as malaria, tuberculosis or HIV/ Aids and those who are undernourished or anaemic, are at greater risk. Religious and cultural beliefs and practices prevent pregnant women from visiting health units.

Every mother and child has the right to survival and well-being and this right is central to dealing with broader social, economic and developmental challenges. When mothers and children die or fall ill, their families, communities and nations suffer as well. Improving their well-being will not only improve their health and that of their society, but it will also decrease inequality and poverty. When a mother is ill or dies, her productive contribution to the home, workplace, economy and society is lost and the survival and education of her children are jeopardized. In homes where a mother is ill or has died, children spend significantly less time in school compared to children from homes where the mother is alive (UNICEF, 2001). The most affected is the girl-child, who is usually forced to drop out of school to care for the ill mother, or take care of siblings after the mother has died.

Frequent illness and malnutrition has a negative effect on the cognitive development, body size and strength of young children. This reduces final educational achievements and productivity or work capacity in later life. Mothers should be supported and encouraged to report for treatment when they or their children are ill. All mothers require access to quality health care during pregnancy and after delivery. Women should be attended to by skilled health workers. Women should be helped to avoid unwanted pregnancies and births through the use of family planning. Mothers who are ill should be provided with information about the causes and treatment of illnesses. Mothers also need to know where treatment is offered.

All children must be immunised against diseases to ensure healthy growth and development. Children and mothers should sleep under insecticide-treated mosquito nets to prevent malaria. This will result in healthier and better-educated children, fewer maternal and child deaths, greater economic opportunities and enhanced well-being of families. Men and the general community have a role to play in promoting the well-being of mothers and children. As decision-makers, the community, husbands, household heads and partners have a key role to play in promoting the health of their spouses and children by ensuring good nutrition, treatment, housing, sanitation and immunisation.

Ssentumbwe (2005) says that one-quarter of all adult women living in the developing world today suffer from some kind of illness or injury related to pregnancy and childbirth. Each year, maternal health complications are responsible for the deaths of 585,000 women, contribute to the deaths of at least 1.5 million infants in the first week of life and 1.4 million stillbirths. The social and economic cost of these disabilities to a labour force and country is enormous.

In developing countries, pregnancy and childbirth account for at least 18% of diseases suffered by these women. Maternal health interventions are among the most cost-effective investments in health. At least 30-40% of infant deaths are the result of poor care during pregnancy and delivery. These deaths could be avoided by improved maternal health, adequate nutrition and health care during pregnancy and appropriate care during childbirth. Poor maternal health and nutrition contributes to low birth weight in 20 million babies each year, almost 20% of all births.

Women account for 70% of the 1.3 billion people who live in absolute poverty. When women cannot work because of health problems, the loss of their income and the cost of treating the illness can drive their families into debt. At least 60% of pregnant women in the developing world are anaemic, which reduces their energy and can depress their incomes. When women cannot work, the consequences can be severe for children. Women are more likely than men to spend their own income on improving family welfare through additional food, health care, school supplies and clothing for children. Millions of premature deaths, illnesses and injuries can be avoided if women prevented unwanted pregnancies and obtained prompt treatment . Governments and other role players should allocate resources to make maternal health services available, especially in poor rural areas. Existing health-care resources should emphasize the most cost-effective interventions. Every woman should have access to a good quality safe motherhood, services offered at the community-level in health centers and in district and regional hospitals.

Most maternal deaths occur during or shortly after delivery, as women do not receive the essential health care needed at this time. Few rural women seek out medical services, because of the distance to a health centre, the costs of consultation, which include consultation fees, drugs and supplies and transportation. Women lack decision-making powers within the family and most husbands are unwilling to provide money for the wives' treatment or to pay for their antenatal and postnatal care. Experience of poor quality services makes women even more reluctant to visit health centers.

To promote maternal health and sustainable development, the government and other role players should improve women's status and raise awareness about the consequences of poor maternal health. Families and communities must encourage and enable women to receive proper care during pregnancy and after delivery (Ssentumbwe, 2005). They should address the religious and cultural issues that prevent women from visiting health centers.

Kurtz and Prather (1995) state that, unless girls are valued by their families and societies for the critical roles they play in social development and the potential they have for adult roles, and unless they are given opportunities for education, they will become mothers with children who are more likely to die in infancy because they are malnourished and unhealthy - and the cycle will be repeated. An investment in girls should be considered as an investment in national development. Investment in the education of girls implies an investment in the health of children and the nation, and this investment yields high economic returns.

Everyone who cares about women and girls should have a vision for them that sets their bodies free, so that they can be healthier, be productive economic role players, be able to care for their children. Parents should give equal attention to girls and boys. Given equal biological advantages and treatment, more girls will survive gestation and the first few years of life. United Nations Commission for Africa (1994), Statistics suggest that sons are preferred and girls receive inadequate care relative to boys.

According to Hill and Upchurch's (1995) research in Egypt, Jordan, Morocco, Pakistan and Tunisia, girls in these countries received less health care, less nutrition and fewer immunisations than boys, thus they have higher mortality rates, die from neglect or are even killed. Female infanticide has been documented in parts of China, India and Pakistan (George, Sabi and Millet, 1992 and Black, 1993). In China and India, sex-selective abortions are performed once the sex has been detected by amniocentesis . A Bombay clinic performed many abortions of female foetuses in the late 1980s. Some Indian sex-detection clinics advertise boldly that it is better to spend 38 dollars on terminating a pregnancy than 3,800 dollars later on a girl's dowry. Thus, during infancy, boys receive more care than girls, which is blatant discrimination against the girl-child. Research shows that when boys are ill, parents rush them to clinics, but girls are first treated at home. Girls in Asia and the Middle East are less likely than boys to be taken for health care when ill and their lower nutritional status over the long term becomes the cause of a higher mortality, indicating that more girls than boys die in early childhood.

Women have the right to access the highest attainable standard of physical and mental health. The enjoyment of this right is vital to their lives and well-being and their ability to participate in all areas of public and private life. Health is a state of complete physical, mental and social well-being and not merely the absence of disease or infirmity. Women's health involves their emotional, social and physical well-being and is determined by the cultural, religious, social, political and economic circumstances of their lives and their biology. Health and well-being elude the majority of women. A major barrier to the achievement of the highest attainable standard of health is inequality between men and women and among women in different geographical regions, social classes and indigenous and ethnic groups. In national and international forums women have emphasised that, to attain optimal health throughout the life cycle, equality, including the sharing of family responsibilities, development and peace are necessary conditions.

Women have different and unequal access to and use of basic health resources, including primary health services for the prevention and treatment of childhood disease, malnutrition, anaemia, communicable diseases, tuberculosis and other tropical diseases. Women also have different and unequal access to opportunities for protection, promotion and maintenance of their health. Health programmes and policies often perpetuate gender stereotypes and fail to consider socio-economic disparities and other differences among women and may not fully take into account the law of autonomy of women regarding their health. Women's health is also affected by gender bias in the health system and by the provision of inadequate and inappropriate medical services to women.

In many developing countries, a decrease in public health spending and structural adjustment contributes to the deterioration of public health systems. Privatisation of health care systems without appropriate guarantees of universal access to affordable health care further reduces health care availability. This situation not only directly affects the health of girls and women, but also places disproportionate responsibilities on women, whose multiple roles in the family and community are seldom acknowledged, hence they do not receive the necessary social, psychological and economic support.

Women's right to the enjoyment of the highest standard of health must be secured throughout the whole life cycle in equality with men. Women are affected by many of the same health conditions as men, but women experience them differently. The prevalence among women of poverty and economic dependence, their experience of violence, negative attitudes towards girls, racial and other forms of discrimination, the limited power many women have over their sexual and reproductive lives and their lack of influence in decision making are social realities which can have an adverse impact on their health. Lack of food and inequitable distribution of food in the household, inadequate access to safe water, sanitation facilities and fuel supplies, especially in rural areas and poor urban areas, and deficient housing conditions, all overburden women and their families and have a negative effect on women's health. Good health is essential for a productive and fulfilling life and the right of all women to control all aspects of their health, in particular their own fertility is a prerequisite for their empowerment.

According to the Inter-parliamentary Council (1994), 99% of women who die from the aftereffects of pregnancy, delivery or abortion live in developing countries. This state of affairs not only has an effect on women's availability to participate in political life, but also presents a major factor for diverting them from activity in civilian life.

Discrimination against girls resulting from the preference for sons leads to unfair distribution of food and access to health care services, endangers the girls' current and future well-being. Counseling and access to sexual and reproductive health information and services for adolescents are inadequate or completely absent, and young women's right to privacy, confidentiality, respect and informed consent is often ignored. Adolescent girls are both biologically and psychologically more vulnerable than boys to sexual abuse, violence, rape and prostitution and to the consequences of unprotected and premature sexual relations. The trend towards early sexual experience, combined with a lack of information and services, increases the risk of unwanted and early pregnancy, HIV/Aids and other sexually transmitted diseases and unsafe abortions. Early child-bearing continues to impede improvement in the educational, economic and social status of women in developing countries like Uganda.

In rural areas, most girls between 12-19 years are mothers, some with more than four children. Early marriage and motherhood curtails educational and employment opportunities for women. Most of the young mothers are also poor and lack everything necessary for good health. Their young husbands also lack education regarding respect for their wives' right to self-determination and sharing responsibilities regarding sexuality, reproduction and domestic work.

The United Nations Commission for Africa (1995) reports that Africa has the world's highest fertility rate, lowest life expectancy (49 years for males and 52 for females), the highest infant mortality rate (about 103 deaths per 1,000 live births), one of the highest maternal mortality rates and one of the highest dependency ratios (47% under 14 years and 3% over 65 years). Africa also has the highest rates of unsafe abortions, which account for 30% of maternal mortality and teenage pregnancy. In most African countries, nearly two-thirds of cases of septic abortions occur in the 15-19 age group. In this context, government and other role players should provide the youth with information required for informed decisions and choices about their own sexuality and fertility. Parents should be sensitised about the value of women in society. The gap between fertility and mortality rates is widening, since more children are being born and fewer people are dying. This gap doubled between 1972 and 1994 and is expected to redouble by 2017. This has had negative consequences for the health and quality of women's lives. The fact that health services are inadequate and people lack information, coupled with the presence of chronic diseases such as malaria and malnutrition, leave many women unable to cope with the physical demands of pregnancy. Consequently maternal morbidity is widespread and the lifetime risk of maternal death for African women is one in 20 compared to one in 10,000 in developed countries. The effects of sexually transmitted diseases and HIV/Aids compound the already vulnerable status of women's health. The rates of unwanted and unplanned pregnancies among women under 20 years of age not only compromise their reproductive health but also deny a majority of them opportunities to complete their education and acquire skills which would enable them to make informed choices about their fertility.

Reproductive health is a state of complete physical, mental and social well-being in all matters relating to the reproductive system and to its functions and processes. It involves a variety of methods, techniques and services that contribute to reproductive health and wellbeing by preventing and solving reproductive health problems. Reproductive health implies that people are able to have satisfying and safe sex lives and that they have the capacity to reproduce and the freedom to decide if, when and how often to do so. In this context women and men should be informed about their rights regarding access to legal methods of family planning and regulating fertility. Men and women should be informed about their right to access appropriate health care services that will enable women to bear healthy children safely.

According to the United Nations Commission for Africa (1995) population and development-related policies and programmes in Africa in general, and Uganda in particular, must strive to improve the status of women while at the same time seeking to reduce the rates of population growth, infant and child mortality and maternal morbidity. Full participation and partnership of men and women are required in both the productive and reproductive areas, including shared responsibility for the care and nurturing of children and the attainment of reproductive health and rights. In this context, the provision of quality family planning services is essential. Such services must ensure that both men and women are informed and have access to safe, effective and affordable methods of family planning. Women and men should also be protected against sexually transmitted diseases, especially HIV/ Aids. However, in many cases women and men avoid contraception or family planning because of religious and cultural beliefs which attach value to having many children. The Roman Catholic Church does not support the use of artificial contraceptives.

However, Africans are producing so many children that families are unable to support them financially or socially. The integration of the full range of reproductive health services into the primary health care system, including decentralised delivery and management, should contribute significantly to the promotion of women's health in general, reproductive health, safe motherhood and the achievement of responsible parenthood.

In the context of the definition of reproductive health, reproductive rights should embrace certain human rights that are recognised in national laws, international human rights documents and other consensus documents. These rights are founded on the recognition of the basic right of all couples and individuals to decide freely and responsibly on the number of children, spacing and timing of their children and to have the information and means to do so and the right to attain high standards of sexual reproductive health. It also includes the couples right to make decisions concerning reproduction, free of discrimination ,coercion, and violence as expressed in human rights documents. In this respect couples should exercise their rights by taking into account the needs of their children and their responsibility towards the community. Promotion of the responsible exercise of these rights should form the fundamental basis for support policies and programmes in the area of reproduction and health, including family planning, by the government and other role players.(http://www.un.org/womenwatch/beging/plafform/ health.htm.page 49//)

Reproductive health eludes many of the world's people because of:

(i)   inadequate levels of knowledge about human sexuality.

(ii) inappropriate or poor-quality reproductive-health information and services.

(iii) the prevalence of high-risk sexual behaviour.
(iv) discriminatory practices.
(v) negative attitude towards women and girls.
(vi) the limited power many women and girls have over their sexual and reproductive lives.

Equal relationships between women and men in sexual relations and reproduction, including full respect for the integrity of the person, consent and shared responsibility for sexual behaviour and its consequences. Unfortunately, in Uganda, few women control their sexuality and reproduction. It is the men who determine how women should behave towards them. In some cases involving couples infected with HIV/Aids, the man may receive treatment without the knowledge of the woman.

Women in rural and urban areas are subject to particular health risks due to lack of services to meet health needs related to sexuality and reproduction. Unsafe abortions threaten the lives of a large number of women, thus represent a grave public health problem, especially among young women. Most of these deaths, health problems and injuries are preventable by improved access to adequate health-care services, including safe and effective family planning and emergency obstetric care. HIV/Aids and other sexually transmitted diseases are sometimes the consequence of sexual violence and have a devastating effect on women's health. Many women find it impossible to insist on safe and responsible sex practices and lack information and services for prevention and treatment. Women who are infected with HIV/Aids have said that social vulnerability and the unequal power relationships between men and women are obstacles to safe sex. The consequences of HIV/Aids reach beyond women's health to their roles as mothers and their contribution to the economic support of their families.The social, developmental and health consequences of HIV/Aids and other sexually transmitted diseases need to be tackled from a gender perspective. The Ministry of Health should mainstream its policies and programmes within the framework of a gender perspective so as to address women's health.

Sexual and gender-based violence, including physical and psychological abuse, trafficking in women and girls and other forms of abuse and sexual exploitation, place girls and women at high risk of physical and mental trauma, diseases and unwanted pregnancy. Such situations deny women the opportunity to use health and other services. Mental disorders related to marganalisation, powerlessness and poverty, overwork and stress, domestic violence and substance abuse are among the other health issues of growing concern to women. Occupational health issues are becoming increasingly important as a large number of women work in poorly-paid jobs under tedious and unhealthy conditions in either the formal or the informal labour market. Cancer of the breast and the reproductive system, and infertility, affect many women. These conditions are preventable or curable if detected early. In developing countries women are often denied treatment because of lack of funds, while men pay for their own treatment and that of their children.

The government and other role players should:

(i)   provide free medical services to the poor under its jurisdiction.

(ii) create and reinforce health systems so that the systems are capable of preventing maternal and child mortality and ensuring that mothers do not suffer major health concerns that prevent them from competing in political and economic activities.

(iii) promote family planning to allow women to organise their domestic lives and their professional and political careers around fewer children.

(iv) reaffirm the right to the enjoyment of the highest standards of physical and mental health; protect and promote the attainment of human rights for women and girls and incorporate it in legislation review; and ensure that health legislation and policies reflect a commitment to women's health and to meet the challenges and changing roles and responsibilities of women.

(v)   design gender-sensitive health programmes, including decentralised health services that address the needs of women throughout their lives and take into account their triple roles and responsibilities: the demands on their time, the special needs of rural women and women with disabilities and the diversity of women's needs arising from age and socio-economic and cultural differences. Include women, especially local and indigenous women, in identifying and planning health-care programmes. Remove all barriers to women's health services and provide a broad range of health- care services. Allow women to assess social security systems in equality with men throughout the life cycle.

(vi) provide accessible, available and affordable primary health care services of high quality, including sexual and reproductive health care, which includes family planning information and services, paying particular attention to maternal and emergency obstetric care. Health workers should be trained in gender concerns.

(vii) ensure that all health workers conform to human rights and ethical, professional and gender-sensitive standards in the delivery of women's health services aimed at ensuring responsible, voluntary and informed consent. Encourage the development, implementation and dissemination of codes of ethics guided by existing international codes of ethics and ethical principles that govern other health professions.

(viii) strengthen primary health care in order to ensure universal access to quality health services for women and girls. Prevent unwanted pregnancies by providing information and counseling to young girls. Promote healthy behaviour, treat physical and social needs and close the gender gap in morbidity and mortality, which disadvantages girls.

(ix) sensitise men and women about the need for good health and nutrition for children of all sexes and women. Promote public information on the benefits of breast-feeding babies without bias of sex.

(x) ensure that population policies and programmes advance gender equality and equity and improve the quality of women's lives by enabling them to exercise rights to plan and control their own fertility and to participate fully at all levels of the implementation of population and human development programmes.

(xi) develop strategies for decision making at all levels in order to meet the needs and improve the quality of life of present and future generations. All aspects of health development planning should promote social justice and eradication of poverty through sustained economic growth in the context of sustainable development.

(xii) improve women's reproductive health, including family planning and integrated population programmes.

(xiii) raise the quality of life of all people through appropriate population and human development policies and programmes targeted at the eradication of poverty and human resource development. Eliminate all gender imbalance and discrimination against women as a prerequisite for eradicating poverty and achieving sustainable human development.

(iv) strengthen preventive programmes by designing both formal and informal educational programmes for mothers to enable and support women to develop self-esteem, acquire knowledge, make independent decisions and take responsibility for their own health, achieve mutual respect in matters concerning sexuality and fertility and educate men about the importance of women's health and well-being. Support programmes for both men and women that emphasize the elimination of harmful cultural and religious practices and attitudes, including female genital mutilation, son preference which results in female infanticide and antenatal sex selection, early marriages, child marriages, violence against women and girls, sexual abuse, discrimination in food allocation, etc. All these practices are violations of human rights and go against medical principles.

(xv) ensure good working relations for professional women at all levels of the health system, including remuneration and promotion of women.

(xvi) ensure that curricula of medical schools and other health-care training facilities include gender-sensitive, comprehensive and mandatory courses for women.

(xvii) promote research about traditional medicine and health practices.

(xviii) ensure equitable representation by women in professional and management positions in the health sector.

(xix) sensitise 95% of the adult and youth population by 2015 about the dangers of HIV/Aids, how it is transmitted and how to protect themselves against it.

(xxi) incorporate population and gender concerns into all national development strategies, plans, policies and programmes and ensure women's full participation as decision makers in these processes.

(xxii) promote safe motherhood by ensuring antenatal, prenatal and postnatal care. Increase the awareness and emphasize significance of immunisation programmes.

(xxii) promote community-based family services aimed at providing information about family planning methods in order to space, postpone or limit pregnancies, especially in rural or urban slum areas, involving both men and women.

Gender, Politics and Development

According to Rodfeudd (1992), the French revolution effected considerable changes in the world by introducing the notion that man's participation in the politics of the day led in his political behaviour and that democracy was a prerequisite. The French revolution gave birth to a very important component of modern civilization, the concept of human rights. But did this revolution ever consider women's status? Rodfeudd (1992) argues that the democracy that arose from the French revolution was limited to using the figure of a woman as the symbol of revolutionary France. The French women's clubs that began in 1789 were all closed by 1795, on the grounds that women did not possess enough physical or mental strength to exercise their rights.

Up to the beginning of the nineteenth century women were barred from taking part in politics.When Olympe de Gouges, a pioneer of feminism, submitted the first draft Declaration of the Rights of Women to the French National Assembly in 1791, it led nowhere. She was condemned as outrageous and scandalous and was sent to the guillotine in 1793. The revolution which promised human rights did not recognise the status of women. French women had to continue fighting for their rights until the 1930s, when they made headway for the first time. It was not until after the First World War that women were able to prove their worth. During the war, women did men's jobs in the factories. During the Second World War, women once again took over men's responsibilities on the home front while the men were fighting at the front line. Women's suffrage was the first and most important of the political rights demanded by women because the vote is the very source of power in a democratic system.

Nassali (2000) says that, for a long time women in Uganda were excluded from participating in politics and democracy. They were marginalised in the electoral process as voters. In the first nationwide Legislative Council (LEGCO) elections held in 1957, women were denied the right to vote on account of the restrictions imposed on franchise, which included property, income and work as a pre-qualification for voting. Ugandan women could not vote because they were uneducated, had no jobs and owned no property. Political violence continues to deter women from participating at equal footing with men. Ignorance, lack of education, property and income, and subordination are the major factors hindering women from realising their equal potential with men.

Lipsitz Bem (1993) mentions that, in the 19th and 20th centuries in the USA, white women and black men were not permitted to participate in politics because they were regarded as inferior, weak, of low intelligence and because they owned no property or land. Women's roles were interpreted in terms of their reproductive function, caring for children and husbands and carrying out domestic chores. Their physical, biological and intellectual make-up was not considered fit for politics.

National Statistics (1998) reveal that women continue to be grossly under-represented in decision making, policy formulation and implementation relating to various functions of local government. The number of women participating as candidates in politics overall is less than 20%.

According to Kwesiga (2000) women's power to make decisions is reduced if they do not own property or land. Some men prohibit their wives from tilling their land or selling the agricultural products raised on it. The United Nations (2000), Nassali (2000) and Kwesiga (2000) agree that the low representation of women in the political decision-making process can be attributed to factors such as lack of employment, low salaries, socio-cultural perceptions, illiteracy, lack of finances, confidence and political commitment and negative social attitudes towards women.

In the realms of culture and religion women have traditionally played no public role. Decisions and laws concerning their well-being were passed by men. Many women still fear to participate in politics because of religious and cultural dictates. Those who dare to participate are rebuked by society or labeled, being called Kyakurasajja, literally meaning behaving like a man.

Kwoba and Kashagire (1998) evaluated civic education and found that most women are unwilling to participate in politics because of domestic responsibilities. Their husbands may also refuse to give them permission or support them financially. Those women, who do try, find other women reluctant to vote for women to represent them. Many women still believe in the superiority of men. Many women lack confidence and skills, and some are unwilling to participate in Local Council politics because they cannot read or write well.

Women, who enter politics against their husbands' will, or support candidates approved by their husbands, may be divorced, harassed, tormented or beaten by their husbands. According to Peacock (1990), the French philosopher Rousseau stated: "Men are born free and equal but everywhere they are in chains". Indeed, although women are born free, they are in chains everywhere.

Moghadam (1992) claims that stakeholders have realised why women's participation is important and why consideration of gender is essential in the analysis of political and cultural movements, transition and social change. It is in this context, of the intensification of religious, cultural, ethnic and national identities, that we see clearly the uneven foundation of development and social change and the way gender, the family and the position of women has been politicised.

Tambouka (2002), poses the following questions regarding women's participation in politics:

(i)   What are the dominant concepts relating to this issue?

(ii)   What are the common ideas that prevail regarding the place of women in the political field?

(iii) Are women instinctively hostile to women candidates in politics? Or is this the result of highly internalized domination by all and for all?

A survey conducted by Tambouka (2002) shows that women and men perceive politics differently. Women are relatively reserved about politics. Few women are as concerned about politics as men are. Women are less interested because of their domestic responsibilities. Women find a favourable environment in the family. Views on the equality and inferiority relationship among women in society differs from one social category to another. Males and females in top executive positions believe that all are equal, more men than women believe that the struggle for equality is showing progress. Echo (2002) states that gender issues, women's rights and social gender relations are of real concern to the government and Non Government Organisations. There are various impediments to women's participation in politics. Male and female representation systems, which clearly differentiate the areas of competence of each, still persist, reinforcing the popular perception that politics is for men while domestic affairs are for women. Women still act conservatively within the family unit, but protest more in the public arena. Globally only 10% of the members of legislative bodies and a lower percentage of ministerial positions are held by women. Although women are the majority of voters at the grassroots level, they continue to be under-represented as candidates for public office. Women's involvement in politics in Uganda has been boosted by affirmative action, with each district sending a woman representative, but few women compete with men in politics. Discriminatory cultural and religious attitudes, responsibilities relating to family and childcare and agricultural work and the high cost and demands of holding a public office, discourage women from participating.

Socialisation and negative stereotyping of women reinforces the tendency for political decision making to remain the domain of men. The under-representation of women in decision making positions in the areas of art, culture, religion, education, health, sports, the media and law have prevented women from having a significant impact on opinions. Inequality in the public arena often begins with discriminatory attitudes and practices and unequal power relations between women and men within the family.

The unequal division of labour and responsibilities within households, based on unequal power relations, limits women's ability to find the time to develop the skills required for participation in decision making in public forums. Non-formal networks and patterns of decision making at the local level reflect male dominance, restrict women's ability to participate equally in political, economic and social life. The low proportion of women among economic and political decision makers at the national, regional and international levels reflects structural and attitudinal barriers that need to be addressed by positive measures.

The Universal Declaration of Human Rights states that everyone has the right to take part in the government of his or her country. The empowerment and autonomy of women and the improvement of women's social, economic and political status is essential for the achievement of both transparent and accountable government and administration and sustainable development in all areas of life. The power relations that prevent women from leading fulfilled lives operate at many levels of society, from the most personal to the highly public. Achieving the goal of equal participation of women and men in decision making will provide a balance that reflects the composition of society necessary to strengthen democracy, equality in political decision making, a leverage function which integrates women and men on an equal footing. Without the active participation of women and the incorporation of women's perspectives at all levels of decision making, the goals of equality, development and peace cannot be achieved (http://www.vn.org/women/dawbeijing/platform/decision/html,)

The Inter-parliamentary Union (1994) comments that cultural and religious values of utilisation tend to assign more or less rigidly specific roles and tasks to men and women. Thus these values tend to limit women's participation in political life or even to exclude them from political governments. Participants should enhance women's dignity at the social level and allow the emergence of a more balanced image of the capacity of men and women to participate in the management of both their public and private lives and affairs.

Despite widespread movement towards democracy in most countries, women are largely under-represented at most levels of government, especially at ministerial and in the upper echelons of politics. Governments, transnational and national corporations, the mass media, banks, academic and scientific institutions, and regional and international organisations, fail to make full use of women's talents as top-level managers, policy-makers, diplomats and negotiators. The equitable distribution of power and decision making at all levels is dependent on governments and other role players. Undertaking statistical gender analysis and mainstreaming a gender perspective into policy development and implementation of programmes is important. Equality in decision making is essential for the empowerment and development of women. Existing databases and methodologies should be used more in the sphere of decision making.

In addressing inequality between men and women regarding the sharing of power and decision making at all levels, governments and other role players should:

(i)   promote a policy of mainstreaming a gender perspective into all policies and programmes of politics and decision making or the democratic process.

(ii) establish the goal of gender balance with government bodies. The number of women in all political sectors must be increased to achieve equal representation of women and men through affirmative action, where necessary.

(iii) promote equal rights for both women and men in political activities and freedom of association and encourage political parties to integrate women in their activities.

(iv) encourage the sharing of work and parental responsibilities between men and women, equal participation in public life and the reconciliation of family and professional lives.

(v) restructure recruitment and career-development programmes to ensure that women have equal access to managerial, entrepreneurial, technical and leadership training. Develop career advancement programmes for women of all ages, including career planning, tracking, mentoring, coaching, training and retraining.

(vi) collect and disseminate quantitative and qualitative data on women and men in decision-making positions, analyse their differential impacts on decision making and monitor their progress. Half of managerial and decision-making positions should be filled by women by the year 2015.

(vii) build and strengthen solidarity among women through education, information and sensitisation activities. Advocacy at all levels will enable women to influence political, economic and social decision-making processes and systems and seek accountability from elected representatives regarding their commitment to gender concerns.

(viii) increase women's capacity to participate in leadership by providing leadership skills and enhancing self-esteem. Help women to develop high self-esteem and the power to make decisions and take up political positions, through gender-sensitive training. Women and men should participate equally in the electoral process, political activities and in leadership areas.

(ix) emphasize two complementary concepts: the concept of parity, that recognises that persons are sexually different but equal, and that of partnership which shows that a creative synergy can be created between men and women so that they can solve community problems effectively. In this context the historical role played by women in society must be recognised, for example, women's participation in national liberation struggles, in rebuilding a nation after past and present development.

(x)   change the images and models of men and women transmitted through education in the family, formal education and the media by emphasizing equality in advertising messages. Any suggestion that one sex is superior to the other must be avoided and the notion of equality and complementarity between the sexes must be promoted.

(xi) take specific and critical measures to enable women's full participation in decision-making and policy formulation and access to all organisations of society, given the long-standing discrimination against women in Africa. The concept of civil, political, economic, social-cultural and religious rights has provided individuals and groups subjected to discrimination with the means for correcting injustice and enhancing social integration. Governments should therefore create a climate of tolerance for the rights of all persons, especially women.

(xii) Address the low representation of women in the political decision-making process, which is attributed to factors like socio-cultural perceptions and inhibitions, illiteracy, lack of finance, lack of political commitment and consciousness, religion, lack of goodwill towards women, lack of scholastic materials and rural infrastructure.

Gender, Economy and Development

The Ministry of Gender, Labour and Social Welfare (1999) and Kwesiga (2002) report that women continue to lag behind in terms of economic growth and development because they do not have access to land, agricultural produce or markets, earn low incomes, have no assets and do not inherit any land or property. Women are the poorest members of society.

Moser (1989) says that women are not primary owners of land, property and rights to land inheritance.Without land rights women cannot develop and realise equality with men. They cannot access credit and land ownership. If their husbands are handicapped, women cannot meet family obligations. Businge (2003) observed that Bakiga men do not give women land but make money from the women's labour. Bakiga women and children till the land owned by men, but the men sell products of their wives' and children's labour and spend the money on alcohol or to marry more wives.

Table 4.1: Contribution of women to Agricultural Development in Uganda

Parameter	Percentage of Total	
	Female	Male
Agricultural labour force	80%	20%
Planting	60%	40%
Weeding	70%	30%
Harvesting	60%	40%
Processing	90%	10%
Access to land ownership	8%	92%

Source: Ministry of Gender , Culture and Labour (2000)

Research carried out in Arua, Mbarara, Hoima and Kapchorwa confirms the data from the Ministry of Gender, Culture and Labour (2000) that women, who carry out most of the agricultural work, have no land.

Access to land by women is largely determined by kinship rights and marriage. Women neither own land nor inherit it. In some cases husbands prohibit wives from tilling the husband's land if the wives do not give the returns to the husbands. If women refuse to hand over the produce they have produced, the wives are beaten, divorced or neglected (Tuhaise, 2000).

In rural areas micro-finance projects run by non-governmental organisations lend money to poor women. But few women apply for loans because they are too poor and fear they might mismanage the money, or they fear that their husbands might appropriate the money and squander it. In villages, women are overwhelmed by poverty, which affects them physically, psychologically and spiritually. This disempowerment of women affects their advancement and equality with men.

Depressed economic conditions and extreme poverty, coupled with cultural and religious values in developing nations, have increased the burden on girls and women who, from an early age, have to contribute to family fortunes by working as domestic workers or hawkers, or by marriage and bride price. Businge (2003) observes that gender inequality hampers household productivity. She notes that the export drive favors men, while women are pushed deeper into poverty. She mentions Kabale district, where the government provided arabica coffee beans to households for cultivation. Wives and children planted and cared for the coffee trees, but the sale of coffee improved only the financial status of men. Instead of these men using the money from coffee sales for their families, paying fees, buying clothing and building houses, they enjoyed their new economic status in trading centers, by drinking alcohol, eating pork, philandering and marrying other wives. As a result of this economic inequality, the Bakiga women and children no longer spend time on the men's coffee shambas, as they see little of the money that accrues from coffee sales. Some women have asked their husbands to give them land on which to grow their own coffee, but the men have refused. This demoralizes women, as they work for nothing. Denying women a share of what they have worked for is an act of economic violence. Women's rights are violated when they are used as beasts of burden and servants of men to better the men's lives. Many women, despite their strenuous efforts, cannot improve their welfare because of gender-based constraints, like limited access to productive resources, including land, capital and unequal power in household decision making.

According to an ex ante poverty and social impact analysis (Businge, 2003) which analysed Uganda's strategic exports initiative (Stratex), the initiative may not lead to the expected development if gender concerns such as women's access to and control of land and capital are not tackled. Researchers have observed that cash crops benefit men relatively more than women and therefore the initiative is unlikely to encourage women to participate more in cash crop production. The report says that export promotion results in improvement in income, which is controlled by men, who use the money to satisfy their own needs, and therefore the increased income does not enhance the welfare of other household members, especially women and children.

Research found that women's and children's needs are not addressed by the increased incomes of men. Businge (2003) found that, in fishing communities, the growth of export-oriented fishing and factory-based processing has reduced women's employment in fish processing and marketing. This increase in income is fuelling greater recreational expenditure by men, with a reported increase in alcoholism and womanizing. If the income was being shared with other family members, the negative impact of poverty on the family could be moderated.

In many fishing areas there is a belief that a woman swimming in the lake would cause the fish to disappear. Such cultural taboos hinder women's equal participation in export-oriented ventures "We have all to rely on the men all the time because we cannot get the riches ourselves from the lake. Our poverty will continue until we are able to go to the lake ourselves," one woman lamented.

Researchers argue that increasing market and export-oriented activities may force women to shift their labour away from important family-care activities. Because women do not benefit from working for export products, they may withhold their labour and sabotage cash crops, as they do not earn or benefit from the income earned from them (Kasente, 2003).

Since 1989, the World Bank has been emphasizing the need for development initiatives to close the links between macro-economic policies and social issues, including gender. Today it is recognised that persistent inequality between women and men in developing countries constrains productivity and improvement and ultimately slows down the country's rate of economic growth (Businge, 2003).

When Pope John Paul II (1996) addressed a women's conference on peace, he said that greater efforts are needed to eliminate discrimination against women in areas such as education, health care and employment. He lamented that certain groups or classes are systematically excluded and where communities or countries lack basic social infrastructures and economic opportunities, women and children are the first to experience marganalisation. Yet where poverty abounds, in the face of devastation caused by conflict and war or the tragedy of migration, it is often women who maintain vestiges of human dignity, defend the family and preserve cultural and religious values. The Pope acknowledged that history is written almost exclusively as the narrative of men's achievements when, in fact, it's better part is often molded by women's determined and persistent action for good. However, women's greater presence in the workforce, in public life and in decision-making, on an equal footing with men, will continue to be problematic as long as the costs of commodities continue to burden the private sector. In the perspective of uncontrolled free-market policies, there is little hope that women will be able to overcome the obstacles in their path. (The Pope Speaks to Women, 1996).

Ministry of Finance and Economic Planning (1995) found that many women aged between 15 and 19 years were mothers or pregnant with their first children. Fertility rates for illiterate women were too high, with each woman giving birth to 7-10 children during her reproductive years. Urban women, with a total fertility rate of 5 births per woman, had smaller families than rural women. Fertility rates were lower in the central region, at 6.8-7.4. Women with secondary education had lower fertility, at 5.2 births per woman, than those with either no education or only primary school education (over 7 births per woman). The majority of women in Uganda marry before they are 18 years, especially illiterate women. Because many women are unaware of the risks of producing many children, they tend to prefer more numbers of children than what their husbands want. Thus most illiterate women do not use contraception. Producing many children binds women to the home caring for babies, or they are weakened by pregnancies or delivery and are thus unable to compete with men in societal activities.

Population statistics reported in September 2004 indicated that Uganda's poor and illiterate produce many children, thus having a permanent effect on women's performance in the employment sector. UNFPA (2004) reported to the population census in 2002 that rural women are likely to have nine or more children, who do not go to school, or who do not pass beyond primary school level. These children are inadequately fed, have poor clothing and live in poor housing facilities. Rural women also have less access to maternity services. On the other hand, urban women produce fewer children, between two and four, are better educated, better fed, enjoy good housing facilities and have access to maternity services. This explains why the UN considers population reduction as the focus of the global plan of action against poverty, especially that of women. Enabling women to have fewer children helps to stimulate development and reduce poverty, both in individual households and in societies.

Both the Global Population Report by the United Nations Population Fund (UNFPA) and the State of Uganda's Population of 2004, released on Wednesday 15 of July 2004, call for a reduction in population growth rates to enhance women's empowerment. Poverty increases women's chances of dying dramatically. In West Africa, a woman's lifetime risk of dying during pregnancy or childbirth is one in twelve (1:12). For women in developed regions, the comparable risk is one in four thousand (1:4,000). The UNFPA (2004) population report shows that lack of reproductive health care will continue to be the leading cause of death among women in developing countries. Regarding infant mortality, 86 babies out of 1,000 live births in Uganda die before they reach their first birthday. In Tanzania even more infants die, i.e. 100 per 1,000 live births, Kenya's infant mortality rate is 69:1,000 and Rwanda has an infant mortality rate of 112 out of 1,000 births. In Sweden and Japan, only three babies out of 1,000 die at birth. Although fertility is falling in many developed countries, it remains high in poorer countries, which will add 1.7 billion people to the total world population in the next 40 years. Developed countries like Sweden and Japan have only 0.1% population growth, hence a positive lifestyle for women. Although a big population of skilled people is an asset, rapid, unplanned population growth is a liability. It stresses women who produce many children at short intervals.

Uganda with an average HIV/Aids prevalence rate of around 6%, has an average annual population growth rate of 3.4% and a fertility rate of 7:10. Marriage of young girls of 15-19 years makes Uganda one of the most fertile countries in the world and this undermines sustainable development and gender equality.

According to UNFPA (2004), Uganda's fertility rate is the highest of all East African countries, with the population growing at 1.5% per year, due to a fertility rate of 4:10. Tanzania's population is growing at 1.9% due to a fertility rate of 5:11, which means more babies are being born in Uganda than in other East African countries. Population analysts attribute this growth to the fact that Ugandans have little access to family planning and high levels of illiteracy, which undermines women's power to understand the negative impacts of giving birth to several children. At least 41% of Ugandan women and 21% of Ugandan men are illiterate, compared to 31% women in Tanzania and 21% women in Kenya.

According to UNFPA (2004), rapid population growth perpetuates and is exacerbated by poor health and gender inequality and therefore steps should be taken to strengthen women's rights to reproductive health and education and gender balance within the family and society. Whereas smaller families can invest more in each child's education and health, those with several children have to spread meager resources so much further, hence inadequate access to social services and shorter life expectancy, especially for women, who are overworked and weakened by producing many children.

There are considerable differences in women's and men's access to and opportunities to exert power over economic structures in society. In most parts of the world, women are virtually absent from or are poorly represented in economic decision making, including the formulation of financial, monetary, commercial and other economic policies and tax systems and rules governing pay. The actual development of these economic structures and policies has a direct impact on women's and men's access to economic resources, their economic power and consequently the extent of equality between them at the individual and family levels and in society as a whole.

In many regions, women's participation in remunerated work in the formal and non-formal labour markets has changed and increased significantly during the past decade. While women continue to work in agriculture they have also become increasingly involved in micro, small and medium-sized enterprises and, in some cases, have started playing more dominant roles in the informal sector. Owing to difficult economic conditions and lack of bargaining power resulting from gender inequality, many women have been forced to accept low pay and poor working conditions and thus have often become preferred workers. On the other hand, women have become aware of and demand their rights. Some women have succeeded in entering and advancing in the workplace and improving their incomes and working conditions. However, women have been particularly affected by economic upheavals and restructuring, which have changed the nature of employment and in some cases led to job losses, even for professional and skilled women. Many women have entered the informal sector owing to lack of opportunities.

Women's participation and gender concerns are still largely absent from and should be integrated into the policy formulation processes of the multilateral institutions that define the terms of cooperation with governments and which set the goals of structural adjustment programmes, loans and grants.

Discrimination in education and training, remuneration, promotion and horizontal mobility practices, inflexible working hours, lack of access to productive resources, inadequate sharing of family responsibilities, a lack of or insufficient provision of services such as child care, continue to restrict employment, economic, professional and other opportunities and mobility for women and make their involvement stressful. Moreover, attitudinal obstacles inhibit women's participation in developing economic policy and in some regions restrict the access of women and girls to education and training for economic management.

Women's share of the labour force continues to rise and women are working more and more outside the household. Although there has not been a significant parallel reduction of responsibility for unremunerated work in the household and community, women's incomes are becoming increasingly necessary to households of all types. Some regions have experienced a growth in women's entrepreneurship and other self-employment activities. In many countries, women form the majority of workers in non-standard work such as temporary, casual, multiple, part-time, contract and home-based employment.

Insufficient attention paid to gender analysis has meant that women's contributions and concerns are often ignored in economic structures, such as financial markets and institutions, labour markets, economics as an academic discipline, economic and social infrastructure, taxation and social security systems and in families and households. As a result, many policies and programmes continue to contribute to inequalities between women and men. Where progress has been made in integrating gender perspectives, programme and policy effectiveness has also been enhanced.

Although many women have advanced in economic structures, the majority of them continue to face obstacles that hinder their ability to achieve economic autonomy and to ensure sustainable livelihoods for themselves and their dependants. Women are usually active in a variety of economic areas, which they often combine, ranging from wage labour and subsistence farming and fishing to the informal sector. However, legal and customary barriers to ownership of or access to land, natural resources, capital, credit, technology and other means of production and wage differentials contribute to impeding the economic progress of women. Women contribute to development, not only through remunerated work, but also through a great deal of unremunerated work. Additionally, women participate in the production of goods and services for the market and household consumption, in agriculture, food production or family enterprises. Women still perform the majority of unremunerated domestic and community work, such as caring for children and the elderly, husbands, the ill, preparing food for the family, protecting the environment and providing voluntary assistance to vulnerable and disadvantaged individuals and groups. This domestic work is seldom measured in quantitative terms and is not valued in national accounts. Women's contribution to development is seriously underestimated and its social recognition is limited (http:

//www/un.org/womenwatch/daw/beijing /platform/economy/ htmm page 2 of 15).

Although new employment opportunities have been created for women by globalisation, other trends have exacerbated inequalities between men and women.globalisation, including economic integration, can create pressures on the employment opportunities for women, who have to adjust to new circumstances and to find new sources of employment, as patterns of trade change. More analysis needs to be done on the impact of globalisation on women's economic status. These trends have been characterized by low wages, little or no labour standards, protection, poor working conditions, particularly with regard to women's occupational health and safety, low skill levels, a lack of job security and social security, in both the formal and informal sectors.

Women's unemployment is a serious and increasing problem in many countries, including Uganda. Many women have certificates that can help them acquire jobs, but most of them are unemployed. Employment opportunities for some women, such as those who are heads of households with young children, are limited for reasons that include inflexible working hours in the formal sector and inadequate sharing, by men and by society, of family responsibilities. In countries undergoing fundamental political, economic and social transformation, the skills of women, if better utilized, could constitute a major contribution to the economies of their respective countries. Women's input should continue to be developed and supported and their potential realised.

Lack of employment in government and the private sector, reductions in public servants and moratoriums on recruitment in the public service have affected women too. In some countries women have taken on more unpaid work, such as the care of children, the ill and the elderly, while in most developing countries women loiter on the streets and some become prostitutes. Women in paid work experience obstacles that hinder them from achieving their potential, some have succeeded in being promoted to lower levels of management; nevertheless attitudinal discrimination often prevents them from being promoted further.

Sexual harassment is an affront to a worker's dignity and prevents women from making a contribution commensurate with their abilities. The lack of a family-friendly work environment, including the lack of appropriate and affordable child care and inflexible working hours, further prevent women from achieving their full potential.

In the private sector, including transnational and national enterprises, women are largely absent from management. Policies and practices relating to hiring and promotion are still discriminatory. The unfavorable work environment and a limited number of available employment opportunities in formal employment have led women to seek alternative income-generating activities. Women have increasingly become self-employed, owners and managers of micro, small and medium-scale enterprises. The expansion of the informal sector and of self-organised and independent enterprises experienced in many countries is in a large part due to women, whose collabourative, self-help and traditional practices and initiatives in production and trade represent a vital economic resource. When they gain access to and control over capital, credit and other resources, such as technology and training, production, marketing and income can increase and sustainable development can become possible.

http;IIwww.Un.org./Womenwatch/daw/Beijing/platform/decision.htm.(2005) ,suggests the following measures for addressing gender issues in the economy:

(i)   addressing the economic potential and independence of women. Governments and other role players should promote an active and visible policy of mainstreaming a gender perspective into all policies and programmes so that before decisions are taken, an analysis is made of their effects on women and men respectively.

(ii) promoting women's economic rights and independence, including access to employment, appropriate working conditions and control over economic resources.

(iii) adopting and implementing laws against discrimination based on sex in the labour market. This would involve enacting and enforcing legislation to guarantee the rights of women and men to equal pay for equal work.

(iv) renewing and amending laws governing the operation of financial institutions to ensure that they provide services to women and men on an equal basis, enacting and enforcing equal-opportunity laws, taking positive action and ensuring compliance by the public and private sector through various laws, enacting policies that support the establishment of national labour laws to ensure the protection of all women workers, including safe work practices and the right to organise and have access to justice.

(v) eliminating discriminatory practices by employers and taking appropriate measures in consideration of women's reproductive roles and functions, to prevent denial of employment and dismissal owing to pregnancy or breast-feeding, requiring proof of contraceptive use.

(vi) enable women to have access to full and equal participation in the formulation of policies and the definition of structures through bodies like the Ministry of Finance, national economic commissions, economic research institutes and other key agencies and through their participation, undertaking legislative and administrative reforms to give women equal rights with men regarding access to economic resources, ownership and control of land and other forms of property, credit, inheritance, equal resources and appropriate new technology and reviewing national income and inheritance tax and social security systems to eliminate any existing bias against women. Governments and other role players should seek to develop a more comprehensive knowledge of work and employment through, inter alia, efforts to measure the distribution of unremunerated work of reproductive and domestic work and work done on farms.

(viii) ensuring that national policies related to international and regional trade agreements do not have an adverse impact on women's traditional and new economic activities. Gender impact analyses should be used in the development of macro and micro-economic and social policies in order to monitor such impact and identify restrictive policies in cases where harmful impact occurs. Gender-sensitive policies and measures should be used to empower women as equal partners with men in technical, managerial and entrepreneurial fields.

(ix) supporting women's self-employment and the development of small enterprises and improving their access to capital and credit. This would involve encouraging women's income-generating projects at national and local levels by facilitating equal access to and control over productive resources, land, credit, capital, property rights and development programmes. This can also be done through strengthening micro-enterprises, new small businesses, cooperative enterprises, expanded markets and facilitating the transition from the informal to the formal sector, especially in rural areas.

(x) supporting programmes and policies that recognise women's vital roles and strengths in ensuring food security. Assisting paid and unpaid women who are involved in food production by, for instance, providing transportation to markets, extension services and credit facilities and other loans in rural areas. Mobilizing the banking sector to increase lending to and financing of women's projects and training women to manage their businesses and finances. Including women in leadership, planning and decision making. Ensuring equal access for women to effective job training, retraining, counseling and placement services that are not limited to traditional employment.

(xi) promoting respect for workers' rights including prohibition of forced labour and child labour, freedom of association and the right to organise and bargain collectively. Discrimination in employment should be eliminated.

(xii) reaching out to rural and urban women involved in micro, small and medium-scale enterprises, paying special attention to low-income women, the marganalised and those who lack access to capital, land, loans etc. Expanding women's access to financial markets and supporting them in their small and large enterprises, paying attention to women's needs while disseminating market and trade information. Providing business services, training and access to markets, information and technology, especially to low-income women.

(xiii) ensuring equal access of women to ongoing training in the workplace, including unemployed women, single parents, those re-entering the labour market, those displaced by new forms of production or retrenchment. Increase incentives to enterprises to expand the number of vocational and training centers that provide training for women in non-traditional areas.

(xiv) integrating or mainstreaming all economic activities with a gender perspective and all economic restructuring and structural adjustment policies. This implies supporting programmes that enhance self-reliance of special groups of women e.g. young women, the disabled, the elderly and minority women. Supporting the economic activities of indigenous women to improve their situations and development. Encouraging participation by women, irrespective of their backgrounds, in production and marketing cooperatives, by providing marketing and financial support, especially in rural areas. Providing networking arrangements for entrepreneurial women, including opportunities for monitoring of inexperienced women by the more experienced.

(xv) analysing and reformulating wage structures in female-dominated professions such as teaching, nursing, secretarial work and childcare, with a view to raising their low status and earnings, promoting the equal sharing of responsibilities by both men and women, changing people's attitudes away from division of labour based on sex to promote the concept of shared family responsibility for work in the home.

(xvi) using educational programmes, media campaigns, school and community education programmes to raise awareness about gender equality and non-stereotyped gender roles of women and men within the family. Encouraging women to report cases of gender violence, sexual harassment and all forms of harassment at home and at the workplace. The following action must be taken:

a) Society should challenge the injustices and religious and cultural beliefs that leave women economically dependent on men.

b) The government, non-governmental organisations and religious institutions should provide an economic alternative (micro-economic projects) to help women free themselves from abusive relationships.

c) Administrators and other people in responsible positions should enable women to obtain trading licenses, travel documents, credit facilities, land and property. Married couples should be able to own property jointly, especially land, housing, businesses, etc.

d   Encourage and sensitise spouses to the need for contraception, so that poor families stop producing more children than they can care for.

e) The government and society at large should eliminate laws, procedures and practices that discriminate against women in all workplaces.

f) Women should be encouraged by their spouses and society to study and obtain qualifications that will enable them to compete successfully with men in the job market.

g) Society should advocate employment policies that enhance gender balance in senior and middle level management everywhere.

Gender, Poverty and Development

Today more than 1 billion people worldwide, the majority of whom are women, live in unacceptable conditions of poverty, mostly in developing countries like Uganda. Poverty has various causes, including structural factors. Poverty is a complex, multi-dimensional problem with origins in both national and international domains. The globalisation of the world's economy and the developing interdependence among nations present challenges and opportunities for sustained economic growth, development and risks and uncertainties for the future of the world economy. The uncertain global economic climate has been accompanied by economic restructuring and persistently unmanageable levels of external debt and structural adjustment. In addition, conflicts, displacement of people and environmental degradation have undermined the capacity of governments to meet the basic needs of populations. Transformations in the world of economics are changing the parameters of social development in all countries profoundly.

A significant trend has increased poverty of women .Migration and consequent changes in family structures have placed additional burdens on women, especially those who provide for several dependants.

Macroeconomic policies need rethinking and reformulation to address poverty. These policies focus almost exclusively on the formal sector. They also tend to impede the initiative of women and fail to consider the differential impact on women and men. The application of gender analysis to a wide range of policies and programmes is therefore critical for poverty reduction strategies. In order to eradicate poverty and achieve sustainable development, women and men must participate fully and equally in the formulation of macro-economic and social policies for the eradication of poverty. The eradication of poverty cannot be accomplished by poverty programmes alone, but will require democratic participation and changes in economic structures to ensure access for all women to resources, opportunities and public services. Poverty has various manifestations, including lack of income and production, lack of sufficient resources to ensure a sustainable livelihood, hunger and malnutrition, ill health, limited or lack of access to education and other basic services, increased morbidity and mortality from illness, homelessness and inadequate housing, unsafe environments and social discrimination and exclusion. It is also characterised by lack of participation in decision making and in civil, social, religious and cultural life. Poverty may be caused by an economic recession that result in loss of livelihoods or by disaster or conflict. The poverty of the low-wage workers and people who fall outside family support systems, social institutions and safety nets, must also be borne in mind.

In the past decade, the number of women living in poverty has increased disproportionately compared to the number of men in the same position in developing countries. The feminine face of poverty recently becomes a significant problem in countries with economies in transition, as a short-term consequence of political, economic and social transformation. In addition to economic factors, the rigidity of socially ascribed gender roles, women's limited access to power, education, training and productive resources, and other emerging factors that lead to the insecurity of families are responsible. The failure to adequately mainstream a gender perspective into all economic analysis and planning to address causes of poverty is also a contributing factor. Empowerment of women is a critical factor in the eradication of poverty. While poverty affects households as a whole, women bear a disproportionate burden. In attempting to manage household consumption and production in conditions of increasing scarcity, women face the kind of poverty that is particularly acute.

In most countries, social welfare systems do not take sufficient account of the specific conditions of women living in poverty and there is a tendency to scale back the services provided by such systems. The risk of falling into poverty is greater for women than for men, particularly in old age, where social security systems are based on the principle of continuous remunerated employment. In some cases women do not fulfill this requirement because of interruptions in work history and the fact that many women are involved in unremunerated work all their lives.

In countries with economies in transition and those undergoing fundamental political, economic and social transformation, this upheaval has often led to reductions in women's income or women being deprived of income. Development and economic growth that is both sustained and sustainable are possible only by improving the economic, social, political, legal and cultural status of women. Equitable social development that recognises that the poor, particularly women, must be empowered is an essential foundation of the utilisation of environmental resources. The success of policies and measures aimed at supporting or strengthening the promotion of gender equality and equity and the improvement of the status of women should be based on the integration of the gender perspective in general policies relating to all spheres of society and the implementation of positive measures, with adequate institutional and financial support, at all levels.

Poverty in Africa, particularly in Uganda, manifests itself in different ways and has its essential origins in lack of income, exclusion from markets, social and political life, unequal distribution of wealth and income from global, regional, sub-regional to local levels, economic recession, drought and other disasters, heavy debt burdens, structural adjustment programmes that are incompatible with sustainable development, rapid population growth, armed conflicts and civil strife. The factors are, in turn, linked to general political and social conditions of a given country. More than a third of the people in Africa either live in abject poverty and are unable to meet their most basic needs. Notably, the poor are usually associated with high levels of malnutrition, illiteracy, poor sanitation and socio-economic activities. The heavy burden of poverty falls disproportionately on women, especially female-headed households, which number about 35% of households today. Although women constitute more than half of the population and have limited access to ownership and co-ownership of land and housing, they nevertheless provide 60 to 80% of the food supply. Women are the backbone of both cash crop and subsistence farming, yet their productive and reproductive activities are neither marketable nor recognised as economic outputs.

Women are concentrated in low-pay, low-grade job sectors and have poor promotion prospects. They are denied the tools and means to sustainability and confront considerable discrimination, which constitutes a major obstacle to increased productivity. Many African countries continue to experience critical situations in terms of food security, accessibility and distribution. Hunger and malnutrition continue to be a critical issue, affecting men, women and children. According to the United Nations Economic Commission for Africa, African Centre for Women (1994), Africa's population has increased at an annual rate of 3% since 1960, while food production grew by only 1.8%, with the food self-sufficiency rate dropping from 100% in 1960 to 81% in the 1990s. Scarce exported agricultural products are marketed at low prices, while foreign exchange earnings accruing from such commodities are diverted from more important uses to pay for food imports. Security and self-sufficiency are therefore not related to food alone but to the pervasive problem of poverty, unequal distribution of income, weaker purchasing power and unfavourable terms of trade and the burden of external debt servicing.

Women in Africa, as the main providers and traditional managers of food at family and household levels can play an important role in the equitable distribution and redistribution of scarce resources. Strengthening of women's potential for management of food and resources can ensure that women's priorities and their families' well-being are better.

Women in Africa must be empowered to participate in economic structures, policy formulation and in the productive process itself. It is now recognised that the contribution of rural women in Africa is critical for development. The United Nations Economic Commission for Africa (1994) emphasizes the economic empowerment of women through stimulating, consolidating and coordinating the entrepreneurial spirit and skills of African women and providing adequate access to both formal and informal sector resources. Women's empowerment will enhance their capacity to alter the direction of change for their well-being and the improvement of society as a whole in a realistic way. It is crucial to engage the younger generation of women as active partners in change. Strategies and actions are needed to move away from the current welfare orientation to address the economic empowerment of women and, in particular, strengthen and support their participation in trade and industry. The struggle against poverty by the economic empowerment of women and the promotion of sustainable livelihoods for women and youth is a moral, political and economic obligation and the responsibility of national governments and the international community and the individual women at the grassroots. Women and other people living in poverty represent an under-utilized productive potential.

Measures to reduce or eliminate poverty are major parameters of growth, empowerment and overall political stability. Women's right to development, of which they are being deprived, should be recognised explicitly. This requires policies that are gender-sensitive, that accommodate the needs and interests of women living in poverty, as defined and articulated by the women themselves. It also requires specific and gender-based anti-poverty policies, programmes and actions that are integrated into overall economic planning at local, national, regional and international levels. The realities of people and women living in poverty are specific, complex, diverse and dynamic and involve more than a lack of income. Disadvantage, deprivation and poverty as experienced by women and their dependants have many facets. These include social discrimination, exclusion, desertion, isolation, physical disability, vulnerability and maternal deprivation. Poverty is also associated with war, famine, drought, refugees and displaced persons, imbalance in trade relations and structural adjustment policies.

The following ways of eradicating poverty would go a long way to eliminate explicit and implicit discrimination against women as suggested on the website,hht;//www,un.org/women watch/daw/ Beijing/platform/poverty/htm(2005) .

(i)   support the full participation and empowerment of women and girls in society in order to make full use of all human resources in the struggle against multi-dimensional poverty, trade, productive employment, public service, basic health-care services, reproductive health, including maternal and child health care and family planning services; providing greater and better opportunities at each stage of girls and women's lives, thereby redressing the fundamental gender-based inequalities.

(ii) supporting women's sustainable livelihoods and other coping strategies in both the market and non-market sectors.

(iii) enforcing laws that will remove barriers to the economic participation of women, particularly laws that relate to property rights, asset holdings, inheritance, credit, labour, zoning and export processing zones. By equipping women in both rural and urban areas with the means required for participation in the process of economic growth, their participation in economic activities will be facilitated. Other measures include, ensuring access to assets and the effective enforcement of related legislation; access to special credit opportunities, information, water supply, agricultural extension (especially for women smallholders), acquisition of techniques for processing agricultural products, and upgrading rural roads. Gender mainstreaming must be implemented in all societies' activities to improve the condition of women by providing basic social services, such as education, health, nutrition and child-care facilities.

(vi) reducing girls' and women's workload by provision of appropriate technologies for certain farming and household tasks. This would promote more equitable sharing of work and family responsibilities between men, women, girls and boys.

(v) designing special economic schemes for poor women, taking into consideration their multiple responsibilities. This would involve forging links with existing facilities and creating new structures suitable to the needs of the poor. Such should reflect the reality of young women and girls who were forced to abandon their education in order to take care of family members.

(vi) facilitating women's decision-making roles at all levels – the family, community, marketing organisations and public, and political spheres. Improving their capacity to promote change and manage development in and through the public sectors.

(vii) analysing, from a gender perspective, policies and programmes, including those related to macro-economic stability, structural adjustment, external debts problems, taxation, investment, employment markets and all relevant sectors of the economy, regarding its impact on poverty, inequality and particularly on women. Assessing its impact on family well-being and conditions and effecting adjustments so that the policies and programmes promote more equitable distribution of productive assets, wealth opportunities, income and services, and target the allocation of public funds to promote women's economic opportunities and equal access to productive resources. Address the basic social, educational and health needs of women, particularly those living in poverty.

(viii) pursuing and implementing sound and stable macro-economic and sectoral policies that are designed and monitored with the full and equal participation of women; encouraging broad-based sustained growth, addressing structural causes of poverty and reducing gender-based inequality within the overall framework of achieving people-centered sustainable development.

(ix) providing adequate safety nets and strengthening state and community-based systems as an integral part of the social policy in order to enable women living in poverty to withstand adverse economic environments and retain their livelihoods, assets and revenues in times of crisis.

(x) protecting women against gender violence and exploitation and ensuring the full realisation of their human rights.

(xi) Integrating women into all programmes that generate money.

(xii) ensuring access to free or low-cost literacy programmes specially designed for education of women living in poverty.

(xiii) promoting and strengthening policies and programmes for indigenous women, eliciting their participation and respecting their cultural diversity.

(xiv) structural adjustment programmes should be designed to minimise negative effects on vulnerable and disadvantaged groups.This means taking action to reduce inequality and economic disparity. It is also significant to review the impact of structural adjustment programmes on social development by means of gender-sensitive social impact assessments and other relevant methods.

(xv) creating an enabling environment that allows women to build and maintain sustainable livelihoods.

(xvi) making it easier for disadvantaged women to access financial services through strengthening links between the formal basic and intermediary lending organisations, providing legislative support and training for women and with a view to mobilizing capital for institutions and increasing the availability of credit.

(xvii) developing conceptual and practical methodologies for incorporating gender perspectives into all aspects of economic policy-making, including structural adjustment planning and programmes.

(xviii) collecting gender and age-disaggregated data on poverty and all aspects of economic activity and developing qualitative and quantitative statistical indicators to facilitate the assessment of economic performance from a gender perspective.

(xix) promoting rural industrialization schemes to reduce rural-urban migration of women.

(xx) promoting all policies and programmes and recommendations that are geared towards the eradication of poverty, with special emphasis on women.

5

World Religious Teachings on Gender

Hinduism and Gender

Traditionally, Hindu religion held women in high esteem, as shown by a Hindu saying that, "Where women are worshipped, there the gods dwell". In Vedic times, scholarly women existed and were respected by society. They were equal in their rights, privileges and duties to men. Female gods bring peace, prosperity and harmony. Woman is considered to be the goddess of fortune and wealth. When she imparts knowledge, she is the goddess of learning, Saraswati. In managing a household, she is considered to be the goddess of power, Parrati. Women are seen as half-men (Lewis, 1983).

Today, however, Hindu women no longer enjoy revered status, due to the way certain scholars interpreted the religious texts such as law books like Manu. The relegation of women to a lower order is, however, also a universal phenomenon. In India the oppression of women increased during Moghul rule. Women were placed on a pedestal by Hinduism but, at the same time, their freedom was curtailed, ostensibly to protect them.

Traditionally, Hindu women accepted marriage as their natural destiny. A man could be unfaithful, but for a woman, it was considered a disgrace. During a marriage ceremony, a woman would take a vow of undying fidelity to her husband, who she would promise to serve, protect and care for. Hindu women regarded their husbands as the masters of the household. They created a religious aura at home, built small altars for worship and sat with their husbands in all religious ceremonies.

Women would undergo severe rites to maintain their vows of fidelity. Because of the spiritual nature of this union, divorce was rare. The Hindu mother was an object of reverence. Mother gods were highly respected and worshipped. In the same way that a Hindu worshipped his god, he also paid reverence to his mother.

According to the code of Manu, Hindu men have to pass through four stages of life to have lived successful lives. In the first stage, the typical Indian man studied the Vedas. In the second stage, a man was expected to become a householder and marry a proper woman from his own caste. In the ideal marriage described in the code of Manu, the man is supposed to be older than his wife. A man of thirty years is supposed to marry a girl of 12, while a man of 24 is supposed to marry a girl of eight.

The third stage involves the man taking up the role of provider and cornerstone of society. Once his duties as a householder are completed and he has reached old age, he is to retreat to the forest and live there as a hermit, meditating and offering sacrifices.

Fourthly, when his days as a hermit are completed, the Indian man is to become a wandering beggar (Lewis, 1983).

Women do not pass through the four stages of life. They are to stay at home under the control and protection of the chief male of the household. According to Lewis (1983), even at home, women may not do anything independently of men. Married women are controlled by their husbands, while young maidens are controlled by their fathers. A widow is protected by her sons.

Hindu women never desire separation from their husbands or children. Separating from the husband would bring the family name into disrepute. Women were meant to procreate. They were for the good and light of the home. Marriage and child-rearing are women's primary roles (Lewis, 1983).

Certain Hindu women played distinguished roles as shown by Vishwa, (2001).

a) Gargi was an intellectual woman in the time of the Upanishads. She astonished her male counterparts by the depth of her learning and debating power.

b) Maitreyi of the Upanishads renounced the pleasures of the world and followed her husband Yajnavalkya into the forest in search of God.

c) Sarifri was an Indian woman of great courage, who gladly faced dangers which a man might shrink from.

d) Ran-Rasimani was a great administrator in the 19th century and one of the pillars of the Rama Krishna mission.

e) Rani Lakshimi Bai of Jhansi was a queen who defied the British in India.

Hinduism and Gender Violence

Religion poses a challenge to feminist theology as it touches on all aspects of women's lives, such as imaging, symbolism, rituals, liturgy, myths, and the status and role of women within the cultural and religious group.

Shanti (1998) explains that, before the establishment of Hinduism as a religion during the Vedic period, women enjoyed high status. The female child was welcomed with as much enthusiasm as the male. Monogamy was practised and widows could remarry. Women chose their husbands and participated actively in religious worship. Women were treated with respect within and outside the home. Couples owned property jointly. However, as world religions such as Hinduism spread, there was a decline in the status of women. According to Hindu scriptures violence against women is intrinsic. Veda 10:10 describes woman as a temptress and seductress who even tempts sages and gods. Sathapatha 13.1, 21 records the way men control and subjugate women. It describes how the divine Raja Varuna seized the woman who had had adulterous unions with other men, leaving the men unpunished. This Hindu notion is common to all religions. Men control their wives as far as adultery is concerned, but men are not controlled by women. Bhagavata Purana 3.31, 39-42 texts describe the woman as the door to hell, "like the grass which is well covered, leading the man to sure death, and like the alluring call of a hunter out to trap its victim". Text 6:18, 30 explains that woman was created by Brahma to arouse desire in man. (Shanti, 1998).

Hindu teaching, exemplified by Manu, upholds that a woman is created for procreation. If she is barren, the husband may take a second wife. The woman's life is determined by procreation of descendants. Males are more desired since they are the heirs of the father's property. Because the woman's sole role is procreation, young girls are married off at puberty. Unless they fall pregnant within a year of marriage, they experience harassment, abusive language and physical violence. The Hindu religion upholds that no woman can survive on her own without a husband or male caretaker. When husbands die, widows have no lives of their own. Every young girl must go around the Fulasi plant and pray for a good husband. Hinduism is patriarchal in nature. According to Manusmritis 9:138, the son is welcome for he frees his parents from hell and inherits his father's property. But a daughter is the property of her husband, since she moves from her natal home to her marital home upon marrying. Giving birth to a son means status and recognition for the woman, thus a daughter is less welcome.

Dowry has become a major source of violence for women in India. Dowry is claimed by the husband and his family, and it is not uncommon for the husband's family to demand a great deal from the prospective wife's family. Hence many parents in India consider girls liabilities, and female foeticide and infanticide are widespread. Families unable to pay dowry demands face the possibility that their daughter may commit suicide.

To ensure that Hindu women remain pure and their sexuality under the control of men, women are not permitted to participate in social activities, and are kept in seclusion. Consequently, women lack wealth and exposure, men use their wealth to control and dominate women, a form of gender violence that is endemic to the Hindu faith.

In India today, marriages between young girls and rich, elderly Arab sheiks are not uncommon. (Shanti 1998:10). The Brahaminic-Hindu patriarchal ideology has, over the centuries, developed stringent laws that hold the seeds of gender violence, domination, oppression, control and discrimination, which are difficult to uproot (Shanti, 1998).

Although female feminists have started to protest by means of counter-cultural expressions such as street theatre, liberation songs and role plays, much work lies ahead. Indian women need education, exposure, access to opportunities, participation in public activities, and skills for self-liberation and empowerment.

Gender in the Near East, Greece and Rome

In the ancient Near East, women had no rights as free people. They were the subjects of men, who were their fathers, husbands, or sons. The inferior position of women in ancient law was under adultery, divorce, dowry, family, inheritance, prostitution and widowhood. Some Mesopotamian laws ascribed high status to women for example, if a widow had property of her own and moved into the new husband's house, he acquired all her property. But if the husband moved into her house, she acquired all his property. Other laws permitted a woman to act as a legal agent. Women appeared as owners, buyers, sellers, defendants and plaintiffs in contracts.

Under Mesopotamian laws women of the temple personnel, whether priestesses or cultic prostitutes, possessed a high degree of freedom and positions of greater esteem and dignity. In Athens, Greece, women had a low social position, their lives were strictly confined to the home, and their responsibility involved producing and looking after children. As in the Near East, marital fidelity was not expected from husbands, though Greek marriage was monogamous. A popular belief among Greeks was that women, by instinct, were nymphomaniacs, thus no woman could be trusted to remain faithful unless she was watched closely (Lipsitz Bem, 1993).

Roman law and custom bestowed a great deal of power on fathers, over both sons and daughters. The status of women was higher, both in terms of legal rights and dignity, than in Greece or the East. By the time the New Testament was being written, women could associate freely with men, they would partake in social activities and public entertainment. The freedom of women in Rome imposed no restraints upon sexual license either for men or women.

Buddhism and Gender

Gautama Buddha was the founder of Buddhism, one of the great religions of India. Buddhism is known for the significant role it has played in uplifting the status of women. Chatsumarn (1998) notes that, in the Vedic and Upanishadic periods, women had considerable intellectual and spiritual freedom, although this freedom was restricted to domestic life, which was conditioned by the supremacy of the husband and the technicalities of household activities.

In ancient India, before Buddhism, all religious rites were conducted jointly by couples, with the woman playing a supportive role to her husband. Brahmanism asserted that, to have a genuine guarantee to heaven, a woman must bear a son, who performs all rituals after the death of his father. However, females also had a share in the performance of rites, though they depended on males. The belief that only sons could perform rites after the death of a husband exerted pressure on women to marry and produce at least one son.

The Hindu ethical code (Manudharma) agrees with Confucius' teaching that a woman must be under the protection of parents when young, of her husband when married, and of her son when old.

That such beliefs exist in all world religions reflects the understanding that a woman cannot lead her life independently and cannot make serious decisions without men. These beliefs indicate clearly that, in India, women were treated as subordinates, depended on men, could not make independent decisions and lived lives imbedded with societal restrictions sanctioned by religion. Women in India were subjugated to cultural and traditional values prevalent in society.

For the first time in the history of world religions, Buddha admitted women into his community (Sangha) on the grounds that they were equal to men and could attain spiritual enlightenment (Chatsumarn, 1998:105). This step was similar to that of Jesus, who freed women from cultural and religious beliefs that bound them. Buddha declared that a woman's spiritual behaviour depended on herself. She did not have to marry or be forced to have a son to ensure her husband's or her own salvation. This kind of teaching opened new possibilities for living, opportunities seized by many women, who opted for this new lifestyle instead of lives of household drudgery prescribed by social commitment and tradition.

Buddha also founded an order of nuns in his religion and female communities comprising nuns (*bhikkunis*) preached *dharma* (Buddhism, or the teachings of Buddha) successfully. They played a large role in spreading Buddhism in Indian society. They spread Buddhism as members of *sangha* (orders of nuns). However, some have criticized the rules of the order of nuns for being oppressive to women. These rules are:

(a)   A nun should salute a *bhikku* (monk) and rise before him.

(b)   A nun should not spend a retreat in a place where there is no monk.

(c)   Every fortnight, a nun should ask from the order of monks, the time of *uposatta* (a weekly assembly of the *sangha*) and when a monk (*bhikku*) would come to admonish them.

(d)   The *pavarana*, a ceremony after the retreat, in which members of the *sangha* ask each other's forgiveness for offences committed, should be held by a nun in the presence of the order of both the *bhikkus* and *bhikkunis*.

(e)   Major offences by nuns should be dealt with by the order of both *bhikkus* and *bhikkunis*.

(f)   A female novice, who remains on probation for two years, should receive the higher ordination from both orders.

(g)   A nun should on no account rebuke or abuse monks.

(h)   Nuns may not admonish monks but monks may admonish nuns (Chatsumarn, 1998:107-108).

Although Buddha had done the unthinkable and unacceptable to Indian society by stating that men and women are equal, women still lived in a society full of social gender bias. So, to meet the social, cultural and historical norms of the time, he had to apply double standards by providing rules to keep nuns under the guidance and protection of men/monks. Nevertheless, the idea that nuns and monks were equal, originated in India through Buddhism.

Feminists argue that women are oppressed by Buddhist structures and texts (Chatsumarn, 1998:110). In Samyutta Nikaya Vol. 37, Buddha is quoted as having reminded monks that "women are a stain on celibacy". In places like Thailand, the fact that Buddhist monks avoid contact with women cause damage to women's self esteem and sense of value. Like Biblical and Koranic sacred writings, Buddhist texts were written by men, who expressed andocentric or male-centered practices, beliefs, attitudes and assumptions. Some monks complain that the presence of female nuns awaken their sexual desires and could entice them into acts of sexual misbehaviour. But Buddha himself never discriminated against women. He moved with them everywhere he went. He did not view them as sex objects. He had self-control and was deeply spiritual. Chatsumarn (1998) argues that, even when monks are separated from nuns, the monks face problems originating from their imaginations, because some of them lack control over their thoughts and desires. Buddhism presents women as a hindrance to monks' spiritual growth and a source of impurity. However Buddha is recorded as having warned monks against coming into contact with women or spending time talking to them. He said, "Nothing binds men as strongly as women", while nuns teach that "Nothing binds women as strongly as men".

Buddhist texts stress categorically that women are the supreme commodity. Manudharma Sastra texts in Buddhism views women as commodities to be handed down from parents to husbands and then on to sons. Women are completely dependent on family members for their survival because they are not considered capable of making independent decisions. Such beliefs about women found in Buddhist texts are shared by Islam, Judism, Christianity, Confucianism and African traditional religions. For instance, in some African societies, a brother-in-law or eldest son of a woman whose husband has died takes control of the widow herself and her household matters.

Buddhism has five "woes" about women which are rooted in Indian culture, and they are considered as subjecting the woman to suffering. The woes are the woman parting with her family after marriage, and going to work for other people's family, menstruation, childbirth, pregnancy and caring for her husband and children. Among the woes is the pain that women undergo while giving birth, although this is compensated by the woman receiving a child. (Chatsumarn, 1998: 110-111).

In the text of Anguttara 11, 80, Buddha is recorded as having said that "Women are selfish and poor in wisdom so they cannot assume a seat in an assembly and they cannot work in or be trained to go to faraway countries." Some of Buddha's teachings are treasured by men in some cultures. However, the rise of modern feminism and resultant emancipation and empowerment of women have seen women breaking through such cultural constraints and participating in societal activities ,although much work lies ahead to ensure equal opportunities for men and women.

Buddha is recorded to have said that "A woman cannot become a Buddha". What women are aiming for all over the world is not to become men, because God created men and women for complementary purposes, but women are working to access the privileges that men enjoy as men.

Chatsumarn (1998) lists local beliefs prejudicial to women under Buddhism in India and Thailand, including the following:

(i)   Women were born from a bad Karma, a belief that distorted women's self-image and hindered their spiritual and social development. According to Buddhist teaching, people are born from both bad and good Karma. With a bad Karma, a person will be born in hell, and with a good Karma a person will be born in heaven. Buddhist preachers or monks supported this belief. On the other hand, women, convinced of their bad Karma, worked hard to make up for their unworthy past by showing more goodness or becoming enlightened. Monks, as recipients of such goodness or efforts, became the benefactors in this vicious conviction.

(ii) Women were considered to be of lower birth (*hinajati*).

(iii) Women were regarded as unclean in a religious sense. Because of this belief many Buddhist temples in Thailand prohibit women from moving around the *stupa* (monument) or entering the *uposatha* hall. Monks insisted that the relics of Buddha were stored in the centre of the *supa* at the time of construction, and if women were permitted at these monuments, the women would be walking at a higher level than the relics, and because they were unclean they would actually compromise the power of the relics.

Chatsumarn (1998) indicates that there are Buddhist passages that convey positive things on women. But since women were not permitted in temples and denied education, these passages were only read by monks (men) who could not deliberate on them to uplift women. Like in Judaism, Buddhist women were not exposed to religious texts. Among the Buddhist there are texts that praise women, which show religious and social values that gave preference to a baby girl. For example, when king Pasendi approached Buddha, complaining about the birth of a baby girl, Buddha consoled him, saying,

> Do not be perturbed, O King, a female child may prove even better than a male, for she may grow up wise and virtuous, her husband's revering and faithful wife. The boy that they may bear may do great things and rule great realms, such a son of noble wife becomes his country's guide.

In true Buddhist teaching there is no difference between a girl and a boy. Indeed, in most cultures and religions, parents are beginning to realise that there is no difference between girls and boys, thus they treat their children equally while exposing them to equal opportunities.

Confucianism and Gender

Confucius was born in 551 BC, when feudal societies were being formed in China (Sun Ai-Lee-Park (1998). Confucius saw an urgent need to establish law and order among peoples and nations. He developed a legal system and taught people how to rule themselves, the family and the earth. Over the past 2,000 years, his teachings have become the foundation of the political and ethical principles guiding Chinese history. Other Northeastern Asian countries, like Korea and Japan, were also influenced by his teachings.

Confucianism represents aggressive, outgoing, formalistic law and order. It typifies the male culture of hunters and male gods in heaven. In contrast, Taoism, founded by Laozi, represents the female culture of agrarian gods and the mother earth religion. According to Confucian cosmology, heaven, earth and humans are intimately linked and humans are to learn from heaven and earth. Heaven and earth are also self-giving continually, bringing new life, and by nature neutral. Nothing is isolated. Confucius' ideology of the cosmic order embraces yang (masculine) and yin (feminine) elements. From this pattern it was deduced that the position of a woman in the human order should be lowly and inferior, like the earth. The proper behaviour for a woman was to be yielding and weak, passive and still. It was left to men to be active and strong, and to initiate activity, like heaven. Though men were considered superior, they could not do without women as their complementary opposites (Sun Ai-Lee-Park, 1998).

Confucianism as a religion upheld women in the context of the family, while men were encouraged to be active in the wider socio-political order, girls were educated to prepare them to be wives and mothers. Boys learnt history and girls classics. Girls were confined to women's quarters. They learnt domestic skills and good manners. At 15, a girl received a hairpin in a coming-of-age ceremony and at 20, she married. Three months before her wedding, she was instructed in four aspects of womanly character, i.e. virtue, speech, comportment and work.

Like in other world religions such as Judaism, Islam and Christianity, Confucianism differentiates between men and women. A fundamental Confucian view is that women are not equal to men. Confucianism stresses that the role of a woman is to produce male heirs for her husband's family. She must look after children and family matters, including servants, dogs and chickens. The woman's achievements were limited to the boundaries of the extended family. Confucianism played a role in spreading and enforcing discrimination, inequality, violence and oppression of women throughout China and neighbouring states.

According to Sun Ai-Lee-Park (1998) every woman following Confucianism had to obey the following four principles:

(i)   As a child, a woman should obey her father, as a wife, her husband, and as a widow her son. There is always a man whom a woman should obey in her life. She can never act independently. She cannot do anything important by herself without a man. In the Confucian cosmology, woman is lowly and subservient, like the earth.

(ii) The five cardinal relationships that a woman should observe are those between ruler and subject, husband and wife, old and young siblings and between friends. Those persons mentioned first should bestow *jen* on the ones mentioned second, who have to obey all the rules.

(iii) There are seven grounds for divorce in Confucianism. Marriage is viewed as a sacred event, registered in the cosmic order and with the ancestral line. Hence it is permanent. However, if a wife commits one of the seven evils, she should be sent back to her native home, which is a great dishonour. The seven grounds for divorce are disobedience to one's parents, failure to bear a male child, promiscuity, jealousy, having an incurable disease, talking too much and stealing. Confucianism does not indicate what happens to a male who commits any of these evils, which is taken to embody discrimination and inequality between the way society and religion treat men and women.

(vi) Confucius stressed that women should guard their chastity and personal integrity. It meant more than sexual continence, but embraced a general sense of honour.

Sun Ai-Lee-Park (1998) outlines the rites of passage a girl underwent from birth that prepared her for womanhood, as described by the first female instructor, Pan Chaa, in 116 AD, in her book, *Instructions for Women*:

(i)   On the third day after birth, she was placed under the bed. This indicated that she should be in a lower position, subservient like the earth, humbling herself before others, especially the husband.

(ii) The baby girl was given a potsherd to play with, which meant that she should work hard, performing her domestic chores.

(iii) Her birth was announced to her ancestors by an offering, which meant that they had recognised her duty to assume a wife's responsibility to the other members of her husband's family (Nu-Chieh 1:26-3a, Swann 19:32, 83).

Confucianism spread to Korea around 1 BC – 6 AD. It became a national religion and a political and ethical orthodoxy during the Lee dynasty. It became rooted in people's lives in Korea and in their thoughts in the 16th century. Although Confucianism has weakened in Korea, the predominance of its practices, behaviours, customs and attitudes still reflect its influence. People still think that the place of a woman, whatever her level of education or status, is the home, while a man is valued for his wider role in society. Many Koreans still believe that a woman should behave in a traditional manner and men should remain dominant. Koreans still prefer boys to girls. If many girls are born consecutively, the mother becomes very anxious, while her husband begins to look around for another woman who can produce a son. In some cases, women continue having children endlessly in the hope of producing a baby boy. Because women and the men have no control over the sex of the baby, they end up with more children than they can afford.

Women worldwide have been brainwashed by androcentrism, to the extent that they undervalue their lives, status and contribution to society. These threats from parents, fellow women and husbands exert stress on these women, who are victims of nature, and they sink into self-pity.

Feminists and theologians have a role to play in emancipating and sensitizing women worldwide, so that humanity nurtures the positive aspects of religions and cultures and combats the dehumanizing aspects of religions and cultural interpretations that relegate women to the periphery of society.

The Jewish Religion – The Old Testament and Gender

In Old Testament times, women were subordinate to men, a woman was a man's property (Genesis 12:12-20, 20:2, 19:8; Judges 19:24-27). In the Decalogue, the woman was counted alongside the man's property.

Women did not eat with men. Genesis 3.76, 18:9 and Ruth 2:4 reports that women were the mentors of disobedience and sin. These verses refer to the inferiority of a woman, her subservience to the man and her dependence upon him for sexual fulfillment, which was the cause of her subjection, which is attributed to a curse. The inferiority of woman is presented as deterioration from the primitive and unspoiled nature of man. The work of women was long and hard; it included milling, baking, procuring fuel and water, spinning, weaving, sewing, taking care of the household and the children. They shared the work involved in tilling the land, sowing, harvesting and processing with men.

In wisdom literature, men are warned against being seduced by prostitutes and the adulterers (Prov. 6:24-26, 7:5-27). Proverbs 11:22 says that a golden ring in a swine's snout is a woman fair and foolish. The sages were aware of the monotony of the nagging wife (Prov. 19:13, 21:9, 25:24, 27:15). Ben Sirach warned people about the danger of wine and women and the ease by which man is seduced by feminine beauty. Sirach found women quarrelsome, talkative, malicious, deceiving men by their beauty, envious, drunken and promiscuous (Ben Sirach 26: 6-12), and he concludes that sin began with a woman and because of her, we all die. Amos 4:1ff and Isaiah 3:16ff criticize the frivolity and extravagance of the women of Samaria and Jerusalem.

Teaching in matters of wisdom and participation in synagogues and temples began at home. Men would be trained to become scribes, rabbis or priests, but the Jews believed that it was extravagant to teach women the law. Men would teach both sons and daughters, but sons received more attention. "When the Lord corrects you my son, pay close attention and take it as a warning" (Proverbs 3:11).

Women were not supposed to teach their children Jewish law because they were not permitted to study it. The Book of Leviticus indicates clearly that only men could be priests. Women could not become priests because they were unclean during their monthly periods, neither could they offer sacrifices.

Women were also excluded from positive ordinances of the law which were regular in nature for example, daily appearances in the synagogue and periodical prayers, as these required holiness and cleanliness. Palestinian women were considered inferior, despite the fact that the scriptures record the heroic deeds of several women. According to most rabbinical customs during Jesus' time, and for a long time thereafter, women could not study the Torah. A rabbi, Eliezer, made his point sharply when he said,

> Rather should the words of the Torah be burned than entrusted to a woman ... whoever teaches his daughter the Torah is like the one who teaches her lasciviousness (African Ecclesiastical Review, 1971).

In the vital religious area of prayer women were so poorly valued that their obligations were less important than that of men for example, women, along with children, were not obliged to recite the *schema*, the morning prayer, or say grace at meals. The Talmud states "Let a curse come upon the man whose wife or children say grace for him." Jewish daily prayers contain a three-fold thanksgiving for men:

(a) Praise be to God that he was not created a gentile man;

(b) Praise be to God that he was not created a woman;

(c) Praise be to God that he was not created an ignorant man (Afer, 1971).

However, in the New Testament, Paul said to the Galatians: "There is neither Jew nor Greek, there is neither slave nor free, there is neither male nor female; for you are all one in Christ."(Gal.3;28).

In Judaism public prayer by women was grossly restricted. It was not possible for a woman to be included in the number necessary for a quorum to form a congregation to worship communally. Women were classified with children and slaves. Married women were grouped with minors and the insane. In the great temple at Jerusalem women were restricted to one outer portion, the women's court, which was five steps below the court for men. In synagogues, women were also separated from men, and women were not permitted to read aloud or play a leading role. Men were not permitted to speak to women in public. The proverbs of the fathers contained the injunctions:

"Speak not much with a woman", The wise men said, "Whoever speaks much with a woman, draws down misfortune on himself, neglects the words of the law and finally earns hell" Jewish rabbis were not even permitted to speak to their wives, daughters or sisters in the street.

Women were not permitted to bear witness in a court of law. Some Jewish thinkers, like Philo, a contemporary of Jesus, thought that women should not leave their households, except to go to the synagogue. Girls were not permitted to cross the threshold that separated the male and female apartments of the household. Women were always under the tutelage of a man, either the father or husband or, in the case of a widow, her dead husband's brother. A husband could divorce his wife easily by merely presenting her with a written letter of divorce, but women were not permitted to divorce their husbands or practise polygamy. The status of women in Jewish religion was bleak. Rabbis described women in unflattering terms:

• They are greedy at their food
• They are eager to gossip
• They are lazy
• They are jealous

In some cases, the most virtuous of women were labelled as witches. However, women would take part in some ordinances, like home prayers, observance of the Sabbath, preparing the dough and offerings, and lighting the Sabbath lamp.

In terms of politics, women had no role to play. They were not supposed to appear in public, unless they were veiled. They were not permitted to speak in public. God was referred to as male. Women were not circumcised as sign of the covenant. The writers of the Old Testament, including prophets, were men. Children born into a Jewish family belonged to the patriarchal line, thus a boy's birth elicited more joy than that of a girl. This practice underestimated the value of women. Women possessed no property, and they were a source of labour for the patrilineal family (Arche, 1998).

In Genesis 3:1ff the androcentric society of males who wrote the bible blamed woman for the fall of humanity. The writer of Genesis

2:18ff says that woman was created out of man's rib. The fall from the grace of God was caused by the woman and the serpent. Philips (1984) said that the serpent, being shrewd, recognised that the woman was the weaker of the two humans; thus she was inferior to the man, had a delusion in power, rational faculties, lack of self control, piety and moral strength. The serpent's position emphasises the definition of the woman as an inferior departure from the male standard. After being seduced, she was able to seduce her husband because she was filled with the power of the serpent and she was the instrument of Satan. She was possessed with a heightened sexuality that inevitably lured Adam to destroy the state of paradise. This led to the definition of woman in terms of her domestic and reproductive functions within the male-dominated society.

Being created as man's helper made her subordinate and defined in terms of her child bearing function to a greater extent than before she ate the forbidden fruit from the tree of knowledge. Genesis 3:16 says "I will greatly multiply your pain in child-bearing, in pain you shall bring forth children, yet your desire shall be for your husband and he shall rule over you." This stresses the inferior position of the woman, her subjection to the man and her dependence upon him for sexual fulfilment.

However, Genesis 1 and 2 show that men and women are equal, and both were created in the image of God. God created them male and female, and Adam saw Eve as his companion and helper: "This is now bone of my bones, flesh of my flesh, woman is her name" (Genesis 2:21-23). The two became one flesh and this shows the fundamental equality between men and women. Sons were instructed to honour their fathers and mothers (Exodus 20:12), while Proverbs 1:8 says, "My son, hear your father's advice and reject not your mother's teaching." Mothers had a right and obligation to share in the trials of a rebellious child (Deuteronomy 21:19). Women took part in festival celebrations, their singing and dancing were among the principal elements of the celebrations (Exodus15:20; Judges 11:34; Psalm 68:25). They also took part in cultic festivals (Deuteronomy 12:12; Judges 13:20; Sirach 1:1-4, 6:1a).

Hebrew law also contained provisions which afforded women special protection: the law of the captive (Deuteronomy 21:10 ff), the law of the wife who is falsely charged with premarital intercourse (Deuteronomy 22:13 ff) and the law of the girl who is raped (Deuteronomy 22:28 ff). There were laws to protect the women in slavery (Deuteronomy 21: 10-4; Exodus 22:22; Deuteronomy 14:29).

Some texts describe a good wife as a good fortune, a gift to the Jewish tribe and a crown for her husband (Proverbs 18:22, 19:14, 12: 4; Sirach 26:1-4,) and list her virtues (Proverbs 31:10 ff). Sirach states that a man needs a wife and lists her qualities (Sirach 26:13-18), beauty, intelligence, silence, discipline, modesty, diligence as a housekeeper, and faithfulness. Some women in Jewish history played the same role as men, making a significant contribution to the history and religion of Israel.

The Great Women of Israel

Rahab (Joshua 2;1-21)

Rahab is a Hebrew word meaning uncertain. Rahab was the prostitute in Jericho who allowed the spies of Joshua to hide in her house (Joshua 2: 1-21). She was spared, together with her household, when the Israelites occupied the city (Joshua 6:17-25). In those days, women were despised and to make matters worse, Rahab was a prostitute. Because of her intelligence she saved her family from destruction by the Israelites, and Rahab and her family were accepted by and went to live with the Israelites. Through Rahab's marriage into Israel's faith she was saved and her status elevated from the contemptible life of prostitution to one of dignity and grace as mother and as a woman of great faith. Her faith raised her from a lowly position and wretched condition of poverty and immorality, to a position of honour in Israelite society.

Abigail (Ben Sirach 25:14 ff)

Abigail was the wife of Nabul of Carmel in Judah. When her husband refused to assist David and his army, Abigail averted David's intention to massacre the entire household by meeting him with provisions of gifts. After the sudden death of Nabul, David married Abigail and described her as an attractive and sensible wife. Abigail was wiser than her husband. Nabul was rough and ill-mannered; described by his wife as a fool. When Abigail met King David with her gifts she said,

> My Lord, let the blame be on me, let your maid speak to you, listen to her words, let not my Lord pay attention to this ill-mannered man, Nabul, for he is what his name says, he is a fool.

Because of Abigail's diplomacy, tact, and political skill she saved her family from destruction after Nabul had refused to supply provisions to David's men. She was able to sense danger, and had to act to avert it. Abigail was aware of Israel's laws of forgiveness which recommend the reverse of revenge:

> You shall not have hate for your brother in your heart. You shall not avenge yourself and you shall not keep anger against members of your own society. (Leviticus 19:17-18)

Michal (1Sameul 19:11ff)

Michal was the younger daughter of Saul, given to David as wife at the price of a hundred Philistine foreskins, although Saul had promised his elder daughter Merab (I Samuel 18:17-30). Michal loved David (Isaiah 18:20) and proved her loyalty to him when Saul attempted to murder him. She revealed her father's plot to kill David and deceived Saul's army by placing a dummy in David's bed while David escaped (I Samuel 19:11-17).

Deborah (Judges 4:1-5:31)

Deborah was a prophetess and the wife of Lappidoth (Judges 4:4, 5:31). She would sit under a certain palm tree between Ramah and Bethel in the hill country of Ephraim, and the people of Israel would consult her about their problems. When the Israelites were being oppressed by the Canaanites under Jabin and Sisera, they appealed to Deborah for help. She summoned Balak and in the name of Yahweh ordered him to assemble 10,000 men from Zebulun and Naphtali. Barak refused to go unless Deborah accompanied him. Deborah's presence at the battlefield led to total defeat for the Canaanites.

Deborah had various roles as a woman. She was a prophet who spoke God's word, and a counsellor to her people. She was a judge who settled disputes for her people. She was an administrator and a military leader. In her role as military leader and commander, she delivered Israel in times of war. Deborah exhibited great courage and total dependence on God, who delivered her and her people from the Canaanites. Judges 5 records her song of praise and prayer, which portrays the excitement of the battle and the recognition that God is the real leader of the Israelite army. Deborah played the triple roles familiar to modern working women i.e. the roles of reproduction as a mother, production, and engagement with the community.

Jael (Judges 4: 12 ff)

Jael, a Kenite, was another courageous woman, who gave the final blow to the Canaanite commander, Sisera, by hammering a tent peg into his forehead while he was asleep in his tent. She offered hospitality to Sisera but killed him because he was an enemy of her people. The song of Deborah praises her for her courage. Upon Sisera's death at the hand of a woman, God humbled Jabin before the Israelites. Once women decide to act, the effects of their activities are likely to be permanently felt by society.

Esther (Esther1;1ff)

The book of Esther describes the decision by King Ahasuerus of Persia, to divorce his queen because she was disobedient. The king chose Esther a Jew to work in his palace, and her uncle Mordecai, who was a guardian at the king's palace. Mordecai and Haman became enemies, and the king authorized Haman to kill all Israelites, beginning with Mordecai. Mordecai used Esther, the wife of the king, to appeal on behalf of the Israelites so that they would be saved. The king granted Esther her petition but said that Haman, who was an enemy of the Jews, should be hanged on the gibbet on which Mordecai was to have been hanged. The king, under the influence of Esther, offered another decree whereby all Israelites were to defend themselves from their enemies, and the Jews were given freedom to kill all those they regarded as their enemies over two days.

Aware of Haman's plot to kill the Jews, Esther summoned the Jews to join her in prayer and to fast as they sought deliverance from their enemies. Because of her intelligence and courage, Esther delivered her people from an officially sanctioned genocide. She courageously approached the king and pleaded for her people. Burdened with great responsibility to save her own people and wearing garments of distress and mourning at the prospect of her own death and that of her own people, she expressed her supplications in prayer (Esther 14:4-19).

Judith (Judith;9-13)

Nebuchadnezzar, King of Assyria, invaded the countries of Eastern Asia because of their refusal to aid him in his war against the Medes. Horofernes, sent by Nebuchadnezzar with an army of 132,000 men, camped near Bethulia, but the Israelites refused to surrender. Judith, a young widow of Bethulia, urged the Israelites to stand firm and to trust in God, and she promised to deliver the city through the mighty power of God. Judith courageously entered Holofernes' camp and flattered him by promising him victory. Holofernes invited Judith to attend a banquet with him alone in his tent. When he became drunk she used his own sword to cut off his head and ran off with it in a bag. Lacking a leader, the Assyrians were defeated. Judith applied her wisdom, courage and action to save Israel. Many men wanted to marry Judith but she remained single all her life.

The "tricks" Judith used to assassinate Holofernes were criticized - she seduced him and made him drunk before decapitating him in his weakness – the message is that God is the God of the depressed, the helper of the lowly, the avenger of the helpless, the protector of the contemptible, and the saviour of the desperate. Judith had to fast and pray to invoke God's help, and in her prayer Judith stressed hardships her people, particularly the women, had had to suffer at the hand of the enemy, such as indignity, defilement and rape.

The Woman of Shunem (2 Kings 4: 8-37)

This woman gave Elisha food and lodging and, in turn, he raised her son from death. This enabled him to carry on the prophetic work of

272 Gender and Development

God. She provided for Elisha's basic necessities to enable him continue the work of God .In turn she was also blessed with her entire family by prophet Elisha,

Israelite Women of Egypt

Wives of the Israelites who were enslaved in Egypt played an important role in the politico-religious life of their people when they refused to kill their male offspring, in spite of the formal order of the Pharaoh (Exodus 1:15-2:10). There are other prominent women who determined the history of Israel, such as the wives of the patriarchs, e.g. Sarah, Rebecca, Hagar, Leah, and Rachael. The actions of women like Jezebel and Delilah influenced the history of Israel in a negative way.

The New Testament and Gender

God created human beings in his likeness (Genesis 1:27). He made them male and female and blessed them by saying, "Have many children so that your descendents will live all over the earth and bring it under control." When human beings were created, men and women were not assigned different roles. Both female and male were charged with the collective responsibility of harnessing the world. Together male and female were charged to procreate and subdue the world.

According to the New Testament, Jesus was aware of the daily life of women and had an interest in their activities, as evidenced by the parables of baking (Matthew 3:33), the lost coin (Luke 15:8 ff), the widow with a lawsuit (Luke 18:1ff), the girls who formed the bridal party (Matthew 28:1ff). Jesus performed miracles at the request of both women and men, e.g. Peter's mother-in-law (Matthew 8:14 ff), the request of Jairus and the woman with the heamorrhage, the woman of Syria with a deformed back and the widow of Nain. Jesus accepted the anointing offered to him by a woman and defended her against criticism. His needs were served by a group of devoted women, many of whom witnessed his death and resurrection. His relations with Martha and Mary were characterised by close and familiar friendship. He spoke without embarrassment to a strange woman at the well of Jacob, which the disciples thought was a departure from the behaviour of a good man. Jesus' conduct towards women was revolutionary at the time.

From the beginning of the primitive church, women appeared as full members of the church. They took an active part in the life of the church. They were not involved in preaching and teaching, but provided assistance to the apostles in their ministry and rendered practical assistance. Priscilla shared with Acquilla the office of gospel instruction as shown in first Corinthians. Women prayed and were permitted to speak in church.

The gospels clearly indicate that Jesus taught women the gospel, the meaning of the scriptures and religious truths. He challenged the Jewish attitude that only men studied the scriptures. His action stemmed from an extraordinary, deliberate decision to break with a custom invidious to women. Women became disciples of Jesus, not only in the sense of learning from him but also in the sense of following him in his travels and ministering to him.

According to Luke 8:1ff a number of women, married and unmarried were regular followers of Jesus. Mark mentions the disciples and women, like Mary Magdalene out of whom seven demons had been driven, Joana whose husband Chuza was an officer in Herod's court, Susana and others, who used their own resources to help Jesus and his disciples. Some women administered the gospel of Christ as deacons in the early Christian church. By permitting women to act as disciples and ministers, Jesus broke a custom that was disadvantageous to women in the Jewish faith. Jesus' first appearance after his resurrection was to a woman, who was then commissioned to bear witness of the risen Jesus to the remaining disciples (John 20:11ff; Matthew 28:9ff; Mark 16:9ff). In typical male Palestinian style, the eleven disciples did not believe the woman since, according to Jewish law, women were not permitted to bear legal witness. Jesus was aware of the Jewish structure which kept women in an inferior position. His first appearance to and commissioning of women to bear witness was the most important event of his life . It linked, in a dramatic way, to his unequivocal rejection of the second-class status of women, one of the main focus of his gospel and the resurrection.

Three other accounts of resurrections in the gospels involve women. The most well-known is arguably the raising of Jairus' daughter from the dead (Matthew 9:18ft; Mark 5:22ff; Luke 8:41ff). During this miracle, Jesus violated the laws of purity by touching her corpse. The second resurrection Jesus performed was that of the only son of the widow of Nain: "And when the Lord saw her, he had compassion for her and he said to her 'Do not weep'" (Luke 7:11ff). The third resurrection is that of Lazarus, at the request of his sisters Martha and Mary, who sent for Jesus when Lazarus was ill.

Women as Sex Objects in Judaism

The gospels report numerous occasions of men treating women as second-class citizens. In Luke 7:36ff a woman of ill repute washed Jesus' feet with her tears, wiped them with her hair and anointed him. The Pharisees commented that, if Jesus was a prophet he should know that the woman he was touching was a prostitute. Jesus rebuked the Pharisees and spoke solely of the woman's human and spiritual actions, he spoke of her love, being unloved, and forgiving her sins because of her faith.

The Pharisees and scribes brought a woman who had been caught in adultery to Jesus, and said to Jesus that Moses had commanded that such women be stoned to death (with reference to Deuteronomy 22:22ff). The Pharisees wanted to trap Jesus: if he told them to stone her, he would be violating Roman law in which Jesus deserved capital punishment and, if he set her free, he would contravene the Mosaic Law. Opposing the Jewish law and condemning the pharisaic religion, Jesus dealt with both the accusers and the accused directly as spiritual and ethical persons. He spoke directly to the accusers in the context of their own ethical conduct: "If there is one of you who has not sinned, let him be the first to throw a stone at her." He spoke directly to the accused woman, with compassion but without approving her conduct; he did not condemn her, but forgave her sins and challenged her to cease sinning. The adulterous woman confirmed Jesus' reputation for kindness towards women and as a champion of their cause.

Matthew 9:10ff and Luke 5:25ff, 8:43ff contain reports of Jesus being by touched by a woman who had suffered from hemorrhage for 12 years. She had consulted physicians without success. As a woman with constant blood flow, she was constantly unclean (Leviticus 15:19ff). This made her incapable of participating in any cultic action, thus she displeased God. Anything she touched was similarly unclean. Various religions forbade women from worshipping in church during their menstrual periods, because they were considered unclean. Because of her faith Jesus' power healed her, and restored her dignity.

In Luke 13:10-13, when Jesus cured the woman whose back had been bent for a long time, he was indirectly saying to all women: "Straighten your back my daughters! Walk erect now. Be proud of being women, daughters of God!" Every woman should discover Christ personally in his gospel. This message illuminates our own lives and makes us emerge from the backstage of oppression (Mbuya-Beya, 1998).

In John 4:5ff, Jesus violated another code concerning men's relationships with women. He asked for water from a Samaritan woman and talked to her. Jewish society forbade men from associating with Samaritans, neither were Jewish men supposed to speak to women publicly. Jesus startled the woman by initiating a conversation. The woman was aware that Jesus' action was out of the ordinary on two accounts. Jesus' disciples were surprised when they saw him talking to a woman, moreover a Samaritan. He strengthened the bridge over the gap of inequality between men and women when he revealed himself to the woman as the messiah. Just as Jesus revealed himself to Martha as the "resurrection" and to Mary as the "risen one" and bade them to bear witness to the apostles, Jesus revealed himself to the Samaritan woman as the messiah and she bore witness about him to her fellow villagers. Because of her testimony, many Samaritans of that town came to believe Jesus was the messiah.

In Mark 10:2ff and Matthew 19:3ff, the Pharisees challenged Jesus about the legality of divorce. Jesus rejected the practice of divorce and insisted on monogamy. The man and woman were to have the same rights and responsibilities in the marriage relationship.

In his relationship with Martha and Mary, according to Luke 10: 38ff, Martha took the typical woman's role of minding the kitchen, but Mary took the traditional male role. She sat at the Lord's feet and listened to his teaching. Martha thought that Mary was out of place in choosing the role of the intellectual, thus she complained to Jesus about it, but Jesus' response indicates that he refused to force women into stereotypical roles. He treated Mary as someone whose highest faculty was the intellect and the spirit and who was permitted to set her own priorities. In this episode, Jesus called women to the intellectual and spiritual life just as he did men (Afer, 1971).

According to Luke 11:27ff, when Jesus was preaching, a woman in the crowd was deeply impressed, and imagined how happy she would have been to have such a son. So she raised her voice to pay Jesus a compliment, which she did by referring to his mother. But her image of a woman amounted to sexual reductionism as she alluded to female genitals and breasts: "Blessed is the womb that bore you, and the breasts that you sucked." Although it was a compliment uttered by a woman, Jesus felt it necessary to reject this baby-machine image of women and insisted on the personhood, and the intellectual and moral faculties, being primary for all. According to Jesus' response to the woman's compliment, a woman should go beyond producing sons and daughters for society; she needs intellectual and spiritual ability.

I Peter 3:7 affirms woman as a full partner with man in Christian life but urges that she should be cherished because she is the weaker sex. Paul maintains that woman is a subject of man; on the other hand the church upholds the teachings of Genesis 1 and 2 concerning monogamous marriage, where wife and husband share love and companionship. In the history of the church, women are involved in church activities, like in Anglican and Pentecostal churches, where women can be elected wardens or church counsellors, where they may qualify as pastors and deacons, thereby being permitted to baptise, conduct matrimonial ceremonies, preach, etc. However, most senior church leaders are men.

The Catholic Church does not allow women to be ordained as priests. All the high positions in the Catholic Church are reserved for men. Nuns do not officiate at mass or baptise, or conduct holy matrimony services. Christians should preach the gospel of liberation from poverty, gender inequality, politics, etc. They should bring the good news of liberation to the wretched and downtrodden and also make them aware of their rights. It is not surprising that today, most preachers and religious leaders are men. Women should try and venture into these fields which are God-given.

Islamic Teaching and its Attitude towards Women

The Qur'an stipulates that men and women are equal, thus women are not inferior in status to men. The Qur'an says that those who perform deeds of righteousness, whether male or female and have faith will enter heaven and not the least injustice will be done to them (Qur'an 4:4). Islam claims that woman is an equal partner of man in the procreation of mankind – that she is a mother and he is a father. Man and woman are protectors of each other and they enjoy what is good and forbid what is evil. They both observe regular prayers, and their Lord accepts their prayers and answers them saying, "Never will I cause to be least the work of any of you, whether male or female, you are members of one another" (Qur'an 3:195, 9:71). This shows that woman is equal to man in bearing personal and common responsibilities and in receiving rewards for her deeds. The Qur'an stresses equal sharing of the parents' property by both female and male. There should be a share for women, whether the property is large or small. Sura 4:7 says, "In the first time a woman was given a share." Islam stresses that all men and women who surrender unto Allah, men and women who believe, obey, speak the truth, who live in righteousness, who are humble, who fast and surrender to God, qualify for forgiveness and vast rewards.

Regarding marriage, a woman has the right to choose a partner. A woman is also entitled to demand of her prospective husband suitable dowry that will be her own. She is entitled to complete provision and total maintenance by her husband. The 33rd âyat of Islam says "Men are the educators and employers of women, All â hu ta⁻ â lâ has created men superior". But Islamic reformers say that this âyat may change.

In his teachings, Prophet Muhammad emphasized that women were not the agents of the devil. According to Islam, the woman and Satan are at war, but the woman is a conqueror. She is not a subordinate, but an equal partner of the man. Prophet Muhammad also taught that a Muslim who is kind to his daughters, who raises them and educates them without showing partiality towards them and accords them a place of dignity, shall guarantee himself a place of honour. Islam stresses that both men and women should be educated.

In Islam a mother enjoys an exalted place and is described as one beneath whose feet lie the heavens. A man is judged on a scale of virtue and according to the way he treats his wife. Islamic teaching allows women to retain their family names.

A woman is entitled to freedom of expression. Her opinions are taken into consideration and cannot be disregarded merely because she is a female. In times of emergency, women are required to accompany men to the battlefield, to nurse the wounded, prepare supplies and serve the warriors.

Islam grants women equal rights to contract, enterprise, to earn and possess property. If she commits an offence, her penalty is the same as that for a man. If she is wronged, her compensation is equal to that of a man (Qur'an 2:178, 14:45). A woman is free to work or be self-supporting and participate in dealing with family responsibilities; she is free to assume family roles provided her honour and integrity are safeguarded.

In Islam, the woman has the right to seek divorce (Qur'an 4:128), and if anyone questions her chastity, such an individual is liable to severe punishment. Women enjoy certain freedoms which men are deprived. They are exempted from some religious duties like prayer, fasting during their monthly periods, pregnancy or sickness, attending obligatory congregations on Fridays and financial liabilities. The holy scriptures of Islam direct men to be humble and humane towards women. It encourages polygamy with certain restrictions. Islamic teaching stresses that everyone must marry, celibate life is discouraged. It encourages married couples to raise their children together and in love. It has strict regulations regarding sexual practices considered unacceptable. Heavy punishments are given to those who have sex outside marriage. Sex within marriage gives dignity and respect to women and discourages prostitution. The position of a mother is exalted in the Islamic tradition. Prophet Muhammad said, "Be bounteous to your father and mother."

Prophet Muhammad advocated faithfulness between partners. Within the family circle women enjoy the same privileges as men, as illustrated by Ibn Hisham when he said,

> And I command you, treat women well because they are not captives in your houses, possessing them as part of your household, on your part take them as a deposit from God and permit yourself the enjoyment of their persons by means of a word, and have therefore the fear of God with regard to women and I order you to treat them well.

This shows that women should not be discriminated against or looked down upon by men. According to the Qur'an 30:21, women should be respected as equals of men: "And of his signs is this, he created for you from yourselves that ye may find rest in them and he ordained between you, love and mercy". Like in Christian teaching, this shows that males and females are complementary to and companions of one another, and therefore should love each other intimately and without exploitation of either party.

Recent trends in Islamic teaching regarding the position of women in society

In modern society, some religions encourage women to be confident and regard themselves as equal to men. Women are challenged to overcome their feelings of inferiority because both male and female are created in the image of God. Women are reminded by Islam to respect themselves and their husbands. Husbands are also called upon to respect their wives. The most perfect man in Islam is the one with good morals and who treats his wife well (Waqf, 1998). Islamic reformers call for respect and good morals in the family.

In terms of rights, Islam stresses equal rights within the family for husbands and wives. Violence towards women is strongly discouraged, men are urged to give women knowledge in order to show that their words are right and legitimate. Islamic reformers like Waqf (1998) say that women some day will be given independence, knowledge and science.

Economically, women are encouraged to seek gainful employment, female-male relationships are encouraged; females are encouraged to consult, listen and communicate to men in an objective way (Hammuddai, 1986). This modern trend challenges men to help their wives with domestic work. Muslim women are encouraged to look for employment in any field, although Muslim men doubt the competence of a female judge (Waqf, 1998).

Islam allows women to inherit their fathers' and husbands' property. The Qur'an says, "To men belongs a share of which parents and near relatives leave and to a woman a share which they have, whether little or much". The woman is supposed to share half of the man's property. If Muslim women work outside the home, they contribute to the well-being of the family, in both material and financial terms.

Muslim women are warned against exposing their bodies in public places. To enhance their self-esteem, Islam supports a dress code for women. Women are not permitted to dress provocatively, regardless of fashion. The Qur'an says: "Do not show your thighs, nor look at the thigh of a person dead or alive, it is a big sin to uncover one's private parts." Men may not dress as women, and women may not behave like males in terms of dressing or talking. Instead, women and men must develop sexual roles in their natural direction as defined by Islamic teaching.

Islamic teaching and practice emphasises the belief in one God for both male and female, as the only means of salvation for sexes, "There. is no other God but Allah, and Muhammad is his messenger". Treating women fairly is of paramount importance in Islam. Men are called upon to treat women as they would like to be treated. "A woman is not a creation whom man will use as he wishes or dismiss wherever he wants. The will of Allah wants people to be happy".

Men and women are entitled to all prayers because they are considered to have equal spiritual ability. Prayers are said five times a day by both sexes, at dawn, midday, mid-afternoon, sunset and nightfall. It is men who climb to the tops of minarets to call out the times for prayer. Before they pray members of both sexes do ablutions and cleanse themselves of any impurities.

All prayers are supposed to be attended by both men and women, since they have equal spiritual ability. Particular types of food, such as pork, and the meat of animals regarded as unclean are forbidden, and no one may consume alcohol. Instead, men and women are advised to take coffee.

In Islam, repentance is an important practice. Both men and women must repent because they are all capable of sinning against Allah. Idolaters and other wrongdoers are warned of disaster if they do not repent while the monotheistic and "disciplined" believers are promised paradise.

Pilgrimage to Mecca is another important Islamic practice. All men and women are encouraged, though not obligated, to visit Mecca to see their ancestral religious home and origin and their leaders, to socialise and to perform rituals. This shows that the female sex is not discriminated against as women are also permitted to leave the home to go on a pilgrimage.

Both women and men must abide by Islamic law in terms of worship, whether individually, socially or morally. Both men and women must repeat the Islamic creed (Shahaddah) which is "There is no God but Allah, and Muhammad is the messenger of Allah" (La illaha illa). These are the words the first Muslim child should hear, boy or girl, and should be the last words recited by a dying Muslim. The devout will utter this statement as often as possible every day and the mere utterance of it makes the reciter a Muslim.

However, many Islamic practices discriminate against women as shown below;

(i) Women are not permitted to enter mosques for prayers during their monthly periods because they are regarded as unclean, neither are women permitted to sit with men during prayers. Instead, women sit behind men, a situation which suggests that women are inferior before God (Allah).

(ii)   Women's status is mentioned in the Qur'an 1:12. Men are in charge of women because Allah has made them excel over women and because they spend their property for the support of women, so women are supposed to be obedient, guarding in secret that which Allah has guarded.

This shows that women are subordinate to men and cannot survive without them, since men are the ones in charge of women's survival.

(iii) Women in Islamic culture are supposed to cover their heads and wear long clothes. In some Islamic countries, such as Afghanistan, women are not permitted to work in public places, drive vehicles, or appear on street.

(iv)   Women may not fulfill leadership or responsibility in the mosque. For example, they are not permitted to become imams, sheiks and muftis. All these responsibilities are given to men and hence women's potential is not recognised.

(v)   In the pre-Islamic period, education of girls was not regarded as important, it was seen as a waste of time and funds (resources) of parents, because girls were expected to marry and therefore be reliant on their husbands. Girls only received informal education to make them good housewives. However, today the above situation is changing. Muslim girls have attained a high level of education and many hold high-paying office jobs.

In conclusion, Islamic teachings and practices on gender favour women to some extent. For example, the practice of murdering female babies is forbidden by Islamic teachings.

Similarities between Islamic and Christian Teachings on Gender Issues

(i)   Islamic and Christian teaching stress equality of both sexes before Allah or God. They teach that both males and females were created in God's image, so they are supposed to be treated equally.

(ii) Islamic and Christian teachings on gender are similar in that they discourage divorce. They do so in order to protect women.

(iii) Both Islamic and Christian teachings emphasise respect for parents.

(iv) Both males and females are supposed to pray to God daily because they both have equal spiritual needs before God or Allah.

(v) Both religions encourage repentance of sins. They both warn of punishment if sin is not repented, while those with repentant hearts are promised paradise.

(vi) Both Islamic and Christian teaching emphasise monotheism, which is belief in one God as the sole creator of all things, most gracious, omniscient, omnipotent, and omnipresent. Believers are supposed to be obedient to God and to their leaders because authority comes from God/Allah.

(vii) Both religions demand adherence to the law, i.e. sharia law for the Muslims and the Ten Commandments for Christians. Believers must observe the above-mentioned laws to prevent punishment.

(viii) Both religions emphasize charitable works to support the needy like the sick, poor, widows, prisoners, etc. In Islam rich adherents are supposed to share with the poor their possessions and this is called *Zakah* or alms-giving.

(ix) Both Christianity and Islam emphasise the importance of the Holy Scriptures. Christians are supposed to read the Bible daily and Muslims the Qur'an. Everything found in the sacred writings is to be taken as holy and inspired by God.

Differences between Islamic and Christian Teachings on Gender Issues

i) Christian women are permitted to serve God in the church, while Muslim women are excluded from the service of God as leaders.

ii) Christian and Islamic teachings differ on the practice of polygamy. Muslim men are permitted to marry more than one wife if they can care for these wives or treat them equally, but Christian church demands monogamy.

iii) Christian and Islamic teaching differs on the practice of divorce. Although Islam discourages divorce, it is permitted under certain conditions, for instance if the wife has caused long-term problems for her husband or where the likelihood exists that one spouse might kill the other. But in Christianity, and especially in the Catholic Church, divorce is forbidden. Marriage is supposed to be permanent in accordance with Genesis, i.e. that what God has put together no man should put asunder.

Setbacks to the Position of Women in Islam

Although Islam treats males and females on an equal footing, few Muslim women are aware of their rights, thus men continue to exploit them on the basis of this ignorance. In places of worship, women cannot lead prayers or even sit together with men. Polygamy continues to undermine women's status, they cannot share equally in terms of resources and love relationships.

The Islamic religion continues to treat women as unclean. In areas where Islamic fundamentalism prevails women are not permitted to appear in public. They are denied the opportunity to work in offices, to go to markets, to drive cars and to participate in business.

For many Muslim states a female head of a state would be an anathema, because a Muslim head of state also heads the religious establishment.

Many questions are raised regarding the inferior status of women in Islam, because the Qur'an stresses equality between the sexes. The most frequently asked questions are: Why do men go to work, while women are encouraged to stay at home? Why do the women have to wear the hijab? Why does a brother receive a bigger share of an inheritance than the sister? Why are all the rulers men? Answers to these questions lead to the conclusion that the Islamic faith treats women as inferior.

Genesis 1:28 explains that God gave equal power to man and woman, to have dominion over all creation in their created differences. These biological differences are meant to encourage complimentarity, fullness, equality, harmony, joy, pleasure, and procreation with God between man and woman. Neither gender is superior or inferior to the other, but these biological differences are meant to complement one another like the two halves of a whole. Without the woman the man is incomplete, and the reverse is also true.

Kalinaki (2002) continues to urgue that, while men are physically stronger, women's biological make-up has enabled her to excel as a homemaker. It is only the woman who can be impregnated, carry, give birth to and suckle a baby. Her gentle caring and self-sacrificing attitude is best suited to bringing up children and looking after the home. To expect her to earn a living to sustain the family amounts to unacceptable injustice and implies that everything she does for her home and children is worthless and needs to be supplemented by an outside income. A woman already has a role to play in society, the role of mother, which no man can claim.

Therefore Islam encourages a woman to stay at home and play her role as a homemaker, thus giving her honour. In Qur'an 4:34, a man is described as the protector and maintainer of the woman, because Allah designed men to be physically stronger and more inclined to have work outside the home, it is the duty of the man to provide financially for the family, and it is also the man who is required to give a "dowry to his wife at the time of their marriage". Muslims believe that if roles outside the home are assigned to women, she will be burdened; women should therefore stay at home and be protected by their husbands, who are in charge of their homes.

However, many Muslim women are beginning to compete equally with men in the world of work outside the home. They also work for wages to support their homes. Muslim men are beginning to appreciate the roles played by women as mothers and as public workers.

In modern times, Muslim women enjoy the same political rights as men in some countries e.g. the right to vote, right to be elected to particular political positions, the right to work in the judiciary, police, army, the right to be a member of parliament, etc.

The Baha'i Faith and Its Teachings on Gender

Equality of Women and Men Is Essential for Global Peace

The emancipation of women and the achievement of full equality between the sexes is essential for human progress and the transformation of society. Inequality retards not only the advancement of women but the progress of civilisation itself. The persistent denial of equality to women is an affront to human dignity. It promotes destructive attitudes and habits in men and women, that pass from the family to the workplace, to political life, and to international relations.

The Bahai faith stresses that the systematic oppression of women is a conspicuous and tragic fact of history. Restricted to narrow spheres of activity in the life of society, denied educational opportunities and basic human rights, subjected to violence, and frequently treated as less than human, women have been prevented from realising their true potential. Age-old patterns of subordination are reflected in popular literature, art, law and religious scriptures. Although there are policies in place to protect the rights of women in Uganda, equality as a principle has not yet been widely accepted. Attainment of full equality remains a challenge to be achieved. The achievement of full equality requires a new understanding of women, their purpose in life and how they relate with one another, an understanding that will compel them to reshape their attitudes, lives and their society.

Christian and Islamic teachings emphasize the equality of men and women. Baha'ullah, the founder of the Baha'i faith, in announcing God's purpose for this new age, proclaimed the principle of the equality of men and women, which is the will of God. The establishment of equal rights and privileges is a precondition for the attainment of a wider unity that will ensure the well-being and security of all peoples (National Assembly of the Baha'i, 1997).

Baha'i writings state emphatically that, when all mankind enjoys the same opportunity of education and equality of men and women is realised, the foundations of war will be destroyed. Like Christianity, the Baha'i faith emphasises the oneness of male and female.

The Baha'i vision of equality between the sexes rests on the central spiritual principle of the oneness of humankind. Baha'ullah taught that the divine purpose of creation was the achievement of unity among all people:

> Know ye not why we created you all from the same dust? That no one should exalt himself over the other. Ponder at all times in your hearts how you were created, since we have created you all from one same substance, it is incumbent on you to be even as one soul, to walk with the same feet, eat with the same mouth, and dwell in the same land that from your innermost being, by your deeds and actions, the signs of oneness of detachment be made manifest" (National Assembly of the Bahai, 1997).

The full and equal participation of women in all spheres of life is essential to social and economic development, the abolition of war, and the ultimate establishment of a united world.

Baha'i writing states that, to proclaim equality is not to deny that differences in function between women and men exist, but rather to affirm the complementary roles men and women fulfil in the home and in society. Baha'ullah prescribed identical education for women and men but stipulated that, when resources are limited, first priority should be given to the education of women and girls. The education of girls is particularly important because, although both parents are responsible for rearing children, it is through educated mothers that the benefits of knowledge are most effectively diffused through society. Reverence for and protection of motherhood has often been used as justification for keeping women socially and economically disadvantaged. In the Baha'i faith great honour and nobility are conferred on the state of motherhood and the importance of child-rearing (National Assembly of the Baha'I, 1997).

Baha'i writing states that loving mothers are best qualified to educate children and train them in all perfections of human rights (National Assembly of the Baha'i, 1997). The greatest challenge facing society is to make social and economic structures for the full and equal participation of women in all aspects of life, while simultaneously reinforcing the critical function of motherhood.

The Baha'i faith stresses that women should become full participants in all domains of life and important areas of decision making. Baha'i scriptures state emphatically that women will be the greatest contributor to establishing universal peace and international arbitration:

> It will come to pass that when women participate, fully and equally in the affairs of the world, when they enter confidently and capably, the great arena of laws and politics, wars will cease for women will be the obstacle and hindrance to it (National Assembly of Baha'i, 1997).

The elimination of discrimination against women and their elevation into positions of prominence and authority is a necessary step in creating a just social order. Without fundamental changes in the attitudes and values of individuals and in the underlying ethics of social institutions, full equality between women and men cannot be achieved. In the past the world has been ruled by force and man has dominated over woman by reason of his more forceful and aggressive qualities, both of body and mind. But in the modern world, the balance is already shifting; women are beginning to participate fully in societal activities on an equal footing with men.

However, men have an inescapable duty to promote the equality of women. The presumption of superiority by men thwarts the ambition of women and inhibits the creation of an environment in which equality may reign. The destructive effects of inequality prevent men from maturing and developing the qualities necessary to meet the challenges of the new millennium. It is essential that men engage in a careful and deliberate examination of attitudes, feelings and behaviour deeply rooted in cultural habits that block the equal participation of women and stifle the growth of men. The long-standing and deeply rooted condition of inequality must be eliminated to overcome such a condition. This requires genuine love, patience, humility, sound initiative, mature wisdom, and deliberate, persistent and prayerful effort.

The Current Status of Women in Society

Today there are many programmes under many groups like the government and Non government Organisations that are trying to bring about equality between men and women. They compete for the same jobs and sit for the same examinations. Both girls and boys are given equal opportunities with regard to education. Many women participate in politics, cultural activities, in the economy, business, they own property, and men can participate in domestic work. Many women are in positions of responsibility, e.g. they are lawyers, professors, army and police officers and teachers. Women are adequately financially empowered, able to support families; some men are financed by their wives, and even provide accommodation for them.

The 1945 Universal Declaration of Human Rights mentions, under fundamental human rights, the dignity and worth of persons and, under equal rights to life, own property, freedom of expression, education and medical care. Pope Paul XXIII said that women are gaining an increasing awareness of their natural dignity through the world, women are demanding, both in domestic and public life, the rights and duties which belong to them (Wamwe and Gitui, 1996; Tarsisio, 1997). Some women are able to pay rent for accommodation, tax, school fees, to buy clothes for family members, many women are involved in micro-finance projects like raising livestock and poultry.

However, inequalities continue to exist. Many women are exploited and oppressed. Many parents still favour the education of boys. Seventy percent of women in the world are illiterate and most of the agricultural work is done by women. Many men spend their time in bars, drinking, while women and their children work in the fields. Few women are financially empowered. Most women are housewives who depend on men for survival.

Women have limited time for leisure. Upon returning home from their places of work they resume household work, while men go drinking, read the newspaper, watch television or engage in other leisure activities. Many women are still oppressed in offices – they are harassed by their employers and fail to receive the recognition they deserve.

290 Gender and Development

Many men in some developing countries prefer to employ men rather than women, they are prejudiced against women, whom they consider to be weak, lazy, gossips, and liable to fall pregnant and demand maternity leave. Polygamy is still practised and adultery is common among men, although to some extent some women are involved in adultery too.

How Women's Image Can Be Improved

- Women need to develop their confidence and realise that they are equal to men. They should resist thinking that, because they are women, they are incapable of doing certain things.
- The government and other stakeholders should encourage women to participate in decision making at all levels of society. They should be encouraged to take part in politics, government service and the world of employment.
- Men should respect the role of women in society. Men should encourage and support women's efforts to exercise initiative.
- Men should help women with domestic work.
- More women should receive training in professional and marketable skills.
- Women should desist from engaging in activities that cause men to regard them as cheap and inferior e.g. posing naked for advertisements, using their bodies to win favours, provocative dressing, prostitution, fashion shows, etc.
- Women should be sensitised to the importance of nutritious foods. They should eat foods which they were forbidden to eat by traditional society, e.g. eggs, chicken, pork, goat meat and grasshoppers.
- Women should desist from placing themselves in dependent positions, they should participate in economic activities to earn money and become independent.
- Religious and cultural bodies should sensitise their communities about equality between men and women.
- Men should permit their wives to work outside the home.
- Men and women should be sensitised to the need for interacting with each other in all aspects of life on an equal footing.

6

The Women's Liberation Movement: Objective, Causes and Human Rights Laws

The women's liberation movement had its origins in related liberation movements and represents an attempt by women to free themselves from all sources of oppression, whether religious, cultural, economic, political or sociological. Today women still struggle energetically to free themselves from oppression (Jendia, 1995; Mbuya-Beya, 1998).

The women's liberation movement is a complex feminist movement with many layers. The movement is active within liberal democratic societies and endeavours to achieve full inclusion of women in political, economic and religious life and access to equal employment. More radical socialists and liberationists define feminism as a movement to transform the patriarchal political and socio-economic system in which male domination of women is the foundation of all hierarchies. Feminism and women's liberation are viewed in terms of culture, religion and consciousness, charting the symbolic, psychological and cultural connection between the definition of women as inferior – mentally, morally and physically – and male monopolisation of knowledge and power. Culture is a tool of domination; within the culture there is social reinforcement of dominant patterns of behaviour and social structure. It is a tool for domination. As long as cultures are patriarchal, the traditions of those cultures will reinforce the right of men to dominate and oppress women and legitimize sexual violence against women. It is this cultural domination that feminists work to liberate women from. Religion is also a tool for dominating women, since it stresses female subordination and submission through its teaching by male preachers.

Objectives of Women's Liberation Movements

The political, environmental, social, religious and cultural oppression of women led to the women's liberation movement. Its major aim is the elimination of all forms of discrimination against women, since discrimination on the basis of sex is a form of injustice which benefits none and should be opposed using all means. From the start of the movement, women struggled to ensure the creation of a human society established by men and women as equal partners. The movement began as a protest against discrimination and the domination of women by men.

The women's liberation movement emphasizes the following:

a)   The common objective of all women's efforts is absolute elimination of discrimination and injustices against women.

b)   Improvement of women's conditions as a result of a change in mentality and attitude, which must take place first.

c)   The campaign for women's rights is concerned with achieving equality in education, recognition, social awareness, economic independence, employment, business, medical care and politics. In areas of education and instruction, efforts are concentrated on the need to abolish stereotyped role divisions of men and women in society. Families must be persuaded that education of boys and girls are equally important and that both sexes should be prepared for culinary and other domestic chores. Girls and boys should attend the same educational institutions, and both sexes should enjoy the same rights and the same opportunities with regard to education (Oduyoye, 1997).

d)   Considering that most illiterate adults are women, educated women should come together and be the prime motivators in literacy campaigns.

e)   Women's achievements and their contribution to society must be recognised and respected by men.

f)   Exchange and dialogue is essential to raise awareness among women regarding the problems that exist in society, particularly those peculiar to women.

Causes and Background of Women's Liberation Movement

The second half of the nineteenth century was a time of great social upheaval in the United States. Not only did the abolition of slavery and the granting of the vote to black men dramatically alter the relations between races, but it also spurred feminists like Elizabeth, Cady, Stanton, Lucretia , and Anthony to challenge the legal and social inequalities between the sexes . The French revolution of 1789 awakened women to their rights.

The world's first ever women's liberation movement convention was held in 1848 in Seneca Falls, New York, where Stanton demanded women's suffrage and other reforms. By 1861, Stanton and Anthony had founded the National Women's Suffrage Association, which was the beginning of a full-fledged women's rights movement in the United States, It later spread to other parts of the world, and women demanded the same rights as men, to vote, to education, to property, to protection by the law and to participate in politics and other public affairs.

Women the world over face similar problems of oppression and subordination emanating from their cultural, social, religious and biological situations. Women are denied the right to participate in democracy, voting, property ownership, education and other societal affairs. The women's liberation movement that began in 1848 spread as women in different parts of the world struggled for liberation from subordination.

Causes of the Worldwide Liberation Movement

In various religious traditions men subject women to oppression because of the religious teaching that woman was created from man's rib. In Genesis, God gave man the authority to name all the creatures, woman inclusive (Genesis 2:21-23). Genesis 3:16 clearly indicates that woman would be a subject of man: "In spite of this, you will still have desire for your husband, yet you will be subject to him". During the exodus, women were not counted in Jewish censuses. Religions preach that woman has been the weaker sex from the time of creation and that

that is why she fell victim to the serpent's temptation. Scripture (bible) stresses the subjection of woman to man. The Bible often reports slave women being abused sexually by their masters, illustrating that women had no control over their bodies. Women should endeavor to liberate themselves from religions teachings that promote inequality.

In the New Testament, Paul, in accordance with the Jewish tradition, stresses the importance of women's submission to men. In his letter to the Ephesians (5:21-33), he urges wives to submit to their husbands. In his first letter to the Corinthians (11:1-12), he orders women to keep their heads covered in order to reflect the glory of their husbands. 1 Peter 3:1-7 urges women to submit to their husbands and husbands to understand that their wives are the weaker sex.

Throughout human history, women have been dominated, discriminated against, despised and viewed as inferior to men. They have experienced feelings of frustration, particularly when treated as sex objects in a male-dominated society. Women have been treated as second-class citizens, have been bartered and sold for bride wealth.

Before the abolition of slavery in America, many black women were sexually abused, bartered and forced to do surrogate work (responsibilities of their mistresses like child caring). Similarly, world history shows women worldwide being treated as slaves, denied the right to vote and to participate in democracy. In the employment sector women usually occupy inferior positions. Men assign to women the domestic tasks which men believe were destined for women by nature and this domestic work often turns into exploitation. In most areas mothers prepare their daughters to assume the role of motherhood by involving them directly in domestic chores. Girls are involved in the kitchen while boys are either playing or reading. Girls are given the responsibility of taking care of their younger siblings while the boys are free to do as they please. As a result of this, girls learn that they must serve others, that the kitchen, the house and the children are her expected domain. When the girl becomes an adult, she is expected to find and prepare food, fetch water, firewood, pound maize, millet and cassava and bear and raise children (Mbuya-Beya, 1998). These activities wear woman out at a very early age. She has no time to reflect peacefully and judge things with perspicacity, because she has no time for recreation or relaxation.

In urban areas, jobless husbands fail to support their wives financially and many urban wives are ignorant about their husbands' real salaries or income. Some working women use what they earn to meet the bulk of the family's needs, especially food, clothing and school fees, while many men refuse to assume responsibility for their homes. In a patrilineal society even her children are taken away from her and she may have to go back to her birth family, alone and dispossessed.

Many African communities think that the only vocation for a woman is to marry and produce children. Motherhood is seen as both a biological function and a social one, and a woman's duty is to bring children to adulthood. A barren woman does not fit in society, she has no important role to play and, when a couple is childless, it is the woman who is considered sterile since male sterility was historically considered a biological impossibility. If a woman produces only female children, the marriage is in peril.

When women divorce, they take away nothing, even when they have contributed to the acquisition of their husbands' property. In most African societies women are blamed for calamities that befall men, misfortunes, disease, poverty, etc. They are considered as the cause of the suffering which men face and this leads to their oppression.

International Law on the Principles of Equality between Men and Women

Gender violence and international human rights law

The recognition of gender violence as an important issue of the women's rights agenda took different directions in different parts of the world. The international human law emerged in the context of activism and research on issues related to the social status of women and their right to participate in public activities. In Europe and North America, the recognition of rape as a phenomenon affecting large numbers of women in the 1960s marked the beginning of a campaign against gender-based violence. Gender violence was recognised as an instrument of controlling female sexuality. The analysis of gender violence became a useful tool for understanding the mechanisms sustaining violence against women in society and for developing strategies to undermine it (Miranda, 1994). The United Nations Decade for Women (1975) was a catalyst for exposure of gender violence. In 1976, the first international tribunal for crimes against women was organised in Brussels. It united 2,000 women to testify about crimes committed against them.

In the same year and prior to the First World United Nations conference on women, human rights activism gained prominence in the Third World. Many countries in the developing world witnessed brutality as a result of military coups, and the worst affected were women. Against this background, some countries saw women initiating programmes to protect women's human rights, recognising that women's rights were being violated by both the family and the state. In Chile, Argentina and Brazil, women participated in political mobilisation against military brutality and repression. The women noted that violation of their rights was double-edged within the home and the state (Schuler, 1992).

In the mid-1980s, Women in Development (WID) realised that economic constraints, education, religion and culture were the main roots of women's marginalisation. The impact of inadequate economic resources on women was analysed. The importance of understanding the underpinnings of women's subordination in totality - legal, cultural, religious and economic – was better appreciated. This was a breakthrough for women's rights activists, who began to develop new analytical perspectives to mobilise economic and political resources to redress social injustices.

In 1985, the Third World United Nations Women's Conference was held in Nairobi and its major theme was the status of women in third world countries. The United Nations General Assembly passed a resolution (No. 40/36 of 29 November 1985) advocating concerted and multi-disciplinary action, both within and outside the United Nations system, to address violence against women. This United Nations resolution recognised that violence against women was an impediment to their full development and gender equity.

The Convention on the Elimination of all forms of Discrimination Against Women (CEDAW), held in 1989 and 1992, led to the most important legal documents dealing with the human rights of women. These documents describe gender violence and mark steps in the promotion of women's human rights to promote gender equality.

CEDAW (1989, 1992) defines gender-based violence as a form of discrimination that seriously inhibits women's ability to enjoy rights and freedoms from a position of equality with men. It is discrimination directed against women merely because they are women, or that affects women disproportionately. It includes acts that inflict physical, mental or sexual harm or suffering, threats of such acts, coercion and other deprivations of liberty.

CEDAW (1989, 1992) and UNFPA (2003) stress that gender-based violence impairs or nullifies the enjoyment by women of human rights and fundamental freedoms under general international law or under human rights conventions. The Universal Declaration of Human Rights proclaims a broad catalogue of rights, some of which address the issue of violence against women. Article I of the Declaration states that all humans are born free and equal regarding dignity and rights. Article 2 proclaims that all human beings are entitled to enjoy all the rights and freedoms set forth in the Declaration without distinction of any kind, even sex, thereby prohibiting all forms of gender-based violence. Under Article 3, everyone has the right to life, liberty and sexuality of the person. This prohibits all forms of sexual and physical violence, including battery and rape. Article 5 prohibits cruel, inhuman or degrading treatment and thereby prohibits acts of violence against women perpetrated or condoned by a state.

According to CEDAW (1992), Articles 2, 5 and 10 of the Universal Declaration of Human Rights refer to traditional attitudes under which women are regarded as subordinate to men, or which subscribe to stereotyped roles. It also refers to widespread practices involving violence or coercion, such as family violence and abuse, forced marriage, dowry death, acid attacks and female circumcision. Such prejudices and practices justify gender-based violence as a form of protection of or control over women. The effect of such violence on the physical and mental integrity of women deprives them of equal enjoyment, exercise and knowledge of human rights and fundamental freedoms. The document addresses gender violence, and its underlying consequences that maintain women in subordinate roles and contribute to low levels of political participation, education, skills, and work opportunities for women. These attitudes also contribute to the propagation of pornography and other types of commercial exploitation of women as sex objects rather than as individuals. This, in turn, contributes to gender-based violence. Article 6 urges states to adopt measures to suppress all forms of trafficking in women and exploitation and prostitution of women. CEDAW (1992) explains that poverty and unemployment increase opportunities for trafficking in women. In addition to established forms of trafficking, other forms of sexual exploitation such as sex tourism and the recruitment of domestic labour from developing countries to work in developed countries also require attention. These practices are incompatible with equal enjoyment of rights by women and respect for their rights and dignity. These practices put women at serious risk of violence and abuse. Poverty and unemployment force many women, including young girls, into prostitution. Prostitutes are especially vulnerable to violence because of their low status, which may be unlawful, and this tends to marginalise them. They need the equal protection by the law against rape and other forms of violence, wars, armed conflicts and the occupation of territories, trends that lead to increased prostitution. Trafficking in women and sexual assault require specific protective and punitive measures. Article 7 declares that all men and women are equal before the law and are entitled to equal protection by the law, without any discrimination.

Article 11 declares equal opportunities for employment, but equality in employment can be seriously impaired when women are subjected to gender-specific violence such as sexual harassment in the workplace. Sexual harassment includes all unwelcome sexually determined behaviour such as physical contact and advances, sexually coloured remarks and showing sexual demand, whether by word or action. Such conduct is humiliating and constitutes a health and safety problem. It is discriminatory when a woman has reasonable grounds to believe that her objection would disadvantage her in connection with her employment, including recruitment or promotion, or when it creates a hostile work environment.

Article 12 talks of equal rights to medical health care. Violence against women puts their health and lives at risk. In some societies, traditional practices perpetuated by culture and tradition, are harmful to the health of women and children. These practices include dietary restrictions for pregnant women, preference for male children and female circumcision, also called female genital mutilation. Many rural women in countries such as Uganda face gender-based violence because of traditional attitudes towards the subordinate role expected of women. Girls from rural communities – more than boys – are at risk of gender violence and sexual exploitation when they leave the rural community to seek employment in towns.

Article 16 guarantees to all men and women of full age the right to marry and establish families and furthermore provides that both men and women are entitled to equal rights to marriage, during marriage and its dissolution. While equality in marriage is provided by the Universal Declaration of Human Rights, family violence is one of the most insidious forms of violence against women within family relationships. Women of all ages are subjected to violence of all kinds, including battery, abuse, sexual assault, mental and other forms of violence, which are perpetuated by traditional attitudes. Lack of economic independence forces many women to remain in violent relationships. The abrogation of their family responsibilities by men can be a form of violence and coercion. These types of violence pose risks to women's health and impair their ability to participate equally in family and public life. The traditional assumption, that men are breadwinners, inhibits women's participation in providing for the family and participating equally with men in the public sphere. In many rural areas, very few women are free to decide on the number and spacing of their children. Because of the importance attached to dowry and the production of children, men continue to believe that women are factories for manufacturing children. This prevents women from participating equally with men in the public sphere, because they are always pregnant, weakened by pregnancies and are obliged to stay at home to look after young children.

Article 23 says that everyone is entitled to just and favourable conditions of work and to equal pay for equal work. This provision prohibits sexual harassment in the workplace.

Article 25 provides for the right to a standard of living adequate for health and well-being, which can be seen as prohibiting violence against women and girls that involves different access to food as a result of nutritional taboos.

Gender-based violence may breach these provisions of the Convention or the Universal Declaration of Human Rights. Breaching these human rights provisions has a strong bearing on gender equity. According to CEDAW (1992) many human rights instruments have failed to address the interests and experiences of women. Women's rights are routinely and universally flouted.

Universal Declaration of Human Rights (1948)
The interparliamentary union (1994) says "whereas the peoples of the United Nations have in the Charter reaffirmed their faith in fundamental human rights, in the dignity and worth of the human person and in the equal rights of men and women and have determined to promote social progress and better standards of life in larger freedom,"

Article 1
All human beings are born free and equal in dignity and rights. They are endowed with reason and conscience and should act towards one another in a spirit of brotherhood.

Article 7
All are equal before the law and are entitled without any discrimination to equal protection of the law. All are entitled to equal protection against

any discrimination in violation of this Declaration and against any incitement to such discrimination.

Article 21

1. Everyone has the right to take part in the government of his/her country, directly or through freely chosen representatives.
2. Everyone has the right to equal access to public service in his/her country.
3. The will of the people shall be the basis of the authority of government; this shall be expressed in periodical and genuine elections which shall be by universal and equal suffrage and shall be held by secret vote or by equivalent free voting procedures (Interparliamentary Union, 1994).

Convention on the Political Rights of Women (1952)

The Contracting Parties

Desiring to implement the principle of equality of rights for men and women contained in the Charter of the United Nations,

Recognising that everyone has the right to take part in the government of his/her country directly or indirectly through freely chosen representatives and has the right to equal access to public service in his country and desiring to equalise the status of men and women in the enjoyment and exercise of political rights, in accordance with the provisions of the Charter of the United Nations and of the Universal Declaration of Human Rights,

Having resolved to conclude a convention for this purpose,

Hereby agree as hereinafter provided:

Article I

Women shall be entitled to vote in all elections on equal terms with men, without any discrimination.

Article 2

Women shall be eligible for election to all publicly elected bodies, established by national law, on equal terms with men, without any discrimination.

Article 3

Women shall be entitled to hold public office and to exercise all public functions, established by national law, on equal terms with men, without any discrimination (Interparliamentary Union, 1994).

International Covenant on Civil and Political Rights (1960)
The States Parties present at the Covenant,
Considering that, in accordance with the principles proclaimed in the Charter of the United Nations, recognition of the inherent dignity and of the equal and inalienable rights of all members of the human family is the foundation of freedom, justice and peace in the world.

Recognising that, these rights derive from the inherent dignity of the human person ....

Article 3

The States Parties to the present Covenant undertake to ensure the equal right of men and women to the enjoyment of all civil and political rights set forth in the present Covenant.

Article 25

Every citizen shall have the right and the opportunity, without any distinctions and without unreasonable restrictions:

a)   To take part in the conduct of public affairs, directly or through freely chosen representatives;

b)   To vote and to be elected at genuine periodical elections which shall be by universal and equal suffrage and shall be held by secret ballot, guaranteeing the free expression of the will of the electors;

c)   To have access, on general terms of equality, to public service in his or her country.

Article 26

All persons are equal before the law and are entitled without any discrimination to the equal protection of the law. In this respect, the law shall prohibit any discrimination and guarantee to all persons equal and effective protection against discrimination on any ground such as race, colour, sex, language, religion, political or other opinion, national or social origin, property, birth or other status (Interparliamentary Union, 1994).

Convention on the Elimination of All Forms of Discrimination against Women (1979)

The States Parties to the present Convention,
Recalling that discrimination against women violates the principles of equality of rights and respect for human dignity, is an obstacle to the participation of women on equal terms with men, in the political, social, economic and cultural life of their countries, hampers the growth of the prosperity of society and the family and makes more difficult the full development of the potentialities of women in the service of their countries and of humanity, ...

Convinced that the full and complete development of a country, the welfare of the world and the cause of peace require the maximum participation of women on equal terms with men in all fields, ...

Aware that a change in the traditional role of men as well as the role of women in society and in the family is needed to achieve full equality between men and women,

Article 2
States Parties condemn discrimination against women in all its forms, agree to pursue by all appropriate means and without delay a policy of eliminating discrimination against women and to this end, undertake:
a) To embody the principle of the equality of men and women in their national constitutions or other appropriate legislation if not yet incorporated therein and to ensure, through law and other appropriate means, the practical realisation of this principle;
b) To adopt appropriate legislative and other measures, including sanctions where appropriate, prohibiting all discrimination against women;
c) To establish legal protection of the rights of women on an equal basis with men and to ensure through competent national tribunals

and other public institutions the effective protection of women against any act of discrimination;

d)   To refrain from engaging in any act or practice of discrimination against women and to ensure that public authorities and institutions shall act in conformity with this obligation;

e)   To take all appropriate measures to eliminate discrimination against women by any person, organisation or enterprise;

f)   To take all appropriate measures, including legislation, to modify or abolish existing laws, regulations, customs and practices which constitute discrimination against women;

g)   To repeal all national penal provisions which constitute discrimination against women.

Article 3

States Parties shall take in all fields, in particular in the political, social, economic and cultural fields, all appropriate measures, including legislation, to ensure the full development and advancement of women, for the purpose of guaranteeing them the exercise and enjoyment of human rights and fundamental freedoms on the basis of equality with men.

Article 4

1.   Adoption by States Parties of temporary special measures aimed at accelerating *de facto* equality between men and women, shall not be considered discrimination as defined in the present Convention, but shall in no way entail as a consequence the maintenance of unequal or separate standards; these measures shall be discontinued when the objectives of equality of opportunity and treatment have been achieved.

2.   Adoption by States Parties of special measures, including those measures contained in the present Convention, aimed at protecting maternity shall not be considered discriminatory.

Article 5

States Parties shall take all appropriate measures:

a) To modify the social and cultural patterns of conduct of men and women, with a view to achieving the elimination of prejudices and customary and all other practices which are based on the idea of the inferiority or the superiority of either of the sexes or on stereotyped roles for men and women;

b) To ensure that family education includes a proper understanding of maternity as a social function and the recognition of the common responsibility of men and women in the upbringing and development of their children, it being understood that the interest of the children is the primordial consideration in all cases.

Article 7

States Parties shall take all appropriate measures to eliminate discrimination against women in the political and public life of the country and, in particular, shall ensure to women, on equal terms with men, the right:

a) To vote in all elections and public referenda and to be eligible for election to all publicly elected bodies;

b) To participate in the formulation of government policy and the implementation thereof and to hold public office and perform all public functions at all levels of government;

c) To participate in non-governmental organisations and associations concerned with the public and political life of the country.

Article 8

States Parties shall take all appropriate measures to ensure for women, on equal terms with men and without any discrimination, the opportunity to represent their Governments at the international level and to participate in the work of international organisations (Interparliamentary Union, 1994).

African Charter on Human Rights and Peoples' Rights (1981)

Article 2

Every individual shall be entitled to the enjoyment of the rights and freedoms recognised and guaranteed in the present charter without distinction of any kind such as race, ethnic group, colour, sex, language, religion, political or any other opinion, national and social origin, fortune, birth or other status.

Article 3
1. Every individual shall be equal before the law.
2. Every individual shall be entitled to equal protection of the law.

Article 13
1. Every citizen shall have the right to freely participate in the government of his/her country, either directly or through freely chosen representatives in accordance with the provisions of the law.
2. Every citizen shall have the right to equal access to the public service of his/her country.
3. Every individual shall have the right of access to public property and services in strict equality of all persons before the law.

Article 18
3. The State shall ensure the elimination of every discrimination against women and also ensure the protection of the rights of the woman and the child as stipulated in international declarations and conventions ....

Article 29: The individual shall also have the duty: ....
2. To serve his/her national community by placing his/her physical and intellectual abilities at its service .... (Interparliamentary Union, 1994).
(vii) World Conference to Review and Appraise the Achievements of the United Nations decade for Women: Equality, Development and Peace, Nairobi, 15-26 July 1985

Excerpts from the Nairobi Forward-looking Strategies for the Advancement of Women
3.   Equality in political participation and decision making
Paragraph 86: Governments and political parties should intensify efforts to stimulate and ensure equality of participation by women

in all national and local legislative bodies and to achieve equity in the appointment, election and promotion of women to high posts in executive, legislative and judiciary branches in these bodies. At the local level, strategies to ensure equality of women in political participation should be pragmatic, should bear a close relationship to issues of concern to women in the locality and should take into account the suitability of the proposed measures to local needs and values.

Paragraph 87: Governments and other employers should devote special attention to the broader and more equitable access and inclusion of women in management in various forms of popular participation, which is a significant factor in the development and realisation of all human rights.

Paragraph 88: Governments should effectively secure participation of women in the decision-making processes at the national, state and local level through legislative and administrative measures. It is desirable that governmental departments establish a special office in each of them, headed preferably by a woman, to monitor periodically and accelerate the process of equitable representation of women. Special activities should be undertaken to increase the recruitment, nomination and promotion of women, especially to decision making and policy making positions, by publicizing posts more widely, increasing upward mobility and so on, until equitable representation of women is achieved. Reports should be compiled periodically on the numbers of women in public service and on their levels of responsibility in their areas of work.

Paragraph 89: With respect to the increase in the number of couples in which both partners are employed in the public service, especially the Foreign Service, Governments are urged to consider their special needs, in particular the couple's desire to be assigned to the same duty station, with a view to reconciling family and professional duties.

Paragraph 90: Awareness of women's political rights should be promoted through many channels, including formal and informal education, political education, non-governmental organisations, trade unions, the media and business organisations. Women should be encouraged and motivated and should help each other to exercise their right to vote and to be elected and to participate in the political process at all levels on equal terms with men.

Paragraph 91: Political parties and other organisations such as trade unions should make a deliberate effort to increase and improve women's participation within their ranks. They should institute measures to activate women's constitutional and legal guarantees of the right to be elected and appointed by selecting candidates. Equal access to the political machinery of the organisations and to resources and tools for developing skills in the art and tactics of practical politics, as well as effective leadership capabilities, should be given to women. Women in leadership positions also have a special responsibility to assist in this field.

Paragraph 92: Governments that have not already done so should establish institutional arrangements and procedures whereby individual women, as well as representatives of all types of women's interest groups, including those from the most vulnerable, least privileged and most oppressed groups, may participate actively in all aspects of the formulation, monitoring, review and appraisal of national and local policies, issues and activities (Interparliamentary Union, 1994).

Declaration on Equality of Women and Men (1988)

The Council of Europe member states,

1. Recalling that equality of women and men is a principle of human rights, upheld as a fundamental right in many international instruments to which they have subscribed and secured by national constitutions and laws;

2. Mindful of their undertaking, by virtue of the Statute of the Council of Europe, to observe such fundamental rights;

3. Convinced that the betterment and progress of humanity absolutely depend on due consideration of the aspirations, interests and talents of both sexes;

4. Observing that in present-day society, inequalities between women and men persist;

5. Aware that sex-related discrimination in the political, economic, social, educational, cultural and any other fields constitutes impediments to the recognition, enjoyment and exercise of human rights and fundamental freedoms;

6. Convinced that resolute overall policies should be pursued for the effective achievement of equality between women and men, such policies to involve the authorities, groups and individuals;

7. Reaffirm their commitment to the principle of equality of women and men, as a *sine qua non* of democracy and an imperative of social justice;

8. Condemn all forms of sexism, as they have the effect of perpetuating the idea of superiority or inferiority of one of the sexes and justifying the preponderance or dominance of one over the other;

9. Deplore the under-utilisation of human resources by the community resulting from the persistence of sexist attitudes and behaviour patterns;

10. Welcome past and present activities aimed at the achievement of equal rights and opportunities for women and men at worldwide, regional and national levels;

11. Assert to resolve and undertake:

    a) To pursue and develop policies aimed at achieving real equality between women and men in all walks of life;

    b) To continue work in the Council of Europe to further the effective achievement of equality between women and men;

    c) To promote awareness of the imperatives of democracy and human rights in respect of equality of women and men;

12. Declare that the strategies to be applied for this purpose must enable women and men to receive equal treatment under the law and equal opportunities to exercise their rights and develop their individual gifts and talents. These strategies should provide for suitable measures including temporary special measures aimed at accelerating *de facto* equality between women and men relating to the following in particular:

    a) Protection of individual rights;

b) Participation in political, economic, social and cultural life;

c) Access to all levels of the civil service;

d) Access to education and freedom of choice in education and initial and further vocational training;

e) Rights of couples;

f) Eradication of violence in the family and in society;

g) Rights and duties with regard to children;

h) Access to all professions, occupational advancement and remuneration;

i) Promotion of economic independence;

j) Access to information.

13. Stress the importance for the achievement of the above-mentioned strategies of informing and educating people in a suitable way and making them realise the injustices and adverse effects of inequalities of rights, treatment and opportunities, together with the need for unrelenting vigilance in order to prevent or remedy any act or form of discrimination founded on sex;

14. Invite the member states not yet having done so to become parties;

a) To Protocol No. 7 to the Convention for the Protection of Human Rights and Fundamental Freedoms and to the European Social Charter and its additional Protocol;

b) To the United Nations Convention on the Elimination of all Forms of Discrimination against Women;

And to apply the Nairobi Forward-looking Strategies for the Advancement of Women adopted by the World Conference to Review and Appraise the Achievements of the United Nations Decade for Women: Equality, Development and Peace (Nairobi, Kenya, 15-26 July 1985).

Vienna Declaration and Programme of Action, World Conference on Human Rights (1993)

The World Conference on Human Rights, ... deeply concerned by various forms of discrimination and violence, to which women continue to be exposed all over the world, ...

18. The human rights of women and of the girl-child are an inalienable, integral and indivisible part of universal human rights. The full and equal participation of women in political, civil, economic, social and cultural life, at the national, regional and international levels and the eradication of all forms of discrimination on grounds of sex are priority objectives of the international community.

    Gender-based violence and all forms of sexual harassment and exploitation, including those resulting from cultural prejudice and international trafficking, are incompatible with the dignity and worth of the human person and must be eliminated. This can be achieved by legal measures and through national action and international co-operation in such fields as economic and social development, education, safe maternity and health care and social support. The human rights of women should form an integral part of the United Nations human rights activities, including the promotion of all human rights instruments relating to women.

    The World Conference on Human Rights urges Governments, institutions, inter-governmental and non-governmental organisations to intensify their efforts for the protection and promotion of human rights of women and the girl-child.

28. The World Conference on Human Rights expresses its dismay at massive violations of human rights, especially in the form of genocide, "ethnic cleansing" and systematic rape of women in war situations, creating mass exodus of refugees and displaced persons. While strongly condemning such abhorrent practices, it reiterates the call that perpetrators of such crimes be punished and such practices immediately stopped.

36. The World Conference on Human Rights urges the full and equal enjoyment by women of all human rights and that this should be a priority for Governments and for the United Nations. The World Conference on Human Rights also underlines the importance of the integration and full participation of women as both agents and beneficiaries in the development process and reiterates the objectives established on global action for women

towards sustainable and equitable development set forth in the
Rio Declaration on Environment and Development and Chapter
24 or Agenda 21, adopted by the United Nations Conference on
Environment and Development (Rio de Janeiro, Brazil, 3-14 June
1992).

37. The equal status of women and the human rights of women
should be integrated into the mainstream of United Nations
system-wide activity. These issues should be regularly and
systematically addressed throughout relevant United Nations
bodies and mechanisms. In particular, steps should be taken
to increase co-operation and promote further integration of
objectives and goals between the Commission on the Status of
Women, the Commission on Human Rights, the Committee for the
Elimination of Discrimination against Women, the United Nations
Development Fund for Women, the United Nations Development
Programme and other United Nations agencies. In this context, cooperation and co-ordination should be strengthened between the
Centre for Human Rights and the Division for the Advancement
of Women.

38. In particular, the World Conference on Human Rights stresses the
importance of working towards the elimination of violence against
women in public and private life, the elimination of all forms of
sexual harassment, exploitation and trafficking in women, the
elimination of gender bias in the administration of justice and the
eradication of any conflicts which may arise between the rights of
women and the harmful effects of certain traditional or customary
practices, cultural prejudices and religious extremism. The World
Conference on Human Rights calls upon the General Assembly to
adopt the Draft Declaration on Violence against Women and urges
States to combat violence against women in accordance with its
provisions. Violations of the human rights of women in situations
of armed conflict are violations of the fundamental principles of
international human rights and humanitarian law. All violations
of this kind, including in particular murder, systematic rape, sexual

slavery and forced pregnancy, require a particularly effective response.

39. The World Conference on Human Rights urges the eradication of all forms of discrimination against women, both hidden and overt. The United Nations should encourage the goal of universal ratification by all States of the Convention on the Elimination of All Forms of Discrimination against Women by the year 2000. Ways and means of addressing the particularly large number of reservations to the Convention should be encouraged. *Inter alia,* the Committee on the Elimination of Discrimination against Women should continue its review of reservations to the Convention. States are urged to withdraw reservations that are contrary to the object and purpose of the Convention or which are otherwise incompatible with international treaty law.

40. Treaty monitoring bodies should disseminate necessary information to enable women to make more effective use of existing implementation procedures in their pursuits of full and equal enjoyment of human rights and non-discrimination. New procedures should also be adopted to strengthen implementation of the commitment of women's equality and the human rights of women. The Commission on the Status of Women and the Committee on the Elimination of Discrimination against Women should quickly examine the possibility of introducing the right of petition through the preparation of an optional protocol to the Convention on the Elimination of All Forms Discrimination against Women. The World Conference on Human Rights welcomes the decision of the Commission on Human Rights to consider the appointment of a special rapporteur on violence against women at its fiftieth session.

41. The World Conference on Human Rights recognises the importance of the enjoyment by women of the highest standard of physical and mental health throughout their life span. In the context of the World Conference on Women and the Convention on the Elimination of All Forms of Discrimination against Women, as well

as the Proclamation of Tehran of 1968, the World Conference on Human Rights reaffirms, on the basis of equality between women and men, a woman's right to accessible and adequate health care and the widest range of family planning services, as well as equal access to education at all levels.

42. Treaty monitoring bodies should include the status of women and the human rights of women in their deliberations and findings, making use of gender-specific data. States should be encouraged to supply information on the situation of women *de jure* and *de facto* in their reports to treaty monitoring bodies. The World Conference on Human Rights notes with satisfaction that the Commission on Human Rights adopted at its forty-ninth session Resolution 1993/ 46 of 8 March 1993 stating that rapporteurs and working groups in the field of human rights should also be encouraged to do so. Steps should be taken by the states for the Advancement of Women in co-operation with other United Nations bodies, specifically the Centre for Human Rights, to ensure that the human rights activities of the United Nations regularly address violations of women's human rights, including gender-specific abuses. Training for United Nations human rights and humanitarian relief personnel to assist them to recognise and deal with human rights abuses particular to women and to carry out their work without gender bias should be encouraged.

43. The World Conference on Human Rights urges Governments and regional and international organisations to facilitate the access of women to decision-making posts and their greater participation in the decision-making process. It encourages further steps within the United Nations Secretariat to appoint and promote women staff members in accordance with the Charter of the United Nations and encourages other principal and subsidiary organs of the United Nations to guarantee the participation of women under conditions of equality.

44. The World Conference on Human Rights welcomes the World Conference on Women to be held in Beijing in 1995 and urges

that the human rights of women should play an important role in its deliberations, in accordance with the priority themes of the World Conference on Women of equality, development and peace (Interparliamentary Union, 1994).

Rights and Duties of Women as Provided by the Constitution of Uganda, 1995

Article 21 clause (1) says all persons are equal before and under the law in all spheres of political, economic, social and cultural life and in every other respect and shall enjoy equal protection of the law.

Clause 2 of the same article says that without prejudice to clause (1) of article 21, a person shall not be discriminated against on the grounds of sex, race, colour, ethnic origin, birth, tribe or religion or social or economic standing, political opinion or disability.

Clause 3 of the same article says that to "discriminate" means to give different treatment to different persons owing only or mainly to their respective descriptions by sex, race, colour, ethnic origin, tribe, creed, or religion, or social or economic standing, political opinion or disability.

Article 24 says that no person shall be subjected to any form of torture, crude, inhuman or degrading treatment or punishment.

Article 26 states that every person has a right to own property either individually or in association. Clause (2) of the same article states that no person shall be compulsorily deprived of property or any interest in or right over property of any description.

Article 29 clause 1 says that every person shall have the right to:
(a) Freedom of speech and expression, which shall include freedom of the press and other media.
(b) Freedom of thought, conscience and belief, which shall include academic freedom in institutions of learning.
(c) Freedom to practise any religion and such practice which shall include the right to belong to and participate in the practice of any religious body or organisation in a manner consistent with the constitution.

(d) Freedom to assemble, to demonstrate together with others peacefully and unarmed and to petition.

(e) Freedom of association, which shall include the freedom to form and join associations or unions including trade unions, political and other civic organisations.

Article 30 states that all persons have a right to education.

Article 31, clause (1) states that men and women of the age of eighteen years and above have the right to marry and to found a family and are entitled to equal rights in marriage, during and at its dissolution.

Clause (2) says that Parliament shall make appropriate laws for the protection of the rights of widows and widowers to inherit the property of their deceased spouses and to enjoy parental rights over their children.

Clause (3) states that marriage shall be entered into with the free consent of the man and the woman intending to marry.

Clause (4) states that it is the duty and right of parents to care for and bring up their children.

Clause (5) says that children may not be separated from their families or other persons entitled to bring them up against the will of their families or those persons except in accordance with the law.

Article 32 clause (1) says that the state shall take affirmative action in favour of groups marginalised on the grounds of gender, disability, age, or any other reason created by history, tradition or custom, for the purpose of redressing imbalances which exist against them. Clause (2) of the same article says that Parliament shall make relevant laws including laws for the establishment of an Equal Opportunities Commission, for the purpose of giving full effect to clause (1) of article 32.

Article 33, clause (1) states that women shall be accorded full and equal dignity of the person with men. Clause (2) of the same article says that the state shall provide the facilities and opportunities necessary to enhance the welfare of women to enable them to realise their full potential and advancement. Clause (3) says that the state shall protect women and their rights, taking into account their unique status and natural maternal functions in society. Clause (4) states that women shall have the right to equal treatment with men and that right shall include equal opportunities in political, economic and social activities.

Clause (5) says that, without prejudice to article 32 of the constitution, women shall have the right to affirmative action for the purpose of redressing the imbalances created by history, tradition or custom.

Clause 6 states that cultures, customs or traditions which are against the dignity, welfare or interest of women or which undermine their status are prohibited by the constitution (Constitution of the Republic of Uganda, 1995).

Achievements and Negative Effects of and Obstacles to Women's Liberation

Achievements of Women's Liberation

a) Many women have organised themselves into groups for the purpose of generating money by means of small projects undertaken outside their domestic roles.

b) Women are found in all spheres of employment and some are even managers and directors.

c) The low opinion regarding women's performance in public roles is changing and men are beginning to appreciate the work women do.

d) Women are participating in politics and are competing with men for leadership positions at various levels – local council, parliamentary, etc.

e) A good number of women can now express themselves confidently in public; they debate and deliberate on issues that affect their society. Women have greater confidence in themselves and can assert themselves in front of others.

f) In rural areas the government has set up health centres, schools and water projects to improve standards of living. Non-governmental organisations and the government provide women with loans to run projects. Women have organised themselves into associations where they deliberate on issues that affect their progress, and most of these organisations are meant to assist them to become financially independent.

g)   Women's organisations like FIDA deal with women's issues. Women of today have learnt to define themselves in relation to their roles, they feel capable of taking any decisions that affect their lives.

h)   Women attempt to go far beyond the feminist appeal for equality. They insist on a change of mentality. Today some African women refuse to be considered as chattels, meant entirely to profit the male. The communion between male and female must extend beyond the body (Oduyaye 1997, Lipsitz Bem, 1993).

i)   There are great numbers of women who express their views in public. They assert themselves as persons. Discrimination against them will not stop unless they take the responsibility of their education into their own hands. Their liberation depends on reassuring themselves of their own social status, taking into consideration that their reproductive function is not the only thing that defines them as responsible persons, but that productive and community work is also open to them.

Negative effects of women's liberation

(a)   Many families are experiencing instability which often leads to divorce resulting from women and men trying to dominate one another, adultery and misunderstanding of women emancipation and liberation movements.

(b)   Some liberated women look down on illiterate and/or traditional women and are not prepared to help them. Women's liberation poses a threat to the male-dominated society, thus men resist them so as to protect their male domain.

(c)   Some liberated women are boastful and arrogant and do not even contribute to meeting family needs.

f)   Children are left in the hands of domestic workers, therefore children are brought up lacking parental guidance, and learn the behaviour of the domestic workers.

Obstacles to women's liberation

All human relations are affected by sexuality. When men and women are together, sexual identity and differences in roles affect the functions that an individual is expected to carry out. Women should be liberated from all practices that give pleasure to men at the expense of women.

Prostitution hinders women's liberation. It exposes prostitutes to the risk of being infected with sexually transmitted diseases, being beaten or battered, loss of self-worth and moral depravity. The women's liberation movement should endeavour to educate women about the dangers of using their bodies to obtain favors. This education process should start with increasing literacy among women.

Prostitution is not only a consequence of the unfavourable living conditions of women, but is a major reason for the degradation of those involved. Female prostitution destroys their souls. The evil effects of prostitution not only affect the women who practise it, but also the men who are involved in it whatever their standing in society.

Polygamy undermines women's liberation, since it encourages the idea that women are property to be acquired by men for sex and procreation. Women are exposed to sexual pressures in the exercise of their professional duties. Some women are harassed sexually by their bosses who threaten to sack or demote them if they do not comply. Sexual harassment should be strongly condemned by society and women who are victims of this sort of corruption should expose those men who are involved.

Poverty ties down women and makes them dependent on men. The government, religious bodies, institutions and non-governmental organisations should try to help women with finances for small projects.

Bride price still remains a practice that relegates women to a position of subordination. Because men assume that they have bought the women, they treat them as their chattels.

Some women have misunderstood the women's liberation movement, thus they think that the proof of women's liberation is moving half naked on the streets, in offices or classrooms, some women appear in public half-naked while others think women's liberation is about ordering men to cook and look after babies.

Religion and the Women's Liberation Movement

Muslims and Christians should co-operate to achieve women's liberation. The liberation of the African woman cannot be effected within the limited confines of each separate community. All communities and religious bodies should work hand in hand to help women realise the fruits of their struggle.

The teachings of the gospel should present the relationship between men and women in various perspectives to that preached by African traditional men . John 10:10 says, "I have come so that they may have life and they may have it in abundance". Women should also have this life in all its abundance.

The Jewish-based scriptures which advocate oppression of women should be interpreted by modern preachers in terms of today's changes. Islam and Christianity are capable of promoting the woman as an equal partner with man, they should stress in their preaching the importance of equality of the human race.

The gospel of "submissiveness" of Ephesians 5:21-33 and 1 Peter 3:1-7 should be preached within the context of modern changes. Preachers who encourage women to submit to men must understand the background and environment of Paul's and Peter's preaching. In the society of these apostles of Christ, women were the subjects of men. Modern religious preachers should preach a gospel of men and women submitting to one another (Nuefer, 1997).

Religious leaders and Christians should preach the gospel of the liberation of both women and men. In the New Testament the gospel of Christ was meant to liberate the despised and downtrodden (women), the outcasts, the oppressed, exploited and all the wretched of society. It should be the gospel that sets men and women free from the very slavery of humanity; a gospel that promotes good relationships between men and women in all aspects of life, a gospel that increases life instead of diminishing and exploiting it. As a result of faith in Christ, his grace and love for one's fellow man, Christians must be committed to the struggle of liberation of the oppressed and the downtrodden (Witherington, 1984).

Women should preserve their dignity, both physically and spiritually. Religious teachings should stress the scriptures of Genesis 1:26-28, which says that man and woman were created together in the image and likeness of God. They are both co-creators, called to re-create people and their environment. Both man and woman are responsible for confronting their economic needs, to work together and to manage their environments prudently. Both men and women are stewards of the earth.

Jesus Christ allowed himself to be approached and touched by women who, after following him faithfully to Calvary, remained in prayer with the apostles as they awaited the coming of the Holy Spirit (Acts 1:14). Women played an important role in the spreading of the gospel in the early Church (John 4:1ff, 26:17-18). Matthew 5:28 reports that Jesus warned men about their lustful eyes. Confronting a woman who had sinned and the adulterous woman (John 8:1-11), Jesus did not condemn them. Instead, he called upon sinful women and their male accomplices to have a change of heart.

Mark 2:27 reports that Jesus opposed traditional taboos which were not a source of life and liberation. He declared that the Sabbath was made for man and not man for the Sabbath. He criticised the purely external religion and religious practices of the Pharisees that ignored the necessities of life. There are many similar Christian religious practices which tend to undermine women's liberation. The liberation of women and all men who are downtrodden can also be achieved through the blood of Jesus and the cross of Calvary, His blood, the cross and resurrection break the traditions and regulations that cause women and the despised of society to become the servants or subjects of others. All religions have the power to liberate women from oppressive structures.

The Islamic faith should also preach the gospel that removes the curtain separating men and women. Both Christianity and Islam lack women in senior leadership positions.

Men and women should break away from traditional practices that oppress women, and make new choices that promote equality and quality of life. It has always been said that the woman's place is in the home. Women were not considered fit to participate fully in national affairs. One of the greatest early educators in Africa, Dr Aggrey of Achimuta, stated: "If you educate a man, you educate an individual, but if you educate a woman you educate a whole nation" (African Ecclesiastical Review, 1971). All over the world, women have had to fight every inch of the way to be accepted as equal human beings, whether in economic, social, religious or political spheres. Due to traditional customs, religion, apathy and the general attitude of men, women have been lagging behind in development. Governmental and non-governmental organisations have to awaken the womenfolk, through formal and informal education, to a full realisation of their proper place in society, as well as their rights, duties and responsibilities as human beings.

In recent times, in the wake of the introduction of Christianity and western civilization in Africa, evolution has taken place regarding the place of the woman in the family as well as in society. This has brought about emancipation for women, and a tendency towards independence, at both individual and family levels. Christianity and western influences, their system of education, law and administration brought about a conflict between the old and the new. It showed African women and men an alternative to the traditional way of life, but it was not possible for Africans to assimilate fully into the western way of life, thereby creating a vacuum that is still unfilled.

Although Christianity teaches equality of all human beings before God, the woman often finds herself second citizen in the church. The church teaches that all men are equal, but in practice this is only reflected in writing or sermons from the pulpit; women are not fully integrated and involved in every aspect of life. Women can be an effective force in the growth of the church and the nation at large if they are fully mobilised. Women need opportunities, facilities, encouragement, awakening and acceptance in their rightful place in society. Women should not be satisfied with providing exclusive utilitarian services in the church; they should know that they are capable of serving God at all levels.

African women want to be liberated from all practices that aim exclusively at using the women's body as a source of pleasure to men. These preparations may go as far as requiring the mutilation of sexual organs. Such customs are a perpetuation of a kind of slavery which liberated women are not ready to accept.

Contribution of Religion to Women's Empowerment

The Christian church and Islam have established girls' schools and the education of many girls is sponsored by church organisations. The Protestant church, in particular, encourages women to participate in leadership. There are women who serve as priests, deacons and wardens in the Anglican community. Protestant churches also encourage family planning so that parents may have children they are able to look after without much strain.

Some religious bodies promote women's well-being by giving them loans, e.g. the Church of Uganda has played a role in giving women cows and loans for small projects. Gender issues are also handled through women's religious associations, such as Uganda Mothers' Union, which sensitizes women about their roles in families and in society at large. Monogamy is encouraged by most religions, (except Islam) because it gives the woman equal status with her husband.

The Qur'an stresses the equality of women and men. Equal sharing of property and education of both sexes is stressed by Islam. A good number of Muslim women are in school where they compete equally with boys. However in Islamic places of worship, a curtain divides the sexes. There are no women serving in the higher echelons of the religious hierarchy.

The Islamic faith contributes towards the cause of women's empowerment by encouraging women to participate in any profession. For example they work as nurses, teachers and even as combatants. Hammudai (1986) says: "Caliph Umar employed a lady, Shifabint as an inspector in the market at the Capital City (Madinah) as Ibn Hajar (Isa bah) recorded. The same lady had taught Haysan, the wife of the prophet, how to write and read.

Christian religious beliefs teach the equality of all. Men and women were created equal by the same God, they are all redeemed by the blood of Christ, they are all sinners, and they will all be justly punished or rewarded at the end of the world (Judette, 1994). In Galatians 3:28, Paul says, "There is neither Jew no Greek, there is neither bondsman nor free, there is neither male nor female, for you are all one in Christ". The principle of the equality of humans must be understood as meaning that all persons are born free and have equal rights. This means that all human persons are to be treated as equals in opportunities, rights and justice (Tarcisio, 1997).

Women's Emancipation

Women's emancipation refers to efforts to bring about a balance in gender roles in a situation where men are considered as superiors. It can be understood as a movement aimed at empowering women to have equal rights with men in places of work, politics and to property and land.

Positive Effects of Women's Emancipation

Enlightenment among women about their rights as a result of information distributed by the mass media, workshops, seminars, the activities of organisations such as FIDA, has lead to women being sensitised about their rights, like the right to care for their children, the right to inherit property and land and the right to protection from male violence.

As a result of women's emancipation, some economic development of women has taken place. A good percentage of women are employed in various sectors at similar salaries to that earned by men, e.g. they are employed as doctors, teachers, nurses, lawyers, politicians, in the judiciary, police, army and in the private sector. A good number of women are also involved in business, both small- and large-scale. Some women are financially self-sustaining – they no longer depend on men for survival, they are able to improve on the standard of living of their families, they pay school fees, own property and land, run businesses etc.

Women's emancipation has advanced the education of girls. The extent of girls' enrolment at both primary and secondary levels has increased slightly because of the Universal Primary Education Policy though, in technical schools, girls' enrolment continues to be low. Enrolment of girls at university has also increased slightly because of positive discrimination in the form of the 1.5 marks added to every female student. Girls and boys sit for the same examinations and, in many cases, girls' schools perform better than boys' schools. However, a high dropout rate persists among girls, especially in primary and secondary schools. There is still a lot to do in terms of education so as to retain girls at school.

In the political sphere, many women today participate in politics. Through affirmative action, each district has a woman representative in Uganda's parliament and there are women in all local councils. However, lower local councils have only a few women because the majority of women cannot read and write and they are hampered by domestic obligations.

Negative Effects of Women's Emancipation

Women's emancipation has led to some family instability due to uncertainty regarding the rights and responsibilities of wives and husbands. Some men feel threatened by economically active and financially empowered women, they feel they are not respected and can no longer control their wives. On the other hand, when women become financially liberated, some of them look down on their husbands and forget their roles as wives.

If wives and husbands do not have the same level of education family instability could result. Men who tend to marry women whose education is higher than theirs feel inferior and may torture their wives as a way of enforcing their authority and this may lead to divorce or separation.

Women who are well educated and financially independent tend to attach less importance to traditional values. They do not feel the respect that culture has traditionally demanded for men, and they could expect men to assist with household chores.

7

Gender Equality, Empowerment and the Development Process

Gender is about empowerment and the process of sensitisation. Unequal gender relations, which oppress women, are a consequence of cultural and religious teachings. Empowerment theory stresses self-reliance in all aspects of life. The empowerment approach has three basic principles:

(i) Encouraging development of women's abilities and self-reliance through earning, owning assets and managing finances.

(ii) Stressing women's confidence and ability to know and negotiate for their rights in the household, places of work and the community at large.

(iii) Emphasizing women's control over their bodies. Thus women have a right to freedom of movement and freedom from male violence.

There are four types of power in society

(i) Power over and among other people, e.g. with other people, groups and organisations, leading to networking, solidarity, coordination and voluntary cooperation.

(ii) Power within and over oneself, leading to inner energy, self-confidence, personal dignity, self-actualization, self-respect and acceptance of others as equals.

(iii) Power to do things, e.g. to learn, understand and act, leading to the ability to be creative.

(iv) Power wielded by educated people over the uneducated, e.g. male over female, and the rich over the poor.

The adverse effects of power over others include intimidation, unequal participation in decision making, oppression and uneven distribution of wealth and income. Patriarchy, which is prevalent in many countries, is an example of one group of people having power over others. Men have more power and influence than women in most aspects of life.

Gender equality is a national and international concern and an important concern to advocates of women's rights. Equality between women and men is essential for sustainable development. The gender needs expressed by UN conferences and global reports cannot be achieved unless women and the resources they represent are integrated into development processes. There is international consensus that gender equality makes an essential contribution to sustainable development. World reports have pointed out that oppression of women has a negative impact on human development.

Poverty is a greater problem for women than men. Approximately 70% of the world's poor are women. Poverty has a more serious impact on women than men. This is a result of the gender distribution of labour and responsibility at home. In most societies women do agricultural work yet they have no money and because they are not educated and do not receive vocational training, they have no access to productive resources. Poverty relief by governments and other institutions should be channeled towards women. Furthermore, the majority of the world's refugees and those in camps are also women and children; therefore refugees should also be targeted for the purpose of development.

Women make up half of the world's population, but in most countries, they have fewer opportunities than men. There is an imbalance between the work of women and men and women's access to resources and power. In most societies, including Uganda, women lack rights relating to property ownership and inheritance. Women also have fewer opportunities to find paid work and to participate in decision-making processes because they lack education; Women are the minority in key posts in public administration, trade, industry and international organisations.

Stakeholders should initiate special initiatives and measures to compensate women for disparities that disadvantage them in relation to men. Development is only possible if everyone has equal opportunities and obligations in all spheres of life.

Gender inequality acts as a hindrance to progress in health education. It also hinders the fight against poverty, diseases like HIV/Aids, illiteracy, malnutrition etc. Education for all is one of Uganda's millennium goals, and will be achieved by implementing universal primary education by 2015 and eliminating gender disparity at all educational levels, paying special attention to raising the enrolment rate of girls. This strategy is an important step towards gender equality. Education brings broad social benefits, it raises family incomes and leads to improved social and reproductive health. The 2002 Ugandan census indicated that illiterate women tender to bear more children than literate women, yet lacked resources to care for a large family. Education contributes to greater participation by women in decision making, awareness of environmental issues and improved social responsibility.

A number of studies show that investing in women's education is the single investment that yields the highest returns. Educated women have fewer children, whose overall health is better and who are more likely to promote the education of girls themselves. Education leads to higher incomes and opportunities and increases their participation in democratic processes. Education is the primary means of strengthening women's positions.

Governments and other role players should create a school system which ensures that girls can exercise the right to education and are maintained there. They should make sure that the girls' education is at par with that of boys.

Governments should ensure that women have access to higher education and vocational training. More female leaders are needed in the education sector to ensure the safety of girls in schools. Efforts should be made to improve on school female staffing and recognise their achievement. Women must have access to vocational training and to be encouraged to enter the fields of science and technology, to counteract the tendency for women to be marganalised in the technological advances.

The government and non government organisations should have information on the respective positions and status of women and men in society and the relationship between the sexes, in order to form a holistic picture of the distribution of resources, rights, power, privilege and responsibility between men and women.

The Ugandan government has made a significant contribution to the promotion of equal rights and opportunities for men and women in all sectors of society. Women are encouraged to compete with men in all sectors; however, women's main drawback is lack of education.

The subordinate position of women is maintained in many societies by means of discrimination, due to religion and culture. Women and girls are subjected to discrimination and oppression in all contexts and stages of life. They are abused, intimidated, criticized and rebuked for taking up male positions and some women are likely to give up the struggle. Making a contribution towards reducing discrimination against and abuse of women in society poses a challenge to stakeholders and feminists or women's liberation movements. The government should put in place laws that protect women from such abuses and discrimination, and promote their rights.

To enhance gender equality and development, stakeholders should sensitise communities about the right of women to access health services. In many parts of Uganda, health care, rights to and access to services in relation to sexuality, pregnancy and child health care are not available to women living in deep rural areas. Mortality rates among women are alarming owing to unsafe child-bearing and complications associated with pregnancy. The government should try to address this issue so that the millennium goal of health for all is achieved. Cultural discrimination against women often has a serious negative impact on women's health. Wife battering and genital mutilation are examples of cultural practices that militate against women's equality and development. Improving women's health means that men should also be involved. Unless men become involved and change their culturally induced attitudes to women, it will be difficult to address the health problems women experience. Governments and other role players should support and maintain primary health care facilities and services for women. The health centers should be equipped with facilities and trained personnel. Women should be sensitised about the benefits of using contraception.

Development Approaches to Gender

Women in Development

a)   Women in Development (WID) approaches issues from the perspectives of women.

b)   A good number of women are excluded from economic, political and educational opportunities in the development process.

(iv) Women should be integrated into existing development programmes so as to achieve gender equity.

(v) WID emphasizes the need to have women's projects, increase women's productivity, increase their income and their ability to look after the household.

Early approaches to WID recognised that development has ignored the women from the design and implementation of the development programmes. The WID approach recognises that more efficient and effective development requires the active participation of women as well as men.

Gender and Development (GAD)

The 1995 Commonwealth Plan of Action on Gender and Development (GAD)

The 1995 Commonwealth Plan of Action on Gender and Development is a blueprint for Commonwealth action to achieve gender equality. It provides a framework within which member governments and the commonwealth secretariat can harness their resources to transform the Commonwealth vision for women into reality. It is an innovative, complex and forward-looking plan for mainstreaming gender issues into all the policies, programmes and activities of governments and the

Secretariat to ensure social justice, equality and fulfillment for all. It provides flexible mechanisms for monitoring its implementation and emphasizes establishing and strengthening institutional capacity in both governments and the Secretariat to advance gender equality. It stresses that, "The reality for most women is still a long way off from the vision." The 1995 Commonwealth plan of action on gender and development focuses on a vision in which the Commonwealth works towards

.... a world in which women and men have equal rights and opportunities in all stages of their lives to express their creativity in all fields of human endeavor and in which women are respected and valued as equal and able partners in establishing the values of social justice, equity, democracy and respect for human rights.

Within such a framework of values women and men work in collabouration and partnership to ensure sustainable economic and social development for all nations (http:///...STPD Internal.asp%3FNOde ID%3D33981+Gender xx and +Development hl=engie=UTF, Page 1 of 2, Commonwealth plan of Action on Gender and Development, 2005)

The Austrian Agency for International Development Plan of Action on Gender and Development (GAD)

According to the Austrain Agency for International Development (1997), since the mid-1980s, there has been a growing consensus that sustainable development requires an understanding of both women's and men's roles and responsibilities within the community and their relationship to each other. Improving the status of women is no longer seen as just a women's issue but as a goal that requires the active participation of men and women. This approach to development has come to be called Gender and Development (GAD).

a) It deals with relations between men and women.

b) It focuses on the unequal distribution of power between women and men and between the rich and the poor, situations which prevent equal participation and equitable development.

c) It works to empower women and the disadvantaged and transforming unequal relations.

d) It aims to identify problems and needs of both men and women and marganalised groups in order to improve their conditions. It addresses women's strategic interests and the interests of the disadvantaged through people-centered development.

The GAD approach, through gender analysis, seeks to understand the roles, responsibilities, resources and priorities of women and men within a specific context and examines the social, economic and environmental role players which influence women roles and decision-making capacity. The collection of women sex-disaggregated data in the programmes and project cycle is an important part of the GAD approach.

For gender equality and development to take root and realise its goals, the current status of women must be taken into consideration. The UNFPA (2004) described the status of women worldwide:

(a) Of 1.3 billion people living in poverty in the world, 70% are women.

(b) Among the world's 6 billion people, women outnumber men by two to one.

(c) Adult women suffer more than men from malnutrition. Of adults suffering from iron deficiency, 458 million are women and 238 million are men. Of those stunted due to protein deficiency, 450 million are women and 400 million are men.

(d) Each year at least half a million women die of complications caused by pregnancy. In almost all poor countries, pregnancy complications are the largest single cause of death among women in their reproductive years.

(e) Although women represent 41% of all workers in under-developed countries, their wages are 30-40% less than those of men for comparable work.

(f) Women constitute less than one-seventh of administrators and managers in developing countries.

(g) Women hold only 10% of the seats in the world's parliaments and 6% in national cabinets.

It is significant to note that in developing countries men and women have not shared equally in the benefits of development to their countries because of the low status of women. Thus there remain wide disparities in opportunities available to women and men in the economic, social and political spheres. The Uganda government's new gender and development policy should be committed to actions that will meet women's immediate needs and address the underlying causes of women's failure to benefit equally from development.

The objectives of GAD policy of any government or other role players should include:

a) Improving women's access to basic education like universal primary education, literacy programmes for women, vocational, technical and tertiary institutions, providing and supporting health care and services like maternal and child health, primary health care and disease control.The Uganda government has made considerable headway in education by providing every school-age child with free education at primary level. The government has also provided all rural areas with health care centers for maternal care, immunisation, malaria treatment and other diseases.

b) Improving women's access to economic resources.

c) Promoting women's participation in leadership and in decision making at all levels.

d) Promoting the human rights of women and assisting in efforts to eliminate discrimination.

e) Mainstreaming a gender perspective in all development projects and programmes, thereby promoting equal access to education. Education is an essential tool for achieving equality and development. Education enables people to take charge of change and shape their own destiny. It is well known that education for girls and women has a catalytic effect on every dimension of development, such as child and maternal mortality rates, fertility rates, educational attainment by girls and boys, productivity and environmental management.

In developing countries, women have started to enter the workforce and are in occupations previously reserved for men. Women have made significant advances towards achieving better working conditions and improved pay. However, women are still largely absent from decision-making positions and power structures that shape society.

All GAD programmes incorporate a gender perspective in their activities, which involves an understanding of the different roles played by men and women within a given context. Gender analysis, as an essential part of social analysis, is the means by which such an understanding is acquired. A crucial part of gender analysis is the collection of socio-economic data and data by sex. It is important that women and men in the communities themselves participate in data collection as well as in the design and implementation of activities. Women and men should participate in decision making and ensure that women's specific needs are known and respected. GAD programmes also promote gender awareness through workshops, radio, television and dissemination of information by its officers.

The responsibility of achieving gender equity is shared by all role players, men and women, policy analysts, planners, managers and programme staff members. The Austrian Agency for International Development (1997) comments that, in recent years, gender equality has become the focus of the GAD approach, a focus which is reflected in the Platform for Action of the 1995 World Conference on Women held in Beijing.

The Millennium Development Goals (Universal) and Gender Equality

The gender equality and the millennium development goals are concerned with poverty, education, health and nutrition, and the environment. It assesses the extent to which gender concerns and perspectives have been mainstreamed into the programmes of governments' and other role players. The goals have a global partnership to address poverty, illiteracy, inequality, discrimination against women and girls, access to health and education, reduce deadly and other diseases, harness the environment and national and international development and achievement to be shared by all nations and peoples of the world.

The gender millennium goals challenge discrimination against women and seek to ensure that all children have equal access to schooling. Its aim is to see more women becoming literate, having greater say in public policy and decision making and enjoying improved income and projects. It stresses that, without progress towards gender equality and the empowerment of women, all the other millennium goals will not be achieved (http://64:233.161/04) and +development 8=en gie=UTF Page 1 of 2).

GAD addresses practical issues that hinder gender development for example, access to clean water, sanitation, health, transportation, communication and electricity. These are specially intended to help women and children participate fully in communal activities. Many women undervalue themselves because their domestic and agricultural work is not paid for.

The benefits of integrating gender into development

By integrating gender concerns into development:

(a)   Women and men are involved and democracy and human rights are respected.

(b)   Participation by both female and male is promoted and full community participation is ensured.

(c)   Information on who does what, when and where is provided by program managers through documentation.

(d)   People, particularly women and marginalised groups, are motivated.

g)   The flow of information within a given group is improved through continuous teaching and monitoring of the programmes.

h)   Opportunities for fairer access to and distribution of resources and income are provided.

(j)   People find it easier to identify themselves with projects.

Obstacles to Women's Participation in the Development Process

Political obstacles

Few governments involve women in decision-making. Women's interests are usually overshadowed by broader allegiances to class and political movements. Few government policies consider women's interests.

Attitudinal Obstacles

Politicians, intellectuals and development planners are resistant to women's greater participation in economic and political life owing to the defined traditional roles of women. Many men assume that the role of women is child-bearing and the woman's place is at home, thus they should be economically dependent on men. This traditional division of rights and responsibilities based on sex places women in an inferior position socially, economically, legally and politically. Gender inequity is prevalent in most institutions.

Conceptual Obstacles

Assumptions about the social responsibilities of men and women affect employment practices in both public and private sectors. It is, for instance, assumed that only men support families, rather than both men and women, or sometimes even women alone. This leads to the idea that a wife's income is supplemental to that of her husband, and consequently women's wages are generally lower than those of men.

In some societies and families, the male head is considered the primary institution, and the wife and children are considered subordinates. Women are assumed to be dependent on men and this assumption leads to government policies failing to recognise the role played by women in the economy.

Lack of Information

Another obstacle to women's participation in the development process is lack of information about women and their contribution to development. As a result there is a tendency to ignore women. The development planners often see women as passive beneficiaries of social and health services. Women's domestic and reproductive roles are not acknowledged and excluded from development planning.

Gender Structural Constraints

Bride Price

Research carried out in the Ankole region of Uganda by the writer of this text found that a wife for whom bride wealth was paid is expected to produce a great number of children. If bride price has been paid and the husband dies, the wife has limited chances of remarrying outside her husband's family, thus she is "inherited", because the parents and brothers of the woman cannot afford to refund the dowry. Modern women ask why, if dowry is a token of appreciation, and not a sale price, it must be returned after a marriage has failed or if a widow leaves her marital home upon the death of her husband? In rural areas like Kigezi, if the woman leaves her marital home, even in old age, the bride price must be returned.

Research carried out in Uganda's Arua District by the writer of this text confirms the findings of Kasekende (1991) that, culturally, payment of dowry or bride wealth is part and parcel of marriage. Bride price assumes the central role of marriage because it is regarded as a source of security and stability in marriage. It is also cherished as a demonstration of the value attached to wives by their husbands and relatives. However, commercialization of dowry influences fertility because, on payment of bride wealth, the husband gains control of his wife's reproductive behaviour. Research carried out by the writer of this text in Kisoro, Kabale, Rukungiri, Arua and Ankole revealed that, when girls become of age, they become a liability to their brothers and parents, who put them under pressure to marry so that they can become assets for them. The dowry received for girls is used to pay for the wives of sons. It was found that women encourage their daughters to marry at an early age, and girls who delay marriage are harassed by parents to the point where they may decide to marry anyone. Some families secretly arrange forced marriages for their children. Among the Bafumbira, Bakiga, Banyankore and Lugbara, it is customary for the bride to be ambushed and abducted by the bridegroom. Parents support this cultural practice because they receive dowry.

Research carried out by the writer to this text in Mbarara, Isingiro and Ibanda agrees with the findings of Ahimbisibwe (1991) that:

- For the Ankole, payment of bride price is a treasured cultural practice, even though it is costly. Consequently most Banyankore condemn activists who agitate for its abolishment.
- Payment of bride price is a matter of pride to parents, especially mothers. Women say that the payment of dowry for their daughters makes the effort of raising them worth while.
- Payment of bride price demonstrates gratitude for raising a girl. This compulsory cultural rite affirms that marriage has taken place.
- Women do not have influence on bride wealth. They do not even share the bride wealth with their husbands. The husband discusses with other men the amount of bride wealth to be paid, which is related to the educational level of the girl and the family background of the boy. From the dowry the mothers and aunts receive only Kinyankore traditional dresses, a goat, a small amount of money and recognition as mothers.
- In Ankole, bride wealth is communal property. The bride's father may be the controller but the extended family receives its share. The paternal aunt *(ishenkazi)*, as an instructor to the bride, receives a goat and a suit or traditional dress, or its equivalent. (She cannot be given a cow because traditionally women may not own cows.) The maternal uncle is given a goat to please the kin of the bride's mother. Part of the bride wealth is used to meet the expenses of the giving-away ceremony.
- The bride and groom indirectly share the bride price, because part of it is used to buy the things that the bride should bring to the marriage. These items include suits, a suitcase, *ekitambi*, (Western Uganda traditional wear) cooking utensils, bedding and furniture. The girls' parents must balance the expenses of the giving-away ceremony and the bride wealth, as expenses incurred for the

ceremony could exceed the bride wealth. Although payment of dowry and the giving away ceremony are costly for the groom and parents of the bride respectively, they are prestigious customs about which the bride, groom and the community feel pride.

- Payment of dowry unites people, as every member of the community is involved.
- A girl who elopes with a boyfriend prejudices herself and her parents. They lack the prestige accorded to other brides and their parents. Eloping also reflects negatively upon the families from which girls elope. The parents are blamed for bringing up their girls like prostitutes.
- Though men and women attend the meeting at which the bride price is set, women play a passive role. They merely listen and report to other women upon conclusion of negotiations. Women cannot negotiate bride price because they cannot set their own prices and do not own property, thus they lack bargaining power.
- Although the girl's mother may have influence, the final decision is made by the man who pays the dowry. In Ankole, women are treated fairly. Husbands seek their wives' opinion before giving away their daughters.
- Today in Ankole, bride price has become expensive especially for those who come from poor backgrounds. The bride's father undertakes several fact-finding missions to check on the economic status of the bridegroom, evaluating his house, the number of cows he owns, the size of banana plantations, education and salary. Because dowry is expensive, some girls elope with boys who are from poor backgrounds . If a girl who eloped dies before her dowry has been paid, she cannot be buried by the bridegroom's family before it is paid.

Payment of dowry is a cultural and religious practice. The Bible reports men paying dowry before taking girls as wives. Jacob worked for Laban for fourteen years as bride price for Rachel and Leah (Genesis 29:15ff).

Because dowry is becoming a thorn in the flesh of the poor, because of changing situations and modern movements of equality, the men and women intending to marry may discuss it with their parents. Bride price may be paid as a form of "gifts". Men may feel free to discuss their financial standing with the women whom they wish to marry, so that they can go through the cultural and religious processes of marriage without prejudice. For example, if the bridegroom is not in a position to raise the number of cows required for dowry, he may discuss it with the bride and her parents. After all, a good marriage is not built on payment of dowry but a good relationship between the spouses. Women may initiate negotiations with parents on the issue of abolishing dowry, but the bridegroom's side should meet the traditional requirements of the uncles, aunts and brothers. Families who wish to pay dowry may do so, but should remember the implications for their daughters in the event of divorce. No human being can be exchanged for commodities, in this respect dowry payments undermine women's equity with men.

Disadvantages of bride price

Because they paid bride price for a wife, the wife is expected to work hard for the bridegroom's family, they may even be beaten. The father-in-law may demand intercourse with his daughter-in-law to ensure that the cows he paid were not for nothing – this is common practice among the Bakiga and Bafumbira. This is dangerous behaviour in today's society, where HIV/Aids is rampant.

Payment of dowry hinders the emancipation of women since it gives the impression that women are the property of men and that they can be bought. It strengthens men's authority over women. It affirms the dependence of women on men. Women work like hired labourers, as if they have to pay back the dowry. Payment of bride price is a major source of inequality. It also impoverishes the family of the groom. Alyanata and Basilika (2004) state that dowry is a source of marital pain, misery, hard work, misfortune and death.

Polygamy

Polygamy is a common practice among Africans for the following reasons:

(a) It provides status and support for women, thus it is a vocation for unemployed women.

(b) It enables more women to be married, should there be more women than men.

(c) It gives men prestige, as many children are produced, expanding the man's lineage.

(d) It is a source of security, especially for boys.

(e) It case one woman is indisposed; another can fulfill obligations and responsibilities towards the husband.

Consequences of polygamy

(a) It undermines equality between men and women since they are counted amongst men's possessions.

(b) More women have to share the man's property as its custodians, as they wait for the boys who inherit it.

(c) Women are dependent on men for most basics of life, yet in most cases polygamous men tend to ignore their wives and children to struggle on their own so as to make ends meet.

(d) It lowers women's self-esteem since many women have to bend low and compete for one 'bull in the kraal', at times the man may completely abandon some wives and their children.

(e) It causes conflicts and rivalry in families as different women compete to appease one man, and as they also struggle to get property from him.

(f) It creates extended families and large families which may be difficult to look after.

(g) It makes women work like beasts of burden so as to appease the man or if the man has neglected them.

(h) It hinders women's liberation since the wives compete to satisfy the husband.

(i) Men are frequently fed on many love potions by many wives that may affect their health.

(j)   One unfaithful partner may infect all the wives or husbands with HIV.

Religious teaching on polygamy

Islam supports polygamous marriages, but Christianity sanctions monogamy. Christianity's approach is based on Genesis 1:27-28, which states that man and woman were created to live together as partners united by mutual love and respect, therefore the ideal marriage should be monogamous and permanent. Equality is emphasised in marriage and the wife and the husband are partners with each other, with distinctive roles that complement one another. Equality in marriage is the will of God, polygamy was the result of sin and men's selfishness. Malachi 2.13-16 saw marriage as a covenant between two people and he condemned divorce. Hosea 2 emphasizes integrity, justice, tenderness and love in marriage. In the New Testament, Jesus called people to a faithful love; he offered people the power to love unselfishly. Jesus upheld the teaching of Genesis 1:26-28 on monogamous marriage. He emphasised the permanence of marriage and condemned divorce. In Mark 10:6-7 Jesus states that whoever divorces his wife and marries commits adultery. Jesus imbued couples with the courage to reconsider their relationships and begin a new life in the difficult process of loving faithfully and unselfishly.

Gender and Programme/Project Management

Reasons why gender must be integrated into programme/project management

- Lack of gender-related policies in organisations and institutions.
- Absence of gender-sensitive managers in organisations and institutions.
- Low importance assigned to gender issues by organisations and institutions.
- People who are knowledgeable about gender are threatened when they try to promote gender concerns.
- Lack of guidelines for integrating gender into programme/project management.

- Lack of knowledge and skills to deal with gender issues.
- Gender inequality in education, in terms of quantity and quality.
- Inadequate participation by women and marganalised groups in decision making, including inadequate participation by women due to their gender-physiological (domestic) roles.
- Women in rural areas do not have time to attend to activities not related to domestic work.
- Most poor people are women and this brings about inequality in society.
- Female-headed families are not acknowledged by society, therefore development planners tend to ignore these families.
- Cultural gender roles hamper development.
- Failure to acknowledge different income streams and expenditure priorities in households. The role of women in development cannot be understood without acknowledgement that men, women and children are active contributors to survival and progress and economic welfare in developing countries.

Effects of failing to integrate gender into programme/project management or development
- The entrenchment of patriarchy
- Persistent inequality in development
- Uneven access to and control of resources and benefits
- Inadequate community participation
- Unbalanced division of labour
- Low rating of women's economic contributions
- A persistently heavy workload for women
- Family incomes remain low
- Inadequate utilization of resources
- Persistence of high morbidity and mortality rates amongst children and women
- Persistence of high birth rates
- Family instability
- All the above finally lead to poor quality of life

Consequences of integrating women in development, planning and programme/project management

a)   The standard of living for girls, women and the disadvantaged would be improved in the areas of health: family planning, nutrition and immunisation of pregnant mothers.

b)   Improving access to education for women, especially literacy programmes for poor, rural or urban women; once they can read and write, can manage projects.

c)   Making projects accessible to women, who can then broaden their choices, especially regarding income-generating activities.

d)   Factoring gender into every activity would lead to involvement of women in all projects at all levels. This would present women with opportunities for participation in decision makings in all spheres of life – cultural, economic, religious, political and social. Government and non-government organisations should involve women in their programmes and projects.

e)   Discouraging traditional beliefs and customs that hinder women's participation in development, e.g. inheritance of property and men's low opinion of women.

f)   Adequate knowledge about gender issues and how women can be incorporated in development programmes.

Guidelines for Integrating Gender into Programme/ Project Management

Dissemination of information

The dissemination of information strategy aims at initiating and supporting the process of changing negative cultural and gender attitudes.

Relevant information must be developed and distributed to government institutions, non-governmental organisations, religious groups and private firms by means of material such as posters, newsletters and pamphlets.

Programme planners and implementers should be trained to use the information available.

Laws geared at reducing negative gender practices and discrimination against women and the marganalised groups must be advocated.

Education for girls and other marganalised groups should form the basis for reducing inequalities. Positive discrimination should be instituted over a limited period of time in favour of women and other marganalised groups to redress past inequalities.

Matters related to land and property ownership and inheritance must favour men and women equally. Decision-makers should be gender-sensitive and concerned about marganalised groups.

Relevant policies and regulations must be reviewed to determine whether policies and regulations are positive, negative or neutral regarding gender issues.

Relevant programmes must be reviewed and assessed regarding the extent to which they contain gender-relevant components, and what the impact of the programmes is on gender issues. Populations must be analysed by age, sex and occupation, also taking marganalised groups and migrants into account. Criteria for strategy design must include gender sensitivity. Other important criteria are concern about marganalised groups, relevance of strategies to the problems of both men and women.

Strategies and their components must focus on the most disadvantaged and marganalised groups, and address gender imbalances. Design management systems and structures should have a fair representation of both sexes. Outline monitoring and evaluation systems should address gender issues, evaluation teams should be gender sensitive and have a fair representation of both sexes and marganalised groups. The evaluation should be participatory. The feasibility of the proposed programme or project in relation to gender as well as its technical feasibility, acceptability and affordability must be assessed.

Programme or project justification should be gender-related and should benefit men, women, children and other marganalised groups. This involves producing a master document which takes into consideration all gender issues; establishing a schedule of activities which includes gender-orientation activities; paying attention to seasons, e.g. during the planting season women are very busy. Resource requirements must be specified and qualified in terms of gender. Budget must be expressed in terms of money and gender and staff must be paid according to skill, output and position and work, not according to sex.

How to implement a gender-based project or programme

a)   Someone who is gender-sensitive should approve the programme. Sensitize donors to gender issues. Review the document plan, including indicators that may have negative gender implications.

b)   Select or appoint a programme or project manager who is gender-sensitive and who is able to address gender issues in the programme or project. Clarify responsibilities, levels of authority and relationships; review whether the management system and structure respond to gender requirements, e.g. women's participation in the programme. Project management should consider women's access to resources. Prepare work plans which include gender orientation and take the season into consideration. Prepare gender-neutral job descriptions.

c)   Programme or project staff must include women. Staff should be motivated and appraisal, appointment, promotion or dismissal of staff should not exhibit gender bias. Arrange for and manage physical facilities in a way that discrimination does not enter into the allocation of office space. Physical facilities such as toilets should be gender-oriented. Design, implement and manage budgeting and finance accountability systems and avoid preferential access to resources. Trace funds for women and marganalised groups. Provide leadership, build teams, delegate without gender bias, be sensitive to cultural and gender relationships.

d)   Avoid decisions which are gender-biased. Communicate and conduct meetings, be gender-sensitive in speech and words used, encourage participation of both men and women. Coordinate the programme or project without gender bias. Provide guidance and supervision, be generous and encourage participation, appreciate contributions regardless of sex. Time management is very important, take into account the activity of profiles of men and women.

Monitoring and evaluating the project/programme

a) Review the monitoring system of the plan and ensure that it can generate the necessary information, including gender-specific results.

b) Design, implement and manage a programme/project management information system that is gender-neutral. Ensure that women and marganalised groups are involved in the collection and analysis of data. Ensure that information is accessible to all groups. Compare actual performance with the plan, paying special attention to gender issues.

c) Identify supporting and hampering factors, with special emphasis on gender-related factors. Formulate and decide on corrective action, inform relevant persons, groups and organisations and implement corrective action. Positive discrimination may be required temporarily.

d) Prepare, produce and circulate programme/project progress reports, including financial statements. Address gender issues in the reports. Prepare terms of reference, specify the gender issues to be addressed, select members of the evaluation team who are knowledgeable about, skillful regarding and sensitive to gender issues.

e) All the evaluation processes should address gender issues, as stipulated by the plan. The information obtained should be disseminated to all beneficiaries and interested parties.

Gender and Rural Development

Rural development strategies must emphasize marganalised groups or the rural poor in order to overcome poverty. Rural areas must be developed in terms of economy, communication, transport, agriculture and politics. The government, religious institutions and non government organisations must provide the rural poor with services like health centers, education, water, transport and security.

Loans, micro-finance projects and credit facilities should be made available to the rural poor irrespective of sex. If women in rural areas can access loans, they could reduce their dependence on men and improve the standards of living of their families. Projects must be implemented in rural areas so that marganalised people and women can become self-reliant. Non government organisations that are helping the poor should be represented in all rural areas e.g. UWESO, Send-a-Cow, World Vision, Action for Development, Compassion International etc.

Since the 1995 Beijing conference the phrase emancipation of women has been on the lips of modern women, but to what extent have rural women understood its implications? Emancipation programmes should be extended to rural areas, so that women understand their rights, roles and responsibilities, so that they can develop their families, societies and the nation at large.

Gender Issues That Could Hinder Rural Development

Traditionally, most African families are headed by men, thus men control the economy. Husbands are the decision makers and they control agricultural produce. In some societies, such as in Kigezi, men spend most of their time drinking and womanizing, while their wives and children do all the agricultural work. Harvested crops are sold by the men, who use the money obtained to buy alcohol and to marry more wives. Few women in rural areas see the income derived from their agricultural products. Sometimes, the loans given to women for investment in projects are claimed by their husbands because they are the heads of families.

Various traditional practices hinder the development of rural women. Women do not inherit property from either their families or husbands, and the issue of dowry impoverishes both men and women. Lack of opportunities, decision making and the existence of polygamy limit women's freedom of choice in economic terms. Ignorance, poverty and discrimination hinder rural development.

Traditional pride in large families contributes to rural backwardness. To achieve rural development women should be sensitised to the value of family planning. Women should produce the number of children they are able to care for. Having fewer children will enable women to participate in politics, projects and agriculture.

In some countries, state institutions create gender imbalances regarding rural development. These institutions tend to reinforce patriarchal dominance over the labour and earnings of women by limiting membership to co-operatives to heads of households, consequently women cannot receive seeds, credit or agricultural advice. Therefore families headed by women cannot access co-op services. In rural areas women work as beasts of burden, they cook, do all the domestic work, care for children, carry out all the agricultural work, collect firewood and water, graze the goats, etc yet their work is not recognised by men. Women's methods of farming must be improved, so that yields are increased and labour decreased.

Major Causes of Poverty among Women

- Income disparities between men and women. In some private-sector jobs, women earn less than men.
- Prevalence of female-headed households.Many families are headed by women who have low incomes and low education levels, yet with high fertility.
- Gender bias is still an issue. Some people are unwilling to employ women, some families are still unwilling to send girls to school, some non-governmental organisations do not give women loans. Women cannot control family property and other resources. Domestic work is unpaid labour.
- Many religions and cultures discourage women from contributing significantly to family income. Some men prohibit their wives from working because their financial contribution is insignificant while others fear that other men may abuse them sexually. Most government policies and programmes favour men. Traditional culture and legislation prohibit women from owning property.

Eradicating Gender Polarisation

Gender polarisation refers to the way social life is organised around the male-female distinction, the forging of a cultural connection between sex and virtually every other aspect of human experience, including modes of dress, social roles, ways of expressing emotion and experiencing sexual desire. The totality of human experience is divided into cultural categories on the basis of gender, so people of different sexes are culturally identified with different clothes, different social roles, different personalities or different sexual partners and friends, as indicated by gender polarisation. With complete gender depolarisation, the biology of sex becomes a minor presence in human social life.

Lipsitz (1993) observed that gender polarisation prevents men and women from developing their full potential as human beings and encourages androcentrism and patriarchy. She goes on to say that the division of human experience into the masculine and the feminine restricts potential in the following ways:

(a) Gender polarisation categorizes women and men into two homogeneous groups, rather than allowing someone to exhibit diversity that naturally exists within each sex, or the overlap that naturally exists between the two sexes.

(b) Gender polarisation transforms men and women into gender caricatures and thereby denies them the fullest measure of their human possibilities. In contrast, the essence of the specifically feminist objection to gender polarisation is that it aids and abets the social reproduction of male power by providing the fundamental division between masculine and feminine upon which androcentrism is built. Lipsitz (1993) comments that the antifeminist aspect of gender polarisation manifests itself at three levels, i.e. the institutional, the psychological and ideological levels:

- At the institutional level, gender polarisation aids and abets the social reproduction of male power by dichotomising the social world into the masculine domain of paid employment and the female domain of home and childcare, thereby sustaining a gender-based division of labour and obscuring the need for any institutional mechanism, like paid childcare, that would enable an individual to participate in both domains. As long as gender polarisation continues to ensure that there are different groups of people – male and female – who do different things, such a mechanism will continue to promote a sexual hierarchy by denying women access to economic and political power.

- At the psychological level, gender polarisation aids and abets the social reproduction of male power by dichotomising identity and personality into masculine and feminine categories, thereby providing a concept of psychological masculinity and femininity to which the culture readily assimilates its andocentric conceptions of power and powerless. The unholy alliance of androcentrism and gender polarisation predisposes men to construct identities around dominance and women to construct identities around deference.

- At the ideological level gender polarisation aids and abets the social reproduction of male power by prompting the cultural discourse to misrepresent the most blatant examples of sexual inequality. Gender polarisation enables religion, science, law, culture and the media to rationalize the sexual *status quo* in a way that automatically renders the lens of androcentrism invisible.

By polarizing human values and human experiences into masculine and feminine, gender polarisation retains culture in the grip of males and highly polarised masculine values. This gender polarisation must be addressed and this requires a social revolution in all aspects of life, by making laws that favour both sexes, rearranging social institutions and reframing cultural discourses. Gender depolarisation also requires a psychological revolution in the sense of who and what it involves being male and female, a profound alteration in peoples feelings about the meaning of biological sex and its relation to psyche and sexuality. This psychological revolution requires that the biological fact of being male and female is viewed in the same way the biological fact of being human is viewed; biological sex should not be at the core of individual identity and sexuality (Lipsitz Bem , 1993).

Gender, Technology, Agriculture, Environment and Development

Gender and Fuel Energy

To enhance women's development in society, the availability of fuel, which is problematic for rural women, must be addressed. Rural electrification should be the primary objective for most developing countries. Governments should provide subsidized power to all rural areas. The vast majority of people in rural areas depend on wood for fuel. The fact of poverty being gendered and the constitution of the household being patriarchal imply that the brunt of low levels of investment in basic infrastructure is borne disproportionately by the poor in general and by women in particular. The vast majority of rural women face energy shortages for cooking. The fuel crisis must be analysed from a gender perspective, because solving it would·mainly alleviate women's burdens.

The fuel crisis represents the failure of the political system to address the larger issues of marganalisation and subordination of groups by gender. Solving the problem of fuel would lead to gender equity; the effect of the fuel crisis is differential experiences for women and men. The issue of cooking energy and firewood availability has been relegated to the realm of women's issues and therefore deemed to be of peripheral importance.

Systems of land ownership and rural agricultural practices have a direct bearing on the availability of energy to the poor. Most poor people have no or only a few acres of land from which to harvest firewood, and commercial wood resources are inaccessible. In some districts, such as Kigezi, banana leaves and agricultural residues of all kinds are used as firewood.

Lack of cooking fuel leads to deforestation and soil erosion, which, in turn, leads to environmental degradation. Fuel shortage is a cause of the destruction of forest resources. Introduction of biogas in rural areas could make a significant contribution, e.g. banana peels, cow dung and other household organic waste should be utilized to provide fuel for cooking. Solar technology should be introduced in rural areas at a subsidised rate. (Pad Mini, 1999)

Gender and Agriculture

Seventy percent of agricultural produce in Uganda is the result of women's work. While women have, legally, the same rights as men in landholding and management, their effective and customary right to land and other resources at the local level is less secure. Few rural women are landowners. Equal rights to land ownership are only realised by educated women. Rural women, who are the main producers, have only inconsistent and temporary access to land. There is need to modernise rural agriculture in terms of provision of good seed, mechanization, application of fertilizers, removal of weeds and introduction of modern harvesting techniques.

The prime responsibility of most African women is considered to be participation in the family and household economy. When their husbands go to work in non-farm sectors, women's taking up of farm work is recognised as "reasonable" and "sensible". When the value of work is measured in commercial terms, women's work depreciates, as the market ascribes a low value to agricultural products and household work (Wang, 1999).

The agricultural work of women is not given due credit in terms of actual labour contribution. While men are engaged in more profitable non-farming activities, women's responsibilities in agriculture increase total family income by full use of family labour. However, there is no explicit wage that can measure women's contribution to total family income.

In spite of women's devotion to household farming, their share of income contributed to the household is not proportional to the labour effort contributed. In most societies, women think that they do the same amount of work as their husbands, but men evaluate their wives' contribution as much lower than their own.

Women still face the problem of raising standards of living through unrecognised farm labour. Use of machinery is a dream, and in places where it can be applied, water, transport and fuel remain obstacles.

Gender and Environment

The linkage between gender and environment has become a global issue in development. Feminists argue that the scientific revolution is a heralding era in which women and nature came to be dominated, controlled and exploited. The teachings of Genesis 1:28 commit humanity to a stewardship of, rather than dominion over, nature and fellow humans.

Jackson (1981) says, the female to a greater extent than the male is the prey of the species and human race has always sought to escape its specific destiny. The support of life became for man an activity and a project in the invention of the tool, but in maternity, woman remained closely bound to her body like an animal. It is male activity that in creative values has made of existence itself a value. This activity has prevailed over the confused forces of life. It has subdued nature and woman.

Land degradation and deforestation continue to rape nature. Environmentalism is a current development thinking and practice that is concerned with addressing the harsh realities of nature. Ecofeminists link nature with the woman and they oppose the domination and exploitation of both by culture.

Improving the rights and livelihood of women should embrace environmental care. Adverse effects of environmental degradation which fall particularly upon poor women should be addressed. In most societies, it is women and girls who collect wood for fuel. Stakeholders should electrify rural societies to reduce deforestation and ease the burden of women. The impact of environmental degradation is often greater on women because of the over-representation of female-headed household among the poor and because of gender-based division of labour within households, which allocate work such as firewood and water collection to women, tasks which become much more difficult with deforestation and falling water tables.

However, from a gender analysis viewpoint, the costs of degradation cannot be assumed to fall predominantly on women without investigating how the gender division of labour is contested and change under environmental stress. It must be recognised that women are frequently agents of environmental degradation because of family pressures to meet the basic needs of large families. Women know more about the environment because of the gender division of labour, which assigns them to many reproductive tasks, which bring them into daily contact with fields, forests and rivers. Women possess knowledge of plants, animals and the ecological processes around them, a reason why they should be harnessed to conserve the environment.

It is undeniable that, to ensure that progress is an enduring reality in most societies, including Uganda, the living conditions of women, who form the majority in any social group and are ranked among the most vulnerable, must be improved. This vulnerability is illustrated by their lack of an alternative fuel source, food insecurity and all forms of risk to which they are subjected on a daily basis. A sustainable development concept is intimately linked with concerns related to natural resources and the environment, which should be managed properly to avoid endangering the growth and potential for future generations (Tambouka, 2002).

The fight against female poverty through environmental protection should take three essential elements into account:
a) The role of women in environmental degradation.
b) The impact of environmental degradation on the precarious economic situation or on female poverty.
c) The role of women in the sustainable management of natural resources and the environment.

Tambouka (2002) explains that, as harvesters of forestry resources (wood), women determine the functioning of the economic mechanism, while they remain victims of their poverty and task-sharing within the household. Indeed, they are compelled to play this role because of the responsibilities they carry within the family. They are in charge of cooking, thus have to find the required energy, therefore they collect wood fuel. Plunged in this hopeless situation, they find themselves in a vicious circle of poverty; their activity degrades the vegetation, making nature less clement to them. They become poorer than before and exploit the forest even more, thus subjecting it to more intense degradation.

Tambouka (2002) says that the demand must be reduced so that restoration through plantation and reforestation activities can be effected. Stakeholders should involve women in tree planting and soil conservation and also provide alternatives for women to meet their fuel and nutritional needs. Cheap rural electrification should be the goal of government planners.

Women have an essential role to play in the development of sustainable and ecologically sound and productive patterns and approaches to natural resource management. Awareness of resource depletion, the degradation of natural systems and the dangers of pollutants has increased markedly in the past decade. These worsening conditions are destroying fragile ecosystems and displacing communities, especially women, from productive activities, and pose an increasing threat to a safe and healthy environment. For example, Uganda's National Environment Management Authority (NEMA) has displaced people from wetlands and forest resources like Ngahinga, Kibale forest, Mabira. Worst affected are women, who have nowhere to cultivate crops and collect firewood. A major cause of the continued deterioration of the global environment is the unsustainable pattern of consumption and production, especially by industrialized countries, aggravating poverty and imbalances. A rise in the sea level as a result of global warming poses a grave and immediate threat to people living on islands and in coastal areas. The use of ozone-depleting substances such as products with chloroflurocarbons, halons and methyl bromides, from which plastics and foams are made, are affecting the atmosphere seriously. This allows excessive levels of harmful ultraviolet rays to reach the earth's surface. This affects people's health severely, as evidenced by higher rates of skin cancer, eye damage and weakened immune systems. It also has severe effects on the environment, including harm to crops and ocean life.

Hurricanes, typhoons and other natural disasters, destruction of resources, displacement and other effects associated with war, armed conflict, the use and testing of nuclear weapons and foreign occupation can also contribute to environmental degradation. The deterioration of natural resources displaces communities, especially women, from income-generating activities, while adding greatly to unremunerated work in both urban and rural areas. Environmental degradation has negative effects on the health, well-being and quality of life of the population at large, especially girls and women of all ages. Natural hazards, wars and diseases affect women more than men.

Non-governmental organisations and governments should pay attention to the roles and special situations of women living in rural areas and those working in the agricultural sector, where training, land, natural and productive resources, credit, development programmes and cooperative structures can help women increase their participation in sustainable development. Environmental risks in the home and workplace may have a disproportionate impact on women's health. These risks to women's health are particularly high in urban areas and low-income areas where there is a high concentration of polluting industrial facilities.

Through the management and use of natural resources women provide sustenance to their families and community. As consumers, producers, educators and caretakers of their families, women play an important role in promoting sustainable development through their concern for the quality and sustainability of life for present and future generations. According to Pad Mini (1999), Governments have expressed their commitment to creating a new development paradigm that integrates environmental sustainability with gender equality and justice within and between generations.

According to the Beijing Platform (2005), women remain largely absent at all levels of policy-formulation and decision making about natural resources and environmental management, conservation, protection and rehabilitation. Their experience and skills regarding advocacy for the monitoring of proper natural resource management, too, often remain marganalised in policy-making and decision-making bodies, as well as at the managerial level in educational institutions and environment-related agencies. Women are rarely trained as professional natural managers with policy-making capacities such as planners, agriculturalists, foresters, marine scientists and environmental lawyers.

In cases where women are trained as professional natural resource managers, they are often underrepresented in formal institutions with policy-making capacities at the national, regional and international levels. Women are seldom equal participants in the management of financial and corporate institutions whose decision-making affects environmental quality significantly. Furthermore, institutional weaknesses exist in coordinating women's non-governmental organisations and national institutions dealing with environmental issues, despite the recent rapid growth of women's non-governmental organisations working on these issues at all levels.

Women can play leadership roles in promoting an environmental ethic, reducing use of, re-using and recycling resources to minimize work and excessive consumption. Women can have a powerful role in influencing sustainable consumption decisions. Women's contributions to environmental management, including the use of grassroots and youth campaigns to protect the environment, have always taken place at the local level, where decentralized action on environmental issues is most needed.

Women, especially indigenous women, have particular knowledge of ecological linkages and fragile ecosystem management. In many communities women provide the main labour force for subsistence production, hence their role is crucial to the provision of food and nutrition, the enhancement of subsistence and informal sectors and the preservation of the environment. In some regions women are the only stable members of the community, as men go to work in distant locations or urban areas, leaving women to safeguard the natural environment and to ensure adequate and sustainable resource allocation within the household and the community.

The strategic action needed for sound environmental management requires a holistic, multidisciplinary and intersectional approach. Women's participation and leadership are essential to every aspect of that approach. The government policy of gender mainstreaming should address these issues of gender inequality in all programmes. Research has shown that sustainable development policies that do not involve both women and men will fail in the long run. They have therefore called for the effective participation of women in the generation of knowledge and environmental education and in decision making and management at all levels. Women's experiences and contribution to an ecologically sound environment must therefore be central to the government Ten-Point Programme of the National Resistance Movement of Uganda. Sustainable development will be an elusive goal unless women's contribution to environmental management is recognised and supported. Governments and other role players should promote an active and visible policy of mainstreaming a gender perspective into all policies and programmes. To promote gender equity in environmental management, governments and other role players like NGOs should:

(i)   Involve women actively in environmental decision making at all levels as managers, planners, implementers and evaluators of environmental programmes and projects.

(ii) Facilitate and increase women's access to information, education, science, technology and economics and exposure of all types, thus enhancing their knowledge, skills and opportunities for participation in environmental decisions.

(iii) Reduce environmental risks that women encounter at home, workplaces and other environments.

(iv) Empower women as producers and consumers so that they can take objective environmental actions, along with men, in their home communities and workplaces.

(v)   Integrate a gender perspective in the design and implementation of, among other things, environmentally sound and sustainable resource management mechanisms, production techniques and infrastructural development in rural and urban areas.

(vi) Encourage social, economic and scientific institutions to address environmental degradation and the resulting impact on women.

(vii) Sensitise women about environmental and natural resource management issues and degradation, thus providing information to contribute to resource mobilisation for environmental protection and conservation.

(viii) Facilitate the access of women agriculturalists, fishers and pastoralists to knowledge, skills on marketing services and environmentally sound technologies to support and strengthen women's crucial roles and their expertise in resource management and conservation of biological diversity.

(ix) Integrate women, their perspectives and their knowledge equally with men in decision making on sustainable resource management and the development of policies and programmes for sustainable development, in particular those designed to address and prevent environmental degradation. Ensure adequate research to assess how and to what extent women are susceptible or exposed to environmental degradation and hazards, including to research and data collection on specific groups of women, especially those with low income, indigenous women and those belonging to minority groups.

(x) Evaluate policies and programmes in terms of environmental impact and women's equal access to and use of natural resources.

(xi) Integrate rural women's traditional knowledge and practices of sustainable resource use and management in the development of environmental management and extension.

(xii) Promote knowledge of and sponsor research into the role of women, particularly rural and indigenous women, in food production and gathering, soil conservation, irrigation, watershed management, sanitation, coastal management, integrated pest management, land-use planning, forest conservation, land fertilisation, fisheries, natural disaster prevention and new sources of energy, while focusing on indigenous women's knowledge and experience.

(xiii) Eliminate obstacles to women's full and equal participation in sustainable development and equal access to and control over resources.

(xiv) Promote the education of girls and women of all ages in science technology, economic and other disciplines in relation to the natural environment, so that they can make informed choices and offer informed input in determining local economics, scientific and environmental priorities for the management and appropriate use of natural and local resources and ecosystems.

(xv) Develop programmes to involve female professionals and scientists as well as technical, administrative and clerical workers, in environmental management; develop training programmes for girls and women in these fields; expand opportunities for the girls and promote women in these fields; and implement special measures to advance women's expertise and participation in these activities.

(xvi) Identify and promote environmentally sound technologies that have been designed, developed and improved in consultation with women and that are appropriate to both women and men.

(xvii) Ensure that women have access to fuel and clean water to promote environmental protection

(xviii) Involve women in the communication industry to raise awareness regarding environmental issues, especially the environmental and health impacts of products, technologies and industrial processes.

8

Gender Mainstreaming and Development

There is growing need to address global issues that affect women and children, among which are conflict and terrorism, refugee camps, HIV/Aids, human trafficking, domestic violence, prostitution, rape, unwanted pregnancies and marriage, large-scale natural disasters and environmental problems. Since gender inequality is a reality, promoting gender equality and women's empowerment and undertaking activities from a gender perspective are crucial in the joint efforts by the international community towards the achievement of the Millennium Development Goals (MDGS).

In the field of international cooperation since 1980, the gender and development (GAD) approach has become increasingly important, as has Women-in-Development, a development approach working to improve the status of women in developing countries. The GAD approach seeks to analyze the causes of gender inequality within the context of relations between women and men and social structures, to effect changes in stereotyped divisions of laboured institutions and systems that encourage gender disparity. The GAD approach emphasizes empowerment of economically and socially disadvantaged women while considering the role of men in eliminating gender inequality. The 1995 Beijing Conference stressed the importance of gender mainstreaming as means of establishing the GAD approach (http://www.mota.Jp.policy/Oda.category/wid/gadhtml, page 2 of 7).

Gender mainstreaming is a process in which women's and men's development challenges and needs as well as development impacts on both men and women are clarified throughout the process of formulation, project planning implementation, monitoring and evaluation, on the premise that all policies, interventions and projects have different impacts on men and women.

It is important to incorporate a gender equality perspective into all development policies, including those that do not directly target women. Development assistance can be implemented more effectively and efficiently if the differences in livelihood situations and needs of both sexes are addressed as part of planning and implementation. In the process of gender mainstreaming the formulation and implementation of laws, policies, interventions and projects in all fields, such as the political, economical or social, have to be monitored and evaluated, bearing in mind that men and women will participate in and benefit from development equally if the existing gender inequality is abolished.

ESIP (1998-2003) defines mainstreaming, a gender perspective, as the process of assessing the implications for women and men of any planned action including legislation, policies and programmes in all areas and at all levels. It is a strategy for integrating women's and men's concerns and experiences into the design, implementation, monitoring and evaluation of policies and programmes in all political, economic, educational and societal spheres, so that women and men benefit equally and inequality is not perpetuated. The ultimate goal of gender mainstreaming is to achieve gender equality, namely to:

- Identify existing gaps between the genders.
- Promote and carry out gender-oriented research in order to identify gender concerns.
- Establish gender-responsive monitoring and evaluation mechanisms for development.
- Make a conscious effort to address gender disparities.
- Develop policies that promote gender responsiveness.
- Transfer practical skills to those involved in mainstreaming gender.
- Promote a gender-sensitive approach to technical cooperation among the various actors in the development arena.
- Advocate gender equity at all levels.

These strategies for mainstreaming gender are admirable, but may remain mere theories if governments do not put in effort to implement them.

Gender mainstreaming takes into account gender concerns and issues in all policies, programmes, administrative and financial activities and in contributing to profound organisational transformation. By contrast, a radical sense of the term mainstreaming is used by those who see women's development as being essentially concerned with women's participation and empowerment to address issues of gender inequality. From this perspective, the mainstreaming of gender issues entails the transformation of the development process. A gender perspective takes into account the fact that human society is comprised of men and women, girls and boys and that gender roles and status are socially constructed. The perspective enables the identification of gaps and disparities as they pertain to the situation of both males and females. It also views both genders as development partners and targets strategic interventions at both to induce greater acceptability and sustainability (UNICEF, 2002).

Tanzarn (2004) defines gender mainstreaming as a dimension that is explicit and verifiable at institutional and operational levels, including phases of policy formulation, identification, design, appraisal, implementation and evaluation. Ebila and Musiimenta (2004) define gender as a process of integrating gender concerns into every aspect of an organisation's priorities and procedures. It is a process rather than a goal that is undertaken to achieve gender equality. It is not an end in itself, but is intended to transform agenda setting and integrate gender concerns into the mainstream of existing practices within institutional policy, programme initiatives, project approval processes and funded researches. In this context gender mainstreaming comprises two major aspects:

(i) Integrating gender into analyses and formulation of all policies, plans, programmes and projects which are politically, socially and economically just.

(ii) Initiatives intended to enable girls and women as well as boys and men to formulate and express their views and participate in decision making across all programmes and institutional issues.

Gender mainstreaming is significant for our society because it enhances gender equity, justice and efficiency as far as development is concerned. Approaches to gender mainstreaming include challenging gender inequality and inequity through analysis, tools and actions to change and improve the condition and position of girls and women as well as marganalised boys and men in society.

Uganda's National Gender Policy and Gender Mainstreaming

Uganda's National Gender Policy is concerned with guiding and directing all levels of planning, resource allocation and implementation of development programmes within a gender perspective. The policy emphasizes gender as a key factor in the planning process because in Uganda, as a patriarchal society, men are the dominant players in decision making, yet women shoulder most reproductive and community management activities. Women comprise more than half of the population but are under-represented in decision making. The policy aims at mainstreaming women's development, which entails addressing gender issues and concerns in all development projects, programmes and institutions. Gender mainstreaming involves integrating gender issues into existing programmes which involve adaptation and transformation of the development process, in order to address issues of gender inequality.

Gender equity and harmonization of gender concerns with other disciplines are challenges facing Uganda's society. The overall goal of the National Gender Policy is to mainstream gender concerns into the national development process in order to improve the educational, social, legal, political, religious, cultural and economic conditions of the people of Uganda, but in particular women (The Ministry of Gender and Community Development, 1997). The purpose of this policy is to mainstream all levels, including planning, resource allocation and implementation of development programmes, with a gender perspective. The emphasis on gender is based on recognizing that gender as a development concept plays a role in identifying and understanding the social roles and relations of women and men of all ages, and determining how it impacts on development. Sustainable development necessitates maximum and equal participation of both genders in the process of development.

From 1998 to 2003 the government of Uganda embarked on mainstreaming gender into the Educational Strategic Investment Plan (ESIP). Its major emphasis was the Universal Primary Education Policy, which was introduced in 1997. The Education Strategic Plan was formulated within the national context of eradicating poverty. Provision of equal opportunities for marganalised groups was expressed in very broad policy terms through Universal Primary Education, which was the key education programme, and the institution of equity measures to eliminate gender, regional and social inequities.

Additional opportunities and challenges facing the National Gender Policy were brought about by the decentralization process, which commenced in 1992 and was made concrete by the Local Governments Act of 1997. Administrative powers have been allocated to local governments at the district and sub-county levels, so that they have powers over sectors like education, recruitment of staff in various fields, financial management and managing various programmes. Gender-responsive planning is one of the key requirements for policy implementation to promote gender equity.

The National Gender Policy, is defined as the process of assessing the implications for women and men of any planned action, including legislation, policies and programmes in all areas and at all levels (ESIP, 1997). The ultimate goal of the National Gender Policy is to achieve gender equality.

Statistics show that, although women in Uganda constitute 80% of the agricultural labour force, only 7% own land and only 30% have access to and control over land. Women's productivity is further hampered by inadequate access to credit and a general lack of skills and appropriate technology due to a high level of illiteracy, poverty and inadequate flow of and access to information. Few women qualify for loans from the traditional financial institutions because they do not have collateral. The National Gender Policy (1997) quotes a survey on women's participation in the Rural Farmer's Scheme of the Uganda Commercial Bank in 1992, which revealed that, of the 27,233 women who applied for assistance as individuals, only 5,117 were assisted. Of the women who applied in groups, 1,616 in total, only 335 women's groups were assisted, and of mixed groups comprising 50% women, the bank assisted only 727 out of the 2,116 applicants.

The main aim of the National Gender Policy is to address gender imbalances, which are evident in the educational, economical, politic, health and employment sectors. The Population and Housing Census of 1991 shows that illiterates comprised 61.3% women and 38.7% men. According to the Education Review Commission Report, primary level enrolment is 80% for both sexes, but female participation declines progressively, leaving around 22.8% of women to enter higher institutions of learning. Gender imbalances are equally evident in the health sector. Uganda's health indicators reveal that the health status of the population, particularly that of women and children, is very poor. According to the Population and Housing Census of 1991, life expectancy is 50.5 years for men and 45 years for women. The Demographic Health Survey (1995) puts the fertility rate at 6.9% and the maternal mortality rate at 50 per 100,000 live births. Infant mortality is estimated at 97 deaths per 1,000 live births. In addition, the HIV/Aids pandemic has compounded the situation and the most vulnerable to this scourge are women.

According to the Uganda Manpower Survey of 1988, women make up about 20% of formal sector employees and are mainly found in low-paying jobs. According to the National Gender Policy (1997) decision making is still predominantly a male domain. At ministerial level, only six out of the total 54 ministers were women (11%). In the civil service, at the permanent secretary level, women make up only 19.4% of the total number of employees. Out of 39 Chief Administrative Officers (CAOs) only five were women. There were 51 women representatives in Parliament, constituting 18.5%. In the 1994 Constituent Assembly, out of 256 delegates, only 49 were women.

Although the government has instituted measures to promote gender equity, there is much still to be done in terms of sensitisation, education, improving staff welfare, especially of medical workers in health centers, and empowering women in the fields of decision making and poverty reduction.

Through the implementation of the decentralization policy, gender issues should be recognised as part and parcel of sustainable development. Mainstreaming gender concerns into the national development process should be a key factor in improving the educational, economic, social, political and cultural conditions of people, especially women.

According to the Ministry of Gender and Community Development (1997), the objectives of the National Gender Policy are to:

(i) Provide policy-makers and other key actors in the development field with specific reference to identifying and addressing gender concerns when taking development policy decisions.

(ii) Identify and establish an institutional framework with the mandate to initiate, coordinate, implement, monitor and evaluate national gender-responsive development plans.

(iii) Redress imbalances which arise from existing gender inequalities.

(iv) Ensure the participation of both women and men in all stages of development.

(v) Promote equal access to and control over economically significant resources and benefits.

(vi) Promote the recognition and value of women's roles and contributions as agents of change and beneficiaries of the development process. It should be noted that the government of Uganda has taken into consideration Gender and Women in Development issues, which are now being promoted as part of sustainable development.

The Role of the Ministry of Gender, Labour and Community Development in the Implementation of Uganda's National Gender Policy

The government of Uganda created a national department, which is the Ministry of Gender, Labour and Community Development, charged with the responsibility of spearheading and coordinating development and ensuring improvement of women's status. The Ministry must establish and chair a multi-steering committee and to strengthen this, especially the coordinating and collabourative role. It is mandated to coordinate, monitor and review the formulation of gender-responsive policies and their implementation within sectors.

According to the Ministry of Gender, Labour and Community Development (1997) the role of this ministry is to:

(i)   Ensure that the national development process is gender responsive.

(ii) Ensure that all policy formulation and reviews, action plans and other major national planning exercises apply a gender-responsive planning approach.

(iii) Liaise with other sectors in identifying and drawing attention to key gender concerns and related needs, e.g. property ownership, land tenure, credit, legal rights etc. and addressing them in the constitution and in the process of law reform.

(iv) Ensure that the national machinery, together with other actors, play an advocacy role in the promotion of gender equity.

(v)   Provide technical guidance and backup to other institutions. This will include promotion of gender analysis and planning skills among all relevant sections of the society in order to build their capacity to identify, analyze and implement gender-responsive programme interventions.

(vi) Liaise with relevant agencies and coordinate the collection and dissemination of gender-disaggregated data necessary for national development.

(vii) Promote social mobilisation for the purpose of creating gender awareness and thus foster the positive attitudinal and behavioural change necessary for the establishment and maintenance of gender equity.

(viii) Monitor the progress made towards achieving gender-responsive national development targets, in cooperation with other key actors.

Approaches and Strategies for Achieving the Policy of Gender Mainstreaming

Mainstreaming strategies are being adopted by development cooperation agencies and institutions of higher learning, like Makerere University, as a means of supporting efforts to achieve equality between men and women. Yet, even with carefully formulated policies, design and procedures, projects have made minor contributions to changing gender equalities. Equality advocates from both within and outside development agencies have argued that gender disparities need to be addressed at the level of policy, selection of priority areas and overall programme design. One way of understanding gender mainstreaming is to differentiate three targets as institutional areas for action (Goetz, 1997):

(i)   The state, its institutions, laws, government policies and programmes, all with the eventual goal of supporting equality between men and women.

(ii) Development and cooperation programmes, either with partner governments or multilateral organisations.

(iii) The agency itself, its structures and procedures.

Goetz (1977) developed a gendered archaeology of organisations comprising eight elements, which are intended to help in assessing the gender sensitivity of organisations and institutions:

(i)   Institutional and organisational history
(ii) The gender-cognitive context
(iii) Gendered organisational culture
(iv) Gendered participation
(v)   Gendered space and time
(vi) The sexuality of organisations

(vii)   Gendered authority structures

(viii)   Gendered incentives and accountability

Goetz (1997) observes that, in recent times, organisations oriented towards social and human development have been more open to the inclusion of gender perspectives. Gender participation approaches may be a means through which grassroots constituencies and field staff can influence policy decision making to take gender into account. She stresses that, when women are involved in public affairs, the problem of sexual harassment undercuts the identity and effectiveness of women as autonomous and equal public agencies. In general, working women struggle to integrate their work and family lives. The greater significance assigned to male achievements and forms of expression as a consequence of their monopoly in organisations is reflected in organisational value systems and the gendering of particular skills in the symbols of authority. Gendered authority systems affect the nature of relationships between males and females. Men as husbands are the power brokers mediating relations between the household and the outside world. Husbands are generally contacted by their wives for permission to work outside the home.

Gender accountability can be defined as responsiveness to women's interests and the incorporation of gender-sensitive policies, programmes and projects into state institutions and donor agencies. Incentives are usually expressed quantitatively in measurable performance targets, rather than qualitative matters such as promoting empowerment processes. Feminists should use government development and democratization processes to promote gender equity at international level and to express their demands to their own governments. Soliciting women's views on the new constitution and its review in Uganda in the 2000s is an example of an effort made to exploit government and international commitment to extending opportunities for political participation by women.

The influence of supportive donors such as the Nordic countries and Canada have emerged as significant in influencing multilateral organisations such as UNDP, the World Bank and ILO to support gender mainstreaming and WID/GAD issues. In these three organisations, pressure to institutionalize gender mainstreaming has led to the establishment of a range of new organisations with broad powers to mainstream gender training, gender guidelines or tools and new monitoring and evaluation mechanisms (Goetz, 1997).

Development institutions, such as Makerere University, have undertaken initiatives to direct more resources to women and to promote greater attention to issues of gender equality between women and men in the programmes and projects they sponsor. Mainstreaming gender into institutions of higher learning is intended to address inequality issues that exist within institutions. Subsequently, a number of strategies have emerged to bring women into the mainstream and institutionalize women's concerns into development programmes. These include:

(i)   Strengthening women's groups and organisations to ensure gender awareness by acting as pressure groups and monitoring implementation of mainstreaming gender activities.

(ii) Gender awareness and analysis training.

(iii) Promoting a critical mass of women inside development organisations.

(iv) Lobbying and exerting pressure on development institutions.

(v)   Political strategy entries. This is defined as a sustained attempt to enter and gradually transform the host organisation from within, changing its procedures, goals and culture along lines that are more equitable.

(vi) An agenda-setting approach that implies transformation of the existing development agenda to one with a gender perspective. The participation of women as decision-makers in determining development priorities is the key strategy. Women should participate in all development activities and through this process bring about fundamental change in existing development paradigms (Goetz, 1997).

Ministry of Gender Labour and Social Development (1997), provides the following strategies for achieving its objectives of mainstreaming gender concerns:

(i)   Raising sensitivity and consciences on gender issues at all levels.

(ii) Promoting a gender-responsive and development (GRD) approach that is based on an understanding of gender roles and social relations between women and men as well as the Women-in-Development (WID) approach, which focuses on women specifically.

(iii) Ensuring that gender policy is disseminated, translated, understood and implemented by all sections of Ugandan society.

(iv) Promoting appropriate education, sensitisation and creation of awareness of the responsibility of all concerned parties in each sector to address the specific concerns of a sector. This should entail consultation with both men and women in specific areas of relevance to the identification of gender concerns.

(v)   Ensuring gender-responsive development planning at all levels, both district and national.

(vi) Promoting a holistic and integrated approach to development planning to ensure that gender issues common to different sectors are identified, analysed and addressed.

(vii) Encouraging all institutions of learning to incorporate gender concerns into their curriculums, from primary schools to institutions of higher learning.

(viii) Promoting policies that address the issues of sexual harassment in offices, classrooms, compounds, public places, churches, homes, etc.

Specific Approaches to Gender Mainstreaming

Strengthening gender analysis and promoting women's participation

The factors that affect gender inequality are complex, comprising economic structure, politics, religion, culture, society, history and geography of any given country or region. For governments or NGOs to achieve impacts that are equitably beneficial for both men and women, sex-disaggregated information on beneficiary groups, needs and project impact should be assessed during the project planning process. From this perspective integration of a gender perspective into ex-ante evaluation should be strengthened and studies and research relating to analysis of women's social and economic roles and situations should be implemented as the need arises. Government and other actors should promote participation in decision making at the planning and implementation stages of policies, projects and programmes.At implementation of these projects and programmes, progress must be monitored, evaluated and effective feedback, based on a gender perspective, given.

Providing assistance to policies and institutions that promote gender equality

Governments, NGOs and the international community should reinforce the efforts of developing countries towards realising international commitments to achieve empowerment of women and gender equality as stated in the Beijing Declaration and Platform of Action and the Convention on the Elimination of All Forms of Discrimination against Women (CEDAW). International and national communities should assist with the formulation of national policy on the advancement of women. National machinery must be strengthened institutionally by establishing a legal and institutional framework from a gender perspective, upgrading gender statistics, raising gender awareness among government officials through gender training and developing and strengthening gender research centers.

Gender capacity-building

The government, NGOs and the international community should support institutions of higher learning in training gender-sensitive people who will disseminate information on gender issues. In these institutions, action should be taken to raise awareness regarding gender issues. They should also promote and effect gender mainstreaming in institutions of higher learning, monitor progress and gauge extent to which gender mainstreaming is addressing gender concerns.

Addressing poverty issues

Regarding gender mainstreaming, poverty is an issue that requires a multi-dimensional response. Poverty is caused by economic factors such as low income and expenditure, social and political factors, as exemplified by the lack of access to basic social services such as education and public health, and lack of opportunities to participate in decision making. Gender inequality persists in many spheres, such as the economy, society and politics. Research shows that, among the 1.1 billion people globally who are poor, 70% are women, who also account for two-thirds of the illiterate population in the world. While considering gender mainstreaming, governments should formulate policies that aim at poverty reduction, improve women's access to all services and welfare opportunities and promote the participation of women in decision-making processes, so that women and men can benefit equally. Governments should ensure equal access to education for all and, through the creation of a social and economic environment that is gender-friendly, enable girls to attain the highest possible levels of education. Governments and NGOs should eliminate gender disparities in literacy, enrollment, school dropout and completion rates. There is need for a gender-sensitive education law, in institutions and education policies, and development of educational software to promote gender equality and empowerment of women. Gender training of all education administrators and teachers is necessary, to promote an understanding of gender and teaching methods. Stakeholders should also promote awareness in communities, including parents and decision-makers in regions, concerning the importance of education for girls.

Governments and NGOs should work to eliminate disparities in health that are a result of gender, such as the disparity in access to medical and health services or the vulnerability of women to sexually transmitted diseases such as HIV/Aids.

Governments and NGOs should ensure equal access to good quality and affordable medical and health services, that information and education concerning family planning and reproductive health are disseminated to men, women, families and local communities, that maternal and child health services for reducing infant and maternal mortality, especially in rural areas, is strengthened and that institutions and medical facilities that support women's life-long health are established.

To achieve gender mainstreaming, the government should develop rural areas by building feeder roads and fostering agriculture, forestry, fishery and rural development. The role of women in production tends to be underestimated and women are unable to utilize productive resources because they do not have rights to own or inherit land. Moreover, in Uganda, the role of women in agriculture is increasing further, because men migrate to cities to work or move away and join armies to fight wars. The government should strengthen the agricultural sector by modernisation, use of fertilizers, mechanization, cross-breeding, seed improvement and application of modern methods of agriculture.

Sustainable Growth

While drawing up gender mainstreaming policies and programmes, stakeholders should realise that economic policies and the development of socio-economic infrastructure for achieving sustainable growth may affect men and women differently. To achieve gender equality, policies or projects which are planned should incorporate a gender perspective. Different living conditions and needs of women and men must be analysed and taken into account at the planning stage. Thus it is important to have men and women participate equally in decision-making processes at the planning stages of projects, so that the benefits can be shared equally by men and women.

Governments should promote planning and implementation of programmes based on a gender perspective, to ensure that the necessary measures are taken. Governments should establish measures to redress gender inequality resulting from differences in labour conditions such as wages, access to occupations and the formulation of trade and investment policies that benefit poor women. Governments and other sectors should build the capacity of women to expand their opportunities in industry and other employment sectors, promoting women entrepreneurs and micro-finance programmes that target women, promote rights and legal protection of female workers in formal and informal sectors and making work and family life compatible for both women and men.

Addressing Global Issues

A gender mainstreaming approach should have a gender perspective incorporated in its actions to address global issues, like natural disasters, floods, earth quakes, drought, environmental issues such as land degradation and environmental pollution; human right issues; diseases like HIV/Aids, malaria, measles and tuberculosis; violence and human trafficking, etc. Stakeholders should analyze the needs of men and women, to identify and eliminate factors which may threaten women, as well as traditions, religions and customs which are harmful to and discriminatory against women. Stakeholders should conserve the environment and promote measures to protect it .

Promotion of Human Rights

Stakeholders should institute legislation and achieve substantive gender equality based on the Convention on the Elimination of All Forms of Discrimination against Women (CEDAW) and other international human rights documents on issues regarding violence against women, which has its background in traditional religions, gender stereotypes and violation of human rights. Abuse against women should be addressed. Governments and other actors should advocate for women's human rights, elimination of prejudice and discrimination against women. Governments and other actors should reject traditional practices that violate the human rights of women.

Stakeholders should develop comprehensive laws and set up institutions to fight trafficking in persons, prostitution, pornography etc. Legal systems, organisations or shelters for support and protection of victimised women and children should be established.

Achieving Peace

To achieve gender equality in all spheres, gender mainstreaming should be concerned with incorporating women into peace-building processes. Conflicts, like the war in Northern Uganda, has created a large number of displaced persons, lead to sexual violence and abduction, forced marriages and pregnancies, deprivation of rights and freedoms and injury and death from landmines and small arms.

These consequences affect women differently from men, as exemplified by the fact that women are more likely to be victims of violence.

During post-conflict periods, social integration of widows and discharged women soldiers are accorded low priority. Women become victims of physical violence from husbands suffering from post-war trauma. Stakeholders should reflect on the needs of women and men by taking actions that incorporate a gender perspective at all stages of peace-building.

The government and other stakeholders should protect women from sexual abuse in conflict situations and provide support to aid recovery from post-traumatic stress. Refugees, especially women, should be supported by the provision of food, sanitary facilities, clean water and security. Women should participate in decision-making in peace processes to bring about security and peace in war-torn areas.

Challenges of Gender Mainstreaming

Tanzarn (2004) outlines the following challenges to gender mainstreaming:

(i)   Limited awareness, resulting in a misconception that gender mainstreaming is intended to promote alien western culture.
(ii) The misconception that gender concerns are women's concerns.
(iii) The misconception that gender mainstreaming is meant for the elite rather than rural people who are poor.
(iv) Men fear that it might reverse the social order and promote female privilege, thus some people resist change owing to deeply ingrained cultures, norms and values.
(v)   Some ministries and institutions are insensitive to gender policies.
(vi) Inadequate gender-disaggregated data to inform policy-makers so that they can take enlightened action.
(vii) Limited gender capacities of decision makers in administration.
(viii) Governments, NGOs and policy makers face constraints in terms of inadequate technical and financial resources.

Gender Planning: A Strategy for Meeting Gender Needs

Moser (1989) says that, while the role women play in most societies is widely recognised, conceptual awareness of the issues of gender and development has not resulted in planning practice. Absence of an adequate operational framework has been problematic. A gender planning approach which takes into account the fact that women and men play different roles in society and therefore have different needs, provides both the conceptual framework and the methodological tools for incorporating gender into planning.

Gender planning relates to the identification of women's triple roles (Reproduction, Production, and Community work) and the distinction between practical and strategic gender needs. It illustrates the capacity of planning interventions to meet gender needs, with examples from such sectors as employment, housing and basic services. It provides a critique of a number of different policy approaches to women and development from the perspective of gender planning and identifies the potential and limitations of each approach for meeting the needs of the low-income earners, especially in Third World countries.

Moser (1989) says that the United Nations Decade for Women (1976-85) played a crucial role in highlighting and publicizing the important but often invisible role of women in the economic and social development of their countries and communities and the plight of low-income women in Third World countries.

Policy-makers have started to shift their focus from a universal concern with welfare-oriented, family-centered programmes, which assumed motherhood as the most important role for women in the development process, to a diversity of approaches emphasizing the productive role of women. Women are an untapped resource that can make an economic contribution to development. This has an important influence on popularizing income-generating projects for women. The focus on gender rather than women was originally developed by feminists, who were concerned about the manner in which women's problems were perceived in terms of women's sex, i.e. the biological differences between women and men, rather than in terms of their gender, i.e in terms of the social relationship between men and women, a relationship within which women have been systematically subordinated.

For states to plan for gender, they need to stress gender awareness approaches which are concerned with the manner in which relationships are socially constructed.Men and women play different roles in society, their gender differences are shaped by ideological, historical, religious, ethnic, economic and cultural determinants. Few authorities responsible for development planning issues have incorporated the issue of gender into the wide diversity of planning disciplines concerned with the lives of low-income communities. As a result decision-making powers continue to remain not only male-dominated, but also gender-blind. Some stakeholders concerned with planning find it difficult to graft gender into existing disciplines.

Gender planning is based on the underlying conceptual rationale that, because men and women play different roles in society, they often have different needs. Therefore, when identifying and implementing needs, it is important to disaggregate households and families within communities on the basis of gender. To identify these different needs requires an examination of planning stereotypes of low-income households and the division of labour within households.

The fact that women and men have different roles has important implications for policy-makers. Women's unpaid role is seldom recognised by men. Women's roles of reproduction, production and community-managing work are seen as natural and non-productive and are not valued highly. This implies that the work that women do is made invisible and fails to be recognised as valuable work, neither by men in the community nor by planners whose job is to assess different needs within low-income communities. By contrast, the majority of the work done by men is valued and is paid for through remuneration, enhanced status or political power. When planning for gender the following should be taken into consideration:

(i) Identifying practical and strategic gender needs: When planners are blind to the roles and needs of women, they may fail to recognise the necessity of relating planning to women's specific requirements. If planning is to succeed, it must be gender-aware. Gender approaches should be stressed by planners to cater for gender concerns.

(ii) Gender interests: When planning for gender, planners must consider strategic gender interests. Gender interests are those that women or men may develop by virtue of their social positioning as a result of gender attributes. Gender interests can be either strategic or practical, each being derived in a different way and each involving differing implications for women.

Strategic gender needs are those needs which are formulated from an analysis of women's subordination to men, enabling the development of an alternative, more equal and satisfactory organisation of society, in terms of both the structure and nature of relationships between men and women. Practical gender needs are those needs that are formulated from the concrete conditions women experience in their engendered position within the sexual division of labour. Therefore, in planning terms, policies for meeting practical gender needs have to focus on income-generating activities, community-level requirements, like housing and basic services, education, health services, water, food and employment.

Governments should train women in areas traditionally identified as men's work s to widen women's employment opportunities and to break down occupational segregation, thereby fulfilling the strategic gender needs to abolish the sexual division of labour (Moser, 1989).

Role of Uganda's Ministry of Planning and Economic Development in Gender Planning

According to the Ministry of Gender, Labour and Social Development (1997), the Ministry of Planning and Economic Development has a vital role to play in safeguarding the operationalisation of the gender policy, by ensuring that gender issues are mainstreamed throughout the national development process. In collaboration with other sectors, the Ministry of Planning and Economic Development will ensure that women and men are fully targeted and that both genders benefit

equitably from all development programmes and projects. The role of
the Ministry of Planning and Economic Development is therefore to:

(i) Ensure that all policies are gender-responsive. Projects and
programmes must include strategies for addressing gender
concerns.

(ii) Build the capacity of planners and policy analysts in cooperation
with the Ministry of Gender, Labour and Community Development.
Gender analysis skills are needed to establish effective structural
linkages between central and special planning, local authorities
and NGOs, to ensure comprehensive gender-responsive planning
at all levels.

(iii) Establish benchmark data on the relative positions of women and
men in all fields, in order to identify priority areas for gender-
responsive programmes and to allocate resources accordingly.

(iv) Ensure that the available resources are directed to gender-
responsive programmes and institutions. In the planning process,
budgetary resources should only be allocated if programmes are
gender-sensitive.

(v) Oversee the monitoring and evaluation of progress in gender-
responsive policy formulation and programme implementation.

(vi) Ensure that all data collected, analysed and disseminated by the
central statistics office are gender-disaggregated (The Ministry of
Gender, Labour and Social Development, 1997).

Therefore, to realise the national gender policy, all planners in their
areas of mandate should:

(i) Integrate gender issues in their policies and in the development
planning process.

(ii) Formulate implementation strategies to ensure that gender issues
and concerns are addressed routinely in all current and future
activities.

(iii) Ensure that development programmes and projects identify
gender roles in order to address specific gender needs arising
from the multiple roles of women in production, reproduction
and community development.

(iv) Promote gender equity among target groups by taking gender-specific affirmative action on behalf of a disadvantaged gender, in cases where inherent and structural inequalities exist.

(v) Increase awareness, knowledge and sensitivity among the staff of the respective institutions and other actors regarding gender differences and imbalances, to redress the situation.

(vi) Coordinate and facilitate activities of NGOs to ensure effective and efficient resource allocation and use it in conformity with government policies and strategies.

Decentralisation and Gender Mainstreaming

Gender is a global concern and its problems can only be solved in global context. Decentralization is a global solution being implemented in almost all programmes in Uganda. The rationale of decentralization is that empowering weak communities and authorities will increase responsiveness and improve quality of life in all development programmes. Local authorities are expected to participate by being accountable for their programmes. Through the decentralization process the participation of women at all levels should be promoted.

The Local Governments Act of 1997, Part II, Article 5, Sections XXII and XXVI indicate that decentralized services and activities will include women in development and cultural affairs. For the purpose of gender planning, the processes of decentralization and promoting democracy provide important entry points for addressing gender concerns at the local level. This is because, at the local level, communities rub shoulders with gender issues and concerns. At the district, sub-county and local council levels, leaders have the potential to incorporate gender concerns into community development and decision-making. They have also the capacity to identify, analyse, examine and incorporate gender concerns. Thus they are able to:

(i) Identify gender issues and concerns.

(ii) Identify solutions to these gender issues, thus initiating laws at local level that are geared towards addressing the existing gender imbalance.

(iii) Incorporate local community issues and concerns regarding gender into development.

(iv) Address cultural and religious issues that bring about gender imbalance.

(v) Promote gender awareness among all members of the community.

(vi) Promote, collect and analyse gender-disaggregated data (if mandated and well facilitated).

(vii) Carry out participatory gender needs assessments at community level.

(viii) Target community-based organisations and affirmative bodies, like women's and youth councils, to incorporate a gender perspective in their work.

(ix) Encourage and enhance the capacity of women to participate in community activities.

(x) Sensitize men about the need for working with women as equal partners for the purpose of developing the community.

(xi) Focus on the family unit as the basic structure for the social construction of gender relations through community-based initiatives.

(xii) Deal with issues arising from gender confrontation.

(xiii) Ensuring that there is equitable devolution of power to both men and women.

(xiv) Interpreting all policies governing the society from a gender perspective.

(xv) Stressing affirmative action as a way of addressing gender imbalance at village or district level.

(xvi) Involving both genders in the democratization processes.

(xvii) Ensuring that each committee, office, NGO and other body are gender responsive. In this respect men and women should be represented equally within local leadership bodies.

Therefore, within the decentralization process, it is necessary to strengthen the national machinery to reach out to all levels of society effectively. Close cooperation between the national and district authorities is essential if gender concerns and issues are to be addressed.

Decentralization enables policy-makers to reach people at the grassroots level.

Curriculum and Gender Mainstreaming

Curriculum refers to the subjects taught at educational institutions. These subjects are taught using textbooks, teaching aids, brochures, magazines and newspapers. There is also a hidden curriculum that refers to all unintended consequences of learning that goes on in an educational institution. The school, the hidden curriculum and the teaching-learning process are supposed to be neutral and beneficial to girls and boys equally. However, in many African countries both the curriculum and the teaching-learning process tend to be gender-biased to the detriment of girls (UNICEF, The World Bank, 2001).

To ensure gender sensitivity in the curriculum and the teaching-learning process, mainstreaming gender and awareness into all aspects of the educational system is important. This process begins with an analysis to determine what is actually being taught, the bias of texts used, the nature of the hidden curriculum, co-curricular activities, resources and space. Stakeholders need to analyze what brings about gender disparities and discrimination in education and the society as a whole so that suitable strategies for correction can be developed.

According to UNICEF (2001) to ensure gender sensitivity of curricula and teaching-learning processes, the following has to be addressed:

Teachers should:
(i)   Pay equal attention to boys and girls in the classroom.
(ii) Encourage girls to express their feelings freely.
(iii) motivate girls, especially in science subjects and mathematics
(iv) Avoid any speech that demeans girls.
(v)   Emphasize dialogue and participation.
(vi) Avoid sexual relationships with girls in the school or class environment.
(vii) Avoid labeling girls in relation to their sex.

Head teachers should
(i)   Be fully committed to girls' education.
(ii)   Ensure that the staff is gender sensitive.
(iii)   Be aware of problems that women and girls face.
(iv)   Create and sustain a supportive, safe and girl-friendly learning environment.
(v)   Encourage girls to participate in leadership.
(vi)   Have a senior woman handle girls' issues.
(vii) Have a deputy headmistress if the head teacher is male and vice versa.

Curriculum writers and publishers should
(i)   Ensure that all written material is gender sensitive.
(ii)   Incorporate positive role models for girls in textbooks.
(iii)   Sensitise the public to the importance of girls' education.
(iv)   Promote gender-responsive policies.

Textbooks, pictures, figures, photographs and information in most school curriculums portray gender inequality. For example, some pictures may show a man driving a lorry, carrying a gun, or looking after cattle, while other pictures portray a woman cooking, carrying children, kneeling in front of a man, carrying a doll etc. Pictures in textbooks portray gender inequality and the subordination of women, an issue that should be addressed by writers. Often pictorial representation by sex still reflects the traditional division of labour.

According to Mbilinyi and Omari (1993) the impression created by illustrations in textbooks is that more boys than girls take part in school activities. Both male and female learners would like their images to feature in books - pictures are a way of attracting children to use books. Those whose gender features most are, therefore, more encouraged to work hard than those who feature less frequently. This kind of imbalance in textbook illustrations contributes to the existing unequal access to secondary and higher education. From the beginning, girls are discouraged from working hard by the existing educational materials .Textbook design poses a big challenge to the goal of gender equality in the provision of education.

Curriculum planning and administration also contribute to career selection by learners. Traditionally, boys are encouraged to select certain subject combinations, like science, while girls are encouraged to take courses that are assumed to be feminine, such as home economics, needlework, typing, religious studies, history, economics and geography. Subject combinations based on sex influence the future careers of learners. Boys become engineers, doctors, architects and technicians while girls become secretaries, nurses, teachers and waitresses.

Mbilinyi and Omari (1993) indicate that such elements of gender inequality exist in the school curriculum because the designers of the curriculum materials belong to a society that is culturally and religiously gender-biased. They are products of a society that promotes gender inequality and their attitudes are reflected in the curriculum. Men write about what they see around them because of the religious, cultural and traditional gender-biased societal attitudes. Few women participate in writing school textbooks. Book-writing, like other academic undertakings, is dominated by men who have better access to education than women.

In this context, stakeholders should make sure that books which are approved for school use are gender-sensitive. Books can contribute to changing outdated traditional attitudes towards gender.

Parents should
(i)   Treat their daughters and sons the same and encourage children to cross over into other gender roles.
(ii) Support girls' education.
(iii) Expose girls to leadership.
(iv) Abandon outdated traditions and gender discrimination.
(v)   Equip girls with skills that instil in them the confidence to compete with boys in all spheres.

Government, donors and funding agencies should
(i)   Make gender responsiveness an essential criterion when funding educational and other programmes.

(ii)   Support gender sensitisation programmes for policy-makers, education practitioners and administrators.

(iii) Promote girls' enrollment using affirmative action at all levels of schooling.

(iv) Impart entrepreneurial educational and decision-making skills to both sexes at an early age.

(v)   Encourage the adoption and local use of technology. Women could be encouraged to make use of modern technology such as modern cooking stoves that do not consume a lot of fuel, or to repair boreholes instead of men.

(vi) Emphasizing to parents, teachers and communities that basic education is a right of every child. Showing that an educated woman is a resource to the community can help eliminate the negative attitude that many people have towards educating girls.

(vii) Make schools friendlier to children in areas of health, accommodation, security and the teaching-learning process.

(viii) Create awareness among girls and boys about dangers of sexual abuse and harassment and teach them how to avoid it. Teachers and parents should encourage girls to report cases of sexual abuse and harassment to authorities or parents. This can be done through life skills training and sex education.

(ix) Mainstream gender concerns in all institutions of higher learning.

(x)   Empower girls with skills that enable them to resist being used as sex objects by men (UNICEF, 2001).

Gender, Discrimination and Stereotyping in the Classroom

According to UNICEF (2002) there are more boys in school than girls in most developing countries. In science and mathematics lessons, teachers prefer to involve boys rather than girls because boys raise their hands enthusiastically. Girls tend to raise their hands timidly. Sometimes, when the teacher tries to involve girls, they contribute reluctantly and they often fail to solve science or mathematics problems. Instead of encouraging girls, teachers often make derogatory remarks, linking the remarks to their personal appearance, sex or background. Some teachers ignore girls, and eventually the girls give up. When a girl performs well, instead of being positively motivated, some teachers will make comment such as, "She has a woman's body, but the brains of a man" (UNICEF, 2002).

In most schools in Uganda there is gender imbalance in class composition in the teaching-learning process. Some teachers stereotype gender by implying that, owing to their character, women are better at cooking, caring for children and managing the domestic set-up, that they have a greater aptitude for household rather than administrative and technical work. Some teachers urge girls not to argue in class, those that do are told that they will never attract husbands. Some teachers stress that men are breadwinners and heads of the family, while women are mothers, forgetting that, today, some families have women as heads and breadwinners. UNICEF (2002) provides an example. In class, a girl read a passage: "Remember boys, when you are courting, that women enjoy complimentary remarks. They like to talk about themselves and about what men think and feel about life. If you want to win the favour of women talk about interesting experiences, hold interesting conversations. You see a normal girl loving anything of an unusual and thrilling character.

The church also promotes gender inequality. On Sunday 22 August 2004, a preacher in All Saints Cathedral, Kampala, was deliberating on Joshua 24:15: "As for me and my family, we will serve the Lord." He challenged heads of families to bring their family members to the knowledge of God. He asked all family heads to stand up, and although the majority were men, there were a handful of women. The male preacher was clearly gender-biased yet he was preaching to both men and women. As a feminist, the author deduced the following from the sermon:

(i) The preacher had a patriarchal assumption, which is deep-rooted in Christian and other religious teaching, that only men can pass religious messages on to family members.

(ii) He was gender-biased. His sermon did not acknowledge that women could also pass religious messages on to family members, a cause that the women liberation movement and gender activists are advocating.

(iii) Young boys and girls who attended this service learnt from the preacher that only family heads, who are usually men, should give moral and religious instruction to family members.

According to UNICEF (2002), sexual barriers also hinder gender equality. In some cultures, the onset of menstruation coincides with the temporary or permanent withdrawal of girls from school. Many girls in rural schools lack sanitary napkins or gender-sensitive toilet facilities at school. Given the stigma many communities attach to menstrual blood, some girls avoid attending school during their periods for fear of ridicule by boys. Boys do not like to sit near menstruating girls - they allege that such girls stink. The school curriculum does not provide girls with information on and skills for dealing with menstruation. Remote schools often have too few female teachers to counsel girls. Faced with physical and sexual threats, girls feel unprotected, with no trusted adult to turn to.

Ssenkaaba (2005) reports that girls still face a number of barriers to education, including cultural ones.

> .... a school girl who after noticing a huge brownish blood patch on her uniform got scared and immediately ran out of the class with a cloud of boys following her, hounding and making fun of her. Confused and embarrassed, she found her way home and for the next five days, she did not attend school until the completion of her menstrual cycle.

Girl Dropout from Education

According to a UNICEF report (2003) the gross enrolment ratio in Uganda from 1996-2005 was 48% in primary, 40% in secondary and 22% in tertiary education. The female dropout rate is 9.4%, compared to 8.4% for boys. As one ascends the educational ladder, the disparities become even greater.

Causes of dropout for girls in primary schools are ranked as follows: pregnancy (95%), family responsibility (53%), sickness (51%), lack of school fees (47%), lack of interest (46%) and other causes (47%). At secondary school level, pregnancy is the reason for 67% of dropout cases. The key barriers to girl's education have been identified as pregnancy-related factors and the HIV/Aids pandemic. World wide women are at higher risk of infection than men, and the age bracket worst affected is 12-30 years. Other barriers to girl's education include lack of security, especially in rural areas where pupils have to walk long distances to school, culturally and socially prescribed gender roles, early marriage, negative cultural practices and the classroom culture (UNICEF, 2003).

At the launch of the United Nations Girls Education Initiative in 2004, it was reported that despite basic education being free, only 49% of girls of school-going age were in primary school. Ugandan girls are faced with a number of barriers to education including cultural practices, civil strife, child labour, HIV/Aids, an inappropriate learning environment and unclear policies.

The UNICEF report (2003) indicates the following barriers to girls' education, which gender mainstreaming should address:

(i) Poverty, socio-economic factors and the indirect costs of education such as textbooks and uniforms, or losing the labour of the girl in the home. At least 35% of Ugandan households exist below the poverty line. Approximately 30% of families are polygamous and, in a paternalistic society, boys are favoured. Girls are expected to contribute financially to the family income through dowry and as domestic workers.

(ii) Due to HIV/Aids, Uganda has almost 1 million HIV/Aids orphans under 15 years. Girls often stay home to look after sick family members; furthermore, many teachers are falling victim to HIV/Aids.

(iii) Lack of policy in key areas. Uganda has the highest rate of adolescent pregnancy in sub-Saharan Africa. Thirty-five percent of girls are either pregnant or have given birth by the age of 17. Yet educational policies exclude pregnant or girl mothers from education.

(iv) Safety and security issues. Sexual harassment and exploitation are deterring girls from attending school. Corporal punishment, although illegal, is still common. Very few schools have separate latrine facilities for girls, which is especially problematic for adolescent girls.

(v) School-based factors. Retention and performance are matters of concern. The curriculum is rigid and lacks clearly articulated quality learning outcomes, competencies and assessment criteria. Classrooms are still characterized by gender-insensitive, non-participatory and non-interactive methodologies.

(vi) At least 1.5 million children work, mainly as domestic workers in urban areas. It is estimated that 80% of underage domestic workers are girls. According to UNICEF (2001, 2003), girls in Uganda experience inequalities at an early age and the discrimination persists into their adult years.

(vii) Most schools levy mandatory fees that pose barriers to children attending school, such as building or construction funds, food funds, PTA levies, uniforms, books and other instructional materials. Because of these costs, poor parents send only their sons to school.

Traditional practices also affect school attendance by girls. Some girls drop out of school in order to get married. Because parents anticipate this occurrence, they attach little value to the girls' education from the start. Girls are needed at home, to work alongside their mothers in basic subsistence farming or taking care of siblings.

Efforts to institute universal primary education by 2010 need strengthening through gender mainstreaming. Achievement of this overall objective will result in tangible benefits for Ugandan women and girls. Expected outcomes in the long term include an increase in the overall enrolment of girls in and out of the formal school setting, higher incomes for women and increased participation of women and adolescent girls in civil life. Provision of basic education to all Ugandan girls will hasten achievement of these outcomes, thus bringing about gender equality (UNICEF, 2001).

Statistics from the Ministry of Education and Sports of 2003 indicate that 3,872,589 boys and 3,760,725 girls were enrolled. The transition rate of Primary Seven stands at 20.9% for girls and 24.1% for boys. Studies show that gender disparity patterns vary according to districts, with the districts of Moroto, Lira, Nebbi, Kotido, Katakwi, Kyenjojo, Masindi, Gulu and Kitgum having the least favourable school environment for girls.

Table 8.1: Trends in enrolment, transition and completion (2001-2004)

Indicators	2001	2002	2003	2004
Survival rate to P5	58%	68%	52%	55.7%
Boys	58.9%	65%	52%	55.2%
Girls	58%	70.8%	51%	56.2%
Transition rate (P7-S1)	61%	69%	59%	64%
Boys	56%	65%	57%	61%
Girls	66%	74%	63%	68%
Gross enrolment (S1-S6)	13%	13.6%	18%	21%
Boys	15%	15%	20%	23%
Girls	12%	12.2%	17%	19%
Completion rate (S4)	21%	22%	18%	25%
Boys	23%	25%	20%	28%
Girls	19%	19%	17%	22%
Transition rate (S4-S5)	31%	41%	42%	39%
Boys	34%	43%	45%	43%
Girls	28%	49%	39%	33%

Source: The New Vision, January 3, 2005

However, as a result of universal primary education, Uganda has made progress towards gender parity. The major challenge to the education sector today is keeping boys and girls in school.

The Ministry of Education has created a gender desk to address the issue of gender parity. The gender desk cited domestic chores, sexual harassment by teachers, violence, and gender discrimination in the classroom, poor enforcement of policies regarding child labour and girls' re-entry to school after pregnancy as some of the factors preventing girls from completing secondary school. Nampala (2005) reports that 40 teachers in Kayunga district were reported for defiling girls in the year 2004.

Through the Education Sector Investment Plan, there are now several interventions in place to address gender disparity in schools. These include the Sexual Maturation Project, which will provide incinerators for safe disposal of sanitary materials, and the Girls Education Movement (GEM), a child-centered grouping aimed at empowering girls on issues affecting their education. The National Strategy for Girls' Education is a partnership programme that regulates activities by different stakeholders in educating girls (Ssenkaaba, 2005).

Gender Analysis

Gender analysis is the systematic examination of the roles, relations and processes relating to the imbalance of power between women and men in society. Gender analysis is a tool that enables research into gender differences, of the nature of relationships between women and men and their different social realities, life expectations and economic circumstances. It is a tool for understanding social processes and for responding with informed and equitable options (Ebila and Musiimenta, 2004). Gender analysis examines problems or situations in order to identify the gender issues involved.

According to UNICEF (2002), gender analysis is the whole process of collecting and analysing gender-disaggregated data so that the interventions that are designed by planners take into consideration the specific needs of girls and boys and men and women. It is a systematic process of identifying the differences therein and examining the related needs of the roles, status, positions and privileges of women and men. The analysis is based on the fact that gender is a critical variable in the development process. A gender analysis process should provide information and analysis about families and communities that will be forged or affected by initiative activities, needs and priorities whether and how these differ by gender and initiative. Gender analysis should identify local and national initiatives for gender equality, the efforts made by the government, NGOs and civil society to pursue these issues and how such initiative can complement these efforts. Gender analysis forms the basis for planning initiatives that have realistic objectives, and activities related to gender equality. In order to design and implement effective interventions for promoting women's participation in all programmes, it is necessary to identify specific gender-based problems and barriers, at family, village, regional, sub-national levels. This means that stakeholders should collect relevant data, both quantitative and qualitative, on the participation of women in societal programmes. For example, planners need data on women's literacy rates, access to resources, employment, leadership and participation in national programmes and politics. Analysis of such issues will help planners to identify problems hindering women's participation and how they can be overcome. Gender analysis is significant for:

(i) Understanding the gender power dynamics underlying the development process and how gender relationships must be transformed to ensure equitable distribution of resources and opportunities in national programmes and interventions.

(ii) Assessing whether girls and women are enjoying the benefits of national programmes and interventions.

(iii) Understanding the extent of gender equality and discrimination in a given context and how community gender values, norms, beliefs and attitudes and socio-economic inequalities are evident in national programmes, and developing responsive and equitable programmes and interventions that promote gender equality.

(iv) Raising sensitivity and consciousness among men about the need for working with women as equal partners to develop the community.

(v) Focusing on the family unit as the basic structure for the social construction of gender relations through community-based initiatives.

(vi) Dealing with issues arising from gender confrontation.

While addressing gender concerns in the decentralization process at the local level, it is important that the following strategies be taken into consideration:

(ix)   Equitable devolution of power to both men and women.

(x)   All policies governing society must be interpreted from a gender perspective.

(xi)   Affirmative action is necessary to address gender imbalances identified at village or district level.

(xii) Men and women must be equipped with skills to handle gender issues.

(xiii) Both genders must be involved in promoting democracy and political processes, while women must be encouraged to participate in politics and politicians must be sensitised all about gender issues.

(xiv) Age and gender-disaggregated data must be collected, completed and disseminated at all levels.

Gender Analytical Tools

Gender analytical tools address the biases portrayed by gender roles, relationships and stereotypes. A gender analytical tool provides guidelines to enhance gender mainstreaming in all programmes, education, decentralization, management, planning, resources and community activities.

Gender mainstreaming as a national concern should address the following questions to provide stakeholders with direction in incorporating gender concerns into planning and policy formulation. These questions may act as tools to deal with gender mainstreaming.

(i)   When the government plans national and other budgets, are the budgets gender-sensitive? Are the government, NGOs and other stakeholders aware of different gender needs? Are stakeholders gender-conscious when planning the budget? Does the budget reflect women's as well as men's interests and needs? Are there gender gaps in the national budget or those of NGOs? Does the national budget demonstrate sensitivity to gender concerns? Is there a dedicated budget specifically for gender issues? What portion of the national budget is allocated to the Ministry of Gender and how is it distributed? How are the government, NGOs and institutions of higher learning strengthening gender? How are gender gaps being bridged?

(ii) Do the Ministry of Education and other Ministries address gender issues? If so, how? How does the Ministry of Planning address gender issues? Does it provide scope for research on gender issues so as to plan properly for specific gender needs? Does it have disaggregated data on gender?

(iii) Who makes decisions and how do these decisions benefit and affect gender? Is gender explicit in the national vision and objectives? Do goals, national policy objectives and strategies take into consideration different gender needs? What is the national organisational structure for governance? How many female ministers, permanent secretaries, judicial officers, police, army, lawyers, doctors, teachers, etc. are there? What roles or activities do these women play in relation to the structure? What benefits accrue to women and men in relation to their positioning? What is the level of participation and efficiency in terms of gender in this national structure?

(iv) What role do men and women play in identifying gender concerns that affect development?

(v) What action should the government, stakeholders, community and individuals take to transform existing gender imbalances and gender relations?

(vi) What interventions are needed in terms of goals, objectives, activities, resource allocation, access to opportunities, monitoring and evaluation to transform the present state of gender inequality?

(vii) Do the constitution of Uganda and other laws properly address gender concerns? Does the Domestic Relations Bill address gender concerns properly? Does it benefit both men and women?

(viii) How do the values, traditions, culture, customs and religions in Ugandan society or the social structure affect gender relations?

Who is positioned where in society? Who benefits and accesses opportunities in terms of gender?

Gender- Responsive Interventions

Gender responsiveness is a planning process in which programmes and policy actions are developed to deal with and counteract the problems which are likely to arise if the needs resulting from socially constructed differences between men and women are not met adequately. Gender-responsive interventions by stakeholders may include:

(i)   Identifying gender needs.

(ii) Addressing gender needs, such as equity in the allocation of resources, allocating priorities and access to opportunities and benefits.

(iii) Developing a gender-sensitive management information system.

(iv) Policy-makers assessing gendered outcomes.

(v)   Proper and dedicated funding of gender programmes and investing in gender capacity-building.

(vi) Sensitizing stakeholders, the community and administration to gender relations.

Analytical Frameworks for Gender Planning in the Development Process as a Strategy for Meeting Gender Needs

Gender analysis frameworks are tools that policy-makers, programme planners and managers can use to ensure incorporation of gender concerns into policies, plans, strategies and activities in order to redress gender inequalities in a given situation. Various gender analysis frameworks have been developed (UNICEF, 2002).

The Harvard Analytical Framework

The framework was developed by the Harvard Institute for International Development in 1985. The Harvard Analytical Framework is based on the assumption that allocating resources to women as well as men makes good economic sense. It is a useful tool for gathering data, understanding women's and men's roles in society and taking into account the external forces which affect development planning. It can be used at different levels of planning and analysis and can be expanded to disaggregate data by religion, culture, ethnic and economic factors as well as gender and age. The Harvard Analytical Framework analyses women's and men's control and access to resources. In analyzing the gender division of labour and the roles of women and men, it provides insights into the power relationships within society and what these relationships are based on. Power is vested in control over resources, such as land, equipment, other assets or labour and over benefits such as cash or political prestige. If women lack access to these resources for example, land, they will be unable to assert their priorities for its use and their access to the benefits will be restricted, since men will be the controllers. The Framework can be used as planning and implementation tool for programmes and projects. The Framework has four interrelated components:

Activity profile
This component is based on the gender division of labour and delineates the economic activities of the population in the project area. Within this component a major question to be answered is raised: "What do women and men, girls and boys do in a given situation, programme or intervention?" Answering this question amounts to delineating the productive and reproductive roles by gender and age. It considers the time taken to perform the various roles and the locus, i.e. where the work is done. It provides for disaggregating activities by sex, age and other factors, thus it records the amount of time spent on activities and the location of activities.

Access and control profile
This component identifies the resources individuals command to carry out their activities and gain benefits. By distinguishing between access to resources and benefits and control over resources, it is possible to assess the relative power of members of a society or economy. Four questions which should be answered under this component are:
- Who has access to the resources she/he needs to do his/her work?

- Who has control over the resources that women and men, as well as girls and boys, need to do their work?
- Who has access to the benefits derived from the work?
- Who controls the benefits derived from the work?

Influencing factors on activities, access and control

This component seeks to identify factors that influence the division of labour and access to and control of resources. Such factors include economic, social-cultural, political and institutional factors. Such factors create different opportunities and constraints for women and men's participation in development. The impact of changes over time in the broader cultural and economic environment must be incorporated into this analysis.

Project cycle analysis

This component focuses on the need to apply the foregoing three types of analysis to the entire project cycle, from project identification, through design and implementation to evaluation. It consists of examining a project proposal or area of intervention in the light of gender-disaggregated data and social change.

The Longwe Framework

According to UNICEF (2002), this framework was developed by Zambian women's rights activist Sara-Hlupekile Longwe. The Longwe or the women's empowerment framework identifies five levels of equality that can be used to determine how empowered women are in a situation or programme. The framework can be used to identify strategies that increase women's empowerment. The five levels of the framework are hierarchical, thus the higher levels suggest more power for women. Within a development project and, by extension, in social life, the attainment of one level is the beginning of the next; comparable to Maslow's hierarchy of needs motivational theory. The five equality levels are:

Welfare
This is the lowest level of empowerment. At this level interventions are directed towards enabling women to meet material needs.

Access
At this level of empowerment, interventions assist women in gaining access to resources needed to produce goods and services.

Conscientisation
This refers to awareness of being dominated and determined to act towards the liberation of self. At this level of empowerment women become aware of male domination and seek equality with them.

Participation
Conscientised women seek to participate in total project life and in social life. They gain some control of the process.

Empowerment and control
This is the highest level of equality. Through participation women gain control over their own development and are fully empowered.

The Longwe Framework is a useful tool for assessing the quality of the education girls receive, by assessing the outcomes of education and how empowering the curriculum and the teaching-learning process are. The Longwe Framework raises questions such as "Are girls in schools competing with boys in science subjects, or they are offering courses that will eliminate women from the job market?" The Framework can be used to plan for empowerment for girls and women in all programmes.

The ABC of Gender Analysis Framework
The Forum for African Women Educationists (FAWE) developed the ABC of Gender Analysis Framework in 1995 (UNICEF, 2002). The Framework allows for both quantitative and qualitative gender analyses of education by analysing educational materials. Aspects of a text, such as the author, the narrator, actors and locus of activity, power relations and language use are investigated, as are the teaching-

learning environment and classroom dynamics. It covers aspects such as teacher expectations and behaviour, student participation in the teaching-learning process, seating arrangements and use of educational space and resources.

FAWE (2004) adapted the ABC tool to raise the consciousness of teachers, authors and curriculum developers about the dangers of a biased curriculum. It was noted by FAWE that biases and educationally damaging portrayals of gender roles occurred within texts. The ABC Framework is designed to guide gender mainstreaming in education, management, decision-making, NGO programmes and the decentralization process. The Framework uses the following questions to analyse the educational curriculum: Who tells the story, female or male? From what perspective is the story told? Who is the main actor who has the upper hand? Who is compromised or dependent? Who is emphasised? Who initiates an action? Who acts? Does the action require technology? Does the action require skills? How are the skills acquired? Who acquires the skills? Why? What are the implications of acquiring or not acquiring the skills? How does this affect males and females? What gender relations are there?

FAWE (2004) shows language as one of the most important and subtle way of portraying gender biases through conventions of speaking and writing. For example, who is named and who is not named in a text? What are the implications and assumptions of naming? What advantages and disadvantages does naming have for a character? Does the nameless lack anything?

FAWE (2004) also shows that generic terms, which are supposed to be neutral, have a clear male or female stamp, e.g. early man, businessman, mankind and chairman .In the texts analysed men may be addressed as "Sir" whereas women are called by their names or just ignored. In Christian songs all people are called brothers. The Anglican prayer of confession reads, "Almighty God, our Heavenly Father, we have sinned against you and our fellow men..."

According to FAWE (2004), male-oriented productive activities, like the production of goods and services, and income awards status and value to men; while activities of women, like reproductive activities, maintenance of the family, collecting water and firewood, nursing children and cooking, are deemed to be of low status. Community activities, in which most women participate, are not paid for but valued to some extent. It is in this context of division of labour or the roles inherent in the socialisation process, that attitudes and expectations in areas of work and professions are formed. It determines the educational level and professions girls and boys aspire to.

FAWE (2004) states that power is crucial, because social gender relations are maintained by prevailing power relations and structures, which shape the course of events. Thus questions of gender sensitivity in power relations are raised: What is the source of power? Is it status, economics, politics or gender? Who has the power? Who receives power? Why? What is the nature of the power? How is power exercised, maintained, perpetuated, distributed or shared?

In terms of education, FAWE (2004) states that classrooms or lecture rooms show gender discrimination, and can be analysed to identify gender gaps. For example: Who sits where? Who answers the questions? Who volunteers? Who asks questions? How does the teacher sample responses? How does he/she praise the learners? Whom does the teacher pay attention to? What forms of reward or punishment are used for boys or girls? At whom are most jokes or anecdotes directed? What is the gender perspective? How much time is allocated to boys or girls to answer questions? What comments does the teacher make with respect to boys or girls? What is the level of gender relations in the classroom or school? Are there gender biases in the way the teacher exercises his/her power in class? What is the dress code for boys and girls? What message does it portray? Does it affect gender relations and performance? What resources are available for boys and girls in terms of dormitories, classrooms, labouratories, football or netball pitches, dining hall and toilet facilities? Information gathered on these analytical gender tools is significant for gender mainstreaming and addressing gender gaps.

The People-Oriented Analytical Framework

The People-Oriented Analytical Framework was devised by Mary B. Anderson and the United Nations High Commissioner for Refugees senior co-coordinator for refugee women, following the adoption by the UNHCR of a policy on refugee women which called for the improvement of participation and access to resources by refugee women. It is based on the Harvard Analytical Framework and is intended to be a practical planning tool for refugee workers in a society like Uganda, which has many refugees, most of whom are women and children. The tool would be of much use to access resources for women. Women in refugee camps face challenges and changes, therefore they need protection and social concern. The People-Oriented Analytical Framework has three components:

(a) Activities analysis: This component acknowledges that the existing gender division of labour and roles have been disrupted by flight. It is therefore essential to find out what men's and women's roles were before the flight and how they have changed for men and women as refugees.

(b) Use and control of resources analysis: This involves gathering data on the resources used and controlled by women and men before flight and as refugees. Women and men may have lost control permanently over resources in their places of origin and may be unable to regain it. Refugee status affects gender relations and may introduce opportunities for positive change. Meeting gender needs in camps raises the following questions:

- Who accesses land, equipment, food, utensils, clothing, shelter, income, education and power? Is it the male or female?

- Who claims the most benefits in the camp? Who is in control of resources and donations? Is it the female or male? Who manages distribution? Who receives the resources and donations and how much?

Determinant analysis

Determinants are factors, both within the refugee camp and in the receiving country, which determine or influence the roles and responsibilities of women and men and change their use and control of resources. Included are economic and demographic factors, institutional structures, socio-cultural factors in refugee camps, legal factors and international political events and trends. It helps to identify external opportunities and constraints which must be considered in planning. Factors such as economic conditions, for instance poverty, inflation rates, income distribution, international terms of trade; infrastructure and demographic factors such as community norms, social hierarchies in families and the community, power structure and religious beliefs will all affect the activities of the Framework (Oxfam, 1994).

The Moser Framework for Gender Analysis and Planning
The Moser Framework was developed by Caroline N. Moser of the London University School of Education and Political Science. She describes the development of gender planning by stating that women and men in Third World countries play different roles and therefore have different needs, women being engaged in triple roles while men are engaged in productive and community roles.

The Framework sees the goal of gender planning as the emancipation of women from subordination by men and women's achievement of equality, equity and empowerment. Moser (1989) says that, while the important role women play in the Third World development process is widely recognised, conceptual awareness of the issues of gender and development have not necessarily lead to its incorporation in planning practice. For stakeholders in different aspects of socio-economic development planning, the lack of an adequate operational framework has been problematic. The Moser Framework is a tool stakeholders can apply to address gender concerns. This observation provides both the conceptual framework and methodological tools needed for incorporating gender into policy-making. The Framework illustrates the capacity of different interventions to meet gender needs, with examples from sectors such as employment, housing and basic services. It provides a critique of a number of different policy approaches to development from the perspective of gender planning and identifies the potential and limitations of each approach for meeting the needs of low-income Third World women.

Moser (1989) is of the opinion that the United Nations Decade for Women, from 1976 to 1985, played a crucial role in highlighting and publicizing the important but invisible role of women in the economic and social development of their societies. However, since then many researchers have moved away from a preoccupation with the role of women within the family, towards an understanding of the complexities of women's employment. Policy-makers have moved the focus away from family-centered programmes, which assume motherhood as the most important role for women in the development process, to a diversity of approaches emphasizing the productive role of women. Today, most men encourage women to engage in productive roles rather than staying at home as mothers, waiting for men to return from work with food and other family necessities. A good number of men are striving to identify themselves with women who can earn. Moser (1989) comments that the Women in Development (WID) approach adopted by United States Agency for International Development (USAID) with its underlying rationale that women are an untapped resource that can provide an economic contribution for development, has had an influence in popularizing income-generating projects for women.

In recent times, it has been recognised that focusing on women in isolation has its limitations and this led to gender in development being investigated in general. Moser (1989) shows that the focus on gender, rather than women, was developed by feminists who were concerned that the problems of women were being perceived in terms of sex, i.e. their biological differences from men, rather than in terms of their gender, i.e. the social relationship between men and women, a relationship in which women have been subordinated systematically. It is imperative that planners take into account gender approaches which are concerned with the manner in which male-female relationships are socially constructed, that men and women play different roles in society and that gender differences are shaped by ideological, historical, religious, ethnic, economic and cultural determinants.

It is significant to note that, in Africa and other developing countries, authorities responsible for development planning have been reluctant in recognizing gender as an important planning issue. Decision-making powers continue to remain not only male-dominated but also gender-blind in orientation. Planners should use gender analysis tools to translate gender awareness into practice. Unless gender is grafted into existing planning disciplines, women will always be marginalised in planning theory and practice.

Moser's rationale for gender planning

Moser and Levy's (1986) approach to gender planning is based on the underlying conceptual rationale that, because men and women play different roles in society, they have different needs. Therefore, when identifying and implementing planning needs, it is important to disaggregate households and families within communities on the basis of gender. To identify these needs it is important to examine two planning stereotypes relating, firstly, to the structure of low-income households and secondly, to the division of labour within the household. While planning for gender, it is important to note that some families are nucleur, consisting of husband, wife and children, while others are extended, consisting of husband, wife, relatives and other kin. Secondly, it is important to note that there is division of labour within the household of which the man is the head of the family and the breadwinner and is primarily involved in productive work outside the home. The wife or wives take(s) responsibility for the reproductive and domestic work involved in the organisation of the household. In this type of family organisation there is unequal control over resources and power between the man and woman in matters affecting the livelihood of the household. Moser and Levy (1986) state that such a sexual division of labour reflects the natural order and is ideologically formalized through such means as the legal and educational system, the media, family planning programmes, politics and economy, without recognizing that, within it, the woman's position is subordinate to that of the man.

The Moser Framework challenges traditions of planning as inadequate, because they do not address gender issues in the planning process. Stakeholders must take into consideration the triple roles of women, strategic gender needs and categories of policy approaches to women and development when planning for gender needs.

The triple roles of women

The Moser framework indicates that in most low-income societies, women have three main roles, namely reproductive, productive and community-managing activities, while men primarily undertake only productive and community activities.

Reproductive role

This role includes child-bearing and rearing responsibilities. It also embraces maintenance of household activities, food preparation, collection of water and fuel, shopping, caring for the husband, family health care and housekeeping. The reproductive role produces labour force through child bearing and rearing, yet it goes unrecognised by society. In poor communities it is labour intensive, tedious and time consuming. It is carried out by women and girls. The woman is the beast of burden under the headship of the man. Reproductive work is unpaid labour. Men will take up this role, acting housekeeper, cook, water carrier, baby-sitter etc. only as paid employment.

Productive role

In their productive role, women produce labour for productive roles. Productive roles offer a secondary income for women. The role takes the form of agricultural work for most poor rural women, and work in the informal sector for urban women. Women may be involved in farming, fishing, business or trade, be employed by NGOs or the state, or be self-employed. Some men limit their wives' activities outside the home, expecting them to concentrate on their reproductive role. In most societies in developing countries the stereotype of the male as a breadwinner or as the productive worker predominates, the man sees his role in the household to be that of the primary income earner. This is common even if the husband is unemployed and the wife's productive work provides the primary income. Both men and women engage in productive activities but their functions and responsibilities differ.

Community roles

Women are also involved in community work in both urban and rural contexts. Community work involves the collective organisation of social events and services such as ceremonies, celebrations, community improvement activities, participation in groups and organisations, politics, village meetings, etc. Some of these community activities are paid roles in which both men and women participate. Women within their gender-ascribed role of wives and mothers struggle to manage productive and community roles, therefore accepting the sexual division of labour and nature of their gender subordination. Men are also involved in community activities but in markedly different ways from women, reflecting a further sexual division of labour. Moser and Levy (1986) show that the special division between the public world of men and the private world of women (where the neighbourhood is an extension of the domestic area) means that women and men undertake different types of community work.

Moser and Levy (1986) point out that, while women have a community-managing role based on the provision of items for collective consumption, men have a community leadership role in which they organise at the formal political level, normally within the framework of national politics.

The fact that men and women have different roles has important implications for policy-makers, because the triple role of women is not recognised and the fact that women, unlike men, are severely constrained by the burden of balancing the roles of reproductive, productive and community-managing work is ignored. Reproductive and community-managing work are seen as natural and non-productive, therefore is accorded no value, yet this is an area where most women participate. Only productive work is valued and this is where most men concentrate. The consequence for women is that most of their work is not recognised by men, the community and planners who assess different needs within low-income communities. On the other hand,

most of the men's work is valued and it is directly or indirectly paid
for by status or political power.

Moser's approach to identifying practical and strategic gender needs for the purpose of planning

It is unfortunate that most planners are blind to the various roles of
women and the fact that women's needs are different from that of men.
Most development planning has failed to integrate gender concerns into
its programmes. If planning is to succeed, it has to be gender-sensitive
and take gender concerns into consideration.

Gender needs

Moser and Levy (1986) stress that planning for low-income women
in developing countries must be based on the women's interests.
Planners should prioritise gender concerns. They should identify the
different needs of women and then translate them into planning needs.
Thus planners need gender policy planning tools and techniques for
implementing policies. They should be in a position to differentiate
women's interests and practical gender interests.

Molyneux (1985) defines gender interests as those that men or
women develop by virtue of their social positioning through gender
attributes. Gender interests can be either strategic or practical, each being
derived in a different way and each involving different implications for
women's subjectivity. There is a distinction between gender interests
and women's interests. The concept of women's interests assumes
compatibility of interest based on biological similarities. The position
of women in society depends on class, ethnicity, culture, gender and
religion. Moser (1989) identifies different areas of women's needs:

- Gender needs in employment: Most low-income women are faced
  with the fundamental problem of lack of adequate skills due to lack
  of education and exposure. The provision of skills training is an
  important gender need, which would enable women to compete
  in the world of employment. Women need training in productive
  skills that can help them earn incomes. Low-income women need
  skills in nursing, teaching, tailoring, bakery, brick-making, animal

husbandry and other self-help projects that can generate income. In some communities women are trained in home economics by NGOs and hospitals, but this only strengthens the reproductive roles and gender needs related to health and nutrition but does not earn women any income.

Planners and policy-makers should train women in areas traditionally identified as men's work to widen employment opportunities. This may break down existing occupational segregation, thereby fulfilling strategic gender needs to abolish the sexual division of labour.

- Gender needs in human settlements and housing: When planning human settlements and housing, planners should bear in mind that women have particular needs. Women need space that offers good accommodation, sanitary facilities, private offices, etc. Women should also have rights to land and ownership of houses with their husbands. Most low-income women stay with their husbands but they do not own houses. Planners should promote housing projects that provide for ownership regardless of the sex of the household head.

- Gender needs in basic services: Planning for child-care facilities and centers is an important step in meeting gender needs. Such facilities should be located in the women's working place, so that they can undertake paid employment. Men should also be encouraged to take care of their children if the child-care facilities are located in their workplace.

- Moser (1989) states that transport is the most critical problem faced by women. Planners should take into consideration the necessity of transport services to meet the needs of men and women. Buses with low fares should operate in rural areas and urban centers during morning and evening peak periods.

- Strategic gender needs: Molyneux (1985) says that strategic gender needs are those needs which are formulated from the analysis of women's subordination to men, arising from strategic gender interests. Strategic gender needs are used to overcome women's subordination in different cultural and socio-political contexts. Satisfying gender needs would lead to a more equal and satisfactory organisation of society, regarding both the structure and nature of relationships between men and women. These needs must be identified by planners and policy-makers to transform the existing unequal relationships between men and women. The strategic needs Molyneux (1985) identified include the abolition of the sexual division of labour and child-care, spreading the burden of domestic labour, removal of institutionalised forms of discrimination such as the right to own property, access to credit, opportunities for education, the establishment of political equality, freedom of choice regarding child-bearing and the adoption of adequate measures against male violence and control over women.

Such strategic gender needs are often identified as feminist because of the level of consciousness required to achieve these needs. In modern society, it has become popular for policy-makers and the media to label any programme or policy associated with women as "feminist", a term that is used in a derisory manner that could provoke hostile and negative reactions from female and male planners. Moser, Levy and Molyneux (1985) agree that identifying the triple roles of women and the differences between practical and strategic gender needs can assist practitioners to understand that planning for the needs of low-income women is not feminist in content, because it benefits the whole family.

Today, governments, feminists, NGOs, policies, programmes and projects worldwide are concerned with women because of their engendered position in the sexual division of labour as wives and mothers. Practical needs are related to unsatisfactory living conditions and lack of resources. Meeting practical needs is a response to an immediate necessity and aim to address women's needs in areas of inadequacy.

Practical gender needs

According to Moser (1989), that practical gender needs are those needs which are formulated from the concrete conditions that women experience in their engendered position within the sexual division of labour. These are formulated directly by women in their positions rather than as a result of external intervention. Molyneux (1985) argues that practical gender needs do not involve strategic goals such as women's emancipation or gender equity, nor do they challenge the prevailing forms of subordination, although they arise directly from them. Practical gender needs arose in response to an immediate perceived necessity identified within a specific context. They are practical in nature and often are concerned with inadequacies in living conditions such as water, health-care and employment. Planners should bear in mind that sexual division of labour within the household gives women the primary responsibility not only for domestic work involving child-care, family, health and food provision but also for community management of housing and services, along with earning an income through productive work. Thus, in planning terms, policies for meeting practical gender needs should focus on the domestic arena, income-generating activities and community-level requirements of housing and basic services. Basic needs such as food, shelter and water are required by all family members, therefore meeting women's practical needs benefits the wider society.

Moser's policy approaches to low-income women and gender planning

In many developing societies the people worst affected by poverty are women. This is because they are marginalised and lack land, property and employment. In this respect, Moser (1989) identifies five approaches to gender planning:

The welfare approach

The underlying rationale of this approach reflects its origins, which are linked to the social welfare. It was introduced in early decades of 1900 by colonialists in Third World countries and its main targets were vulnerable groups such as women. During the First World War, One of its aims was to provide relief aid to low-income women who, in their engendered roles as wives and mothers, were seen as the people primarily concerned with the welfare of the family. Social welfare was emergency relief initiated in Europe after the Second World War, accompanying the economic assistance. This relief aid was undertaken by international private relief agencies and relied on volunteer by the middle class women for effective and cheap implementation. The welfare approach is based on three assumptions:

- That women are passive recipients of development, rather than participants in the development process.
- That motherhood is the most important role of women in society.
- That child-rearing is the most effective role for women in all aspects of economic development, while the man's role is assumed to be productive.

The welfare approach is family-centered in orientation. It targets non-working housewives and mothers to improve family welfare, particularly relating to children and household property. It stresses the physical survival of families through direct provision of food. It meets the needs of people in refugee camps because the majority of refugees are women and children. It also meets the needs of women-headed families since they look after the elderly and children. The welfare approach planning policy is implemented by projects of the United Nations High Commissioner for Refugees (UNHCR) and non-government organisations. These focus on women in their reproductive role, with special attention being paid to pregnant or lactating women. Malnutrition is addressed by food and nutritional education and distribution of food to medical health centers or hospitals to benefit children under five years, pregnant mothers and nursing mothers..

Moser (1989) reports that, since the 1970s, the welfare policy towards women has been extended to include population control by family planning programmes. Development agencies responded to the world's population problem by identifying women in their reproductive role as primarily responsible for limiting the size of families. They assumed that poverty could be reduced through the widespread dissemination of contraceptive knowledge and technology. However, the planners of the welfare policy did not take into consideration the religious and cultural values and women's status in the family and society, education and labour force participation, factors that also affect fertility differentials. Some religions, such as Catholicism, forbid the use of contraceptives. Some cultures expect women to produce as many children as possible in order to counteract high mortality rates and to provide labour. Uneducated women are generally unwilling to use contraceptives because of ignorance as well as cultural and religious beliefs. Some men forbid their wives to use contraception.

Critics of the welfare planning policy and development economists and planners observed that the policy failed to meet the needs of women. For example, women need more than food aid and charity handouts; they need security and skills to become more productive.

It is argued that welfare programmes tend to create a culture of dependency. Such assumptions regarding women's reproductive role exclude them from development programmes operated by mainstream development agencies providing a significant proportion of development. The welfare approach is not concerned with meeting strategic gender needs for example, the right of women to control their own reproductive roles.

The equity approach
The purpose of the equity approach is to gain equity for women who are seen as active participants in development. It recognises their triple roles and seeks to meet strategic gender needs through direct intervention involving giving political and economic autonomy and combating inequality. Moser (1989) based the equity approach on the following assumptions:

- Colonialism and neocolonialism contributed to the decline in women's status in developing countries.
- Modernisation was equated with gender equality, asserting that capitalist development models imposed on Third World countries had exacerbated inequalities between men and women. United

States Agency for International Development (USAID) had ignored women in its first development projects, something which was challenged by Women in Development (WID).

The equity approach was the original Women in Development approach applied during the United Nations Women's Decade from 1976 to 1985. The equity approach recognises that, although women are often the main contributors to the basic productivity of their communities, especially in agriculture, their economic contribution was referred to neither by national statistics nor in the planning and implementation of development projects.

Economic strategies have had a negative impact on women. Women should be brought into the development process by provision of access to employment and the marketplace. The equity approach is also concerned with fundamental issues of equality which transcend the development field. Its primary concern is addressing the inequality between men and women in the public sphere of life and across socio-economic groups. It identifies the origins of women's subordination as lying not only in the context of the family, but also in relationships between men and women and in the marketplace, thus places considerable emphasis on economic independence as being synonymous with equity.

According to Moser (1989), in focusing on reducing inequality between men and women, especially in the sexual division of labour, the equity approach meets important gender strategic needs. Equity programmes are identified as uniting the notions of development and equity, the underlying logic being that women have lost ground to men in the development process. Therefore policy-makers should identify women's concerns and incorporate them in the planning process. The approach stresses that women should receive a fair share of the national and natural resources.

In developing countries, the approach is criticized as representing western feminism and threatening to the male domain. It is also unpopular with governments. USAID (1978) notes that some development agencies are hostile to equity programmes because of their intention to meet not only practical gender needs but also strategic needs. Because of widespread criticism of the equity approach, it was abandoned, in spite of the fact that it stressed the right to own property, legal rights, right to divorce, custody of children, voting, participation in politics and economic activities for women. It meets strategic gender needs rather than actual needs.

The anti-poverty approach

This approach links economic inequality between men and women, not to subordination, but to poverty. Its major concern is eradicating poverty. Through the World Bank, the policy works to eradicate absolute poverty by funding projects and programmes, especially those involving women, to reduce income inequality and increase productivity.

The anti-poverty approach targets low-income women and assists them to escape absolute deprivation that is the result of men ignoring the contribution made by women in meeting the basic necessities of the family. This approach stresses reducing inequality between men and women by reducing income inequality.

Underlying this approach is the assumption that the origins of women's poverty and inequality is their lack of land and capital, sex discrimination in the labour market and religious and cultural beliefs. Women's poverty is seen as a problem of underdevelopment, not subordination. It recognises the reproductive role of women and seeks to meet practical gender needs to earn income, particularly from small-scale, income-generating projects. In this respect it addresses women's education and employment, which may simultaneously increase women's economic contribution and reduce fertility rates.

Critics of the poverty approach policy comment that the approach cannot succeed because of particular constraints facing women in their engendered roles:

- Most women lack education and property and therefore do not qualify for credit.
- Men control household budgets. Even if a wife could obtain credit, it is likely that her husband will claim the money.

- Cultural constraints restrict women from moving freely outside the domestic arena and compete with men.
- Many governments and NGOs consider women's productive work of less importance than that of men, and view it as a secondary source of income.

Income-generating programmes based on the anti-poverty approach may provide employment for women, but unless the employment leads to greater autonomy, it does not meet strategic needs. The anti-poverty approach ignores women's reproductive roles. Income-generating projects, which assume that women have time available to manage the projects, may increase their triple burden. Unless an income-generating project also alleviates women's burdens of domestic labour and child-care, practical gender needs would not be realised, particularly not that of earning an income. Women need support from men regarding domestic work and child-care. Some women cannot work in offices, projects or business because they have nobody to care for their children.

The efficiency approach

In the efficiency approach the emphasis shifts away from women to development, on the assumption that increased economic participation for women in Third World countries is linked to equity. Organisations such as USAID, the World Bank and the Organisation for Economic Co-operation and Development (OECD) propose that an increase in women's economic participation in development links efficiency and equity. The efficient approach shifts from a paid to an unpaid economy by making use of women's unpaid time. It emphasizes women's increased participation, not only as mothers but also as community managers. It promotes self-help projects.

Moser (1989) reported of a serious deterioration in living conditions of low-income populations resulting from a decline in income levels. Within the household, a decline in consumption often affects women more than men, while the introduction of charges for education and health-care can reduce access more severely for girls than for boys. The capacity of households to shoulder the structural adjustments can have detrimental effects on human relationships, expressed by domestic violence, lower mental health, the breakdown of family structures, resulting in increasing numbers of single-parent households.

The efficiency approach argues that women's concerns, both in the household and in the workplace, need to be consciously made part of the formulation of structural adjustment policies which, in turn, will require the direct involvement of women in both the definition of development and adjustments to its management. The efficiency approach relies heavily on the elasticity of women's labour in both reproductive and community managing roles. It only considers gender practical needs and unpaid work. The major purpose of the efficiency approach is ensuring that development is more efficient and effective as a result of women's economic contribution, with participation equated with equity. It seeks to increase practical gender needs while relying on domestic roles and an elastic concept of women's time. Women are seen entirely in terms of their capacity to compensate for declining social services by extending their working day.

The empowerment approach planning policy

The empowerment approach policy differs from the equity approach not only in its origins, but also in the causes, dynamics and structures of women's oppression which it identifies in terms of strategies.

Moser (1989) explains that, since the late 19th century, Third World feminism has been an important force for change regarding gender, with women participating in nationalistic and patriotic struggles. Although the empowerment approach acknowledges inequalities between men and women and the origins of women's subordination in the family, it also emphasizes the fact that different women experience oppression differently, according to their role, class, colonial history and current position in the international economic order. It also maintains that women have to challenge oppressive structures and situations simultaneously at different levels.

The empowerment approach stresses that women's experiences are tempered by several factors, such as class, race and age, and that action is necessary at different levels to combat oppression. The approach openly acknowledges that women need to obtain more power if they are to improve their position. It recognises women's triple roles and seeks to meet strategic gender needs indirectly through bottom-up mobilisation of women.

The empowerment approach questions some of the fundamental assumptions concerning the interrelationship between power and development that underlie other approaches. While it acknowledges the importance of power to women, it seeks to identify power less in terms of domination over others (with its implicit assumption that a gain for women implies a loss for men) and more in terms of the capacity of women to increase their own self-reliance and internal strength. This is linked to the right to determine choices in life and to influence the direction of change, through the ability to gain control over crucial material and non-material resources. It places less emphasis on the equity approach of increasing women's status, but seeks to empower women through the redistribution of power within as well as between societies.

The empowerment approach was well articulated by the Development Alternatives with Women for a New Era (DAWN), a loose coalition of individual women and women's groups set up prior to the 1985 World Conference of Women in Nairobi.

DAWN (1985) analysed the conditions of the world's women and formulated an alternative future society which it identified thus:

> We want a world where inequality based on class, gender and race is absent from every country and from the relationships among countries. We want a world where basic needs become basic rights and where poverty and all forms of violence are eliminated. Each person will have the opportunity to develop her or his full potential and creativity and women's values of nurturance and solidarity will characterize human relationships. In such a world, women's reproductive role will be redefined. Child care will be shared by men, women and society as a whole. Only by sharpening the links between equality, development and peace can we show that the basic rights of the poor and the transformation of the institutions that subordinate women are inextricably linked. They can be achieved together through the self-empowerment of women.

DAWN (1985) believes that strategies are needed to break down the structures of inequality between genders, classes and nations. These strategies include national liberation from colonialism, neo-colonialism, control over exports, agriculture and other multinational activities.

The new era envisaged by DAWN (1985) also requires the transformation of the structures of subordination that have been inimical to women. Changes in legislation, civil and labour codes, systems of property rights, control over women's bodies and the social and legal institutions that underwrite male control and privilege are essential if women are to attain justice in society.

According to the empowerment approach, policy-makers must develop strategies to empower women with skills so that they can compete equally with men. It also seeks to assist traditional organisations to move towards a greater awareness of feminist issues. Like other approaches, its implementation would be sustained through women's organisations and groups. These organisations would use legal changes, political mobilisation, consciousness-raising and education for women to realise equality.

In the context of these approaches, the National Gender Policy should use its machinery to identify gender concerns and incorporate them in the planning and implementation process. In the world of women's empowerment and the need for equity, men and women should work together harmoniously. Men should not feel robbed of their authority as providers, rulers, defenders and decision-makers but should recognise that the present generation of women are overcoming the hurdles posed by cultural and religious boundaries and are able to also contribute to the needs of the family, even when their salaries are lower than those of their husbands. Women's empowerment should encompass all economic, spiritual, cultural, intellectual, political and religious spheres. Women's empowerment and equity does not mean women becoming men, being arrogant or dominating others, but acting responsibly in a world characterized by gender equality.

According to Graham (1998), empowering women should involve the capacity to counter power over others with a countervailing power of autonomy and power over self. In families where men suppress their wives' achievements there is usually tension and such families could even break up. On the other hand, if women look down on their husbands because they are educationally, politically, economically and culturally empowered, their families will crumble like a pack of cards. Women's empowerment means building up self-respect, self-sufficiency and fearlessness, caring for others and resisting power over others. When empowerment is perceived as involving superiority and domination over others, it leads to violence in families, offices and other social groups. Women's empowerment involves acquiring skills for peace, love and awareness, being conscious of factors that hinder personal development, such as sexism, religious and cultural bigotry, ageism, militarism, imperialism, and environmental degradation, and counteracting them. The wellbeing of both genders at all levels should be promoted and human wellbeing must be promoted over developmental and technological processes. Skills necessary to address the issues that hinder human development must be developed.

Empowerment is an important element of development, being the process by which people take control and action in order to overcome obstacles. It is the collective action by which the oppressed and deprived overcome the obstacles of structural inequality which have placed them in disadvantaged positions. The women's equality and empowerment framework considers the empowerment policy and goal to be an essential process for advancement. It is the process by which women are mobilised to understand and overcome gender discrimination to achieve equality of welfare, efficiency and access to resources.

Deductions from Moser's framework

(i)   Women experience competing demands between productive, reproductive and community-level responsibilities. Balancing these roles constrains women severely.

(ii) Planners should take into consideration activities taking place at home and workplace and factors such as transport and the environment. Unless they are considered, they will impact on women's performance.

(iii) NGOs and planners should incorporate practical gender and strategic needs in their planning processes, and should define the goals of intervention. Practical gender needs include providing rural women with access to water, seedlings, fertilizers, firewood, improved ovens, markets for their product, training and skills, paid work and information and environmental conservation. On the other hand, strategic gender needs, which include women's collective organisation, the right to speak and skills in leadership, management and education, should also be emphasised,

(iv) Women should be supported by planners and policy-makers to identify their own needs and interests.

(v) Gender-disaggregated data for planning purposes is very important.

(vi) Planners and NGOs should assist rural women to improve their productivity and fight inequality and dependence.

(vii) Planning of gender concerns should be linked with women's triple roles (although Moser's framework does not address these concerns).

(viii)Gender awareness must be incorporated into all planning conducted by the state and NGOs. Women should be included so that they deliberate on issues that affect them. Moser's framework can be used for planning at all levels. It can also be used concurrently with the Harvard Framework for project planning. The framework stresses gender planning as a way of challenging unequal gender relations and supporting women's empowerment. It shows practical and strategic gender needs as powerful tools for addressing women's short-term needs, to bring about equality between men and women.

(ix) Moser's frame work indicates to planners that productive, reproductive and community work are interrelated, a reminder to planners that household work should be as highly valued as productive and community work. The framework recognises that institutions, political bodies, cultures and religions could resist incorporating gender concerns into programmes.

Limitations of Moser's framework

(i)   It does not take into consideration men's strategic and practical needs, one reason why men are likely to resist women's empowerment and equality.

(ii) Not all women fulfill three roles as the framework claims. In rural and urban areas the majority of women are housewives who participate in agricultural work or remain at home doing housework. Some women do not participate in community activities because of cultural, religious or community dictates which prohibits them from appearing in public.

(iii) Moser only refers to inequality arising in households but ignores other forms of inequality like class, race, ethnicity, employment and power differentials in households.

(iv) The framework refers to what people do and what resources they have, but ignores relationships through which people act and how decisions are reached.

Conclusion: A Theoretical Overview

In this study of religion, culture, gender and development, the role played by religion and culture in relation to social structure, occupational integration, education, economics and the political socialisation of men and women was examined. These factors influence gender roles, relations, structure and authority and raises questions about gender inequality, violence and subordination, which affect national development. Several theoretical propositions are given below regarding the relationship between religion, culture, gender and development and the role of education and the media in transforming people's attitudes to enhance gender equality and in creating strategies for the development of both genders.

The interplay of religion and culture can create or reinforce as many gender problems as it can overcome. Religion, which has been identified as the champion of gender imbalance and subordination, has the capacity to promote gender equality.

Attending school can be a great equaliser, as it increases social and economic mobility and hastens the integration of women in programs and equal distribution of educational opportunities. Education also distributes vertical social privileges more widely, also to the disadvantaged of society. Education should be used as a tool to sensitise people about religions and cultural practices that keep women in a subordinate position. Governments and NGOs should address uneven distribution of educational opportunities. Future politicians, religious and cultural leaders, educators, parents and the community at large should address the demands of the underprivileged, especially women, regarding equality. While primary education has been decentralized, secondary education must also be transformed so that girls can continue to access education.

In cultural and religious spheres, women assume the position of subordinates, and feminists are addressing this by women's emancipation, gender mainstreaming, decentralization, state programmes and NGOs. As women struggle for liberation, they should retain responsibility for their domestic roles. Working women should supplement their husbands' income by contributing to the provision of basic necessities of the family. The family as basic unit of the society will benefit if husbands and wives improve their communication skills.

Cultural and religious values that assign specific roles to men and women should change to permit both sexes fulfill any role regardless of sex. The concepts of parity and partnership must be developed. Parity refers to the fact that persons are different but equal, and partnership means that a creative synergy can be created between men and women if they work together.

Traditional roles and tasks assumed by women at home and their activities outside the home, whether professional, political or communal should not be stereotyped as conflicting activities. The government should organise public information campaigns for this purpose. The government must ensure that the portrayal of women in the media and textbooks corresponds with reality and encourages girls to achieve their full potential (Interparliamentary Union, 1994).

Men should support women's participation in social activities and share with them obligations and responsibilities, as well as authority, with regard to domestic work and the rearing and education of children. It is equally important to recognise and enhance the role and activities of women inside the home. Governments, parliaments and non-governmental organisations should campaign for recognition of the importance of this role.

The images and models of women and men which are transmitted by education in the family, formal education and the media should be gender-responsive and gender-aware. They should not portray one sex as being superior to the other but should promote the image of equality and complementarity between the sexes. Cultural and religious customs, practices and laws that discriminate against women should be revised. It is important for men and women to receive sufficient information about their rights and responsibilities.

In a rapidly changing and unstable world, education and training should be broad-based and designed as a system of lifelong learning, to strike a balance between practical and academic skills. Education should be linked to sustainable development, now requiring, among other things, fresh dimensions to close the gap between male and female. Equal access to school for boys and girls must be emphasised and girls should be assisted so that they are retained in schools. The government should sensitise people and campaign for girls' education. NGOs and the government should make special provisions, such as awarding grants or special allowances for girls' schooling, or supply of educational materials free of charge. In schools, boys and girls should be allowed access to all subjects and teachers should not bias girls against taking science subjects. The curriculum should be gender-sensitive. All the educational materials in all institutions of learning should be scrutinized to determine whether messages suggest men's superiority over women. Educational material should be the same for both boys and girls.

Mortality among women in developing countries is high, mainly due to pregnancy, delivery or abortion. Governments should strengthen health care in all sub-counties with facilities to prevent maternal and child mortality. Feminists, the government, NGOs and religious leaders should promote the use of family planning in rural areas to allow women to organise their personal, professional and domestic lives.

No act of violence against a woman should go unpunished. It is imperative for women to be sensitised about their human rights as declared by the United Nations (1948), the Convention on the Political Rights of Women (1952), the Convention on the Elimination of All Forms of Discrimination Against Women (1979), regional instruments concerning the status of women and the Ugandan constitution (1965). The principle of equality between men and women should be set out explicitly in the national constitution. In revising or drafting legislation, the government should consult with women's organisations to ensure that principles of equality and justice are included.

All citizens should participate fully in the political, economic, social, religious and cultural affairs of their society. The language used in legislation should avoid discriminating between men and women. In areas where too few women are involved, affirmative action should be considered.

Today society as compared to the past has greatly changed. Women appear in public with unveiled heads, they ask sensitive questions regarding their status, they are involved in national development, cultural and religious teachings should suit modern times. The word of God that talked to biblical women in subordinate situations, like Hagar, Deborah, Esther, Vashti, Jael, Susan and others, has not changed. It continues to talk to women in precarious situations and He will come down to liberate them.

Feminists, the state and NGOs should stress gender mainstreaming of all programmes, projects, and policies to counteract gender imbalance. The decentralization process should be an entry point for reaching women at grassroots level.

References

Action Aid Uganda (2003) *Thinking Aloud*. Centre for Domestic Violence Prevention. Kampala, Uganda, New Vision Publications. Vol. 12 No. 47.

Adhiambo, O. (1995) *Girls and Schools in sub-Saharan Africa, Analysis Action*, Washington D.C, The World Bank.

African Eccesiastical Rwview (1971), *African Ecclesiastical Review*. Masaka, Uganda.

African Platform for Action (1994) *Fifth African Regional Conference on Women*. 16-23 November 1994. Dakar, Senegal, United Nations Economic Commission for Africa Centre for Women.

Ahimbisibwe, D. (1991) I Can't Give Away My Daughter For Nothing. *Arise, A Woman's Developmental Magazine*. Volume, date etc Kampala: ACFODE. pp. 9-10.

Alda, A. (1995) *What Every Woman Should Know About Men* ,October 1995. pp 15-16.

Alyanata, and Basilika, A. (2004) Dowry, Source of Marital Pain, Misery. *The New Vision*, Vol. 17 No. 234 ,Tuesday14 September 2004. p. 21.

Anarfi, J.R. (1994), HIV/Aids in Sub-Saharan Africa. Its Demographic and Socio-economic Implications. *African Population Paper No. 3*. African Population and Environment Institute (APAI).

Anderson, C. (1992) *Practical Guidelines on Gender and Development, A Practical Guide*, New York, Routledge.

Anderson, M.B. and Chen, M.A (1988*)* *Integrating WID or Reconstructing Development?* Paper Presented at the Association for Women in Development (AWID) Conference, April 1988. Washington, DC , USA.

Anderson, M.B., Overholt, C., Cloud, C. and Austin, J. (1994) *Gender Roles in Development Projects*. UK: Oxfam.

Arche, L. (1998) Women in Biblical Patriarchy. *Women and Religion*. Institute of Women's Studies, St Scholastica's College Manila. Mandaluyong City, Philipines: Raintree Publishing. p. 15

Barton, T. and Mutiti, A. (2000) *Northern Uganda Psycho-social Needs Assessment*. Uganda, Kampala, UNICEF Publications.

428

Basilika, A. (2004) Was it a Dowry Death? *The New Vision,* Vol. 15 No. 225, 4ᵗʰ September 2004. p. 19.

Baylies, C. and Bujra, J. (1984) *Challenges, Gender Inequalities.* ROAPE Publications.

Bem, S.L. (1972) *Psychology Looks at Sex Roles: Where have all the Androgynous People Gone?* Los Angeles: UCLA Symposium.

Black, M. (1993) Girls and Girlhood, Time We Were Noticed. *The New Internationalist.* No. 240, 8 th February 1993. p. 7

Boserup, E. (1970) *Women's Role in Economic Development.* New York: St Martin's Press.

Businge, G. (2002) Where is the Man? *The New Vision.* Vol. 17, No. 205. Tuesday 27 August 2002. p. 11

Businge, G. (2003) Domestic Chores Hinder Women's Empowerment. *The New Vision,* Vol. 11 No. 222 Tuesday 17th August 2003 pg 9.

Bagyendera, C.H. (1991) What it Takes to be a Good Wife. *Arise, A Women's Developmental Magazine,* No. 4, October-December 1991. Kampala: ACFODE. p. 25.

Byamukama, D. (1999) The Buganda Ritual Discriminates Against Women. *The New Vision,* Vol. 5, No. 68 Thursday 15 April 1999. p. 27.

Byamukama-Asiimwe J, Kiyimba A. (1999) 1slam polygamy ,and the Domestic relations bill, *Arise, A woman's development magazine* published by ACFODE, Kampala.

Byamukama Asiimwe J. and Kiyimba. A. (1999) Islam, Polygamy, and the Domestic Relations Bill, Eradicating Violence Against Women, The Police and Family Protection, Feeding Pregnant Adolescents, *Arise, A Women's Development Magazine,* No. 27, Kampala: ACFODE. p. 8-14

Canadian International Development Agency (2001) *Questions about Culture, Gender Equality and Development Co-operation.* Canada: Minister of Public Works and Government Services.

Caplan, P. (1982) *Women's Organisations in Madras City India.* In Caplan, P. and Bujra, J. (eds.) *Women United, Women Divided.* Bloomington: Indiana University Press. p.p. 99-128.

CEDAW (1989, 1992) *Convention on the Elimination of Discrimination Against Women.* Vienna and Nairobi: Kenya.

CEDAW (1999*) The United Nations convention on the elimination of all forms of discrimination against women,* third country status report of the government of the Republic of Uganda.

Chapman, G. (1989) *Christian Living Today.* Pastoral Institute of Eastern Africa., Cassel publishers Limited,London.

Chatsumarn, K. (1998) Women in Buddhism. *Woman and Religion,* Institute of Women's Studies, St Scholastic College, Manila. Mandaluyong City, Philipines: Raintree Publishing. p. 104.

Collier, J.F. and Yanagisako, S.J. (1988) Theory in Anthropology Since Feminist Practice. *Critique of Anthropology,* 9(2);260-272

Connell, R.W. (1985) *Theorising Gender,* Stanford University press, Stanford. p.p. 260-272.

Constitution of the Republic of Uganda (1995), Kampala, Uganda.

Davidson, M.J. and Cooper, C.L. (1992) *Shattering the Glass Ceiling. The Woman Manager.* London: Paul Chapman Publishing.

DAWN (Development Alternatives, with Women for a New Era) (1985) *Development, Crisis and Alternative Visions, Third World Women's Perspective.* Delhi: Eastern publication, London.

De Beavoir, S. (1988). *The Second Sex,* London: Picador.

Diehl-Huwe, U. (1991) *Equality and Differences.* Berlin: Kassel publications.

Dorr, J. (2002) *Women Seeking Justice.* Nairobi, Kenya: Pauline Publications.

Dortzbach, D. (1996) *Aids in Africa: The Church's Opportunity.* Nairobi: MAP International.

DOSSIER.,(1997) *Violence,* What a Waste of Energy*: Leadership for Christian Leaders,* March 13, p. 13, Kampala Uganda

East African Standard (2004), Gunmen Raped my Wife, says Ngugi. *The Monitor,* Tuesday 17August, 2004. p. 13.

Eastern and Central Africa Women in Development Network (ECA-WIDNET) (1997), *Violence against Women Trainers Manual.* Nairobi: Pauline Publications.

Ebert, F. (1998) *Women's Landmarks in the Democratization Process in Uganda.*

Ebila, F. and Musiimenta, P. (2004) Basic concepts of gender, *A paper presented at the Gender Analysis Workshop for Sentinel Sites,* Makerere University, 21-24 July 2004, Mukono, Uganda.

EDIRISA Organisation (2003) *Lake Bunyonyi and Kabale in Your Pocket.* Bunyonyi Safari Resort.

Emasu, A. (2004), Battered for being HIV/Aids Positive. *The New Vision,* Vol. 19, No. 281, 23rd July 2004. p. 19.

ESIP (1998-2003) *Mainstreaming Gender into Education Strategic Investment Plan.* Uganda: Ministry of Education and Sports.

Fatima, B.M. (1991) African Women and Feminist Schools of Thought. *Alternative Development Strategy for Africa Institute of African alternatives,* London:

FAWE (Forum for African Women Educationists) (2004) *A Gender Analysis Tool: ABC of Gender Analysis,* Kampala: Makerere University,Uganda.

Ferree, M. and Hess, B. (1987) *Analyzing Gender: A Handbook of Social Science Research.* Newbury Park: Sage Publications.

Fiorensa, S.E. (1987) *In Memory of Her.* New York: Crossroad.

Francia. M, Ocarm. C, Larson. M., and Chlefe.R (1998) Woman and Religion, p.55-64, Insitute of women's studies, St scholastic college, Manila, Raintree publishing company, Philippines.

Fredrick, V.G. (1968) *Marriage Partnership.* Cork publications.

Freedman, E.B. (1990) *Theoretical Perspectives on Sexual Difference: An Overview. In Rhode,* p.p. 257-261.

Freeman, J. (1996) Aids, Women's Vulnerability and Human Rights. *Earthtimes News Series.* Lutheran World Education Women's Magazine, No. 46, Department for Mission and Development, Geneva, Switzerland. p. 42.

Freud, S. (1965, 1977) *Three Essays on the Theory of Sexuality,volume 7of the standard Edition of complete psychology works of Sugmund Freud.* Translated by James Strachey. The Institute of Psychology and Hogarth Press 1977.

Gallin, R.S. (1986) Mother-in-law and Daughter-in-law. Intergenerational Relations within the Chinese family in Taiwan. *Journal of Cross-cultural Gerentology.* Boulder,Westview press.

Gallin R.S, and Ferguson.A.(1989) *Women and International Development, creating an agenda in; The women and international development* p.122, vol.1,Boulder ,Westview press.

Gallin, R.S. and Ferguson, A. (1992) *Conceptualizing Difference: Gender Class, and Action.* ,Boulder,West view press.

George, E.L., Sabi, R. and Millet, B.D. (1992). Female Infanticide in Rural South India. *Economic and Political Weekly*, Vol 2 No. 5, 30 May 1992. pp. 1,153-1,156.

Giovana, D.C. (1985), *Environmental Education and the Question of Gender: A Feminist Critique.*

Goetz A.M. (1997) *Getting Institutions Right for Women in Development*, UK: ZEB Books.

Gray, H.L. (1989) *Gender Considerations in School Management Masculine and Feminine Leadership Styles in riches*, Human Resource Management, in Ozgal, Open University press,C (Educs),and Morgarn.

Gray J. (2000)Gender difference, The Mars-Venus perspective. http: //psychology.about.comlibrary/weekly aa 080102a.rhtm.

Graham, H. (1998) Empowerment of Women for Peace. *Woman and Religion.* St Scholastica's College, Manila. Mandaluyong City, Philipines: Raintree Publishing. p. 24.

Hill, K. and Upchurch, D.M. (1995) Gender Differences in Child Health: Evidence from Demographic and Health Surveys. *Population and Development Review,* p.p.127-215.

Hammuddai, A. (1986) *Islam in Focus*, Islamic Foundation.

Hutchins, R.M. (ed.) (1952a) Laws. In *Great Books of the Western World*, Vol. 7. Chicago: Encyclopedia Britannica. p.p. 640-799.

Hutchins, R.M. (ed.) (1952b) On the Generation of Animals. In *Great Books of the Western World*, Vol. 9. Chicago: Encyclopedia Britannica. p.p. 225-331.

Hutchins, R.M. (ed.) (1952c) On the Origin of Inequality. In *Great Books of the Western World*, Vol. 38. Chicago: Encyclopedia Britannica. pp 323-366.

Interparliamentary Union (1994), *Plan of Action to Correct Present Imbalances in the Participation of Men and Women in Political Life.* Paris 26 March, Report Series and Documents No. 22,

Jackson,C.(1981)W*omen,Nature, Gender/History? A Critique ofEcofeminist Development.* School of Development Studies, University of East Anglia, Norwich. London: Frank Cass.

Jackson C. and Pearson R.(eds) (1998), Feminist Visions of Development; Gender Analysis and Policy, Routledge, London and New York.

Jaquette, J.S. (1988) *Gender Issues in Development Cooperation.* Colloquium Report, Occasional Paper No. 3. Washington DC: Association for Women in Development.

Jendia, C. (1995), *Behind the Scenes: The Problems Facing Women in Church Ministry in Uganda.* Spokane: W.A. Gamaga University.

Jones, E. (1961), *The Early Development of Female Sexuality,* papers on psycho-analysis (page 438-451) Boston, Beacon.

Judette, A.G. (1994) *Images of Faith, Spirituality of Women in the Old Testament.* New York: Claretan Publishers.

Kakaire A.K. (2004) Sabiny Men Speak Out on Female Genital Mutilation. *TheMonitor,* p. 10.

Kakwenzire.J.(1991), Arican leaders accused of double standards, *Arise ,A woman's magazine,* pp 3-6, No .4, Oct-Dec ,published by ACFODE,Kampala Uganda.

Kalinaki, D.K. (2002) Islam Does Not Distinguish Between Men and Women. *The Monitor.* ,No. 67,23rd May 2002. p. 17.

Kameo,E.(2003)UNOfficialAppealsAgainstViolencetowardsWomen on Wednesday. *The Monitor,* No. 330, 26 November 2003. p. 5.

Kamla, B. (1991) *Education's Empowerment: Some Reflections.* Colombia, Sri Lanka: ASBAE.

Kamya, I.R. (1999) Culture hinders women empowerment, *Arise ,A Woman's Development Magazine,* Published by ACFODE. p.p. 52- 53

Kanter, R.M. (1977) *Men and Women of the Corporation.* New York: Basic Books.

Kasekende, E.N. (1991) Bride Price Adds Value. *Arise, A Woman's Developmental Magazine.* Published by ACFODE. p.p. 23-24.

Kasente, D. (2003) Gender Inequality Hampers Productivity of Households. *The New Vision,* Vol. 18, No. 268, Tuesday 11 November 2003. p. 6

Kawamara,S.(1991), Facing River Kisizi. *Arise, A Woman's Developmental Magazine.* October-December, Published by ACFODE. p.p. 21-22. Kampala Uganda.

Kikampikaho, M. and Kanyike, F. (2004), *A Gender Analysis Tool Adapted from the FAWE ABC of Gender Analysis. Kampala:* Makerere University Gender Mainstreaming

Kurz, K.M. and Pratter, C. (1996) *Improving the Quality of Life of Girls.* USA: United Nations Children's Fund Publications.

Kwesiga. J.C (1998) Women's empowerment ;The link between theory and practice; In ACFODE, Arise magazine No 2,3, pp7-9, Kampala Uganda.

Kwesiga, J.C. (2002) *Women's Access to Higher Education in Africa: the Ugandan Experience*. Kampala: Fountain Publishers.

Kwoba, N. and Kashagire, H. (1998) *Report on the Valuation of Civic Education Programme and its Impact on the Community*. September Kampala ,Uganda,ACFODE.

La Fontaine, J. (1960) Homicide and Suicide among the Gisu. In Bohannan, P. (ed.), *African Homicide and Suicide*. Princeton, New Jersey: Princeton University Press.

Lewis, J. (1983) *Women's Welfare: Women's Rights*. Kent, UK: Croom Helm.

Lipsitz .S.B. (1993) *The Lenses of gender ,transforming the debt on sexual inequality* ,Yale University press, New haven and London.

Lirri, E. (2004) Femrite Condemns Ngugi Attack. *The Monitor*, Wednesday 18August 2004. p. 4.

Longwe, H. (1995) The Evaporation of Policies for Women's Advancement.; In *A Commitment to World Women*. Oxford: Wolfson College.

Lungaho, R.H. (2001) *The Gender Issues in Domestic Labour, Focus on Uasin Gishu District, Kenya*. Working Paper No. 73. Kampala: Kenya Centre for Basic Research.

Maccoby9, E.E. and Jacklin, C.N. (1974) *The Psychology of Sex Differences*. Stanford: Stanford University Press.

McKenzie, S.J. (1965), *Dictionary of the Bible Inc*. New York: Publisher.

Maicibi.A. (2005) *Pertinent issues in management ; Human Resource and Educational management, Net Media publishers* Ltd, Kampala,Uganda.

Mananzan, M.J. (1998), *Woman and Religion*, Institute of Women's Studies, St Scholastica's College, Manila. Mandaluyong City, Philipines: Raintree Publishing.

Mananzan, M.J. (Sr.) (1998) Towards an Asian Feminist Theology. *Woman and Religion*. Institute of Women's Studies, St. Scholastic College, Manila. Mandaluyong City, Philippines: Raintree Publishing.

Mananzan, M.J. (Sr.) (1998) The Religious Woman Today, and Integral Evangelism. *Woman and Religion.* Institute of Women's Studies, St. Scholastic College, Manila. Mandaluyong City, Philippines: Raintree Publishing.

Mannathoko, C. (2001) Gender and HIV/Aids within the Context of the Safety and Security of girls. *A paper presented in a coference on Girl's Education Movement inAfrica*, 15th-17th, Kampala- Uganda, UNICEF/ESARO.

Mbilinyi, D.A. and Omari, C. (2000) *Gender Relations and Women's Image in the Media.* Tanzania, Dar-es-Salaam University.

Mbilinyi, M. (1992) Research Methodologies in Gender Issues. In Meena, R. (Ed.) *Gender in Southern Africa, Conceptual and Theoretical Issues.* Harare: SAPES Books.

Mbiti, J. (1988) *African Religion and Philosophy.* Heinemann: London.

Mbughuni, P. (1979) *The Image of Women in Kiswahili Prose Fiction.* Paper presented at a Workshop on Women's Studies and Development. Dar es Salaam, Tanzania.

Mbuya-Beya, B. (1998) *Woman, Who Are You? A Challenge.* Nairobi: Pauline Publications.

Merril, C.T. (1989) *The New Testament Survey*, Northwestern College, WM B. Cerdmans Publishing Company, Inter-varsity Press.

Mifumi Project (2003) Domestic Violence and Police Work, the Tororo Declaration, Tororo, Uganda. *The New Vision*, Vol. 18, No. 268, Tuesday 11 November, 2003. p 17.

Millet, K. (1969) *Sexual Politics.* New York: Ballantine Books.

Ministry of Education and Sports (2000), *Education Statistical Abstract,* The Republic of Uganda.

Ministry of Education and Sports (2003), Education Statistical Abstract, Pre-final draft, The Republic of Uganda.

Ministry of Finance and Economic Planning (1995) *Demographic and Health Survey.* Entebbe: Statistics Department.

Ministry of Gender Labour and Social Development, (1997) *The National Gender Policy.* Kampala.

Ministry of Gender, Labour and Social Development (1999), *The Country Report on the Convention on Elimination of Discrimination Against Women,* (CEDAW), Kampala, Uganda.

Miranda, D. (1994) *Women and Violence, Realities and Responses Worldwide*. London: ZEB Books.

Moghadam, M. (1988) *Patriarchy and the Politics of Gender in Modernizing Societies: Iran, Pakistan and Afghanistan.*, West view Press,U.S.A.

Moghadam, M.V. (1990) *Introduction: Women, Identity and Politics in Theoretical and Comparative Perspective*. USA: West View Press.

Molyneux, M. (1985) *Mobilisation Without Emancipation?* Women's Interests, State, and Revolution in Nicaragua. Feminist Studies. Vol II No. 2.

Mombasa proceedings (1995) Regional Consultative Meeting on Integrating Gender into Programme/Project Management. 19-23 June. Mombasa,

Moser C.N. and Levy, C. (1986) *A Theory and Methodology of Gender Planning: Meeting Women's Practical Needs.* DPU Gender and Planning Working Paper No.11. London: Development Planning Unit.

Moser, C.N. (1989) *Gender Planning in the Third World: Meeting Practical Needs and Strategic Needs.* London: Pergamon Press.

Mueller, D. (1993), *The Sexuality Connection in the Productive Health Studies in Family Planning*.

Mugenyi, M.R. (1991) Media Rapped for Lack of Objectivity, The Role of Media in Promoting Social Change. *Arise, A Woman's Developmental Magazine*. Published by ACFODE. p.p. 10-11.

Muhwezi, J.M.K. (2005) Message of the Honourable Minister of Health on the occasion of World Health Day', 3rd May, 2005. *The New Vision*, Vol. 20, No. 254, 2nd September 2005. p. 11

Mukasa, S. (199) Violence Against Women and many profound effects ;Arise ,Awoman's magazine publication by ACFODE,Vol 28 Kampala Uganda.

Munyambabazi, C. (2004) What Has Gone Wrong With Our Youth? Let's Go Back To Our Roots. *The New Vision*, Vol. 15 No. 227 Wednesday 13 September 2004. pp. 9.

Mushanga, T. (1974) *Criminal Homicide in Uganda: A Sociological Study of Violent Deaths in Ankole, Kigezi, and Toro Districts of Western Uganda.* Nairobi: East African Literature Bureau.

Mwagale, R. (2004) Revealing the Female Face of the HIV/Aids Epidemic. *The New Vision*, No. 19, No. 287, 30th April , p. 21.

Myrna F, Cwefe, R., O'Carm and Lason, M. (1998) *Woman and Religion*, Institute of Women's Studies, St Scholastica College, Manila. Mandaluyong City, Philippines: Raintree Publishing. p. 64.

Nalugo, M. (2004) The Domestic Relations Bill; Do you know what the Parliament has in store for you? *The Monitor*, Saturday 4 December 2004. p.p. 4-5.

Nampala, M. (2005) Forty Teachers Defiled Pupils in Kayunga. *The New Vision*. Vol. 19 No. 314, Monday 3 January 2005. p. 42.

Nandutu, A. (2004) Female Genital Mutilation Still Rife in Kapchorwa. *The Monitor*, 4th October No 167 p.p. 8-9.

Nassali, M. (2000) Gender and Grassroots Democracy *Documenting Women's Experiences in Decentralization and Local Government in Uganda*. Kampala CBR Publications.

National Assembly of the Bahai's of Uganda (1997) *Why Gender Balance is Essential for Global Peace*. Uganda: Baha'i Publications.

National Statistics (1998) *Women and Men in Uganda*. Ministry of Gender and Community Development and the Statistics Department, The Ministry of Planning and Economic Development.

Nida, E.A. (1983) *Customs and Cultures, Anthropology for Christian Missions*. California: William Carey Library.

Ninsiima, J. (2001) African Women Being Sold into European Sex Slavery. *The New Vision*, Tuesday 18th March 2001, Vol. 16 No. 74, p. 19.

Nkonok, S. R. (1991) The Ecology Strategies for Environmentally Balanced Development. *Alternative Development Strategies for Africa*. London: Institute of African Alternatives.

Nansubuga, L. (2000) Uganda Girls are Trafficked for Sex. *The Other Voice*, Vol. 8, No. 9, 31 July 2000.

Nuefer, E.S. and Neufer, E.T. (1997) *Woman and Worship*. San Francisco: Harper and Row.

Ocheng, R. (2000) 'Impact of Culture on Women's Empowerment', *Arise, A Women's Development Magazine*, No. 30, November. Published by ACFODE. p. 5.

Ocwich, D. (2003) Ann Wants Gender Balance. *The New Vision*, Tuesday, 16 December, Vol. 18 No 2,981, p. 10.

Oduyoye, A.M. (1997), *Transforming Power*. Accra, Ghana: S.W.1, Press.

Ogen K.A. (2002) 'Women meet to save animal life', Friday, August 23 *The Monitor.*

Oxfam (1994) *Oxford Gender Training Manual.* Oxfam: UK and Ireland.

Pad Mini (1999) *Gender, Technology and Development.* Vol. 3 No. 1 , May-August 1999. Thailand: Asian Institute of Technology Publication. p. 166

Paul John II (1995) *Letter of Pope Paul II to Women.* Kampala: Pauline Publications

Paul John II (1995) *Apostolic letter milieris dignitatem of the Supreme Pontiff John Paul II on the dignity and vocation of women on the occasion, of the Marian year.* Africa: St. Paul's publication.

Peacock, H.L. (1990) *A History of Modern Europe 1789-1981.* Heinemann Educational Books.

Pearson, R., Whitehead, A. and Young. K. (1984) *Of Marriage and Market.* London: Routledge and Kegan Paul.

Philips, J.A. (1984) *Eve: The History of an Idea.* San Francisco: Harper & Row.

Preston, R. (1984) *Gender Ideology and Education, Implications at the Ecuadorian Periphery,* Gender in Latin America.

Radford, R.R. (1996) Ecofeminism, First and Third World Women, Women Resisting Violence, *Spirituality for life.* New York: Orbis Books.

Raymond, J.G. (1979) *The Trans Sexual Empire: The Making of the She-male.* Boston: Beacon.

Reuters (2004) Violence Against Women abets HIV. *The New Vision,* Vol 23 No 287, p. 23.

Rhode, D.L. (1989) *Justice and Gender: Sex, Discrimination and the Law.* London, Harvard University.

Riffat, H. (1998) *Women and Religion,* Institute of Women's Studies, St Scholastica College, Manila. Mandaluyong City, Phillipines: Raintree Publishing.

Roberts, E.D. (1993) Motherhood and Crime. *LOWA Row Review.* Vol. 79 p.p. 95-141.

Rodfeudd. A. (1992) *Women in Politics in Asia and the Pacific.*

Rwendeire, M. (2001), *Gender Sensitivisation,* A Paper Presented at the Induction Course for the Newly Recruited Members of Staff at the Ministry of Education and Sports Headquarters. Sports View Hotel, Kireka, 23-25 January 2001. Uganda.

Sanga, E. (1995) Women and Gender Relations in Radio Programmes In Mbiliny, D.A. and Omari, C. , *Relations and Women's Images in the Media.* Oxford: Africans Books Collective.

Sayers, J.(1982) *Biological Politics, Feminist and anti-Feminist Perspectives.* New York: Tavistock.

Sayers, J. (1984) The Psychology and Gender Division'. In *World Yearbook of Women and Education.* London: Kogan Page. p.p. 40-51.

Schmuck, R.A. (1986) School Management and Administration: An Analysis by Gender. In Hayle, F. and Nation, M.C. (Eds.) *The Management of Schools World Year Book of Education.* Kogan Page.

Schuler, M. (Ed.) (1992) *Freedom from Violence, Women's Strategies from Around the World.* New York: UNIFEM.

Scott, J. (1986) *A Useful Category of Historical Analyses: American Historical Review.*

Shakeshaft, C. (1987) *Women in Educational Administration.* Newbury Park: Sage.

Shanti, M. (1998) Hinduism, Caste, Gender and Violence. *Woman and Religion.* Institute of Women's Studies, St Scholastica College, Manila. Mandaluyong City, Philippines: Raintree Publishing. p.104.

Shisanya, C. (2001) *Violence against Women: Implications of Socio-religio-cultural Practices on HIV/Aids Infectors Among Women in Kenya.*

Shiva, V. (1989) Staying Alive: Women Ecology, and Development, London: Zed Books.

Ssali, H.H. (2002), Sex on the Streets. *The Monitor.* No. 165 Friday 23 August 2002. p.6.

Ssali, S.N , Mulyampiti.T. (2004), *Introduction to gender Analytical skills.* A Paper Presented at a Workshop on Gender Mainstreaming. Colline Hotel, Mukono, 21–24 July, 2004. Kampala: Women and Gender Studies Department, Makerere University.

Ssejoba, F. (2004) Shame, a Priest Caught in Lodge with a P.6 Girl of 15 years *The Sunday vision,* Vol. I No. 60, Sunday, 18, December 2004.p.1.

Ssemanda. G. (2003) Men Served Before the Rest of Family Members. *The New Vision,* Vol. 17 No. 234 Saturday October, 2003. p.3.

Ssenkaaba, S. (2005) Gender Parity Still a Dream in Uganda. *The New Vision*. Vol. 19 No. 314, Monday 3 January 2005. p. 23.

Ssentumbwe, O. (2005) Material Health, a Vital Social and Economic Investment. *The New Vision*, Tuesday 3 May, Vol 16, No. 53 p. 16

Stacey, J. and Thorne, B. (1985) The Missing Feminist Revolution. In *Sociology, Social Problems.* . p.p. 301-316.

Stahly G.B. (1978) A Review of Select Literature on Spousal Violence. *Victimology, An Internal Journal*. Vol. 2, No. 3-4. p.p. 591-607.

Straus, M.A. (1978) Wife Beating: How Common and Why? *Victimology, An International Journal*. Vol. 2, No 3-4. p.p. 443-458.

Sun Ai-Lee-Park (1998) Confucianism, Woman's Way, the Liberative and the Oppressive. *Woman and Religion*, Institute of Women's Studies, St Scholastica College, Manila. Mandaluyong City, Phillipines: Raintree Publishing.

Susie, J.(1992) *Gender and Land Reform, Zimbabwe, and Some Comparisons*, Zimbabwe

Tambouka.Diwara.A.(Dr) (2002) Gender and Governance of political behaviour of men and women in Morocco, *Gender and environment management in Togo*, series No.9,published by Ford foundation, Dakar, Senegal, Echo magazine, Dossier.

Tanzarn, N. (2004) *Understanding the Gender Mainstreaming Strategy*. A Paper Presented at the Gender Analysis Workshop for Sentinel Sites, Makerere University, 21-24 July 2004, Mukono, Uganda.

Tarcisio, A. (1997) *Every Citizen's Handbook, Building Peaceful Society*. Nairobi: Pauline Publishers.

The Pope speaks to women (1996). *Letters and Addresses of Pope John Paul II*. Africa: Nairobi , Pauline Publications.

The Star and Supa AFP (2003) 'Girls haunted by Kony ordeal, hate their lives', *The Monitor*, No 329, Uganda.

The World Bank (2001) *Secondary Education in Africa Strategies for Renewal*, World Bank presentations at the December 2001, UNESCO IBREDA, World Bank regional workshop in Mauritius on the renewal.

Tibatemwa Ekirikubinza, L. (1999) *Women's Violent Crimes in Uganda: More sinned against than sinning* Fountain Publishers, Uganda.

Tim and Beverly Lahaye (2003) *The Act of Marriage: Experience the Beauty and Joy of Sexual Love*, Christian Art Publishers, China.

Tinker, I. (1987) *UN Decade for Women: Its Impact and Legacy,* Washington DC. Oxford University press.

Tinker, I. (1990) *Persistent Inequalities, Women and World Development,* Oxford: Oxford University Press.

The Guardian, (2004) Aids May Wipe out Women. *The New Vision.* Vol. 19, No. 287, 3rd Feb,2004. p. 23.

The United Bible societies (1999) Good News Bible ,with Deuterocanonical books ,Africa Inter-regional services.

Tuhaise, L. (2000) Which Way Forward for Ugandan Women? *,Arise A Women's Development Magazine,* No. 30, November, published by ACFODE. p. 14

Uganda Bureau of Statistics (2001), *Uganda Demographic and Health Survey,* Entebbe, Uganda.

Uganda Bureau of Statistics (2001) *Uganda Demographic and Health Survey 2000-2001,* Entebbe, Uganda.

Ultimate Media (2003) Women Want a Law against Marital Rape. *The New Vision.* Vol. 28 No., Tuesday 18 November 2003, p.17.

UNAIDS (2003) Peer education and HIV/Aids, Concepts, uses, and challenges, UNAIDS' report on global estimates of HIV/Aids, Geneva. Switzerland.

UNESCO (2000) *World Education Report 2000,* The Right to Education, Towards Education for All Through Life. Paris:

UNESCO (2001), UNESCO's strategy for HIV/Aids, Preventative Education, Paris, France, Institute for Educational planning.

UNFPA (2003) International Day for Elimination of Violence against Women. Statement by Thoraya Ahmed Obaid, UNFPA Executive Director. *The New Vision,* Vol. 18, No. 280, Tuesday 25 November 2003. p.6.

UNFPA (2004) Global Population Report and the State of Uganda's Population. *The New Vision,* Vol. 12 No.56, Wednesday 15 April 2004. p.17.

UNICEF ESARO, (2000), Young people, gender sexuality, and HIV/ Aids in Education, Regional study in Rwanda, Kenya, Botwana, Tanzania, South Africa, Zambia, and Zimbabwe.

UNICEF (2001) Girls' Education Movement in Africa, Girls Education the Best Single Investment Conferences 15-17 August 2001 Uganda.

UNICEF (2002) Eastern and Southern Africa Regional Office, (2002) *Girls' Education Training Manual: focus on the African girls' education initiative,* April, Draft one, Nairobi.

UNICEF (2002) *Girls' Education Training Manual. Focus on the African Girls' Education Initiative, Eastern and Southern Africa.* Regional Office, Nairobi: UNICEF.

UNICEF (2003) *African Girls Education Initiative.* Regional Monitoring and Evaluation Technical Team Assistance (ESARO) Regional Report 2002,. Uganda: UNICEF.

UNICEF Report (May, 2003) *Taking Girls' Education Movement to Scale,* Uganda, UNICEF Publications.

United Nations Commission for Africa (1994), *Platform for Action, Report of the fifth Regional Conference for African women, Dakar, Senegal.*

United Nations Commission for Africa (1995) *Gender in Africa,The issues and facts, A pocket conference in collabouration with World Bank.* AddisAbaba, Ethiopia.

United Nations (2000) *Equality, Development and Peace in the 21st Century,* Beijing +5 Conference, China.

United Nations Population Fund (UNFPA) 2004 Population Explosion Hinders. *The New Vision,* Vol. 28 No. 364 Tuesday 9 2004. p. 21.

USAID (1982) The gender information framework pocket guide, Washington, D.C, USAID Office of Women Department.

Vishwa. H.P (2001) *Hindu Darma,* VHP, publications, India.

Wamahiu, S. and Miriti, L.G. (2001) *Assessing Quality.* Basic Education Training Manual for Fellows and Partners in Gender and Education. Nairobi: CARE.

Wamwe, G. and Gitui, M. (1996) *Violence against Women.* Nairobi: Action Publishers.

Wang. N. (1999) *Gender Technology and Development.* Vol. 3, No. 2, May-August 1999. Thailand: Asian Institute of Technology. p.p. 200-215.

Waqf, I. (1998), *The Religious Reformers in Islam.* Turkey.

Wayne. S. (1998), *A Systematic Theology: An Introduction to Biblical Doctrine.* Intervarsity Press.

Weiss, and Raogupta, (1998) *Bridging the Gap: Addressing Gender and Sexuality in HIV Prevention,* Washington DC: International Center for Research on Women.

Witherington,. A. (1984) *Women in the Ministry of Jesus.* Cambridge: Cambridge Press.

Women's Vision (2003), "Microbicides: New Hope against HIV/Aids for Women" *The New Vision.* Vol. 18, No. 280,Tuesday 25 November 2003, p.7

World Health Organisation (1968) *Reproductive Health and Development.* WHO.

Wave, H. (1981) *Demography and Development.* Canberra: Australia National University.

Williams, D.S (1993) *Sisters in the Wilderness, The Challenge of Womanist God Talk,* Mary Knoll, New York: Orbis Books.

htt://www.un.org./womenwatch/daw/beijing/platform/ health.html,Women and Health, page 1 of 16 –10 of 16.

http://www.un.org/womenwatch/daw/beijing/platform/economy.htm page of 15 (2005) *Women and Economy.*

http://www.un.org/womenwatch/daw/beijing/platform/violence.htm, Violence against women, page 1 of 9.

http.../STPDiNTERNAL.ASP%3fnODEid%3d33981+GENDER++an d+development&h1=en&i.e=UTF page 1 of 2, *Commonwealth 1995 plan of Action on Gender and Development.*

http/www/msc Gender Development and Globalisation.html Gender++and+development&hl=en&hl=UTF, MSC Gender, Development and Globalisation.

http://64.233.161.104/search?q=cac.../+gender+equality+and development&hl=en&hlen&i.e=UTK MD *Gender Net, Gender Equality and Millemium Development Goals,* page 1 of 2.

http://www.un.org/womebnwatch/dew/beijing/platform/educ.html, pages 1 of 10–100flo Education and Training of women.

http://www.un.org./womenwatch/daw/Beijing/platform/ poverty.htm, *women and poverty.*

Index

CPSIA information can be obtained at www.ICGtesting.com
Printed in the USA
BVOW05s0343250714

360461BV00002B/96/P